Elements of Quality Online Education:

Practice and Direction

Edited by *John Bourne & Janet C. Moore*

D1451251

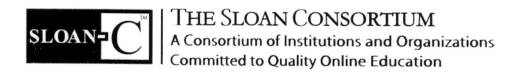

THE SLOAN CONSORTIUM
A Consortium of Institutions and Organizations
Committed to Quality Online Education

Volume 4 in the Sloan-C Series

This book contains information obtained from authentic and highly regarded sources. Reprinted material is quoted with permission, and sources are indicated. A wide variety of references are listed. Reasonable efforts have been made to publish reliable data and information, but the authors and the publisher cannot assume responsibility for the validity of all materials or for the consequences of their use.

Neither this book nor any part maybe reproduced or transmitted in any form or by any means, electronic or mechanical, including photocopying, microfilming, and recording, or by any information storage or retrieval system, without prior permission in writing from the publisher.

The consent of Sloan-C and the Sloan Center for OnLine Education (SCOLE) does not extend to copying for general distribution, for promotion, for creating new works, or for resale. Specific permission must be obtained in writing from SCOLE for such copying. Direct all inquiries to SCOLE, at Olin Way, Needham, MA 02492-1245, or to publisher@sloan-c.org. Online at http://www.sloan-c.org.

Copyright ©2003 by Sloan-C™

All rights reserved. Published 2003

Printed in the United States of America

0 9 8 7 6 5 4 3 2 1

International Standard Book Number 0-9677741-5-2

Elements of Quality Online Education:

Practice and Direction, Volume 4 in the Sloan-C Series

This is the fourth volume in the annual Sloan-C series of case studies on quality education online. In 1999, 2000, 2001, and 2002, the Sloan Foundation selected expert contributors to report on work in progress and to collaborate on research of importance to asynchronous learning networks. Each volume publishes contributions in the form of documented, peer-reviewed scholarly studies of learning and cost effectiveness, access, and faculty and student satisfaction.

Other titles available in this series:

Elements of Quality Online Education
Volume 3 ISBN 0-9677741-2-8
Online Education: Learning Effectiveness, Faculty Satisfaction, and Cost Effectiveness
Volume 2 ISBN 0-9677741-1-X
Online Education: Learning Effectiveness and Faculty Satisfaction
Volume 1 ISBN 0-9677741-0-1

This book was made possible by a grant from the Alfred P. Sloan Foundation.

SCOLE
Sloan Center for OnLine Education
at Olin and Babson Colleges

Sloan-C has its administrative home at the Sloan Center for OnLine Education (SCOLE) at Olin and Babson Colleges. SCOLE has been established as a center that spans the two campus of Olin College and Babson College. SCOLE's purpose is to support the activities of the Sloan Consortium, a consortium of higher-education providers sharing the common bonds of understanding, supporting and delivering education via asynchronous learning networks (ALNs). With the mission of providing learning to anyone anywhere, SCOLE seeks to provide new levels of learning capability to people seeking higher and continuing education. For more information about SCOLE, visit www.scole.olin-babson.org.

For more information about Olin and Babson Colleges, visit www.olin.edu and www.babson.edu.

Elements of Quality Online Education: Practice and Direction

Volume 4 in the Sloan-C Series

Contents

INTRODUCTION

Frank Mayadas
President

John Bourne
Executive Director

Janet C. Moore
Chief Leaning Officer

Sponsored by the Alfred P. Sloan Foundation and hosted by the State University of New York, the fourth annual Sloan workshop focused on the Sloan-C quality framework for online education. This September 2002 workshop convened at Lake George, New York, bringing together more than 40 invitees who are veteran practitioners and leaders in online education to review work in progress and to forecast needed developments in research and practice.

The Sloan-C quality framework has evolved with online learning, and it continues to evolve as technology enables innovations in teaching and learning for more—and more diverse—kinds of learners. Beginning in 1993 with the coining of the term "asynchronous learning networks" (ALN), the Sloan-C vision of quality is now understood as a synergy among five elements: learning effectiveness, cost effectiveness, access, faculty satisfaction and student satisfaction. These elements are known as the five pillars of quality; they are the values, principles and goals of asynchronous learning networks. ALN networks are not only technological channels; ALN emphasizes the special quality of communicative, asynchronous interactions among people. ALN is online learning that is accessible, affordable for anyone, any time, and anywhere, in a wide variety of disciplines. Thus, the quality framework is an instrument for continuous quality improvement—strategic planning with continuous feedback from all members of the institution.

Sloan-C values research and innovations that provide evidence of excellence. Channels for sharing empirical knowledge include annual volumes based on the workshops; the online, peer-reviewed *Journal of Asynchronous Networks*; the Sloan-C website, and more. To enable Sloan-C members to exchange knowledge, editors for each of the pillars gather effective practices for display at http://www.sloan-c.org/effectivepractices. The editors led the 2002 workshop and presented overviews of the state of practice and challenges in online education; authors invited from ten institutions supported the overviews with perspectives from two- and four-year, public, private, and research institutions.

Karen Swan of Kent State (and formerly, of the SUNY University at Albany) and Sloan-C editor led the discussions of learning effectiveness. Roxanne Hiltz of the New Jersey Institute of Technology (NJIT) and the Learning Networks Effectiveness Research Web Center and Randy Garrison of the University of Calgary provided supporting perspectives. According to Swan, research demonstrates that outcomes from online learning are at least as good as face-to-face learning outcomes. Online communities of inquiry are characterized by "social presence"—the perception of immediacy that reduces perceived psychological distance. Social presence results from interaction with peers, with teachers, with content, with interface, and with witness learning. Witness learning, also known as vicarious learning, is interaction that occurs when people learn by observing interaction among others.

Swan cites studies that demonstrate how online communities develop trust and engagement, leading to measurably higher levels of learning. We know online learning is effective, says Swan, "What we need to know is what makes it good, and how can we make it better?"

- Roxanne Hiltz of NJIT addresses this question in her survey of the research designs that measure learning with a variety of indicators. While most studies examine a single course or a single program, Hiltz proposes that more a generalizable, theoretical model will enable multi-course, multi-institutional, multi-national, performance and archival based, longitudinal research. This kind of context-based research will discover more exactly what is most effective about asynchronous learning, and thus spur continuous improvement.

- Randy Garrison of Calgary University finds online learning "uniquely suited to create a cognitive presence for higher order learning." In online communities of inquiry, the climate of social presence is enhanced by teaching presence that creates structure and process in the group; teaching presence and social presence create cognitive presence, the selection of content and discourse uniquely suited to the community. Teaching presence is "conceptually rich, coherently organized, and persistently exploratory." This online model of presence goes beyond some traditional models for classroom learning; online learning better enables reflection and collaboration, as it helps bring learners' attention not only to what we learn but how we learn. Thus Garrison advises going beyond traditional models. "Start with the big ideas, start with the learning outcomes," says Garrison; this enables learners to construct content and take advantage of the "multiplicative properties of communicative freedom, information access, and individual control of time and space."

Melody Thompson, Director of Quality and Planning at the Pennsylvania State University World Campus and Sloan-C editor, led the discussions of faculty satisfaction. Marie Fetzner of Monroe Community College (MCC) and Erv Boschmann of Indiana University Purdue University Indianapolis (IUPUI) provided supporting perspectives. According to Thompson, faculty satisfaction means concentrating on making teaching online a satisfying experience for faculty by providing access to new student populations; training and technical support; policies, including intellectual property, that include recognition and reward; and opportunities for professional development, research, and publication. Thompson shows that these provisions help faculty "feel positive about what they do and to do their jobs well."

- An initial difficulty for faculty is the increased time it takes to develop and conduct online courses. Marie Fetzner reports on Monroe Community College's organizational model that is designed to lighten faculty's administrative burden. A support team helps faculty concentrate on teaching and provides help for managing large discussions and providing timely feedback. The team is designed to emulate the structure of an online problem solving community— "team-based, collaborative, comprehensive, action-oriented and non-hierarchical in nature." The replicable model shares some resources centrally with SUNY, such as a faculty guidebook and support, technical infrastructure with a consistent template for learner interface, and operational and administrative support. Locally, team members help faculty schedule training, design courses, and obtain library and technical support; the team also acts as the liaison and advocate for students with support services.

- Erv Boschmann reports on the incentives that IUPUI provides for promotion and tenure. At IUPUI, faculty satisfaction is an institutional focus that recognizes that advances in information and instructional technology are an important facet of scholarship. Annual surveys of faculty contribute to policies that include internal and external peer review, personal statements of teaching philosophy, student advising, professional service and collegiality, and sound pedagogical procedures for course development and refinement. Continuous institutional responsiveness to the pace of change leads IUPUI to ask: "What will technology *not* be used for?"

Tana Bishop, of the University of Maryland University College and Sloan-C editor, led the discussions about cost effectiveness. Chris Geith of Michigan State University (MSU) and Greg Waddoups of Brigham Young University (BYU) provide supporting perspectives. The goal of cost effectiveness means institutional commitment to improving learning while reducing costs to the institution and to students. According to Bishop, now that we know that online learning results in significant, positive outcomes, institutions need to learn better how to leverage the technological resources, particularly in curriculum and course design, student access and support, library and IT, and consortia and partnerships. Creating frameworks for analyzing costs, identifying distinctive and key institutional goals, and linking course outcomes with costs help institutions meet their respective missions. In fact, Bishop says, asynchronous learning networks are an opportunity for leadership in higher education. Robert Ubell of the Stevens Institute commented that ample opportunities for return on investment are real because online programs eliminate infrastructure costs associated with campus instruction: "the four *P*s, pizza, pillows, parking, and pool." Cost effectiveness is a ratio of value divided by expense, as defined by institutional context and purpose.

- Chris Geith describes how MSU's Global Connection links learner-centered customized online program with costs in the initial stages of planning. To create learner-centered rather than teacher-centered curricula, MSU focuses on self-directed, student control of learning purpose, content as a means to knowledge, teachers as facilitators, and evaluation as a means for learning. Choosing appropriate pedagogies for corporate training and higher education significantly impacts how effectively faculty and students spend time, how many media are developed, and how technology supports learning.

- Greg Waddoups of BYU illustrates how the design of a basic reading and writing course at BYU improves learning outcomes and convenience for students *at the same time* it significantly reduces instructor time traditionally spent on preparation, instruction, grading, office hours, email, conferencing, and course development. Noting that student writing is better in the online courses, Waddoups identifies a delicate balance among learning effectiveness, cost effectiveness, and student satisfaction, concluding that "systematic course redesign, including the integration of technology, can create efficiencies."

Joeann Humbert, of the Rochester Institute of Technology (RIT) and Sloan-C editor, led the discussions of student satisfaction. Eric Fredericksen and Peter Shea of the State University of New York Student Learning Network (SLN) and Karen Vignare of RIT provide supporting perspectives. Humbert pointed out that while research demonstrates that there is a great deal of satisfaction with courses, levels of interaction, community and support services, it is important to continuously study student expectations to determine appropriate levels of interaction and learning community involvement. Student expectations are rising and it is essential for institutions to determine the difference between student needs and desires. Humbert calls for longitudinal studies, studies of multiple models, studies of the value of automated interactivity, studies of online student services, and studies of blended learning.

- Eric Fredericksen and Peter Shea of SLN, a program of 40000 learners and 2500 courses, and winner of the 2002 Sloan-C award for excellence, report on how SLN works within a framework that continuously examines how effective teaching and learning practices create high levels of satisfaction among students and faculty. Social presence, including building environments of trust, is critically important for success.

- Karen Vignare of RIT reports on the integration of online learners with face-to-face learners in at RIT where 25% of students enroll in online courses, resulting in an increase in RIT's graduation rates. Students report strong satisfaction with online learning. Vignare also details the process of longitudinal measurements of completion rates, retention, attrition, customer service, gender, status, and comparisons with face-to-face learning.

John Sener, consultant for the Sloan Center for OnLine Education and Sloan-C editor, led the discussions of access. Merrily Stover of the University of Maryland University College (UMUC) and Bruce Chaloux of the Southern Regional Electronic Board (SREB) provide supporting perspectives. Sener defines access as connecting learners with education anywhere by reducing barriers to courses, programs, learning and self-assessment resources, administrative and academic services, technical infrastructure and support services. Technology opens doors for more students and enables institutions to accommodate different learning needs; thus finding ways to bring greater attention to their programs becomes an institutional imperative.

- Merrily Stover reports that the University of Maryland University College has successfully launched and scaled a variety graduate and undergraduate programs for more than 87,000 enrollments in liberal arts, in business and computing, and in niche markets like fire science and legal studies. Outreach, student services, comprehensive web services, career development and student success centers, disability support, and library support for online learners are intrinsic to UMUC's commitment to ensuring "that no student is disadvantaged by his or her choice of delivery format, and that all students, wherever they are, have seamless access to the UMUC experience."

- Bruce N. Chaloux, Director of the Electronic Campus of the Southern Regional Education Board reports that "the 'digital divide' is real and growing. Differences in computer ownership and Internet access across racial, geographic, and income groups are larger in the South than the rest of the nation." In an effort to redress unequal access, SREB invites national participation in designing policies for credit transfer and articulation; for finance; for reaching the underserved; for faculty; for student services; for financial aid; and for quality assurance. "The goal of universal access through the development of an accessible and affordable ubiquitous technical infrastructure will take many years," says Chaloux; meanwhile concerted efforts at the national, regional, state and institutional levels can overcome a number of policy barriers. Policies to address pricing, access to financial aid for part-time distance learners, and more equitable, fair and just credit transfer and articulation arrangements can be addressed successfully. People "in the broader academic and policy communities will need to join forces to help make the needed changes a reality. The *hard* work is about to begin."

The purpose of the Sloan Consortium (Sloan-C) is to help learning organizations continually improve quality, scale, and breadth according to their own distinctive missions, so that education will become a part of everyday life, accessible and affordable for anyone, anywhere, at any time, in a wide variety of disciplines. You are welcome to join.

Learning Effectiveness

LEARNING EFFECTIVENSS: WHAT THE RESEARCH TELLS US

Karen Swan
Kent State University

- Knowledge is constructed through social interactions among people. Better quality learning results from the greater personalization of learning experiences.

- Rather than being impersonal, computer-mediated communication often seems "hyper-personal."

- Online education seems particularly well constructed for social learning because all students have a voice and no student can dominate the conversation. Online discussion creates certain mindfulness and a culture of reflection.

- Learning communities, both virtual and traditional, are defined by interaction, spirit (the recognition of community membership), trust, and learning.

- Online discussion may be more supportive of experimentation, divergent thinking, exploring multiple perspectives, complex understanding and reflection than F2F discussion.

I. INTRODUCTION

"LEARNING EFFECTIVENESS means that learners who complete an online program receive educations that represent the distinctive quality of the institution. The goal is that online learning is at least equivalent to learning through the institution's other delivery modes, in particular through its traditional face-to-face, classroom-based instruction.. . . Interaction is key." [1]

The goal, the *raison d'etre*, the stuff of education is learning. Thus, learning effectiveness must be the first measure by which online education is judged. If we can't learn as well online as we can in traditional classrooms, then online education itself is suspect, and other clearly critical issues, such as access, student and faculty satisfaction, and (dare we say it) cost effectiveness are largely irrelevant. Indeed, when online learning was first conceived and implemented, a majority of educators believed that it could never be as good as face-to-face learning. Many still do. In fact, however, we now have good and ample evidence that students generally learn as much online as they do in traditional classroom environments.

A. "No Significant Difference"

For example, Johnson, Aragon, Shaik and Palma-Rivas [2] compared the performance of students enrolled in an online graduate course with that of students taking the same course taught in a traditional classroom. Using a blind review process to judge the quality of major course projects, they found no significant differences between the two courses. The researchers further found that the distributions of course grades in the two courses were statistically equivalent. Maki, Maki, Patterson and Whittaker [3], in a two-year quasi-experimental study of undergraduate students, found more learning as measured by content questions and better performance on examinations among students in the online sections of an introductory psychology course.

Fallah and Ubell [4] compared midterm exam scores between online and traditional students at Stevens Institute of Technology and found little or no difference in student outcomes. Freeman and Capper [5] found no differences in learning outcomes between business students participating in role simulations either face-to-face or asynchronously over distance. Similarly, Ben Arbaugh [6] compared the course grades of classroom-based and Internet-based MBA students and found no significant differences between them. In a study of community health nursing students, Blackley and Curran-Smith [7] not only found that distant students were able to meet their course objectives as well as resident students, but that the distant students performed equivalently in the field. Similarly, Nesler and Lettus [8] report higher ratings on clinical competence among nurses graduating from an online program than nurses who were traditionally prepared.

Several researchers have used faculty perceptions of student learning as a measure of learning effectiveness in online courses. Dobrin [9], for example, found that 85% of the faculty teaching online courses felt that student learning outcomes were comparable to or better than those found in face-to-face classrooms. Hoffman [10] reports similar findings, as does Hiltz [11]. In this vein, other researchers have surveyed students and used their perceptions of their own learning as an effectiveness measure. Shea, Fredericksen, Pickett, Pelz and Swan [12], for example, found the 41% of 1,400 students enrolled in SUNY Learning Network's online classes believed that they learned as much as they learned in traditional classes. Forty-seven percent thought they learned more. Many researchers [13, 14, 15] have reported similar findings.

Indeed, Thomas L. Russell [16] created a "No Significant Difference" website that presents the results of 355 research reports, summaries and papers reporting no significant differences between the learning outcomes of students learning over distance and students learning in traditional classrooms. Likewise, in a review of distance education studies involving students in the military, Barry and Runyan [17] found no significant learning differences between resident and distant groups in any of the research they reviewed. Most recently, Hiltz, Zhang and Turoff [18] reviewed nineteen empirical studies comparing the learning effectiveness of asynchronous online courses with that of equivalent face-to-face courses. Using objective measures of content learning as well as survey responses by faculty and students, the studies provide "overwhelming evidence that ALN tends to be as effective as or more effective than traditional course delivery."

Of course, there have been instances in which studies have reported significantly poorer learning in online courses. For example, Chen, Lehman, and Armstrong [19] compared traditional, correspondence, and online learners and found that achievement test scores were highest for correspondence students and lowest for students taking courses online. Similarly, Brown and Liedholm [20] report significantly worse performance on examinations for virtual graduate microeconomics classes. These sorts of findings, however, are very much in the minority.

Of greater importance are methodological problems in studies comparing learning from online and traditional courses. Starr Roxanne Hiltz and J. Ben Arbaugh critically examine methodologies for research on the learning effectiveness of online courses in their study in this section. Despite many such problems, however, it is clear that when compared using gross measures of learning effectiveness, students learn as much if not more in online courses as they do in traditional higher education courses.

B. Beyond "No Significant Difference"

Another potential problem with comparisons of the learning effectiveness of online and traditional education is epistemological and involves the notion of no significant difference itself. The "no significant difference" paradigm stems from an article written by Richard Clark [21] for the *Review of Educational Research* in which he argued that media do not make a difference in learning but rather that instruction does. Clark was particularly concerned with several studies of computer-assisted instruction (CAI) that compared it with traditional instruction and found that students at a variety of levels learned more and faster from CAI [22]. Clark argued that these and other findings of significant differences between technology-based and traditional interventions resulted from more rigorously designed instruction, not from media effects. Media, he maintained, were like trucks, they were delivery vehicles and no more.

What mattered, according to Clark, was the quality of instruction, not how it was delivered. The CAI studied, for example, was rigorously designed according to principles of instructional design, while the traditional instruction with which it was compared was not. Thus, Clark argued that media effects were a chimera because if instruction were held constant there would be no significant learning differences between technology-based and traditional education. Early proponents of distance education picked up on Clark's ideas to support their cause. Well-designed instruction, they argued, was well-designed instruction, regardless of how it was delivered. Thus, they maintained, as long as the quality of instruction delivered over distance was as good as the quality of traditional education, there would be no significant differences in learning between them. Indeed, as we have seen, the research supports such a view.

However, many in the educational technology community, notably Kozma [23], have challenged Clark's position. Kozma conceded the importance of instructional design, but argued that media mattered too. What makes CAI so effective, for example, is its ability to deliver instruction that is individualized for every student and that provides each one with extensive practice and immediate feedback. Of course, a human tutor working one-on-one with an individual student could do the same [24], but teachers working in traditional classrooms cannot and the notion of tutors for all students is impractical. All media particularly support specific kinds of instruction and are less supportive of others [25]. Indeed, most educational technologists today agree that instruction should be designed to take advantage of the unique characteristics of media that matter or that can be made to matter in teaching and learning.

The epistemological problem with the "no significant difference" concept, then, is that it glosses over real differences in the asynchronous online medium that might be uniquely supportive of particular ways of knowing and learning. Carol Twigg [26] contends that the biggest obstacle to innovation in online learning is thinking things can or should be done in traditional ways. Trying to make online education "as good as" traditional education often encourages us to make it the same as traditional education. Trying to make online education "the same" most likely will lead to less than optimal learning, when, in fact, online education has the potential to support significant paradigm changes in teaching and learning. Twigg focuses on the potential of online environments to support individualized instruction. Randy Garrison, in his contribution to this section, explores the unique ability of asynchronous online learning to support both reflection and collaboration, and relates these to Dewey's notion of the inquiry cycle. In this study, I will discuss what the research tells us about the effectiveness of asynchronous online learning in terms of interactivity.

C. Online Interactions

Central to the concepts of both learning and computer mediation is the notion of interaction. Interaction refers to reciprocal events involving at least two actors and/or objects and at least two actions in which the actors, objects, and events mutually influence each other [27]. No matter what learning theories we hold— behaviorist, constructivist, cognitivist, or social— reciprocal events and mutual response in some form must be integral to our notions of how we learn. Similarly, interaction is widely cited as the defining characteristic of computing media [28, 29, 30, 31, 32]. What computer can do that other media can not do is to change in response to user input and so interact with users. Computer-based telecommunications connect people beyond the limitations of space and time to promote interactions among people who might not otherwise interact. Because interaction seems central to multiple conceptualizations of both learning and learning online, and because it highlights what is unique in online learning and hence the potential for paradigm change, I will use it as an organizing characteristic in the review of research and program initiatives which follows.

Researchers concerned with computer-based education have identified three kinds of interactivity that affect learning: interaction with content, interaction with instructors, and interaction among peers [33]. Interaction with content refers both to learners' interactions with the course materials and to their interaction with the concepts and ideas that content generates. Interaction with instructors includes the myriad ways in which instructors teach, guide, correct, and support their students. Interaction among peers refers to interactions among learners, which also can take many forms— debate, collaboration, discussion, peer review, as well as informal and incidental learning among classmates. Each of these modes of interaction support learning and each can be uniquely enacted in online learning environments.

Of course, none of the three modes of interaction function independently in practice. Interaction among students, for example, is supported by instructor facilitation and support, and, because it centers on content, can be seen as a variety of that type of interaction. Thus, a useful way of thinking about the three forms of interaction is provided by Rourke, Anderson, Garrison and Archer's [34] "community of inquiry" model of online learning. If one equates cognitive presence in this model with interaction with content, teaching presence with interaction with instructors, and social presence with interaction among students, it gives a good representation of how all three work together to support learning online (Figure 1). At the same time, it should be remembered that both teachers and students have social presence, that in many online courses, both teachers and students teach, and that learning is always learning of content.

This study explores current research concerned with online learning effectiveness in terms of learners' interactions with course content, with their instructors, and with their classmates, as well as briefly examining two other sorts of interaction suggested in the literature— interaction with course interfaces and vicarious interaction— with the hope that such focus will highlight some of the ways in which asynchronous online networks may uniquely support particular kinds of learning. It is important to remember, however, that none of these interactions stands alone and that all of them involve, to greater or lesser degrees, all three sorts of presence identified in the community of inquiry model.

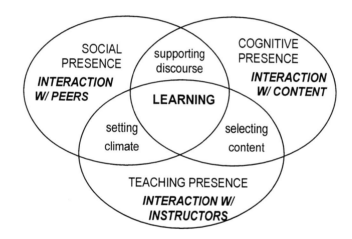

Figure 1: Interactivity and Learning Online
Adapted from Rourke and colleagues (2001) community of inquiry model

II. INTERACTION WITH CONTENT

Interaction with content refers to the learners' interaction with the knowledge, skills and attitudes being studied. In general, this has to do with the learners' interaction with the course materials and so is primarily concerned with course design factors, but it plays out, of course, across all the interactions. Measurement of online content learning has been undertaken in terms of performance (course grades, exams, written assignments, and so on) and perceptions of learning by students and faculty. As noted above, most of this research has involved comparisons of learning online with learning in traditional classrooms, and most has found no significant differences in learning outcomes between the two modes of learning. More recently, however, innovative studies have looked more specifically at particular cognitive skills [35, 36, 37], and these sorts of studies hint at particular affordances and constraints for learning online.

All of us are aware of the enormous amount of content available through the World Wide Web; many of us are overwhelmed by it. Shank [38], however, warns that information is not learning. Indeed, researchers agree that many computer-based educational offerings provide poor learning opportunities

[39, 40]. Much of what we do know about design for online learning has been extrapolated from research on learning in general, and computer-based learning and multimedia design in particular. Janicki and Liegle [40] have synthesized the work of a range of instructional design experts in these areas [22, 41, 42, 43, 44, 45] to develop a list of ten concepts that support the effective design of web-based instruction. These are:

- Instructors acting as facilitators
- Use of a variety of presentation styles
- Multiple exercises
- Hands-on problems
- Learner control of pacing
- Frequent testing
- Clear feedback
- Consistent layout
- Clear navigation
- Available help screens

Chickering and Gamson's "Seven Principles for Good Practice in Undergraduate Education," updated for online learning, are based on research and practice in traditional undergraduate education [46]. These include:

- Contacts between students and faculty
- Reciprocity and cooperation among students
- Active learning techniques
- Prompt feedback
- An emphasis on time on task
- Communication of high expectations
- Respect for diverse talents and ways of learning

Similarly, Keeton, Scheckley and Griggs [47] have adapted and revised the seven principles according to a survey of twenty years of teaching practices, basing their eight principles on the practices they find to have had the greatest impact on learning gains in higher education:

- Make learning goals and one or more paths to them clear
- Use deliberate practice and provide prompt constructive feedback
- Provide an optimal balance of challenge and support that is tailored to the individual students' readiness and potential
- Broaden the learners' experience of the subject matter
- Elicit active and critical reflection by learners on their growing experience base
- Link inquiries to genuine problems or issues of high interest to the learners to enhance motivation and accelerate their learning
- Develop learners' effectiveness as learners early in their education

- Create an institutional environment that supports and encourages inquiry

We can extrapolate from what we know about computer-based learning and learning in higher education and look for intersections across the two domains. What these sets of organizing concepts seem to have in common, then, is that they suggest online developers and instructors provide:

- Clear goals and expectations for learners,
- Multiple representations of course content,
- Frequent opportunities for active learning,
- Frequent and constructive feedback,
- Flexibility and choice in satisfying course objectives, and
- Instructor guidance and support.

Although anecdotal reports on asynchronous learning networks give a good deal of support for such a framework [26, 48], and it is well accepted that these design principles support computer-based learning and adult learning in general, it remains to be seen whether they apply to online courses in particular. Swan, Shea, Fredericksen, Pickett, Pelz. and Maher's [49] research on course design factors affecting student perceptions of learning, for example, suggests that several design characteristics that typically affect student perceptions in traditional, face-to-face classes may be irrelevant online. Research testing the particular effects of specific strategies for online design and instruction needs to be undertaken in a rigorous manner (See Hiltz and Arbaugh in this volume). Each of the above principles, for example, could be explored using experimental or quasi-experimental methods within the asynchronous online framework to test whether they really matter in such format.

Some research of this kind has been undertaken. For example, early research on asynchronous online learning has shown that the structure [50], transparency [51], and communication potential [52] of course designs heavily influence students' learning. Swan, et al. [49] examined the relationships between course design factors and students' perceived learning in 73 different online courses and found significant correlations between the clarity, consistency, and simplicity of course designs and students' perceived learning. Such findings support the above prescription for clear goals and expectations for learners. They also perhaps suggest both a constraint of asynchronous online environments and a way of ameliorating that constraint. Because real-time negotiation of meaning is impossible among instructors and students separated by space and time, clarity of meaning is more important in online classes. Consistent, transparent, and simple course structures add to such clarity as well as insure that learners only have to adapt to such structures once.

Swan and colleagues [49] also found significant correlations between perceived student learning and instructor feedback (interaction with instructors), between perceived student learning and communication with peers (interaction among classmates), and between students' perceived activity in courses (interaction with content) and their perceived learning. Others [35] report similar findings. These results support the above prescriptions for frequent opportunities for active learning, frequent and constructive feedback, and instructor guidance and support.

Thus, these findings support, in part, some but not all of the above prescriptions, and certainly not exhaustively. Specific areas that have not been well explored include the areas of multiple representations of content, student flexibility and choice, and instructors as mentors and guides. Coincidently, online learning affects paradigm change significantly in these areas. They thus very much deserve further investigation.

A. Personalization

As previously noted, one of the unique things that computer supported interactivity allows is the individualization of instruction. Indeed, when Carol Twigg [26] gathered a group of innovative online faculty and administrators in a Pew sponsored symposium to discuss paradigm changes in online learning, their overall conclusion was that individualization was the key to innovation in distance education. Better quality learning, they agreed, would result from the greater personalization of learning experiences for all students. Symposium participants identified five key features of pacesetting programs that support personalization of learning:

- An initial assessment of each student's knowledge, skills, and preferred learning style
- An array of high-quality, interactive learning materials and activities
- Individualized study plans
- Built-in, continuous assessment to provide instantaneous feedback
- Appropriate, varied kinds of human interaction when needed

The University of Phoenix, for example, welcomes students by name. Phoenix accesses and collects learners' personal information to maintain individualized relationships with them and to personalize feedback on their work in progress [53]. At Penn State, David DiBiase [54] inaugurated "student learning e-portfolios" so students could more actively plan their own educational goals, share examples of their work with potential employers, master transferable information technology skills, demonstrate knowledge gained beyond the classroom, present authentic evidence of learning outcomes, and so personalize their learning experiences.

Many online programs personalize instruction by offering much greater flexibility in terms of time as well as space. Rio Salado College's online program, for example, uses a computer-based management system to make ninety percent of its courses available for students to enroll in every two weeks [55]. Similarly, Cardean University permits students in all their online MBA courses to start any time and to progress at their own rate [56]. Excelsior College [57] does not even require academic residency. Rather, Excelsior recognizes student learning from any source by offering standardized credit-by-examination college programs that validate learning through standardized assessment, which is recorded on college transcripts.

Other institutions have used online formats to let students personalize their learning experiences themselves. For example, Ed Kashy and Michael Thoennessen [58] at Michigan State University helped design CAPA, a quizzer, randomizer, grader, and manager that helps students identify their own errors and correct individualized problems. Students in Ohio State University's introductory statistics courses can choose a variety of formats— lectures, video examples, individual or group discovery laboratories, remedial/perquisite training modules, graded homework assignments, individual or group review, individual or group projects— to meet specific course objectives [59]. Stanford University has created "courselets," self-contained, integrated tutorials covering a small set of concepts to be used across science and engineering courses [60]. Students who need particular knowledge can access courselets and/or skills as pre-requisites for other learning, want to extend their knowledge in a particular area, and/or are interested in cross-curricular applications of concepts.

At Virginia Polytechnic Institute, linear algebra students are given flexibility in both time and learning experiences to meet course objectives [61]. Students can choose either traditional instruction or utilize the totally asynchronous online Math Emporium that allows them to work their way through content units. In the Math Emporium, students choose when to access course materials, what types of materials to use, and how quickly to work through the units. Learning is assessed through short, electronically graded quizzes associated with each unit. Final exam scores, general education outcomes, and longitudinal follow-up studies all indicate that the achievement of online students is consistent with that of students, both at Virginia Polytechnic Institute and elsewhere, who learn linear algebra in traditional ways.

While most of these innovative programs and others like them report no significant differences in learning outcomes when compared with traditional instruction, they neither discuss nor explore what specific kinds of learning personalization might support, let alone investigate why they might better support them. For example, studies of student learning from computer-assisted instruction (CAI) suggest that CAI may better support the learning of discrete facts and concrete skills than more complex and integrated kinds of understanding [62]. Research on student choice of learning formats has been mixed in finding any benefit from such choice; indeed the negative results of learner control have been widely reported [63, 42]. Thus, rigorous and specific investigations of the particular benefits, and potential deficits, of personalization in online environments are very much called for.

Another issue surrounding personalization, especially individualization in terms of temporal flexibility, is the trade off between individualization and social learning. As noted previously, and as illustrated in the community of inquiry model (Figure 1), interactions with content overlap with interactions with instructors and peers. Extreme individualization cuts students off from these human interactions, most especially from interactions with classmates. Most contemporary theories of learning maintain that learning is, at least in part, social in nature, and that knowledge is constructed through social interactions among people [64]. It may also be that students enjoy learning with others (See the section on Student Satisfaction in this volume). Thus, future research should examine personalization and learning in relationship to social interactions and student satisfaction.

B. Multiple Representations

Many researchers note that students perceive online learning as more equitable and more democratic than traditional classroom learning [65, 66] because it allows for the presentation and inclusion of multiple points of view. Such a view suggests that online environments may be particularly supportive of what Judith Langer terms "literary understanding" [67], the divergent consideration of a variety of possibilities and perspectives. Similarly, Rand Spiro's [68] cognitive flexibility theory suggests that hypermedia (of which the World Wide Web is the extreme example) can uniquely support learning environments that allow for multiple representations of complex material. Spiro's research on learning from hypermedia found that students who explored complex topics from multiple perspectives through hypermedia programs scored higher on measures of complex understanding then students presented with similar material through a traditional (linear) CAI format. Thus, online environments might be particularly supportive of the development of literary understanding, divergent thinking, and/or complex conceptual knowledge.

Indeed, some researchers have begun exploring learning-specific kinds of content that may support such contention. Drew Parker and Andrew Gemino [41] at Simon Fraser University, for example, compared student learning of both concepts and techniques between traditional and online versions of a course in systems analysis and design for business majors. Although there were no significant differences in final exam scores between classes, on closer examination they found that students in the traditional classes scored significantly higher on the technical part of the exam, while students in the online sections scored significantly higher on the conceptual part of it. Benbunan-Fich and Hiltz [69] found that both individuals and groups working on ethical case scenarios with ALN support produced greater quantity and better quality solutions than either individuals or groups working without such support. Further research into online support for the development of particular kinds of knowledge, skills, and understandings, in particular for learning complex concepts or exploring multiple viewpoints, is clearly indicated.

Indeed, Picciano [37] reports a congruent finding from his study of an online graduate course in educational administration that relates directly to interaction. He found that students classified as highly interactive scored significantly better on a written assignment (an analysis of a particular case study) than students classified as either moderately or less interactive in the course. Picciano attributes the higher written assignment scores of the more interactive students to their greater ability to integrate multiple perspectives in deciding whether and how to implement an academic program, an ability he suggests they may have developed through their extensive interaction with other students' points of view in the course discussions. No corresponding differences were found between these high medium and low groupings on exam scores. Picciano suggests that the kinds of learning assessed by the multiple-choice exams might be done through group interaction as well as individually. Picciano's research suggests interesting directions for future exploration of the potential benefits of multiple representations and individualization, as well as of personalizing online experiences relative to particular learning styles. All these areas clearly deserve further investigation.

III. INTERACTION WITH INSTRUCTORS

A second type of interaction in online environments occurs between learners and their instructors. In any educational setting, the instructor serves as an expert who plans instruction to stimulate students' interests, motivates their participation in the learning process, and facilitates their learning. The relationship between instructor/student interactions and learning outcomes has been well documented in traditional classrooms [70, 71]. It makes sense that interactions with instructors would be equally important online.

Research on learning through interactions with instructors, however, has yet to document clearly the relationships between online teaching behaviors and student learning. Research to date is preliminary but intriguing. It has mostly been correlational and based on interview and survey data and faculty and student perceptions, but these do hint at important relationships between instructor activity and student learning. Initial investigations of instructor roles in online environments also seem quite promising. Nonetheless, much work still needs to be done in this area.

As noted, research that links instructor interactions and student learning is based, for the most part, on perceptions. Richardson and Ting [71], for example compared the perceptions of two groups of students involved in asynchronous learning. They found that students learning through written correspondence with instructors were more concerned with instructor feedback than any other sort of interaction with their instructors, whereas students learning online felt that all interactions with instructors mattered. Shea, et al [72] found significant differences in perceived learning among students interacting with their instructors at differing perceived levels. Students who reported low levels of interaction with their instructors also reported the lowest levels of learning. Conversely, students who reported high levels of interaction with their instructors also reported higher levels of learning from them. Swan, et al. [49] found a strong correlation between student perceptions of learning and their perceived interactions with instructors. Richardson and Swan [73] similarly reported a significant correlation between student satisfaction with their instructors and their perceived learning online, and Jiang and Ting [74] found correlations between perceived interactions with instructors and perceived learning.

A few quantitative studies have gone beyond perceptions to examine actual instructor activity in online classes. Jiang and Ting [74], for example further reported that both perceived learning and perceived interaction with instructors were linked to the actual average numbers of responses per student that instructors made. Swan, et al. [49] also found a weak correlation between students' perceived interaction with their instructors and the actual frequency of instructor interaction in online course discussions. Picciano [14] likewise found that instructors' activity was related to students' perceived learning in an online graduate level course in educational administration. These findings indicate the importance to students of interactions with their instructors in online environments. Connections between student interactions with their instructors and learning outcomes have yet to be documented, however. Also of interest are the ways in which instructors facilitate interaction among classmates in online course discussions and how these relate to learning therein. All are promising areas for further investigation.

A. Teacher Immediacy / Teaching Presence

One aspect of particular importance in understanding the efficacy of teacher/student interactions in face-to-face classrooms is the notion of teacher immediacy and immediacy behaviors. "Immediacy" refers to the "psychological distance between communicators" [75]. Educational researchers have found that both teachers' verbal immediacy behaviors (such as giving praise, soliciting viewpoints, humor, self-disclosure) and their non-verbal immediacy behaviors (such as physical proximity, touch, eye contact, facial expressions, gestures) can lessen the psychological distance between teachers and their students, leading (directly or indirectly, depending on the study) to greater learning.

For example, while early research on immediacy posited a direct relationship (learning model) between teachers' immediacy behaviors and both cognitive [76, 77] and affective learning [77, 78, 79], more recent immediacy research has come to believe that intervening variables mediate the relationship. In motivation models [80, 81, 82], the intervening variable is hypothesized to be state motivation. In these kinds of models, teachers' immediacy behaviors are conceptualized as increasing students' motivation to learn, resulting in greater affective and cognitive learning. In Rodriguez, Plax and Kearney's [83] affective learning model, affective learning itself is seen as the intervening variable; that is, teacher immediacy behaviors are seen as increasing students' affective learning which in turn affects their cognitive learning. Figure 2 graphically represents these proposed models.

LEARNING MODEL

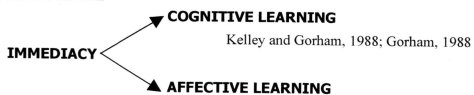

Kelley and Gorham, 1988; Gorham, 1988

Richmond, Gorham and McCroskey, 1987; Gorham, 1988

MOTIVATION MODEL

Christophel, 1990; Richmond, 1990; Frymeir, 1994

AFFECTIVE LEARNING MODEL

Rodriguez, Plax and Kearney, 1996

Figure 2: Research-Based Models of the Relationship between Immediacy Behaviors and Learning

Whatever the proposed model of the relationship between teacher immediacy behaviors and learning, a positive relationship between teacher immediacy and learning has been clearly documented in the research literature. This has led certain theorists to suggest that asynchronous media, because they are less personal than media which transmit non-verbal and/or vocal communications, are less capable of representing teacher immediacy, in the literature of "social presence" [84, 85, 86]. Hence, by implication, asynchronous media are less capable of supporting learning. Researchers and practitioners experienced with online teaching and learning, however, contest this view. They argue that rather than being impersonal, computer-mediated communication often seems "hyper-personal" [87], and that participants in computer-mediated communications create social presence by projecting their identities through verbal immediacy behaviors alone [34, 74, 88, 89, 90].

This latter research, however, centers on online course discussions, hence on interactions among discussion participants, of which interactions between instructors and students are only a small, usually unidentified, fraction. As previously noted, research focusing on the roles instructors play in online discussions and their relationship to knowledge creation and learning within them is definitely a priority. Also of interest are other sorts of interactions between online instructors and students such as instructor feedback on assignments, journaling between instructors and students, and teaching presence in online lectures.

In this connection, several researchers have attempted to categorize the roles online instructors perform to reflect the ways in which they project their presence. Berge [91], for example, maintains that moderators of online discussions must fulfill four major functions— managerial, social, pedagogical and technical. Paulson [92] reduces these to three sets of functions— organizational, social, and intellectual. Rossman [93} provides empirical support for similar categories through the analysis of over three thousand student course evaluations. He found that student comments and complaints concerning their online instructors clustered into three major categories— teacher responsibility, facilitating discussions, and course requirements.

Anderson, Rourke, Garrison and Archer [94] have termed instructors' ability to project themselves in online courses "teaching presence," which they define as "the design, facilitation and direction of cognitive and social processes for the purpose of realizing [students'] personally meaningful and educationally worthwhile outcomes." They conceive of teaching presence as composed of three categories of activities roughly analogous to those defined by Berge, Paulson and Rossman— design and organization, facilitating discourse, and direct instruction— and have created protocols to measure teaching presence in terms of these categories through content analysis of thematic units in online discussions. The protocols have been tested in the analysis of the complete transcripts of two online courses and proved both reasonably reliable and useful in identifying differences in both the quantity and quality of the teaching presence projected by differing online instructors. How such differences might relate to learning has not yet been hypothesized, let alone investigated, but protocols from Anderson and colleagues provide a good beginning.

In a similar vein, Coppola, Hiltz, and Rotter [95] investigated the changing roles of instructors teaching online classes through semi-structured interviews with twenty faculty members who had prepared and delivered at least one online course. They assert that, in any environment, teachers have three roles – cognitive, affective, and managerial. They found that the instructors they interviewed believed that in online environments, their cognitive role shifted to one of deeper complexity, their affective role required finding new tools to express emotion, and their managerial role necessitated greater attention to detail, more structure, and additional student monitoring. Anderson, Rourke, Garrison, and Archer [94] report similar shifts in responsibilities.

For example, at the University at Albany, Donna Rogers [96] responds privately to all her students' discussion postings in online courses on educational computing and media in teaching and learning. Rogers believes this practice allows her to interact with students around issues of content without depressing the range and variety of viewpoints expressed in the public discussion. At the University of Northern Virginia [97], students can elect to take courses in tutorial mode, an electronic extension of the time-honored tradition of mentoring. In tutorial mode classes, students interact in a similar one-on-one manner with their instructors around course assignments. All other interactions are voluntary. Murray Turoff [98] at the New Jersey Institute of Technology believes that a key instructor role is to motivate, encourage and facilitate authentic, active and collaborative interactions among students. He has developed a carefully focused structure for his course in interface design and management of information systems that breaks course activities into small manageable parts associated with discussions of related topics and large course discussions into smaller collaborative groups. This careful structuring, Turoff contends, allows him to teach large enrollment classes in an intimate and interactive way.

Many institutions offering online courses recognize both the importance of interaction with instructors online and changing faculty roles therein. They thus offer extensive trainings for their faculty that go beyond technical training to address issues of online pedagogy at the University of Central Florida [99] Penn State [100], Stevens Institute [101], and the SUNY Learning Network [102], to name just a few. Many institutions also offer online pedagogical support for faculty. For example, the University of Maryland [103] offers nine online training modules at a variety of levels as well as current listings for training opportunities for faculty across the state. Similarly, the University of Washington has created a web-based resource for its online faculty that offers practical advice on design and teaching an online course [104]. The University of Illinois at Springfield provides faculty with a daily review of news, research, and information on asynchronous online learning with links to complete reports [105].

IV. INTERACTION WITH CLASSMATES

Socio-cognitive theories of learning maintain that all learning is social in nature and that knowledge is constructed through social interactions [65]. Online education seems particularly well constructed to support such social learning because of the unique nature of asynchronous course discussions [106]. To begin with, all students have a voice and no student can dominate the conversation. The asynchronous nature of the discussion makes it impossible even for an instructor to control. Whereas discussion in traditional classrooms is, for the most part, transacted through and mediated by the instructor, online discussion evolves among participants. Accordingly, many researchers have found that students perceive online discussion as more equitable and more democratic than traditional classroom discourse [66, 67]. In addition, because it is asynchronous, online discussion affords participants the opportunity to reflect on their classmates' contributions while creating their own, and to reflect on their own writing before posting it. This tends to create a certain mindfulness and a culture of reflection in online courses [107, 108].

However, as Eastmond [51] reminds us, computer-mediated communication is not inherently interactive, but depends on the frequency, timeliness, and nature of the messages posted. Ruberg, Moore and Taylor [109] found that computer-mediated communication encouraged experimentation, sharing of ideas, increased and more distributed participation, and collaborative thinking, but also found that for online discussion to be successful, it required a social environment that encouraged peer interaction facilitated by instructor structuring and support. Hawisher and Pemberton [110] relate the success of the online courses they reviewed to the value instructors placed on discussion. Students in these courses were required to participate twice weekly and 15% of their grades was based on their contributions. Picciano [14] likewise found that students' perceived learning in online courses was related to the amount of discussion actually taking place in them. Likewise, Jiang and Ting [75] report correlations between perceived learning in online courses and the percent of course grades based on discussion, and between perceived learning and the specificity of instructors' discussion instructions.

Similarly, Shea, Swann, Fredericksen and Pickett's [111] study of 268 online courses across the State University of New York system found significant differences in students' perceived learning among differing levels of perceived peer interaction. Students who rated their level of interaction with classmates as high also reported significantly higher levels of learning. Swan and colleagues [49], moreover, found a strong correlation between students' perceptions of their interactions with peers and the actual frequency of interactions among students. They also found correlations between students' perceived interaction with peers and the percentage of course grades based on discussion, the required frequency of student participation in discussions, and the average length of discussion responses.

In their 1996 commentary on the ways technology influences practices, Chickering and Ehrmann [46] noted that "the biggest success in this realm has been that of time-delayed (asynchronous) communication . . . [in which] total communication increases and, for many students, the result seems more intimate, protected, and convenient than the more intimidating demands of face-to-face communication with faculty." Many have perceived interactions among students through asynchronous discussion as unique, and so interesting, sources of learning in online courses [49, 112, 113]. They are also perhaps the best researched to date. Much of that research has been premised on research about the social aspects of learning in face-to-face environments. Because interactions among classmates are arguably significantly different in online environments, research in this area needs, as Picciano [14] argues, to begin relating social concepts to actual learning and actual interactions.

A. "Social Presence"

As previously noted, "immediacy" refers to perceived "psychological distance between communicators" [76]. In traditional, face-to-face classrooms, educational researchers have found that teachers' immediacy behaviors can lessen the psychological distance between themselves and their students, leading, directly or indirectly depending on the study, to greater learning [76, 77, 78, 79, 80, 81, 82, 83, 114, 115].

That the immediacy research in traditional classrooms has implications for learning through online communications has been previously noted. Some communication researchers argue that differing media have differing capacities to transmit the non-verbal and vocal cues that produce feelings of immediacy in face-to-face communication. Short, Williams and Christie [83] refer to these capacities as "social presence," or the "quality of a medium to project the salience of others in interpersonal communication."

They contend that low bandwidth media, such as text-based computer-mediated communication, have less social presence, and by extension promote less learning, than media with greater communication potential. Media richness theory [84] reaches a similar conclusion, as does Picard's [85] more recent notion of "affective channel capacity."

Researchers experienced with online teaching and learning, however, contest this view. Participants in computer-media communications, they argue, create social presence by projecting their identities into their communications. Walther [87], for example, argued that participants in strictly text-based electronic conferences adapt their language to make missing non-verbal and vocal cues explicit and so develop relationships that are marked by affective exchanges. What are important, these researchers contend, are not media capabilities, but rather personal perceptions of presence [34, 74, 88, 108, 115].

Of course, as previously noted, online discussions are qualitatively different from discussions in face-to-face classrooms. In particular, the role of instructors shifts from discussion leader to discussion facilitator, and students commonly assume more responsibility [94, 95, 108, 116]. Research on immediacy in face-to-face classrooms has focused on teacher immediacy behaviors. Research on social presence/immediacy in online environments, however, has accordingly focused on the immediacy behaviors of all discussion participants. In practice, such research has centered on interactions among classmates.

Loni Gunawardena [88, 117], for example, developed a survey to explore student perceptions of social presence in computer-mediated conferences. In two separate studies, she found that students rated the asynchronous discussion as highly interactive and social. Gunawardena concluded that course participants created social presence by projecting their identities to build a virtual discourse community among themselves. Richardson and Swan [74] similarly explored perceptions of social presence among students enrolled in seventeen online courses using a survey adapted from Gunawardena. They found that students' perceived learning, satisfaction with instructors, and perceptions of social presence were all highly correlated. In addition, direct entry regression revealed that students' overall perception of social presence was a strong predictor of their perceived learning in the courses.

To account for such findings, Danchak, Walther, and Swan [118] proposed an equilibrium model of the development of social presence in mediated educational environments (Figure 3). Equilibrium, in this sense, refers to an expected level of interaction in communications [119]. When communicative equilibrium is disrupted (as, for example, when one conversation partner moves closer to another), reciprocal actions to restore equilibrium usually result (as when the other partner moves backward or reduces his gaze). Danchak and colleagues suggest that analogous behaviors preserve the expected (from face-to-face-experience) social presence equilibrium in computer-mediated communications. They argue that when fewer affective communication channels are available to transmit immediacy via conventional vocal and non-verbal cues, participants in mediated communications will increase their verbal immediacy behaviors to the extent needed to preserve a sense of presence.

Figure 3 illustrates this equilibrium model. The model suggests that as the capacity of particular media (the vertical bars) to transmit affective immediacy cues (the dark sections of the bars) decreases, people using such media to communicate increase their verbal immediacy behaviors (the white sections of the bars) and equilibrium is maintained.

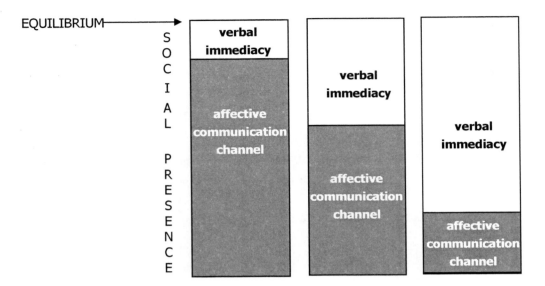

Figure 3: Equilibrium Model of Social Presence

To explore further the function of verbal immediacy behaviors in the development of social presence in online discussions, Rourke, Anderson, Garrison and Archer [34] distinguished among three kinds of immediacy responses. These are: affective responses (personal expressions of emotion, feelings, beliefs, and values), cohesive responses (behaviors that build and sustain a sense of group commitment), and interactive responses (behaviors that provide evidence that the other is attending). They tested these categories in a pilot content analysis of online discussion and found them quite reliable.

Swan, Polhemus, Shih and Rogers [120] used the categories devised by Rourke and colleagues [34] to develop protocols for the content analysis of online discussion. Swan [115] applied these to the analysis of discussions in a graduate education course. She found an average of six verbal immediacy indicators per discussion, lending support to the equilibrium model. In addition, the analyses revealed that, although the use of affective indicators mirrored the general flow of the course discussions as the course progressed across time, cohesive indicators declined in frequency, while the frequency of interactive indicators increased. These findings suggest that different kinds of immediacy indicators perform different functions in the development and maintenance of social presence and that the importance of these functions varies across time and context.

Most studies of social presence in online discourse are premised on the assumption that social presence enhances learning. The premise, of course, derives from research on immediacy in face-to-face classrooms. As we have seen, however, online discussion is significantly different from traditional classroom discussion. In addition, the immediacy research in traditional classrooms has focused exclusively on teacher behaviors, whereas the social presence research in online courses examines the behaviors of all discussion participants. Thus, a relationship between social presence and learning through online discussion has yet to be empirically identified and defined.

An important and interesting step in this direction was undertaken by Picciano [37] who related student perceptions of social presence to actual and perceived interactions and learning in an online, graduate level course in education. Picciano analyzed the relationships among survey data on students' perceived social presence, learning, and interaction and measures of their actual interactions in course discussions and performance scores on exams and a written assignment. He found that perceptions of social presence were correlated with perceptions of learning and interaction, and that perceived learning and perceived interactions were also correlated, but that perceived social presence was correlated with neither actual interactions nor performance. He did find, however, that when learners were split by their interactivity into high, moderate, and low groupings, students in the highly interactive group significantly outperformed the others on written assignments. When students were similarly grouped by perceptions of social presence, students experiencing the highest levels of social presence also scored significantly higher than the other students on written assignments. There were no such differences in exam scores. As previously noted, Picciano relates these findings to the potential for interactions in online discussion to support complex understanding, divergent thinking, and the development of multiple perspectives. Such findings clearly deserve further investigation, as does the whole area of the relationship between social presence and learning in online courses. A critical element of that relationship may be instructor behaviors, another factor deserving of future research.

In any case, support for interactions among students and the development of social presence is a priority for many online programs. At Stevens Institute, for example, faculty are specifically encouraged to model verbal immediacy behaviors in course discussions [101]. Similarly, faculty development in the SUNY Learning Network emphasizes socio-cognitive theories of learning and pedagogies designed to support the development of social presence and learning communities [121]. At the University of Phoenix, students are organized into learning teams to provide support and help for one another [53]. Students at the New Jersey Institute of Technology are similarly organized into collaborative groups in which they are encouraged to share their knowledge and experience as well as their learning [98]. At NJIT, students are required to participate in asynchronous discussions and are graded not on the number or size of their contributions but on their quality and timeliness. Similarly, Mercy College's distance learning program has institutionalized a set of criteria for evaluating the quality of discussion postings [122]. According to these criteria, good postings are substantial, concise, provocative, hermeneutical, timely, logical, and grammatical. Only postings that meet these criteria receive full participation credit.

B. Virtual Learning Communities

The concept of social presence leads to that of virtual learning communities [123, 124, 125, 126, 127, 128, 129]. Virtual learning communities have been variously defined by differing authors, and variations on the term, such as "virtual classrooms" [107], "computer-supported knowledge-building communities" [130], or "communities of inquiry" [34] may confuse the concept. Most conceptualizations, however, seem to center on one of two foci relating to research on learning communities in general.

Some researchers focus on learning, more specifically, they focus on Scardemalia and Bereiter's [130] notion of learning as collaborative knowledge building. Beverly Hunter [131], for example, asserts that a defining characteristic of a virtual learning community is that "a person or institution must be a contributor to the evolving knowledge base of the group . . . that there is a mutual knowledge-building process taking place". Hoadley and Pea [128] likewise are concerned with knowledge construction. Such definitions are commonly operationalized in terms of evidence of knowledge construction and/or support for knowledge building processes. Other researchers base their work on Lave and Wenger's groundbreaking research on learning communities and on the social relationships that support them [132, 133]. Caroline Haythornthwaite [127], for example, contends that the best way to understand virtual learning communities is to focus on the underlying social networks developing within them. Haythornthwaite suggests studying online learning communities by mapping the social and task support relationships within them.

Some recent, promising notions of virtual learning communities combine the concept of learning with that of community. Nolan and Weiss [129], for example, locate virtual learning communities at "the intersection of the social organization of an environment and the activities expected and conducted by participants in a particular setting. Likewise, Renninger and Shumar [134] view virtual learning communities as lodged in the particular interactions of participants within them. Indeed, it seems that the dual notions of learning and community both rest on and return us to the notion of interaction.

Interaction is one of four components used by Alfred Rovai [135] to define learning communities, both virtual and traditional. The remaining components include spirit (the recognition of community membership), trust, and learning. Rovai designed a survey instrument, the Sense of Classroom Community Index (SCCI) to measure participants' sense of each of these elements, such that comparisons between learning communities could be made both in terms of overall sense of community and/or on each of the subscales. Using the SCCI, he compared classroom communities among adult learners enrolled in a mix of fourteen traditional and asynchronous undergraduate and graduate courses at two urban universities. While Rovai found no differences in overall sense of community between the two media formats, he found greater variability in overall SCCI scores among the online courses. Indeed, the five (of seven) online courses with the highest SCCI scores had significantly higher sense of community ratings than did the seven traditional courses. Rovai suggests that this indicates that the development of community in online courses is more sensitive to course design and pedagogical factors than its development is in traditional environments. In this vein, he also found a moderate positive correlation between classroom community ratings and interactivity (as measured by the number of discussion postings) in the online courses.

In addition, Rovai [135] discovered significant differences in conceptual community structure, as indicated by items on the subscales, between the online and face-to-face classes he studied. Specifically, discriminate analyses revealed significant differences in scores on individual survey items indicating that student perceptions of learning and trust were higher in the online classes, whereas student perceptions of community membership was higher in the traditional classes. Rovai suggests that these findings indicate that online instructors should particularly work to promote feelings of community among online students while supporting and building on their perceptions of learning and trust.

Indeed, many online programs specifically support activities aimed at the development of feelings of community. Faculty in the SUNY Learning Network, for example are encouraged to foster a sense of learning community in their courses through such activities as ice-breaker discussions and monitoring of individual students' class participation [102]. The Penn State World Campus wants its online students to identify with Penn State and with each other as members of a community. The World Campus website thus provides them with activities and services specifically designed to encourage that identification, such as news about people in the World Campus community, online student groups, career and leadership opportunities, and other co-curricular learning experiences comparable to those available to resident students [136]. The University of Illinois, Champagne-Urbana's LEEP3 online masters degree program in library and information science uses face-to-face meetings to build community among cohorts and classes of students [137]. Student cohorts begin their program with a twelve-day stay on campus dedicated to developing community while acclimating them to the technology they will use online. All subsequent courses student take include one on-campus session. LEEP3 administrators attribute the program's greater than ninety-five percent retention rate to its attention to community building.

V. OTHER INTERACTIONS

There is a large body of research on learner interactions with course content, with their instructors, and with other learners in traditional educational settings, and, as we have seen, there is a growing body of research on student-content, student-teacher, and student-student interactions in online learning environments. Two other sorts of learner interactions that have recently garnered the interest of the distance education community also deserve mention. These are learner-interface interactions and vicarious interactions.

A. Learner-Interface Interaction

In reviewing the concept of learner interactions as they pertained to distance education, Hillman, Willis, and Gunawardena [138] noted that new and emergent technologies had, at least temporarily, created a fourth type of interaction, learner-interface interaction, which they defined as the interaction that takes place between a student and the technology used to implement a particular distance education process. Interface in this sense thus refers to specific technologies, platforms, and applications students must use to interact with course content, instructors and classmates online and in other distance learning situations, as illustrated in Figure 4. Interactions with an interface thus afford or constrain [139] the quality and quantity of the other three interactions.

Hillman and colleagues [138] maintained that user-interface interaction involved more than just the mediation that occurs between senders and receivers in all communication, but rather entailed genuine and ongoing interactive processes through which users developed mental models of the interface based on their interpretations of its structure and actions. They further contended that learner-interface interactions were critical because failure to interact successfully could dramatically inhibit learning. For example, a student who has difficulty navigating folders or asynchronous conferences may completely miss vital course content or instructions. At the very least, students who must devote significant mental resources to interface interaction will have fewer resources to devote to learning. On the other hand, productive interactions with well-designed interfaces can enhance learning by elucidating knowledge structures or scaffolding knowledge creation. Thus, Hillman and colleagues argued for both well-designed course interfaces and prerequisite orientations to their use.

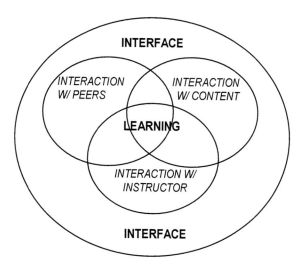

Figure 4: Interaction with Interface Conceptualized

Many online programs have responded to these suggestions. For example, students at Washington State University can access online course information, including syllabi, topics to be covered, resources to be used, and tips for success in online learning, as well as short video introductions to the professor and the course, before enrolling in them. This allows students to become comfortable with the interface (or to reject it) before they commit to its use [140]. Mercy College employs students who are comfortable with both learning online and with Mercy's Merlin system interface to serve as course "wizards". Wizards tutor student newcomers in the use of course interfaces, trouble-shoot and problems they might be having, and support student learning across time. Wizards also help instructors with course design, contributing a unique and important perspective on interface design in particular [141]. At the University of Illinois Virtual Campus (IVC), students are welcomed to online learning through a carefully designed set of online resources including tutorials on the use of technology tools, a "Getting Started" guided orientation to the IVC interface, help with academic success skills, career and life planning, and extensive additional resources specifically geared for online and/or distant students. In addition, forty IVC student support centers across the state provide local face-to-face, phone, and/or email support for online students who desire personal contact [142]. These are just a few examples of student orientation and support systems associated with most online education programs. The ubiquity of these services indicates the necessity for helping students develop effective mental models of course interfaces and so offers pragmatic evidence to support Hillman and colleagues's notion of interaction with interface.

There is likewise some empirical support for the notion of learner-interface interaction. Swan, Bowman, Vargas, Schweig and Holmes [143], for example, developed a user response model of the ways in which people make sense of electronic texts from rich observations of students searching for information on the Internet. User response models view meaning as jointly residing in the "reader" and the electronic "text". The authors' "reading the Internet" model also identifies the social, physical, and cognitive contexts surrounding this interaction as contributors to the meaning-making process. Their grounded research found that unlike printed texts which most readers engage singly, users engage electronic texts at three levels, each of which affect meaning making— the content or page level, the design or website level, and the interface level. Together the design and the interface levels identified in this model involve what Hillman and colleagues [138] consider interactions with interface. Observations of user reactions at these levels support their contentions. The researchers found that students not only needed to navigate and make sense of each of these levels before they could process content, but how they interacted with platforms/browsers and the structure of particular websites affected the meanings they eventually developed from that content.

Such findings raise interesting questions and suggest directions for research concerned with learner-interface interactions and their effects on learning. How, for example, might course delivery platforms affect the quality of learning? Most commonly used delivery platforms, for instance, separate course activities by function. Discussions are separate from course documents are separate from written assignments are separate from exams. It could be argued that such structure neither supports knowledge integration nor multiple representations of ideas, but rather constrains them. Investigations into whether this is, in fact, the case, and if, so how that affects learning would be both interesting and informative. Another interesting and potentially rich area for investigation involves the linking of concepts within and beyond online courses. Many scholars [for example 28, 29] believe that linking by association is the most unique and promising attribute of computer-based environments because it allows us to develop ideas in ways that mirror but extend the ways in which we think [144]. We have some evidence that student use of extensively linked hypermedia develops their abilities to make connections between ideas and think in more complex ways [69, 145], but we have not explored the effects of linking in online courses.

The growing convergence of media formats, bringing with it the possibility of the integration of print, audio, video, and interactive elements with synchronous and asynchronous communication and links to the vast information resources of the Internet, suggests that understanding learner-interface interaction may likewise be increasingly important in conceptualizing learning online. In particular, it would be beneficial to have a better understanding of the specific learning benefits (and constraints) that can result from learner interactions with a variety of media and combinations of media within such environments.

B. Vicarious Interaction

In traditional classroom discussion, vicarious learning is the norm. An instructor poses a question and a student answers it. Perhaps the instructor leads the student to a deeper understanding of a concept, corrects a misconception, or helps the student clarify an idea. Thus in traditional classroom discussion, teacher-student interaction takes place with a single student at a time, and yet we view such discussion as both highly interactive and an important part of the educational experience for all students. We do so because we believe that students who actively process these individual interactions will learn from them. Leah Sutton [146] argues that, even though online discussion is qualitatively different from face-to-face discussion, even though it encourages greater and more equitable participation, and even though the concrete record it produces might tempt us to forget what we cannot see, the same principle applies to asynchronous discussion online. Sutton suggests that direct participation in online discussion is not necessary for all students all of the time. She further contends that those who actively observe and process both sides of direct interactions among others will benefit from that process which she calls "vicarious interaction".

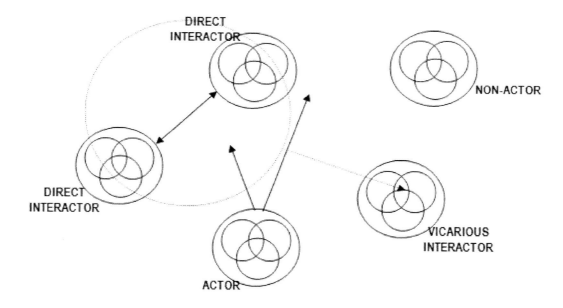

Figure 5: Four Types of Interactors (adapted from Sutton, 2001)

Indeed, in a pilot study of student behaviors in online discussion, Sutton [146] identified four different types of interactors that emerged from her data— direct interactors, students who directly interacted with other students and/or the instructor; vicarious interactors; actors, students who provided unilateral input regardless of the reactions or comments of others; and non-actors, students who did not participate in the communication process. Figure 5 illustrates these types. Notice that direct interaction is reciprocal, and that vicarious interaction processes that reciprocity. For this reason, Sutton argues that students learn almost as much from vicarious interaction as from direct interaction, and more from vicarious interaction than from either action or non-action, by relating her findings to Bandura's [147] theory of observational learning. According to Bandura, observational learners go through four stages— attention, in which a learner analyzes and absorbs the behavior of a model; retention, in which the learner mentally represents that behavior; production, in which the learner overtly enacts the behavior; and motivation, in which the learner anticipates reinforcement. Direct interactors, Sutton maintains, go through all four stages as they process and respond to others messages and anticipate responses to their own. Vicarious interactors go through three of the four stages. They attend to and process their classmates messages, as well as anticipate reinforcement if only vicarious reinforcement. Actors, however, only produce without attending or processing. Actors, she argues, thus learn little from online discussion. Non-actors, of course, learn nothing.

Sutton [146] concludes that direct interaction in online discussion is not necessary for all students as long as they observe and actively process the interactions of others. In particular, she recommends vicarious interaction for students who are passive or reluctant to participate in overt interaction. Bandura's work [147] suggests another purpose. Bandura's theory of observational learning derives from his notion that novices learn by observing expert modeling. Thus, vicarious interaction might be particularly recommended to novices in a field or in a particular topic. Similarly, the notion clearly relates to the concept of legitimate peripheral participation, which Lave and Wenger [132] identify as an accepted way for novices to enter communities of practice. In their studies of informal learning within such communities, Lave and Wenger noticed that the initiation of new members was a gradual process that began with observation at the periphery of community activity and progressed slowly through increased levels of participation. Thus, vicarious interaction might also be a means of initiating new students to online learning. In any case, a better understanding of vicarious interaction in online discussion might make us better able to assist certain kinds of learners.

Of course, all online discussion participants interact vicariously to greater or lesser degrees. Interestingly, there is some evidence to indicate that all such vicarious interaction plays a significant role in student satisfaction and learning. For example, Fulford and Zhang [13] explored the relationships between learners' perceptions of interaction and their satisfaction with distance courses delivered through interactive video. Their results indicate that students' perception of the general level of student-student and student-instructor interaction within classes had more influence on their satisfaction with them than did their perceptions of their own specific interactions. Similarly, when Helmut Fritsch [148] asked students enrolled in online distance education courses what parts of the courses they thought they learned the most from, they ranked their general reading of message postings higher than their own active participation in the discussion. Fritsch terms such vicarious interaction, "witness learning," and like Sutton [146], notes that it is an integral part of learning from face-to-face discussions. He is interested in how witness learning is enacted in online environments and how online instructors can support and enhance it. Such questions clearly deserve further study.

VI. SUMMARY AND IMPLICATIONS

What does the research tell us about learning effectiveness in asynchronous online environments? On the one hand, it tells us that online environments support learning outcomes that are generally equivalent to those resulting from traditional, face-to-face instruction [16, 17, 18]. On the other hand, the research suggests that unique characteristics of the medium may afford and constrain particular kinds of learning [139]. Such affordances and constraints, in turn, suggest certain strategies and approaches that might enhance the learning effectiveness of online instruction. These are summarized in Tables 1 through 3 which connect what we know, or think we know, about learning in asynchronous online environments with suggestions for practice that might either capitalize on unique their affordances or ameliorate their unique constraints.

RESEARCH FINDING	IMPLICATIONS FOR PRACTICE
Interactions with course interfaces are a real factor in learning; difficult or negative interactions with interfaces can depress learning.	Work with major platforms to improve interfaces to support learning. Develop consistent interfaces for all courses in a program. Provide orientations to program interfaces that help students develop useful mental models of them. Provide 24/7 support for students and faculty. Make human tutors available.
Greater clarity and consistency in course design, organization, goals, and instructor expectations lead to increased learning.	Review courses being taught and/or being developed to insure clarity and consistency. Establish quality control guidelines that address issues of clarity and consistency. Address issues of course design and organization and instructional goals and expectations in faculty development.
Ongoing assessment of student performance linked to immediate feedback and individualized instruction supports learning.	Automate testing and feedback when possible. Provide frequent opportunities for testing and feedback . Develop general learning modules with opportunities for active learning, assessment and feedback that can be shared among courses and/or accessed by students for remediation or enrichment.

Table 1: Interaction with Course Interfaces and Content:
Research Findings and Practical Implications

Table 1 summarizes findings relating to interactions with course interfaces and interactions with content. Interactions with course interfaces relate to a constraint of asynchronous learning. In traditional, face-to-face classrooms, instructors and students can negotiate meanings in real time. This allows instructors to make goals and expectations clear and to remediate student misconceptions and confusions as they occur. In asynchronous courses, this kind of negotiation of meaning is not possible. In addition, course interfaces and course design add another layer of information students must interpret and navigate. Thus, careful attention to these features in course design and implementation can make important differences in learning from online courses.

On the other hand, online environments can take advantage of the unique ability of the computing medium to respond to users and so individualize their learning according to their particular learning needs and styles [26]. Computers also can provide students with almost unlimited opportunities for active learning linked to immediate feedback and assessment which we know leads to improved learning outcomes. These capabilities of computers should be capitalized on.

Table 2 summarizes research findings relating to interactions with instructors in asynchronous learning networks and their implications for educational practice. Interactions with instructors are critical in all learning environments. They are perhaps more critical online [14, 49, 75]. Because there is no classroom in which students can connect with their instructors, guidelines for instructor-student interactions must be made explicit. Frequent and supportive interactions with instructors thus support online learning.

RESEARCH FINDING	IMPLICATIONS FOR PRACTICE
The quantity and quality of instructor interactions with students is linked to student learning.	Provide frequent opportunities for both public and private interactions with students. Establish clear expectations for instructor-student interactions. Provide timely and supportive feedback. Include topic of instructor interaction in faculty development.
Instructor roles change in online environments.	Include the topic of changing roles in faculty development and provide examples of how other instructors have coped. Provide ongoing educational technology support for faculty. Develop forums for faculty discussion of changing roles – online and F2F.

Table 2: Interaction with Instructors:

Research Findings and Practical Implications

Instructor roles change online [95]. In many ways, these changes have to do with the unique affordances and constraints of the environment itself. Instructors need to be clearer, to provide greater structure for their students, and to find new ways to express emotion and otherwise connect with students. In particular, instructors need to develop new ways to project teaching presence [94] in asynchronous online learning environments.

Figure 3 summarizes research findings and practical implications concerned with interactions among students in asynchronous learning networks, including those involving vicarious learning [146, 148]. Indeed, interactions among students through asynchronous discussion have been perceived by many authors to be uniquely interesting sources of learning in online courses [49, 66, 106, 107]. Participants view online discussion as more equitable and democratic and as more mindful, and reflective than discussions in face-to-face classrooms. Research also suggests that asynchronous learning environments might be particularly supportive of experimentation, divergent thinking, and complex understandings, and less supportive of convergent thinking, instructor directed inquiry and scientific thinking than face-to-face discussions [36, 37].

However, researchers remind us that learning through online discussion depends on the frequency, timeliness, and nature of the messages posted, hence on the value instructors put on it [12, 75, 110]. In addition, the development of social presence and virtual communities among discussion participants has been shown to support learning through online discussion. [34, 37, 74, 88].

RESEARCH FINDING	IMPLICATIONS FOR PRACTICE
Learning occurs socially within communities of practice; there is greater variability in sense of community ratings among online courses than in F2F courses.	Design community-building activities. Model the use of cohesive immediacy behaviors in all interactions with students. Develop initial course activities to encourage the development of swift trust.

	Address issues of community in faculty development.
Verbal immediacy behaviors can lesson the psychological distance between communicators online; overall sense of social presence is linked to learning.	Develop initial course activities to encourage the development of swift trust. Model and encourage the use of verbal immediacy behaviors in interactions with students. Encourage students to share experiences and beliefs in online discussion. Introduce social presence and verbal immediacy in faculty development.
Student learning is related to the quantity and quality of postings in online discussions and to the value instructors place on them.	Make participation in discussion a significant part of course grades. Develop grading rubrics for participation . Require discussion participants to respond to their classmates' postings and/or to respond to all responses to their own postings. Stress the unique nature and potential of online discussion in faculty development.
Vicarious interaction in online course discussion may be an important source of learning from discussion.	Encourage and support vicarious interaction . Require discussion summaries that identify steps in the knowledge creation process. Use tracking mechanisms to reward reading as well as responding to messages.
Online discussion may be more supportive of experimentation, divergent thinking, exploration of multiple perspectives, complex understanding and reflection than F2F discussion.	Encourage experimentation, divergent thinking, multiple perspectives, complex understanding and reflection in online discussion through provocative, open-ended questions, modeling support and encouragement for diverse points of view. Develop grading rubrics for discussion participation that reward desired cognitive behaviors . Develop initial course activities to encourage the development of swift trust.
Online discussion may be less supportive of convergent thinking, instructor directed inquiry and scientific thinking than F2F discussion.	Use other course activities to support these such as written assignments, one-on-one tutorials, small group collaboration and self-testing. Develop grading rubrics for discussion participation that reward desired cognitive behaviors .

Table 3: Interaction with Classmates and Vicarious Interaction:
Research Findings and Practical Implications

All of these areas of inquiry are young as online learning itself. Further research, more rigorous research, and more creative research are definitely needed. In particular, researchers should explore the unique characteristics of asynchronous online environments that matter or that can be made to matter in learning and instruction. Robbie McClintock [149] writes, "Digital technologies are for education as iron and steel girders, reinforced concrete, plate glass, elevators, central heating and air conditioning were for architecture. Digital technologies set in abeyance significant, long-lasting limits on educational activity." We need to explore the new, wonderful kinds of learning asynchronous environments make possible.

VII. REFERENCES

1.   **Moore, J.C.** *Elements of Quality: The Sloan-C Framework.* Needham, MA: Sloan-C Press, 2002.
2.   **Johnson, S. D., Aragon, S. R. Shaik, N. and Palma-Rivas, N.** Comparative analysis of learner satisfaction and learning outcomes in online and fact-to-face learning environments. *Journal of Interactive Learning Research, 11* (1) 29-49, 2000.
3.   **Maki, R. H., Maki, W. S., Patterson, M., and Whittaker, P. D.** Evaluation of a web-based introductory psychology course. *Behavior Research Methods, Instruments, and Computers, 32,* 230-239, 2000.
4.   **Fallah, M. H. and Ubell, R.** Blind scores in a graduate test: Conventional compared with web-based outcomes. *ALN Magazine, 4* (2), 2000, http://www.aln.org/alnweb/magazine/Vol4_issue2/fallah.htm
5.   **Freeman, M. A. and Capper, J. M.** Exploiting the web for education: An anonymous asynchronous role simulation. *Australian Journal of Educational Technology, 15* (1), 95-116, 1999. http://www.ascilite.org.au/ajet/ajet15/freeman.html
6.   **Arbaugh, J. B.** Virtual classroom versus physical classroom: an exploratory study of class discussion patterns and student learning in an asynchronous Internet-based MBA course. *Journal of Management Education, 24,* (2), 213-233, 2000.
7.   **Blackley, J. A. and Curran-Smith, J.** Teaching community health nursing by distance methods: Development, process, and evaluation. *Journal of Continuing Education for Nurses, 29* (4), 148-153, 1998.
8.   **Nesler, M. S. and Lettus, M. K.** A follow-up study of external degree graduates from Florida. Paper presented at the 103rd Annual Convention of the American Psychological Association, New York: August, 1995.
9.   **Dobrin, J.** Who's teaching online? *ITPE News, 2* (12), 6-7, 1999.
10.   **Hoffman, K.** M. What are faculty saying? *eCollege.com,* May, 1999.
11.   **Hiltz, S. R.** Impacts of college-level courses via asynchronous learning networks: some preliminary results. *Journal of Asynchronous Learning Networks, 1* (2), 1997.
12.   **Shea, P., Fredericksen, E., Pickett, A. Pelz, W. and Swan, K.** Measures of learning effectiveness in the SUNY Learning Network. In J. Bourne and J. Moore (Eds) *Elements of Quality Online Education: Volume 3 in the Sloan-C Series.* Needham, MA: Sloan-C Press, 2002.
13.   **Fulford, C. P. Y Zhang, S.** Perceptions of interaction: the critical predictor in distance education. *The American Journal of Distance Education, 7* (3), 8-21, 1993.
14.   **Picciano, A. G.** Developing an asynchronous course model at a large, urban university. *Journal of Asynchronous Learning Networks, 2* (1), 1998.
15.   **Dziuban, C. and Moskal, P.** Emerging research issues in distributed learning. Orlando, FL: Paper delivered at the 7th Sloan-C International Conference on Asynchronous Learning Networks, 2001.
16.   **Russell, T. L.** *The No Significant Difference Phenomenon.* Montgomery, AL: IDEC, 1999. http://teleeducation.nb.ca/nosignificantdifference/
17.   **Barry, M. and Runyan, G.** A review of distance-learning studies in the U.S. military. *The American Journal of Distance Education, 9* (3), 37-47, 1995.
18.   **Hiltz, R., Zhang, Y., Turoff, M.** Studies of effectiveness of learning networks. In J. Bourne and J. Moore (Eds) *Elements of Quality Online Education: Volume 3 in the Sloan-C Series.* Needham, MA: Sloan-C Press, 2002.
19.   **Chen, H., Lehman, J. and Armstrong, P.** Comparison of performance and attitude in traditional and computer conferencing classes. *The American Journal of Distance Education, 5* (3), 51-64, 1991.

20. **Brown, B. W. and Liedholm, C. E**. Can web courses replace the classroom in principles of microeconomics? *American Economics Review*. May, 2002.

21. **Clark, R. E**. Reconsidering research on learning from media. *Review of Educational Research, 53* (4), 445-459, 1983.

22. **Kulik, J. A.; Kulik, C. C.; and Bangert-Drowns, R. L**. Effectiveness of computer-based education in elementary schools. *Computers in Human Behavior, 1* (1), 59-74, 1985.

23. **Kozma, R. B**. Learning with media. *Review of Educational Research, 61*, 179-211, 1991.

24. **Anderson, J. and Reiser, B**. The LISP tutor. *Byte Magazine, 10* (4), 159-175, 1985.

25. **Salomon, G**. *The Interaction of Media, Cognition and Learning.* San Francisco: Jossey-Bass, 1981.

26. **Twigg, C**. *Innovations in Online Learning: Moving Beyond No Significant Difference.* The Pew Learning and Technology Program, 2000. http://www.center.rpi.edu/PewSym/mono4.html

27. **Wagner, E**. D. In support of a functional definition of interaction. The American Journal of Distance Education, 8 (2), 6-29, 1994.

28. **Bolter, J. D**. *The Writing Space: The Computer, Hypertext and the History of Writing.* Chapel Hill, NC: University of North Carolina Press, 1991.

29. **Landow, G. P**. Hypertext: The Convergence of Contemporary Critical Theory and Technology. Baltimore, MD: Johns Hopkins University Press, 1992.

30. **Lanham, R. A**. *The Electronic Word: Democracy, Technology, and the Arts.* Chicago: University of Chicago Press, 1993.

31. **Murray, J. H**. Hamlet on the Holodeck: The Future of Narrative in Cyberspace. New York: The Free Press, 1997.

32. **Turkle, S**. Life on the Screen: Identity in the Age of the Internet. New York: Simon and Schuster, 1997.

33. **Moore, M.G**. Three types of interaction. *American Journal of Distance Education, 3* (2), 1-6, 1989.

34. **Rourke, L., Anderson, T., Garrison, D. R. and Archer, W**. Assessing social presence in asynchronous text-based computer conferencing. *Journal of Distance Education, 14* (2), 2001.

35. **Garrison, D. R., Anderson, T. and Archer, W**. Critical thinking, cognitive presence, and computer conferencing in distance education. *The American Journal of Distance Education, 15* (1), 2001.

36. **Parker, D. and Gemino, A**. Inside online learning: Comparing conceptual and technique learning performance in place-based and ALN formats. *Journal of Asynchronous Learning Networks, 5* (2), 64-74, 2001. http://www.aln.org/alnweb/journal/jaln-vol5issue2v2.htm

37. **Picciano, A. G**. Beyond student perceptions: Issues of interaction, presence and performance in an online course. *Journal of Asynchronous Learning Networks, 6* (1), 2002. http://www.aln.org/alnweb/journal/jaln-vol6issue1.htm

38. **Shank, R**. Horses for courses. *Communication of the ACM, 41* (7), 23-25, 1998.

39. **Bork, A**. Advantages of computer-based learning. *Journal of Structured Learning, 9* (1), 63-76, 1986.

40. **Janicki, T. and Liegle, J. O**. Development and evaluation of a framework for creating web-based learning modules: a pedagogical and systems approach. *Journal of Asynchronous Learning Networks, 5* (1), 2001.

41. **Gagne, R., Briggs, L. and Wager, W**. *Principles of Instructional Design.* New York: Holt, Reinhard and Winston, 1988.

42. **Hannafin, M. and Peck, K**. The Design, Development, and Evaluation of Instructional Software. New York: MacMillan Publishing, 1988.

43. **Tennyson, R**. Cognitive science and instructional technology: improvements in higher order thinking strategies. *Proceedings of the Association of Educational Communication and Technology*. Dallas, TX: AECT, 1989.

44. **Jonassen, D., Davidson, M., Collins, M., Campbell, J. and Haag, B**. Constructivism and computer mediated communication in distance education. *American Journal of Distance Education, 9* (2), 7-25, 1995.

45. **Ward, E. and Lee, J.** An instructors' guide to distance learning. *Training and Development, 29* (1), 40-44, 1995.

46. **Chickering, A., Ehrmann, S. C.** Implementing the seven principles: Technology as lever. *AAHE Bulletin*, October, 3-6, 1996. http://www.tltgroup.org/programs/seven.html

47. **Keeton, M.T., Scheckley, B.G., Krecji-Griggs, J.** *Effectiveness and Efficiency in Higher Education for Adults.* Council on Adult and Experiential Learning. Chicago: Kendall-Hunt, 2002.

48. **Schrum, L. and Hong, S.** Dimensions and strategies for online success: voices from experienced educators. *Journal of Asynchronous Learning Networks, 6* (1), 2002.

49. **Swan, K., Shea, P., Fredericksen, E., Pickett, A., Pelz, W. and Maher, G.** Building knowledge building communities: consistency, contact and communication in the virtual classroom. *Journal of Educational Computing Research, 23* (4), 389-413, 2000.

50. **Romiszowski, A. J. and Cheng, E.** Hypertext's contribution to computer-mediated communication: in search of an instructional model. In Giardina, M. (Ed.) *Interactive Multimedia Learning Environments.* Berlin: Springer, 1992.

51. **Eastmond, D. V.** Alone but Together: Adult Distance Study through Computer Conferencing. Cresskill, NJ: Hampton Press, 1995.

52. **Irani, T.** Communication potential, information richness and attitude: A study of computer mediated communication in the ALN classroom. *ALN Magazine, 2* (1), 1998.

53. **Trippe, T.** Student satisfaction at the University of Phoenix Online Campus." In J. Bourne and J. Moore (Eds) *Elements of Quality Online Education: Volume 3 in the Sloan-C Series.* Needham, MA: Sloan-C Press, 2002.

54. **DiBiase, D.** Using e-Portfolios at Penn State to Enhance Student Learning: Status, Prospects, and Strategies. February 16, 2002. http://www.e-education.psu.edu/portfolios/e-port_report.shtml

55. **Scarafiotti, C.** Rio Salado College: a systems approach to online learning. In Twigg, C. *Innovations in Online Learning: Moving Beyond No Significant Difference.* The Pew Learning and Technology Program, 2000. http://www.center.rpi.edu/PewSym/mono4.html

56. **Duffy, T. M.** Cardean University: problem centered pedagogy. In Twigg, C. *Innovations in Online Learning: Moving Beyond No Significant Difference.* The Pew Learning and Technology Program, 2000. http://www.center.rpi.edu/PewSym/mono4.html

57. **Kashy, E., Thoennessen, M., Alberti, G., Tsai, Y.** Implementing a large on-campus ALN: Faculty perspective. In J. Bourne and J. Moore (Eds) *Online Education: Volume 1 in the Sloan-C Series.* Needham, MA: Sloan-C Press, 2001; *Journal of Asynchronous Learning Networks, 4,* (2), 2000. http://www.aln.org/alnweb/journal/jaln-volume4issue3.htm

58. **OSU Department of Statistics.** Ohio State University: a buffet of learning opportunities. In Twigg, C. *Innovations in Online Learning: Moving Beyond No Significant Difference.* The Pew Learning and Technology Program, 2000. http://www.center.rpi.edu/PewSym/mono4.html

59. **Peinovich, P.** E. Excelsior College: what you know is more important than where or how you learned it. In Twigg, C. *Innovations in Online Learning: Moving Beyond No Significant Difference.* The Pew Learning and Technology Program, 2000. http://www.center.rpi.edu/PewSym/mono4.html

60. **Sloan Consortium Effective Practices:** Learning Effectiveness. 2002b. http://www.sloan-c.org/effectivepractices

61. **Olin, R.** F. Virginia Polytechnic Institute and State University: the Math Emporium; student-paced mathematics 24X7. In Twigg, C. *Innovations in Online Learning: Moving Beyond No Significant Difference.* The Pew Learning and Technology Program, 2000. http://www.center.rpi.edu/PewSym/mono4.html

62. **Swan, K., Guerrero, F., Mitrani, M. and Schoener, J.** Honing in on the target: Who among the educationally disadvantaged benefits most from what CBI? *Journal of Research on Computing in Education, 22*, 4, 381-403, 1990.

63. **Tennyson, R.D. and Buttrey, T.** Advisement and management strategies as design variables in Computer-Assisted Instruction. *Educational Communication and Technology Journal. 28*, 169-176, 1980

64. **Bransford, D., Brown, A. and Cocking, R.** *How People Learn: Brain, Mind, Experience and School.* Committee on Developments in the Science of Learning, Commission on Behavioral and Social Sciences and Education National Research Council. Washington, DC: National Academy Press, 1999.

65. **Harasim, L.** On-line Education: Perspectives on a New Environment. New York: Praeger, 1990.

66. **Levin, J. A., Kim, H. and Riel, M. M.** Analyzing instructional interactions on electronic message networks. In L. Harasim (Ed.), *On-line Education: Perspectives on a New Environment* New York: Praeger, 1990.

67. **Langer J. and Close, E.** *Improving Literary Understanding through Classroom Conversation.* Albany, NY: National Research Center on English Learning and Achievement, 2001.

68. **Spiro, R.J., and Jehng, J.C.** Cognitive flexibility and hypertext: theory and technology for the nonlinear and multidimensional traversal of complex subject matter. In D. Nix and R.J. Spiro (Eds.), *Cognition, Education, and Multimedia: Exploring Ideas in High Technology.* Hillsdale, NJ: Lawrence Erlbaum Associates, 1990.

69. **Benbunan-Fich, R. and Hiltz, S. R.** Impact of asynchronous learning networks on individual and group problem solving: A field experiment. *Group Decision and Negotiation, 8*, 409-426, 1999.

70. **Madden, M. and Carli, L.** Students' Satisfaction with Graduate School and Attributions of Control and Responsibility. New York: Paper presented at the Annual Meeting of the Eastern Psychological Association, 1981.

71. **Powers, S. and Rossman, M.** Student satisfaction with graduate education: Dimensionality and assessment in college education. *Psychology: A Quarterly Journal of Human Behavior, 22* (2), 46-49, 1985.

72. **Richardson J. and E. Ting, E.** Making the most of interaction: what instructors do that most affect students' perceptions of their learning. College Park, MD: Paper presented at the 5th International Conference on Asynchronous Learning, 1999.

73. **Richardson, J. and Swan, K.** An examination of social presence in online learning: students' perceived learning and satisfaction. Seattle, WA: Paper presented at the annual meeting of the American Educational Research Association, 2001.

74. **Jiang, M. and Ting, E.** A study of factors influencing students' perceived learning in a web-based course environment . *International Journal of Educational Telecommunications, 6* (4), 317-338, 2000.

75. **Weiner, M. and Mehrabian, A.** Language within Language: Immediacy, a Channel in Verbal Communication. New York: Appleton-Century-Crofts, 1968.

76. **Kelley, D. and Gorham, J.** Effects of immediacy on recall of information. *Communication Education, 37* (2), 198-207, 1988.

77. **Gorham, J.** The relationship between verbal teacher immediacy behaviors and student learning. *Communication Education, 37* (1), 40-53, 1988.

78. **Kearney, P., Plax, T. G. and Wendt-Wasco, N. J.** Teacher immediacy for affective learning in divergent college classes. *Communication Quarterly, 33* (1), 61-74, 1985.

79. **Richmond, V. P., Gorham, J. S. and McCrosky, J.** The relationship between selected immediacy behaviors and cognitive learning. In M. McLaughlin (Ed.) *Communication Yearbook 10.* Beverly Hills, CA: Sage, 574-590, 1987.

80. **Christophel, D.** The relationship among teacher immediacy behaviors, student motivation, and learning. *Communication Education, 39*, (4), 323-240, 1990.

81. **Richmond, V. P.** Communication in the classroom: power and motivation. *Communication Education, 39* (3), 181-195, 1990.

82. **Frymier, A. B.** (1994) A model of immediacy in the classroom. *Communication Quarterly, 42* (2), 133-144, 1994.

83. **Rodriguez, J. L., Plax, T. G. and Kearney, P.** Clarifying the relationship between teacher nonverbal immediacy and student cognitive learning: affective learning as the central causal mediator. *Communication Education, 45*, 293-305, 1996.

84. **Short, J., Williams, E. and Christie, B.** *The Social Psychology of Telecommunications.* Toronto: Wiley, 1976.

85. **Rice, R. E.** Contexts of Research in Organizational Computer-Mediated Communication. In M. Lea (Ed.), *Contexts of Computer-Mediated Communication.* New York: Harvester Wheatsheaf, 113-144, 1992.

86. **Picard, R. W.** *Affective Computing.* Cambridge, MA: MIT Press, 1997.

87. **Walther, J.** Interpersonal effects in computer mediated interaction. *Communication Research, 21* (4), 460-487, 1994.

88. **Gunawardena, C. and Zittle, F.** Social presence as a predictor of satisfaction within a computer mediated conferencing environment. *American Journal of Distance Education, 11* (3), 8-26, 1997.

89. **LaRose, R. and Whitten, P.** Re-thinking instructional immediacy for web courses: a social cognitive exploration. *Communication Education, 49*, 320-338, 2000.

90. **Swan, K.** Immediacy, social presence, and asynchronous discussion. In J. Bourne and J. C. Moore (Eds) *Elements of Quality Online Education, Volume 3 in the Sloan-C Series.* Needham, MA: Sloan-C Press, 2002.

91. **Berge, S.** L. Facilitating computer conferencing: Recommendations from the field. *Educational Technology, 15* (1), 22-30, 1995. http://www.emoderators.com/moderators/teach_online.html

92. **Paulsen, M. P.** Moderating educational computer conferences. In Berge, A. L. and Ollins, M. P. (Eds) *Computer-Mediated Communication and the On-Line Classroom in Distance Education.* Cresskill, NJ: Hampton Press, 1995.

93. **Rossman, M.** Successful online teaching using an asynchronous learner discussion forum. *Journal of Asynchronous Learning Networks, 3* (2), 1999. http://www.aln.org/alnweb/journal/Vol3_issue2/Rossman.htm

94. **Anderson, T., Rourke, L., Garrison, D. R. and Archer, W.** Assessing teaching presence in a computer conferencing context. Seattle, WA: Paper presented at the annual meeting of the American Educational Research Association, 2001.

95. **Coppola, N. W., Hiltz, S. R. and Rotter, N.** Becoming a virtual professor: pedagogical roles and ALN. HICSS 2001 Proceedings, *IEEE Press,* 2001.

96. **Rogers, D.** Discussion management. Sloan-C Quality Education Online Effective Practices Sharing, 2002. http://www.sloan-c.org/effectivepractices/

97. **Hatheway, B.** Tutorial instruction model. **Turoff, M.** Large enrollment classes. Sloan-C Quality Education Online Effective Practices Sharing, 2002. http://www.sloan-c.org/effectivepractices/

98. **Turoff, M.** Large enrollment classes. Sloan-C Quality Education Online Effective Practices Sharing, 2002. http://www.sloan-c.org/effectivepractices/

99. **Dziuban, C.** Knowing behavior patterns helps teaching and learning. Sloan-C Quality Education Online Effective Practices Sharing, 2002. http://www.sloan-c.org/effectivepractices/

100. **May, J.** Enhancement of faculty satisfaction. Sloan-C Quality Education Online Effective Practices Sharing, 2002. http://www.sloan-c.org/effectivepractices/

101. **Ubell, R.** Faculty modeling of verbal immediacy in online discussions. Sloan-C Quality Education Online Effective Practices Sharing, 2002. http://www.sloan-c.org/effectivepractices/

102. **Fredericksen, E.** Faculty development process. Sloan-C Quality Education Online Effective Practices Sharing, 2002. http://www.sloan-c.org/effectivepractices/

103. **Wells, M**. Online access to faulty technology training opportunities. Sloan-C Quality Education Online Effective Practices Sharing, 2002. http://www.sloan-c.org/effectivepractices/.

104. **Lewis, T.** Online faculty guide to distance teaching. http://depts.washington.edu/ctltstaf/distance_learning/

105. **Schroeder, R.** Up to date information on new and developing initiatives, methodologies, and technologies in ALN. Sloan-C Quality Education Online Effective Practices Sharing, 2002. http://www.sloan-c.org/effectivepractices/

106. **Wells, R.** *Computer-Mediated Communication for Distance Education: An International Review of Design, Teaching, and Institutional Issues (ACSDE Monograph No. 6).* University Park, PA: The American Center for the Study of Distance Education, 1992.

107. **Hiltz, S. R.** The Virtual Classroom: Learning without Limits via Computer Networks. Norwood, NJ: Ablex, 1994

108. **Poole, D. M.** Student participation in a discussion-oriented online course: a case study. *Journal of Research on Computing in Education, 33* (2), 162-177, 2000.

109. **Ruberg, L. F., Moore, D. M. and Taylor, C. D.** Student participation, interaction, and regulation in a computer-mediated communication environment: a qualitative study. *Journal of Educational Computing Research 14* (3), 243-268, 1996.

110. **Hawisher, G. E. and Pemberton, M. A.** Writing across the curriculum encounters asynchronous learning networks or WAC meets up with ALN. *Journal of Asynchronous Learning Networks, 1* (1), 1997.

111. **Shea, P. J., Swan, K., Fredericksen, E. E and Pickett, A. M.** Student satisfaction and reported learning in the SUNY Learning Network. In J. Bourne and J. C. Moore (Eds) *Elements of Quality Online Education, Volume 3.* Needham, MA: Sloan-C Press, 2002.

112. **Hartman, J., Dziuban, C., Moskal, P.** "Faculty satisfaction in ALNs: A dependent or independent variable?" In J. Bourne and J. Moore (Eds) *Online Education: Volume 1 in the Sloan-C Series.* Needham, MA: Sloan-C Press, 2000; *Journal of Asynchronous Learning Networks, 4* (2), 2000. http://www.aln.org/alnweb/journal/jaln-volume4issue3.htm

113. **Hiltz, R., Coppola, N., Rotter, N., Turoff, M.** "Measuring the importance of collaborative learning for the effectiveness of ALN: A multi-measure, multi-method approach." In J. Bourne and J. Moore (Eds) *Online Education: Volume 1 in the Sloan-C Series.* Needham, MA: Sloan-C Press, 2000; *Journal of Asynchronous Learning Networks, 4* (2), 2000. http://www.aln.org/alnweb/journal/jaln-vol4issue2.htm

114. **Christenson, L. and Menzel, K.** The linear relationship between student reports of teacher immediacy behaviors and perceptions of state motivation, and of cognitive, affective and behavioral learning. *Communication Education, 47,* (1), 82-90, 1998.

115. **Swan, K.** Virtual interactivity: design factors affecting student satisfaction and perceived learning in asynchronous online courses. *Distance Education, 22,* (2), 306-331, 2001.

116. **Ahern, T. C. and El-Hindi, A. E.** Improving the instructional congruency of a computer-mediated small-group discussion: a case study in design and deliver. *Journal of Research on Computing in Education, 32* (3), 385-400, 2000.

117. **Gunawardena, C. N., Lowe, C. A. and Anderson, T.** Analysis of a global online debate and the development of an interaction analysis model for examining social construction of knowledge in computer conferencing. *Journal of Educational Computing Research, 17* (4), 397-431, 1997.

118. **Danchak, M. M., Walther, J. B. and Swan, K.** Presence in mediated instruction: bandwidth, behavior, and expectancy violations. Orlando, FL: Paper presented at the Seventh Annual Sloan-C International Conference on Online Learning, 2001.

119. **Argyle, M. and Cook, M.** *Gaze and Mutual Gaze.* Cambridge: Cambridge University Press, 1976.

120. **Swan, K., Polhemus, L., Shih, L-F. and Rogers, D.** Building knowledge building communities through asynchronous online course discussion. Seattle, WA: Paper presented at the Annual Meeting of the American Educational Research Association, 2001.

121. **Fredericksen, E.** Student satisfaction and reported learning: interaction, learning community formation, and beyond. Sloan-C Quality Education Online Effective Practices Sharing, 2002. http://www.sloan-c.org/effectivepractices/

122. **McCluskey, F.** Defining effective participation. Sloan-C Quality Education Online Effective Practices Sharing, 2002. http://www.sloan-c.org/effectivepractices/

123. **Cutler, R.** Distributed presence and community in Cyberspace. *Interpersonal Computing and Technology, 3,* (2), 12-32, 1995.

124. **Moller, L.** Designing communities of learners for asynchronous distance education. *Educational Technology Research and Development, 46* (4) 115-122, 1998.

125. **Wegerif, R.** The social dimension of asynchronous learning networks. *Journal of Asynchronous Learning Networks, 2* (1), 1998.

126. **Brown, R.E.** The process of building community in distance learning classes. *Journal of Asynchronous Learning Networks,* 5 (2), 2001. http://www.aln.org/alnweb/journal/Vol5_issue2

127. **Haythornthwaite, C.** Building social networks via computer networks: creating and sustaining distributed learning communities. In K. A. Renninger and W. Shumar (Eds) *Building Virtual Communities: Learning and Change in Cyberspace.* Cambridge: Cambridge University Press, 2002.

128. **Hoadley, C. and Pea, R. D.** Finding the ties that bind: tools in support of a knowledge-building community. In K. A. Renninger and W. Shumar (Eds) *Building Virtual Communities: Learning and Change in Cyberspace.* Cambridge: Cambridge University Press, 2002.

129. **Nolan, D. J. and Weiss, J.** Learning in cyberspace: an educational view of the virtual community. In K. A. Renninger and W. Shumar (Eds). *Building Virtual Communities: Learning and Change in Cyberspace.* Cambridge: Cambridge University Press, 2002.

130. **Scardamalia, M., and Bereiter, C.** Computer support for knowledge-building communities. In T. Koschmann (Ed.), *CSCL: Theory and Practice of an Emerging Paradigm.* Mahwah, NJ: Lawrence Erlbaum Associates, 1996.

131. **Hunter, B.** Learning in the virtual community depends upon changes in local communities. In K. A. Renninger and W. Shumar (Eds) *Building Virtual Communities: Learning and Change in Cyberspace.* Cambridge: Cambridge University Press, 2002.

132. **Lave, J., and Wenger, E.** *Situated Learning: Legitimate Peripheral Participation.* Cambridge: Cambridge University Press, 1990.

133. **Wenger, E.** *Communities of Practice: Learning, Meaning, and Identity.* New York: Cambridge University Press, 1997.

134. **Renninger, K. A. and Shumar, W.** Community building with and for teachers at the Math Forum. In K. A. Renninger and W. Shumar (Eds) *Building Virtual Communities: Learning and Change in Cyberspace.* Cambridge: Cambridge University Press, 2002.

135. **Rovai, A. P.** A preliminary look at structural differences in the sense of classroom community between higher education traditional and ALN courses. *Journal of Asynchronous Learning Networks, 6* (1), 2002.

136. **Middleton, H.** Student satisfaction is rooted in learning community. Sloan-C Quality Education Online Effective Practices Sharing, 2002. http://www.sloan-c.org/effectivepractices/

137. **Estabrook, L.** S. University of Illinois at Urbana-Champaign: LEEP3 Master of Science Degree. In Twigg, C. *Innovations in Online Learning: Moving Beyond No Significant Difference.* The Pew Learning and Technology Program, 2000. http://www.center.rpi.edu/PewSym/mono4.html

138. **Hillman, D. C., Willis, D. J. and Gunawardena, C. N.** Learrner-interface interaction in distance education: An extension of contemporary models and strategies for practitioners. *The American Journal of Distance Education, 8* (2), 30-42, 1994.

139. **Gibson, J. J.** *The Senses Considered as Perceptual Systems.* Boston: Houghton Mifflin, 1996.

140. **Oaks, M. K.** Flexible enrollment options offer students control of learning. Sloan-C Quality Education Online Effective Practices Sharing, 2002. http://www.sloan-c.org/effectivepractices/

141. **Sax, B.** Wizards: student tutors help peers learn. Sloan-C Quality Education Online Effective Practices Sharing, 2002. http://www.sloan-c.org/effectivepractices/

142. **Gunn, C.** IVC Online Student Resource Center. Sloan-C Quality Education Online Effective Practices Sharing, 2002. http://www.sloan-c.org/effectivepractices/

143. **Swan, K., Bowman, J., Vargas, J., Schweig, S. and Holmes, A.** Reading the WWW: Making sense on the information superhighway. *Journal of Educational Technology Systems, 27*,(2), 95-104, 1998/99.

144. **Bush, V.** As we may think. *The Atlantic Monthly*, July, 1945, 101-108.

145. **Swan, K.** History, hypermedia, and criss-crossed conceptual landscapes. *Journal of Educational Multimedia and Hypermedia, 3* (2), 120-139, 1994.

146. **Sutton, L.** The principle of vicarious interaction in computer-mediated communications. *International Journal of Educational Telecommunications, 7* (3), 223-242, 2001.

147. **Bandura, A.** Social Foundations of Thought and Action: A Social Cognitive Theory. Englewood Cliffs, NJ: Prentice Hall, 1986.

148. **Fritsch, H.** Witness learning. Hagen, Germany: Fern Universitat Central Institute for Distance Education Research, 1997.

149. **McClintock, R.** The Educators Manifesto: Renewing the Progressive Bond with Posterity through the Social Construction of Digital Learning Communities. New York: Institute for Learning Technologies, Teachers College, Columbia University, 1999. http://www.ilt.columbia.edu/publications/manifesto/contents.html

VIII. ABOUT THE AUTHOR

Karen Swan (B.A., Philosophy, UConn.; M.Ed., Curriculum and Instruction, Keene State College; Ed. M., Ed. D., Columbia University, Instructional Technology) of Kent State University as of 2003, was an Associate Professor of Instructional Technology in the Department of Educational Theory and Practice and the Director of the Learning Technologies Laboratory at the University of Albany. Her research has been primarily in the area of educational computing environments-namely, Logo programming, Integrated Learning Systems and hypermedia-on which she has published widely. She is also interested in social learning from broadcast video and has edited a book on that subject with Dr. Carla Meskill. Dr. Swan has published two interactive video disk applications-The Multimedia Sampler for IBM and Set on Freedom: The American Civil Rights Experience for Glencoe. Dr. Swan is a project director for the Technology and Literacy research strand of the National Research Center on English Learning and Achievement (CELA).

COGNITIVE PRESENCE FOR EFFECTIVE ASYNCHRONOUS ONLINE LEARNING:

THE ROLE OF REFLECTIVE INQUIRY, SELF-DIRECTION AND METACOGNITION

D. Randy Garrison
University of Calgary

- Education is a personal and public learning experience; online education nurtures independent thinkers in an inter-dependent collaborative community of inquiry.

- The asynchronicity and connectivity of online learning offer the unique integration of reflection and collaboration that support higher-order learning in an effective and unprecedented manner.

- The challenge is to get beyond imitating traditional approaches to teaching and learning, emphasizing knowledge generation less than control of learning.

- Students need to be "hooked on a big idea" to become reflective and self-directed in constructing meaning; discussing thinking strategies encourages the development of metacognition.

- At the heart of effective learning is that this collaboration is sustained over a longer period. The dialogic writing process is not as spontaneous and fleeting as verbal communication.

I. INTRODUCTION

Education is only now experiencing the early influence of asynchronous learning networks. In this regard, we have much to learn about using this technology for effective learning. At the outset, asynchronous online learning is not just another educational technology to be used as a simple enhancement and then let slide when something new comes along. Asynchronous online learning is here to stay and is forcing educators to reflect on the teaching and learning process and what constitutes effective learning. Moreover, simulating traditional face-to-face classroom methods using asynchronous online learning simply misses the point that we are operating in a new medium with unique properties.

The goal here is to explore issues of cognitive presence in achieving higher-order learning outcomes in an asynchronous learning environment. To start, the properties of asynchronous online learning will be outlined and a framework presented. The focus will then shift to the role of reflective thinking, self-directed learning and metacognition as concepts that help define and shape effective higher-order learning in an asynchronous learning environment. Issues of learning effectiveness and practices associated with asynchronous learning will conclude the paper.

II. BACKGROUND

It has been obvious for some time that asynchronous online learning has the potential to provide access for learners to a wide range of programs and information. What has not been apparent, or at least not well understood, is that asynchronous online learning is more than a means for accessing information. It has the significant potential for enhancing the intellectual quality of learning environments and outcomes. Asynchronous online learning has the properties to support higher-order learning and create the cognitive presence congruent with deep and meaningful learning outcomes. This will most assuredly mean a move from the transmission and assimilation of vast amounts of information to the interactive and constructive potential of asynchronous online learning in virtual communities of inquiry without diminishing the time and space independence of the learner.

At the core of the properties of asynchronous online learning is the ability to provide collaborative learning experiences at the convenience of the individual. That is, we can have both interaction and independence. Not long ago it was impossible to have both; more of one meant less of the other. From a cognitive presence perspective, online learning networks make possible critical discourse and reflective space. Thus, we identify *connectivity* and *asynchronicity* as the core properties of online learning networks; they have the potential to create a uniquely effective higher-order learning environment. The corollaries of connectivity and asynchronicity for purposes of learning online are collaboration and reflection.

The collaborative and reflective properties of asynchronous online learning offer the potential to create an environment with both social and cognitive presence. In this regard, the challenge is to understand the properties and potential of asynchronous online learning that go beyond "infotainment." However, a greater focus must be on the cognitive aspects of the educational process if quality learning outcomes are to result. At issue is learning, rather than connectivity or control for their own sakes. Learning for educational purposes is more than simply accessing information and participating in chat rooms.

It is to this challenge that we turn next. We begin by providing a framework of asynchronous learning and a guide to contextualize cognitive presence.

III. COMMUNITY OF INQUIRY

Education is both a personal and public learning experience. The challenge for educators is to link the properties of asynchronous online learning with the ability to create communities of learning and inquiry that integrate cognitive, social and teaching presence to meet individual and societal needs. Asynchronous online learning has the particular properties to integrate the interactive and reflective characteristics that enhance cognitive presence beyond that in even small face-to-face groups. True communities of inquiry are possible through collaborative and reflective communication. The educational goal is independent thinkers nurtured in an inter-dependent collaborative community of inquiry. This goal speaks directly to the properties of asynchronous online learning.

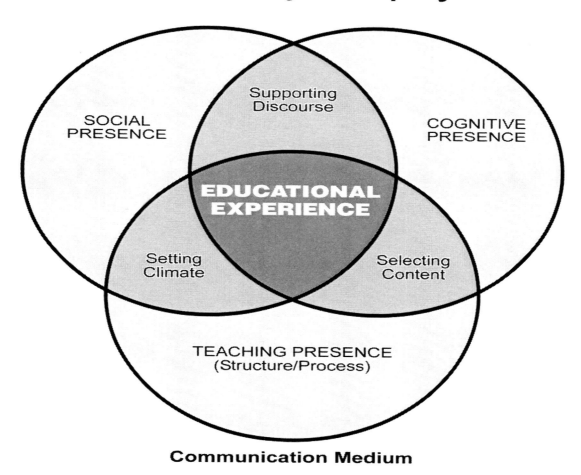

Figure 1: Community of Inquiry
Reproduced by permission from Pergamon [1]

The structural elements of a community of inquiry are cognitive, social and teaching presence [2]. Figure 1 configures these elements. Cognitive presence reflects the intellectual climate and is associated with the facilitation of critical reflection and discourse. Cognitive presence does not occur in isolation. Social presence (personal and emotional connection) is essential in any community of inquiry, and it is a particular challenge for virtual communities. Teaching presence creates and ensures the continued functioning of an educational community. Effective learning depends upon the appropriate balance and integration of all three presences. While the literature is replete with articles and books discussing online learning from the perspective of social and teaching presence, little progress has been made in understanding cognitive presence and higher-order learning effectiveness online.

IV. COGNITIVE PRESENCE

Ultimately, effective learning must take into consideration both the internal cognitive process as well as the external contextual elements that precipitate and shape thinking. Cognitive presence concerns the process of both reflection and discourse in the initiation, construction and confirmation of meaningful learning outcomes. If a deep and meaningful learning outcome is the goal of an educational experience, then an understanding of cognitive presence is a priority. In an asynchronous online learning context, two derivative properties – reflection and collaboration – shape cognitive presence in ways unique to this medium.

A. Reflective Inquiry

According to Dewey, the ultimate challenge is how "shall we treat subject matter … so that it will rank as material of reflective inquiry, not as ready-made intellectual pabulum to be accepted and swallowed as if it were something bought at a shop" [3]. In contrast to the spontaneous verbal communication of face-to-face learning contexts, the asynchronous and largely written communication of asynchronous online learning appears to provide the conditions that encourage reflection. In addition to providing time to reflect, the permanent and precise nature of written communication also enables reflection to interpret and construct meaning.

For Dewey, reflection has to do with the state of learning and one's own mind (knowledge and strategies; to know and use). Learning means inducing reflection through questions and actively monitoring this inquiry for achieving understanding. To understand the reflective process, Dewey proposed a model of inquiry and reflective thinking (see Figure 2) [3]. In an ideal sense, the cycle is initiated with the perception of a need or problem and then proceeds to exploring for relevant knowledge, constructing a meaningful explanation or a solution, and finally resolving dissonance through action. It is important to understand the natural cycle of the learning process to regulate the learning process effectively. Awareness of phases of inquiry or learning can be useful in understanding and selecting specific strategies and activities.

The two dimensions that shape the practical inquiry model are deliberation-action and perception-conception. The deliberation and action dimension is of particular interest here. This axis defines the reflection and collaboration properties of asynchronous learning. This process iterates between thought and action and unifies the private and public worlds of inquiry. Perception and conception operate at the interface of these two worlds. The inquiry model describes the process of creating meaning from experience and the process of creating cognitive presence.

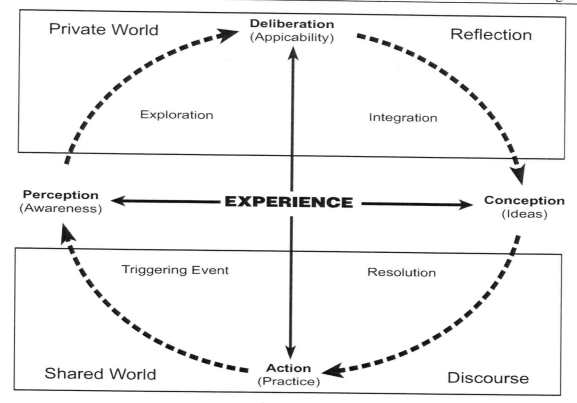

Figure 2: Practical Inquiry
Reproduced by permission from Pergamon [2]

While reflective inquiry represents both constructive (internal) and collaborative (external) aspects of cognition, the perspective here is from the inside out. That is, emphasis is on the generation of knowledge and less so on the control of learning activities. This perspective is reversed in the self-directed learning construct, which looks at learning from the outside in.

B. Self-Directed Learning

The asynchronous and virtual nature of online learning calls on learners to be self-directed and to take responsibility for their learning. That is, online learning calls on learners to assume greater control of monitoring and managing the cognitive and contextual aspects of their learning. This shift in responsibility is both a challenge and an opportunity for asynchronous online learning. The challenge is that educators have the responsibility to provide structure and guidance that will encourage and support students who are assuming increased control of their learning. The opportunity is that asynchronous online learning promotes self-directed and self-regulated learning.

A model of self-directed learning that integrates motivation with issues of reflection and action is provided by Garrison (see Figure 3) [4]. The key dimensions of the model are monitoring (reflection) and managing (action) the learning process. Monitoring is the assessment of feedback information, while managing is controlling learning tasks and activities. Initiating interest and maintaining effort are essential elements in self-direction and effective learning. Without self- monitoring and self-management, learning effectiveness is considerably diminished.

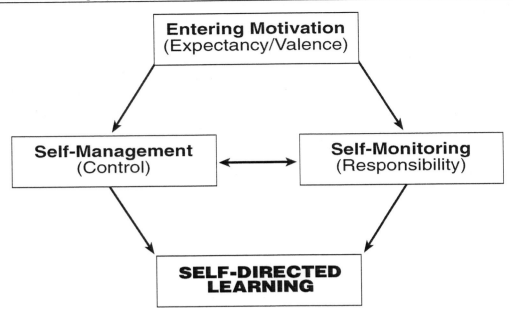

Figure 3: Self-directed learning Dimensions
Reproduced by permission from Garrison, D. R. [4]

The conceptualization and practice of self-directed and self-regulated learning have focused on issues of control, both externally and internally. Garcia and Pintrich [5] make such a distinction and state that self-regulation refers "to students' monitoring, controlling, and regulating their own cognitive activities and actual behavior." That is, self-regulated learners are both active and reflective participants who assume appropriate responsibility and control in the learning process. These are the same essential dimensions of reflective inquiry. As we shall see, they are also the same dimensions of metacognition.

C. Metacognition

In its basic form, two key dimensions or components are associated with metacognition. Schraw describes the two components of metacognition as knowledge of cognition and regulation of cognition. In short, "metacognition consists of knowledge and regulatory skills that are used to control one's cognition". The first includes knowledge of oneself and possible implementation strategies. Regulation of cognition, on the other hand, "refers to a set of activities that helps students control their learning" [6].

Paris and Winograd also believe that metacognition "captures two essential features ... self-appraisal and self-management of cognition" [7]. Self-appraisal is reflection about knowledge and motivational states for resolving a problem, while self-management is the metacognitive orchestration of actually solving a problem. Again, we see the same knowledge and regulatory components of metacognition emerging that are congruent with the dimensions of reflective inquiry and self-direction.

Finally, Hacker sums up understanding of metacognition in these words:

> … there does seem to be general consensus that a definition of metacognition should include at least these notions: knowledge of one's knowledge, processes, and cognitive and affective states; and the ability to consciously and deliberately monitor and regulate one's knowledge, processes, and cognitive and affective states. [8]

In this statement, we see similar dimensions emerging in each of the previous constructs – reflection (knowledge) and regulation (management). More importantly here, they parallel the defining properties of asynchronous online learning. Reflective inquiry, self-direction and metacognition are all associated with internal cognitive and external control issues. At the same time, asynchronous learning is characterized by two properties – asynchronicity and connectivity. For high cognitive presence, both of these properties must be present. Attention must be given to the opportunity to reflect upon and monitor knowledge (re)construction as well as the ability to collaborate and manage the learning process.

In terms of the collaborative property, Schraw emphasizes the importance of interaction in modeling and sharing cognitive experiences. The properties of metacognition are congruent with the individual wanting or needing "to communicate, explain, and justify its thinking to other organisms as well as to itself; these activities clearly require metacognition. … [and] a penchant for engaging in those metacognitive acts termed social cognition" [6]. Learning in an educational context is socially situated, demonstrating the essential importance of interaction and community to reveal cognitive and metacognitive knowledge and strategies. This is further supported by Hartman who notes that discussion about thinking strategies encourages the development of metacognition [9].

D. Summary

Each of the previous constructs are described in terms of essentially two dimensions or clusters of ideas. In the first cluster are the ideas of reflection, monitoring, and knowledge; while in the second cluster are ideas such as collaboration, management, and discourse. On the surface, they appear to break down into internal and external themes. More importantly for our purposes, they correspond to the core properties of online learning in which asynchronicity encourages reflection and connectivity provides unique opportunities for collaboration and discourse. Reflection is enhanced by the asynchronous property and collaboration is made possible by its connectivity.

The properties of asynchronous online learning match well with the characteristics of higher-order learning constructs such as reflective inquiry, self-direction and metacognition. There is every reason to believe that asynchronous online learning can be extremely effective in supporting higher-order learning and creating quality cognitive presence online. Moreover, it could be argued that asynchronous online learning has a unique advantage over face-to-face learning in creating cognitive presence and achieving deep and meaningful learning outcomes through the integration of the asynchronous and connectivity properties. Yet, we know so little about creating cognitive presence in online learning.

The close mapping of online learning properties and higher-order learning dimensions suggest considerable potential in informing and guiding learning effectiveness. In the next section, we explore how these seemingly inherent advantages might be translated to practice.

V. LEARNING EFFECTIVENESS

Most attention in the literature devoted to understanding and facilitating asynchronous online learning has focused on teaching presence and social presence. Social presence is an essential element of any educational experience since, by definition, education is a socially sanctioned and shared process. Similarly, education has an overriding cognitive component associated with constructing and re-constructing societal knowledge for the benefit of the individual and society. Finally, teaching is essential to the educational experience and is the means of bringing together the social and cognitive elements of the learning process in a purposeful and effective manner. Learning effectiveness, therefore, must include consideration of social, cognitive and teaching presence. While the focus in this section is on cognitive presence and its implications for learning effectiveness, it should be realized that it is theoretically and practically impossible to separate this discussion from teaching and social presence.

To understand learning effectiveness for asynchronous online learning is first to appreciate what is unique about this medium. To reiterate, the asynchronous (i.e., reflective) and connectivity (i.e., collaborative) properties of online learning are not to be taken separately. It is how we integrate and use the capabilities of asynchronous online learning in a synergetic manner that makes the online medium unique. How we combine and integrate the reflective and collaborative possibilities of the inseparable private and public worlds makes the learning experience effective for all concerned.

In this regard, it must be made clear that learning effectiveness cannot be accomplished by way of either a "sage on the stage" nor a "guide on the side". Each approach is focuses on only one of the dimensions or properties of an integral natural learning experience. Certainly, using asynchronous online learning simply to access more information is not to improve learning effectiveness. Nor will access to free discussions or chats necessarily provide effective learning. The educational process is far too complex for such slogans to shape an effective learning experience. These simplistic, one-sided views do not help maximize new learning technologies that have the potential to change radically the context and communication of the teaching and learning transaction.

Another effectiveness issue worthy of note is the employment of right to left thinking. That is, being clear and committed to intended learning outcomes (in this case higher-order learning) and then implementing methods (e.g., reflective inquiry and self-direction) that are congruent with achieving such goals. The research on deep and surface learning make it clear that effective learning must have clear expectations and then employ approaches congruent with the intended outcomes [10]. That is, provide time to reflect (avoid excessive workload), have students assume appropriate levels of responsibility and control, and provide opportunities to collaboratively assess the depth of understanding (assess for understanding). This point is made by Ramsden when he states that whatever we say about developing "understanding and critical thinking … our assessment practices and the amount of content we cover . . . demonstrate to undergraduate students what competence in a subject really means" [10].

Finally, there must be an emphasis on inquiry. Inquiry is based on questioning from both teacher and students, individually and collaboratively, seeking answers to these questions, and then confirming understanding, diagnosing misconceptions and testing solutions through applications and/or discourse. In this regard, "Higher-order learning requires systematic and sustained critical discourse where dissonance and problems are resolved through exploration, integration, and testing" [11]. Higher-order learning requires teaching presence and skilled facilitation.

Too often online discussion is concentrated at the exploration or information gathering stage. For higher-level learning, discourse must be seen as a means to resolving issues and testing ideas through vicarious or direct application. Garrison et al. found that only 17% of the online discussions in two graduate level courses were focused on the latter two stages of reflective inquiry [11]. The most likely explanation for this finding is inappropriate teaching presence (i.e., design, facilitation and assessment) in terms of clarifying the intended higher-order learning outcomes, modeling appropriate responses, and then assessing and shaping the discussion for this purpose. All participants must understand their roles and the intended goals of the learning experience.

Taking responsibility and control of one's learning is the core of reflective inquiry, self-directed learning, and the development of metacognitive abilities that ultimately provide the foundation for continued learning. Inquiry requires an environment of both independence and support. Asynchronous online learning integrates the properties of freedom with connectivity, once a logical contradiction.

A. Effective Practices

This discussion is shaped by an appreciation for the properties of asynchronous online learning as well as creating and facilitating cognitive presence for higher-order learning outcomes. Cognitive presence for purposes of higher-order learning is associated with effectively facilitating and developing reflective thinking, self-directed learning and metacognitive awareness. Furthermore, when educators capitalize on the integration of the central properties of online learning and dimensions of higher-order learning – asynchronicity/reflection and connectivity/collaboration – there is a high probability that deep and meaningful learning outcomes will result. In other words, recognizing and utilizing the unique capability of asynchronous learning networks to provide reflective and collaborative learning opportunities is the first step in enhancing learning effectiveness.

Although cognitive presence is created through the dynamic integration of, and iteration between, critical reflection and discourse, we shall discuss the effective use of each separately. Moreover, we shall limit our discussion to key principles and guidelines.

1. Reflection

The first point to be made is that effective learning online must utilize the strengths of written communication, including its asynchronicity. While writing can support collaborative learning, its dominant strength is that writing's permanence and precision encourages reflection. When managed well from a facilitation perspective, written communication has great potential to establish cognitive presence and support reflective inquiry.

To use written communication effectively, learners must be given the opportunity to revise and refine their comments and ideas. The permanent nature of written communication in an online context provides for a systematic approach to constructing meaning, particularly in difficult and ill-defined content areas. However, the use of asynchronous learning requires planning, structure, and the facilitation of the discourse directed toward clear goals.

From a content perspective, the key is not to inundate students with information. The first responsibility of the teacher or content expert is to identify the central idea and have students reflect upon and share their conceptions. Students need to be "hooked on a big idea" [12] if learners are to be motivated to be reflective and self-directed in constructing meaning. Inundating learners with information is discouraging and is not consistent with higher-order learning. Assessment must also be designed to measure depth of understanding if that is the intended learning outcome. Inappropriate assessment along with excessive information will seriously undermine reflection and the effectiveness of asynchronous learning.

Perhaps the most effective practice in establishing an online cognitive presence congruent with higher-order learning is for the teacher or facilitator to model reflective inquiry. This is best done with the teachers objectively providing commentary and insight into their thinking processes (i.e., thinking out-loud). The purpose is to increase metacognitive awareness – a precondition for critical thinking and self-direction. Modeling reflective inquiry provides learners with concrete examples of how to approach subject matter for purposes of constructing personal meaning. Students learn how to manage and monitor their own learning and perhaps to demystify knowledge development. They gain the ability and confidence to be self-directed learners. In this regard, the teacher must participate in, but not dominate, discussions.

Modeling reflective inquiry and increasing metacognitive awareness can be greatly assisted by explicitly sharing a model of the thinking and learning process such as practical inquiry. Insight into the phases of inquiry and learning can help learners appreciate whether they are defining a problem, searching for relevant information, connecting ideas for meaning, or confirming understanding. Metacognitive awareness provided by such models can be an important tool in acting confidently and effectively through the selection and employment of appropriate strategies. This combined with teachers sharing their thinking processes can be of considerable help so learners can develop metacognitive strategies and abilities and become reflective, self-directed learners.

2. Collaboration

Reflective activities can only be artificially separated from the collaborative process of learning. Collaborative asynchronous learning can also be sustained in a unique manner. At the heart of effective learning is that this collaboration is sustained over a longer period. The dialogic writing process is not as spontaneous and fleeting as verbal communication. These characteristics, however, provide new possibilities as well as challenges.

The first challenge is to establish a community of inquiry where learners feel connected and cognitively engaged, where a community supports and encourages ideas to be critically analyzed and meaning to be negotiated. The discourse, however, must be purposeful and focused. The facilitator must be able to interject new ideas, diagnose misconceptions, and move the discussion toward resolution that may or may not be predictable. The role of the facilitator "goes beyond a neutral weaving of participants' contributions" [2]. Clarifying, explaining and summarizing are legitimate functions of a facilitator. As long as this direct intervention is constructive, open communication is not threatened. At the same time, lecturing online or simply providing access to information is a complete misuse of asynchronous learning networks.

One important technique is to allow students to moderate their discussions in small groups. This will actively engage most learners in a committed and free manner. The key is for students to report their progress or conclusions. In this way, they receive appropriate feedback from all participants and confirmation of their understanding. By providing this increased responsibility and control, learners are encouraged to become more self-directed. The same technique can also be used for group projects, which is an excellent way to have learners collaboratively apply their new knowledge.

Establishing cognitive presence online represents a significant shift in the design and delivery of educational experience. As such, the principles and guidelines for learning effectively online require a significant shift in our thinking. That is, online learning effectiveness requires a shift away from information dissemination and assimilation to the collaborative construction of meaning and understanding. The practical challenge is to design the learning activities that provide the right balance and integration of reflection and collaboration.

VI. CONCLUSION

The purpose of this study was to identify the essential properties of asynchronous online learning that will enhance cognitive presence and learning effectiveness. The asynchronicity and connectivity properties of online learning offer the potential for the unique integration of reflective and collaborative learning opportunities. From a philosophical perspective, these properties can be translated into a collaborative-constructivist approach to learning [13] that combines the stimulation and feedback of a collaborative and socially shared approach with reflective inquiry and personal responsibility to construct meaning. Asynchronous online learning has the potential to support higher-order learning in an effective and unprecedented manner.

The challenge is to get beyond imitating traditional technologies and approaches to teaching and learning. We must continue to learn about the multiplicative properties of asynchronous online learning. This means moving beyond the additive novelty of asynchronous online learning "that replicates the delivery of lectures over a computer and the Internet enhanced with multimedia analogues to the overheads of a lecture" [2]. Unreflective adoption of past practices will not help us understand the multiplicative properties of communicative freedom, information access, and individual control of time and space for creating an expanded cognitive presence and effective higher-order learning experiences and outcomes.

It is not a question of simply doing things more efficiently. We must begin to understand the cognitive presence implications of asynchronous online learning and how educators can design and model reflective and collaborative inquiry so learners have the opportunity to reflect and engage in meaningful discourse with metacognitive awareness, taking responsibility to manage and monitor their learning. Asynchronous online learning can create cognitive presence higher-order learning requires. We must learn how to better facilitate such learning in a variety of educational contexts.

VII. REFERENCES

1. **Garrison, D. R., Anderson, T., & Archer, W.** (1999). Critical Inquiry in a Text-based Environment: Computer Conferencing in Higher Education. *The Internet and Higher Education*, 2(2-3), 87-105.)

2. **Garrison, D. R., & Anderson, T.** (in press). *E-Learning in the 21st Century: A Framework for Research and Practice*. London: Routledge/Falmer.

3. **Dewey, J.** (1933). *How We Think* (rev. ed.). Boston: D.C. Heath.

4. **Garrison, D. R.** (1997). Self-directed Learning: Toward a Comprehensive Model. *Adult Education Quarterly*, 48(1), 15-31.

5. **Garcia, T., & Pintrich, P. R.** (1994). Regulating Motivation and Cognition in the Classroom: The Role of Self-schemas and Self-regulatory Strategies. In D. H. Schunk & B. J. Zimmerman

(Eds.), *Self-regulation of Learning and Performance: Issues and Educational Applications* (pp. 127-153). Hillsdale, NJ: Lawrence Erlbaum Associates.

6. **Schraw, G.** (2001). Promoting General Metacognitive Awareness. In H. J. Hartman (Ed.), *Metacognition in Learning and Instruction: Theory, Research and Practice* (pp. 3-16). Boston: Kluwer. Quotation from Flavell, J. Cognitive Development. NJ: Prentice-Hall, 1987.

7. **Paris, S. G., & Winograd, P.** (1990). How Metacognition Can Promote Academic Learning and Instruction. In B. F. Jones & L. Idol (Eds.), *Dimensions of Thinking and Cognitive Instruction* (pp. 15-51). Hillsdale, NJ: Lawrence Erlbaum Associates.

8. **Hacker, D. J.** (1998). Definitions and Empirical Foundations. In D. J. Hacker, J. Dunlosky, & A. C. Graesser (Eds.), *Metacognition in Educational Theory and Practice* (pp. 1- 23). Hillsdale, NJ: Lawrence Erlbaum Associates.

9. **Hartman, H. J.** (2001). Teaching Metacognitively. In H. J. Hartman (Ed.), *Metacognition in Learning and Instruction: Theory, Research and Practice*. Boston: Kluwer.

10. **Ramsden, P.** (1992). *Learning to Teach in Higher Education*. London: Routledge.

11. **Garrison, D. R., Anderson, T., & Archer, W.** (2001). Critical Thinking, Cognitive Presence and Computer Conferencing in Distance Education. *American Journal of Distance Education*, 15(1), 7-23.

12. **Prawat, R.S.** (1998). Current Self-regulation Views of Learning and Motivation Viewed through a Deweyan Lens: The Problems with Dualism. *American Educational Research Journal*, 35, 199-224.

13. **Garrison, D. R., & Archer, W.** (2000). *A Transactional Perspective on Teaching-learning: A Framework for Adult and Higher Education*. Oxford, UK: Pergamon.

VIII. ABOUT THE AUTHOR

Randy Garrison is a Professor and Dean of the Faculty of Extension at the University of Alberta. He previously held the position of Associate Dean (Research and Development), in the Faculty of Continuing Education, at the University of Calgary. He began his academic career at the University of Calgary as Director of Distance Education. There he developed a successful Master's degree specializing in workplace learning that was accessible to working professionals through computer mediated communication. Dr Garrison's areas of research are related to the teaching and learning transaction in the context of adult, distance, and higher education. He has published extensively in these areas.

IMPROVING QUANTITATIVE RESEARCH METHODS IN STUDIES OF ASYNCHRONOUS LEARNING NETWORKS (ALN)

Starr Roxanne Hiltz
New Jersey Institute of Technology

J. B. Arbaugh
University of Wisconsin

- If ALN research is to be useful for informing educational research and practice, it needs greater attention to more rigorous, pedagogically sound measurement.

- Cross-institutional ALN research has yielded valuable insights, such as the usefulness of ALN in cross-cultural settings, the role of interaction in ALN courses, the importance of instructor experience, and the perceived flexibility of the medium in predicting ALN effectiveness.

- While recent advances in multi-course, multi-discipline ALN research are encouraging, it is vital to extend study beyond institutional, state, and even national boundaries.

- An evaluation of the effectiveness of a learning medium ought also to include measures of the costs of the course delivery, including money and time.

- Studies tracking subsequent student performance after their ALN experiences are essentially non-existent.

I. INTRODUCTION AND OVERVIEW

The first year of the Sloan-funded project to "improve the quantity, quality, and dissemination" of research on the effectiveness of learning networks focused on gathering, organizing, and analyzing past empirical studies about ALN effectiveness. These studies are summarized and available for discussion at the WebCenter for Learning Networks Effectiveness Research (http://ALNResearch.org), and an analysis of them was presented at the 2001 Sloan summer workshop and in Volume 3 of the Sloan-C quality series [32].

During the second year, the focus turned to setting an agenda for future research on ALN effectiveness, including how to improve the quality and comprehensiveness of ALN research. The leading researchers on ALN, judged by their production of refereed published articles, were invited to a workshop at NJIT to share ideas and reach consensus on the top research concerns for the next five to ten years. Participants plan to develop a collaboratively written book which describes what we know based on past research, what we need to know, and the methodological techniques (both quantitative and qualitative) needed to improve knowledge about ALN effectiveness. The book about these findings is planned for publication in 2004.

This paper includes selections from the first draft of a key chapter from the book on quantitative methodologies for studying ALN effectiveness. We invite feedback and suggestions that will be useful to ALN researchers.

This paper addresses two main themes concerning quantitative studies of ALNs. The first theme is measuring learning. Most studies comparing online and face-to-face courses suggest either that there is no significant difference, or that ALNs result in significantly higher learning than do traditional classroom settings. While these findings might be encouraging, these comparative studies typically suffer a variety of methodological problems that make it difficult to reach definitive conclusions concerning ALN learning effectiveness.

A second theme is improving the generalizability of findings in ALN studies. Historically, this stream of research has been highly reliant upon single-course studies or on a small number of courses at a single institution. While these studies have provided some insights, the idiosyncrasies of the single course bases complicates generalizing to other learning environments. This paper includes recommendations for improving research methodologies.

II. IMPROVING QUANTITATIVE RESEARCH ON ALN EFFECTIVENESS

The first and most basic measure of learning effectiveness is, "How much did the students learn? How well did they master skills? How well can they apply knowledge?" If we cannot validly measure learning, then we cannot compare the relative effectiveness of learning. Thus, we begin with a review of the major ways in which learning can be measured objectively or quantitatively, including some problems and limitations with each of the possible measures.

Besides the assessment of learning within a course and the assignment of a grade, there are also other effectiveness criteria, including students' own evaluations of the course and of their satisfaction with it, and measures of resource expenditures, such as how much time the students and faculty spent to achieve their learning objectives. If students in "mode A" learn the same as in "mode B," but they spend twice as much time, or it takes twice as much faculty time, then "mode A" cannot really be called "effective." We will thus look briefly at the use of attitudinal surveys and at time logs and other alternatives to measuring effort in a course.

A. Methods of Assessing Student Learning[1]

1. Grades (on exams or in the course)

The most usual way of assessing student learning is to give an examination. This may include "objective" questions such as "true or false" or "multiple choice," or essay questions that are open-ended and require students to compose answers. In the traditional exam, there is a fixed amount of time allowed, and the students are proctored to make sure that they do not cheat.

Many volumes examine the proper techniques for and the limitations of the examination for assessing student learning [16]. Chief among the limitations of the exam are that test taking is itself a skill; many students suffer from "test anxiety" and do not do well under time pressure. Other students are good at guessing the correct answer when they see a list, even if they do not really know the answer. Second, in a limited time such as an hour or two, only simple skills can be tested; often students feel that the questions were "unfair" or "tricky" and did not adequately cover the main learning objectives of the course. Third, for a course conducted as a learning network in which one of the methods and objectives is for students to work as collaborative teams, the individual examination is not in keeping with all of the rest of the course. Fourth, despite proctoring, there may be cheating, on objective exams in particular.

Despite the limitations of the objective examination, it will probably always remain one of the means of assessing student learning, since the instructor effort needed for grading is relatively low; and in fact, if the exam is objective, the task can be offloaded to automation or to teaching assistants. However, in terms of comparing the effectiveness of different teachers or different modes of course delivery, the main problem with test scores, or even course grades, is that instructors tend to curve grades within a section. That is, they tend to add points or make other adjustments so that each section of each course has a grade distribution that looks something like a normal curve, with a sufficient number of A's (although grade inflation skews towards A and away from F). In addition, different instructors have different grading patterns; some are considered "easy graders" and seldom flunk students or give less than a B, whereas others are considered "hard graders" and tend to reserve A grades to designate outstanding work. Thus, even "objective" grades tend to have a strong element of subjectivity.

2. Collaborative Examinations

In a collaborative exam, students work together in all phases of the exam process, although in the version described below, individuals answer the actual exam questions. NJIT experimented with collaborative examinations [41]. In a two-semester study of a graduate information systems course, students designed collaborative exams. First, each student composed essay questions; next, each student selected one question and answered it; third, the student who created the question graded the answer and provided a justification of the grading. Subsequently, Ph.D. students enrolled in the course did an intermediate review of the grading, and lastly, the instructor provided a final grade. If the scores of the grader and intermediate reviewer were within a few points of each other, the instructor assigned

---

[1] Portions of this section are adapted from the online tutorial by Constance Steinkeuler and Sharon Derry created for the WebCenter for Learning Networks Effectiveness Research (www.alnresearch.org).

the higher score. If the two disagreed, then the instructor graded the question. (The instructor regraded between 20-30% of the questions.)

Various advantages of the collaborative exam were reported by students in post-course surveys (N= 138 responses). Results show the majority of students felt that they learned throughout the process including making up questions, and grading others' answers; that the exams were successful in demonstrating what they learned; and that it was an enjoyable process. Students found the collaborative online exam to be a less stressful experience than traditional exams, and a majority recommended that it be used for other courses.

Of course, the collaborative exam would not solve the problem of "curving" and "grade inflation." However, a collaborative exam rather than the traditional exam might more validly measure the kinds of skills taught in online courses.

3. Projects and portfolios

A project is an artifact prepared by an individual student or a collaborative group of students to apply the knowledge and skills in the course. For instance, in a programming course, the student may write a program. In a course on computer ethics, the student may analyze a case scenario and apply ethical principles to arrive at a suggested resolution of the problem situation. In an architecture course, the student may construct a paper or a computerized model of a building. The project has the dual aims of improving the students' skills though practice, and of demonstrating whether the student can actually apply the course knowledge.

Portfolios are student-prepared collections of documents that evidence understanding of important concepts or mastery of key skills; portfolios require students to organize, synthesize, and communicate their achievements throughout the semester. Most portfolios are students' personalized collections of their work over the entire duration of the course. For online courses, these portfolios are often created on a web page so other students and the instructor can view them. A strong motivational factor is that the work done during the course can also be shared with prospective employers and others. For a project or portfolio approach to assessment to work well, instructors must communicate expectations to students at the beginning of the course, outlining (1) the kinds of mastery students are to demonstrate; (2) the types of materials that are considered evidence that those goals have been met; and (3) the criteria by which the portfolios will be evaluated. Because procrastination is more likely in online courses, instructors provide assignments with specific due dates for each the items to include in the portfolio. The portfolio assignment includes scoring rubrics, systematic guidelines for content and evaluation weight. Some or all of the assignments may be collaborative, in which case the scoring rubric needs to describe how the individual contribution to the group project will be assessed.

However, grading portfolios can be time-consuming and often require multiple grading rubrics, one for each type of artifact they may contain. Thus, portfolios are usually best suited for courses with smaller enrollments; however, they can be modified for larger courses by reducing their scope and tightly structuring their format for greater uniformity. If there are group projects, then there are fewer total items to assess, and larger classes become more amenable to a project/ portfolio grading approach. It has been found that assessing on an assignment-by-assignment basis is more reliable than assessing on a portfolio-by-portfolio basis [37].

4. Participation (number, frequency, length of comments)

Since learning networks involve students contributing daily to class discussions and activities, it is possible to directly assess this constant participation, rather than have a separate assessment activity. One can simply count things like the number, regularity, and length of contributions. The problem with this approach is that students may simply load the class discussion with items that are not very thoughtful or original, or perhaps not even on the subject. For a small class, the instructor could grade the quality and relevance of every contribution as if it were an essay. For larger classes, with hundreds of comments every week, such grading becomes an impossible burden.

We are not aware of any studies of the efficacy and methodology for directly assessing online learning from the transcript of the class discussions. Perhaps some software could be developed to aid in this process. For example, the original Virtual Classroom® software counted and displayed the number, length, and percentage of contributions of each student during any specified time. This made it easy for the instructor to use weekly data to encourage more regular or active contributions if students seemed to be lurking rather than actively participating. Conceivably, a program could automatically analyze feedback each week, showing students what their contributions were in comparison to the average for the rest of the class.

B. Methods for Evaluating Course Outcomes

Whatever the method used to assess student learning, there are also other aspects of the course process and outcomes that need to be measured for a complete picture of course effectiveness. These include subjective measures of course satisfaction by both students and faculty, and measures of resource expenditures, particularly time.

1. Attitudinal Surveys: Perceived Learning/Satisfaction

Attitudinal surveys, which are most often post-course student evaluations, can provide valuable information on students' perceptions of the course, the discipline, the instructor, the materials and tools, and individual progress and knowledge gains. This strategy is highly useful for teasing apart which elements of the pedagogy and/or technology students feel are most easily mastered, most comfortable, and/or most personally rewarding, as well as which elements are perceived as most difficult, most frustrating, and/or most futile. In general, such surveys can be administered relatively quickly and conveniently. For instance, computer-administered surveys that are automatically transferred into a statistical database for analysis can simplify the analysis process.

One serious source of invalidity in survey data is that respondents may be different from non-respondents; thus, it is important to take steps to try to get all students to complete a questionnaire. Non-response bias is important because non-respondents may very well have differing perceptions of the ALN experience, thereby making the conclusions drawn from studies of low response rates rather misleading [21, 22].

There are several ways that researchers can address the non-response issue. First, they can increase the level of their own hands-on involvement in the data collection process by means such as personalizing the appeal for participation with letters and initiating additional mailings to boost response rates [21, 46]. An additional benefit of multiple mailings is that they allow for comparisons between early and late responders. Since late respondents often closely resemble non-respondents, these comparisons can be used to test for the likelihood of non-response bias.

Secondly, researchers can decrease the inconvenience of completing and returning surveys, or increase the rewards to students for completing them. Online surveys that can be submitted with a click instead of an envelope and a trip to the mailbox seem to help response rate somewhat, especially if automatic reminders are built into software to notify non-respondents. Another strategy that has worked at NJIT is to have instructors distribute and collect post course questionnaires at proctored final examinations.

Another validity problem is that the data generated through such surveys is *self-reported* rather than direct observation. One problem is the tendency towards a "halo effect;" if the student is generally happy with the course, including the instructor and the grade, then all questions on a survey tend to be answered positively, or if the student is unhappy, the reverse is true. Attitudinal surveys can provide a summative overview of how and/or what students do, think, or feel about a given course, but a more detailed understanding of students' attitudes requires the use of supplementary research methods such as individual or group interviews

2. Measuring Time and Effort

In addition to self-reported outcomes, an evaluation of the effectiveness of a learning medium ought to include measures of the costs of the course delivery. Costs include both money expended to produce and deliver course materials (for example, on-campus courses include the costs of constructing and maintaining the physical plant) and time spent by the instructor and the students specific sections of the course. Both money and time measures are difficult to obtain, though reasonable approximations of the monetary cost of producing and offering a course ought to be obtainable from university accounting records.

3. Experimental Designs

To reach valid conclusions about cause and effect in terms of the medium of course delivery, experimental design is required. However, it is generally very difficult to achieve the standards of a controlled laboratory experiment, which requires random assignment of students to conditions in ALN research. For example, one cannot randomly assign a student to take a face-to-face section of a course that meets at a time and place which conflicts with other obligations of the student. Without random assignment, there is no assurance that the treatment groups are comparable and that the observed differences in learning are the result of the medium. On the other hand, it is possible to experiment with various treatments within the sections of a course. For example, students could be randomly assigned to be graded by exams constructed and graded by the instructor, or by collaborative exams constructed and graded by the students themselves. In addition, a quasi-experimental design that does not use random assignment could be used to measure items such as knowledge gain through pre-course and post-course exams [3, 4].

The guidelines for designing and carrying out experiments are beyond the scope of this paper. However, some of design limitations should be noted. A course is not a "laboratory;" many other things are happening to the student while taking a particular course. In other words, it is impossible to control all of the sources of variance during a semester-long course. To achieve the best chance of finding relationships between variables in field experiments, it is especially important to have a large sample of students, so that the laws of probability can allow the effects of the independent variable(s) of interest to become apparent. It is also important that "instructor" be one of the controlled variables; that is, the same instructor should be offering all of the conditions being studied, rather than say, one instructor offering a face-to-face version of a course and another instructor offering an online version. In past studies, variations among instructors were much larger than variations associated with mode of course delivery (for example, [28]).

4. Expanding the scope and validity of ALN studies

ALN research has generally progressed from anecdotal experiences with single courses to comparisons with classroom learning in single course settings, to multi-course and multi-discipline ALN studies. This pattern first emerged via the efforts of researchers at the New Jersey Institute of Technology beginning in the mid 1980s and progressing through their Virtual Classroom project during the 1990s [27, 28, 30, 31, 11, 18]. This pattern has emerged in other institutional settings beginning in the early to mid 1990s [2, 3, 9, 10, 13, 19, 42, 44].

Based on this progression of research, we would like to help encourage future researchers to build upon this emerging body of knowledge. Part of understanding how to build on this research requires identifying areas where the value added of additional future research would be rather limited. Obviously, ALNs are no longer new. As a result, we are now familiar enough with them to know that anecdotal reports of single course experiences by a single instructor no longer substantially increase knowledge about ALNs.

Nevertheless, single-course comparison studies of ALNs and classrooms are numerous [1, 3. 14, 24, 38, 39, 40, 47]. Reviews of ALN-classroom comparative literature [8, 48], suggest that there is more than enough research comparing student performance in ALN and face-to-face courses to conclude that, the medium at worst has a neutral impact on student performance. The overabundance of single-course studies suggests the need for increased research using multi-course, multi-discipline, and/or multi-institution samples. Therefore, the remainder of this paper focuses identifying issues that should be addressed in future studies.

C. Research needs

1. Multi-course studies

Multi-course studies would provide several methodological benefits for ALN research. Two direct benefits would be increased external validity and statistical power. Since ALN research has historically been reliant upon many studies based on individual courses [3, 12, 20, 45], many findings may be reflecting idiosyncrasies of the instructor rather than accurate prescriptions for best practice in web-based course delivery. Multi-course studies increase the likelihood that these instructor-unique characteristics can be controlled for, thereby allowing for increased generalizability of findings.

2. Multi-institution studies

While the recent trend toward multi-course studies is welcome, other factors must also be addressed to advance the state of ALN research. In addition to providing increased external validity, multi-institution studies provide an opportunity to increase statistical power in studies of ALN courses. Since the concept of online delivery of education in some disciplines is still relatively new, it is somewhat rare that an individual institution would offer a large number of class sections in a web-based format. As a result, most ALN studies have tended to use relatively small sample sizes. These small samples result in low statistical power [17]. Using multiple-institution samples is one way to efficiently increase sample sizes.

In addition to providing statistical benefits, multi-institution studies would provide greater opportunities to generalize research findings. Presently, nearly all multi-course studies have been conducted with a single college or university as a research setting. While the findings of these studies have certainly been fruitful, institution-unique characteristics may limit the generalizability of these findings to other settings. For instance, consider two of the primary sources of multi-course studies, the Virtual Classroom Project at NJIT and the SUNY Learning Network. The majority of published research conducted at NJIT suggests that ALNs have a positive impact on participant satisfaction and student learning [11, 28, 31]. While this is encouraging news for ALN supporters, NJIT is the "perennially most wired campus" in America according to Yahoo. Also encouraging are SUNY's studies that include thousands of students on different campuses of the state university system, and thus are multi-campus if not multi-institutional. SUNY results have also been very positive in terms of satisfaction of students and faculty with ALN [23]. SUNY has won multiple awards for the excellence of its ALN programs, including an award for the best faculty-training program. Of course, one would expect excellent results in schools like these. We have yet to learn, however, what happens on relatively small campuses that may not have similar levels of technical and support resources.

Therefore, collaborative efforts of researchers at different institutions should be particularly encouraged. Historically, there has been a paucity of multi-institution ALN research, and most has been on a rather small scale, usually between two institutions and a limited number of courses. In spite of these limitations, cross-institutional ALN research has yielded valuable insights, such as the usefulness of ALN in cross-cultural settings [49], the role of interaction in ALN courses [28], the importance of instructor experience, and the perceived flexibility of the medium in predicting ALN effectiveness [6, 43, 33, 49].

3. Multi-national studies

If comparisons of institutional practices merit additional research, then certainly an emerging area of future research should be the study of ALN practices in different national or cultural contexts. Presently, much of this research is rather small in scope, often focusing on multi-national collaboration between schools in the context of a single course or activity within a course [33, 49]. However, as more schools seek to deliver education via the internet to a global audience and create collaborative ventures with schools in other countries, opportunities for multi-national ALN studies will certainly increase. In addition to the comparative, statistical, validity enhancements to ALN research previously mentioned, multi-national studies will allow additional research in topics such as cross-cultural learning network selection and development [33, 36], teaching and learning styles of international audiences [15, 25], and technological impacts on learning [49].

4. Longitudinal studies

One consequence of the relative newness of delivery of education via the internet is that opportunities for the study of ALN-related changes in student, instructor, program, and institutional behavior over time have been extremely limited. Researchers associated with the Virtual Classroom project have been among the leaders in longitudinal research [29]. Otherwise, longitudinal studies (which collect measures on the same subjects over a period of time) have tended to be limited to designs such as repeated measurement of subjects over a semester [1, 38, 49] or following a small cadre of students through their ALN experiences over a 1-2 year period of time [34, 35]. How do students, and faculty, change their behavior and attitudes over time, from their first online course to their second, fifth, or tenth?

In addition to seeing changes in student behavior over time, longitudinal research examining program and institutional changes can be very useful for schools beginning online programs. For instance, Arbaugh [5] recently found that the flexibility and convenience of ALN courses were significant predictors of student learning and satisfaction in the first two years of his study, but ceased to be significant predictors after that. This finding suggests that the days in which schools can compete based on the convenience of their ALN offerings may be numbered. In addition, initial work on changes in instructor behavior by Coppola, Hiltz, & Rotter [18] suggest that transitions in teaching styles and personas are very much works in progress. Additional research in these areas will greatly enhance our understanding of how ALNs evolve and provide us with insights on how they may further change in the future.

5. Future performance of ALN participants

Student performance would be a natural extension of increased longitudinal work. Studies tracking subsequent student performance after their initial ALN experiences are essentially non-existent. Multi-year studies would measure the long-term retention of course materials. For instance, students who take an introductory Computer Science course in various modes could be followed through the second and third courses in the typical course sequence, to see if their performance in these subsequent courses is any different.

Universities are interested in loyal alumnae who will contribute time and money to their schools after graduation. Do students who had most of their courses online in contrast to on campus students differ in long-term affiliation? A relatively easy to accomplish study might look, for instance, at the rate at which graduates join the alumnae association within the first year.

6. Increasing the Use of Archival and Interaction Data

One way to improve the validity of research findings is to use multiple methods and multiple sources of data. Archival data related to the study of ALN may be gathered from a number of sources, and has been relatively neglected in past ALN research. Some of these data sources include course syllabi, examination scores, and student records. Such data have already been collected for other purposes, and their use is "non intrusive" as long as strict confidentiality processes are followed. Course syllabi are frequently available publicly on web sites, and can be used to see the number and nature of collaborative assignments in a course, for instance. The use of archival data from institutional records on individual students will probably require a signed consent form, which can be combined with the consent form used with a post course questionnaire or the informed consent procedure for a field experiment.

Other under-utilized sources of data are recordings of raw interaction, online or face-to-face. In the case of online courses, the transcripts of all interactions are preserved and available for analysis; few studies actually take advantage of this rich source of data. Recording face-to-face classes to create a transcript has been very time consuming in the past. With new digital recorders and automatic transcription devices, this source of comparative data on interaction patterns may become easier to obtain.

A Multi-Method Field Experiment with Repeated Measures

We are beginning to see exemplars of excellent methodology in ALN research. Field experiments using "repeated measures" control for many of the sources of confounding of variables. In repeated measures designs, all subjects receive all treatments, and the order of the treatments is counter-balanced to ensure valid results.

A recent study by Heckman and Annabi [26] exemplifies such a field experiment, using content analysis of actual transcripts of discussions as the major method of data analysis. It presents a content-analysis approach to comparing discussions in face-to-face (FTF) classes with ALN classes. The authors worked with eight discussion transcripts from groups that were using the case study method to drive the discussion. Four transcripts were ALN and four FTF; but each of the four groups participated in both modes. Their findings provide evidence that ALNs generate high levels of cognitive activity, at least equal to, and in some cases superior to, the cognitive processes in the FTF classroom.

The research design is innovative and exemplary, because unlike most comparative studies of modes of learning, it did not involve self-selection of mode by students. One hundred and twenty seniors in an information systems capstone class were organized into a 1X2 repeated measures experiment with counterbalanced order of the student sequence. Each student participated in two case study discussions, one in a traditional FTF mode and one via ALN, randomly assigned to control for order effects, group composition effects, and effects of the first case discussion upon the second.

In the FTF discussions the instances of cognitive processes were predominantly in the lower order 'exploration' category while the ALN discussions contained more high-level cognitive processes such as the 'analysis' category. The findings show that even though the same students discussed the same cases, in discussions led by the instructor, following identical discussion plans, that there were substantial differences between the FTF and ALN discussions.

III. CONCLUSION

Improving the scope and validity of quantitative methods for assessing learning effectiveness was one of the top rated research priorities according to the prominent ALN researchers who participated in the NJIT workshop. We have examined two significant criteria that must be addressed if ALN research is to be useful for informing future educational research and practice: more attention to valid and pedagogically sound measurement of ALN learning effectiveness, and increased rigor in studies of ALNs. While the quality of ALN research on these criteria has improved dramatically within the last five years, clearly there is much more to be done. In terms of measuring ALN effectiveness, a clear implication is that multiple measures of effectiveness should be used, preferably collected from different data sources.

While recent advances in multi-course, multi-discipline ALN research are encouraging, extending this research to study ALNs beyond institutional, state, and even national boundaries is vital for understanding the contextual factors that most significantly influence ALN effectiveness.

IV. REFERENCES

1. **Alavi, M., Y. Yoo and D.R. Vogel.** Using Information Technology to Add Value to Management Education. Academy of Management Journal, 40(6): 1310-1333 (1997).
2. **Andriole, S.J.** Requirement-Driven ALN Course Design, Development, Delivery, and Evaluation. Journal of Asynchronous Learning Networks, 1(2) (1997).
3. **Arbaugh, J.B.** Virtual Classrooms versus Physical Classrooms: An Exploratory Study of Class Discussion Patterns and Student Learning in an Asynchronous Internet-Based MBA Course. Journal of Management Education, 24(2), 207-227 (2000).
4. **Arbaugh, J.B.** An Exploratory Study of the Effects of Gender on Student Learning and Class Participation in an Internet-Based MBA Course. *Management Learning,* 31(4), 533-549 (2000).
5. **Arbaugh, J.B.** A Longitudinal Study of Technological and Pedagogical Characteristics of Web-Based MBA Courses. *Academy of Management Best Papers Proceedings.* D. Nagao (Ed.) (2002).
6. **Arbaugh, J.B., and R. Duray.** Class Section Size, Perceived Classroom Characteristics, Instructor Experience, and Student Learning and Satisfaction with Web-Based Courses: A Study and

Comparison of Two Online MBA Programs. *Academy of Management Best Papers Proceedings.* D. Nagao (Ed.), MED A1-A6 (2001).

7. **Arbaugh, J.B., and R. Duray.** Technological and Structural Characteristics, Student Learning and Satisfaction with Web-Based Courses: An Exploratory Study of Two MBA Programs. *Management Learning,* 33: 331-347 (2002).

8. **Arbaugh, J.B., and L. Stelzer.** Learning and Teaching Management Education via the Internet: What do we know? In *Research in Management Education and Development: Educating Managers with Tomorrow's Technologies,* R. DeFillipi & C. Wankel, (Eds). Greenwich, CT: JAI Press, 2003.

9. **Arvan, L., Ory, J., Bullock, C. D., Burnaska, K.K., and Hanson, M.** The Scale Efficiency Projects. *Journal of Asynchronous Learning Networks,* 2(2) (1998).

10. **Bailey, E. K., & Cotlar, M.** Teaching via the Internet. *Communication Education,* 43(2): 184-193 (1994).

11. **Benbunan-Fich, R., & Hiltz, S.R.** Correlates of Effectiveness of Learning Networks: The Effects of Course Level, Course Type, and Gender on Outcomes. *Proceedings of 35th* Hawaii International Conference on System Sciences (2002). Washington, DC, IEEE Computer Society Press, CD Rom.

12. **Berger, N.S.** Pioneering Experiences in Distance Learning: Lessons Learned. *Journal of Management Education,* 23: 684-690 (1999).

13. **Boston, R.L.** Remote Delivery of Instruction via the PC and Modem: What Have We Learned? *The American Journal of Distance Education,* 6(3): 45-57 (1992).

14. **Card, K.A.** Providing Access to Graduate Education Using Computer-Mediated Communication. *International Journal of Instructional Media,* 27: 235-245 (2000).

15. **Carswell, L., Thomas, P., Petre, M., Price, B., and Richards, M.** Distance Education via the Internet: The Student Experience. *British Journal of Educational Technology,* 31(1): 29-46 (2000.)

16. **Clark, J.L.D.** Measures of Student Learning. In Centra, J.A., *Determining Faculty Effectiveness.* San Francisco: Jossey Bass, 1979, pp. 93- 119.

17. **Cohen, J.** *Statistical Power for the Behavioral Sciences.* Second ed. Hillsdale, NJ: Erlbaum (1988.)

18. **Coppola, N.W., Hiltz, S.R., & Rotter, N.G.** Becoming a Virtual Professor: Pedagogical Roles and Asynchronous Learning Networks. *Journal of Management Information Systems,* 18(4): 169-189 (2002.)

19. **Dumont, R.A.** Teaching and learning in cyberspace. *IEEE Transactions on Professional Communication,* 39(4) : 192-204 (1996).

20. **Ellram, L.M., & Easton, L.** Purchasing Education on the Internet. *Journal of Supply Chain Management,* 35(1): 11-19 (1999).

21. **Fowler, F.J. Jr.** *Survey Research Methods* (Revised Edition). Newbury Park, CA: Sage, 1988.

22. **Fraenkel, J.R., & Wallen, N.E.** *How to Design and Evaluate Research in Education.* New York: McGraw-Hill, 1990.

23. **Fredericksen, E., Pickett, A., Shea, P. and Pelz, W.** Student Satisfaction and Perceived Learning with Online Courses: Principles and Examples from the SUNY Learning Network. In J. Bourne and J. Moore (Eds) Online Education: Volume 1 in the Sloan-C Series. Needham, MA: Sloan-C Press, 2000; *Journal of Asynchronous Learning Networks,* 4, 2 (2000).

24. **Freeman, M.A., & Capper, J.M.** Exploiting the Web for Education: An Anonymous Asynchronous Role Simulation. *Australian Journal of Educational Technology,* 15(1): 95-116, 1999.

25. **Hannigan, C., & Browne, M.** Project Management: Going the Distance. *International Journal of Instructional Media,* 27: 343-356. 2000.

26. **Heckman, R. and Annabi, H.** A Content Analytic Comparison of FTF and ALN Case-Study Discussions. Proceedings of the 36th Hawaii International Conference on System Sciences, 2003. Washington, DC, IEEE Computer Society Press, CD Rom.

27. **Hiltz, S.R.** Correlates of Learning in a Virtual Classroom. *International Journal of Man-Machine Studies,* 39:71-98. 1993.

28. **Hiltz, S.R.** The Virtual Classroom: Learning Without Limits via Computer Networks. Norwood, NJ: Ablex Publishing Corporation, 1994.

29. **Hiltz, S.R., Coppola, N., Rotter, N., Turoff, M., & Benbunan-Fich, R.** Measuring the Importance of Collaborative Learning for the Effectiveness of ALN: A Multi-Measure, Multi-Method Approach. *Journal of Asynchronous Learning Networks,* 4(2), 2000.

30. **Hiltz, S.R., Johnson, K.D., & Turoff, M.** Experiments in Group Decision Making: Communication Process and Outcome in Face-to-Face versus Computerized Conferences. *Human Communication Research,* 13(2), 225-252, 1986.

31. **Hiltz, S.R., & Wellman, B.** Asynchronous Learning Networks as a Virtual Classroom. *Communications of the ACM,* 40(9): 44-52, 1997.

32. **Hiltz, S.R., Zhang, Yi, and Turoff, M.** "Studies of Effectiveness of Learning Networks," In Bourne, J. and Moore, J.C., Eds., *Elements of Quality Online Education.* Needham, MA, Sloan-C, 2002, pp. 15-41.

33. **Jarvenpaa, S.L., and Leidner, D.E.** Communication and Trust in Global Virtual Teams. *Organization Science,* 10: 791-815, 1999.

34. **Kazmer, M.M.** Juggling Multiple Worlds: Distance Students Online and Offline. *American Behavioral Scientist,* 45: 510-529. 2001.

35. **Levin, S.R., Levin, J.A., & Waddoups, G.L.** CTER Online: Evaluation of an Online Master of Education Focusing on Curriculum, Technology and Education Reform. *Proceedings of the 34th Hawaii International Conference on System Sciences,* 2001.

36. **Nulden, U.** Thematic Modules in an Asynchronous Learning Network: A Scandinavian Perspective on the Design of Introductory Courses. Journal of Group Decision and Negotiation, 8: 391-408, 1999.

37. **Nystrand, M., Cohen, A.S., and Dowling, N.M.** Addressing Reliability Problems in the Portfolio Assessment of College Writing. *Educational Assessment,* 1(1): 53-70 (1993).

38. **Piccoli, G., Ahmad, R., and Ives, B.** Web-Based Virtual Learning Environments: A Research Framework and a Preliminary Assessment of Effectiveness in Basic IT Skills Training. *MIS Quarterly,* 25: 401-426, 2001.

39. **Redding, T.R., and Rotzien, J.** Comparative Analysis of Online Learning vs. Classroom Learning. *Journal of Interactive Instruction Development,* 13(4): 3-12, 2001.

40. **Sandercock, G.R.H., & Shaw, G.** Learners' Performance and Evaluation of Attitudes Towards Web Course Tools in the Delivery of an Applied Sports Medicine Module. *ALN Magazine,* 3(2), 1999.

41. **Shen, J., Hiltz, S.R., Cheng, K., Cho, Y. and Bieber, M.** Collaborative Examinations for Asynchronous Learning Networks: Evaluation Results. *Proceedings of the 34th Hawaii International Conference on Systems Sciences,* IEEE Computer Society Press, Los Alamitos, CA, (Maui, January 3-6, 2001), CD Rom.

42. **Sorg, S., Truman-Davis, B., Dzubian, C., Moskal, P., Hartman, J., and Juge, F.** Faculty Development, Learner Support and Evaluation in Web-Based Programs. *Interactive Learning Environments,* 7(2-3): 137-153, 1999.

43. **Sullivan, P.** Gender Differences and the Online Classroom. Male and Female College Students Evaluate Their Experiences. *Community College Journal of Research and Practice,* 25: 805-818 (2001).

44. **Swan, K, Shea, P., Fredericksen, E., Picket, A., Pelz, W. and Maher, G.** Building Knowledge Building communities: Consistency, Contact, and Communication in the Virtual Classroom. *Journal of Educational Computing Research,* 23: 389-413 (2000).

45. **Taylor, J.** The Continental Classroom: Teaching Labor Studies Online. *Labor Studies Journal,* 21: 19-38 (1996).

46. **Tomaskovic-Devey, D., Leiter, J., and Thompson, S.** Organizational Survey Nonresponse. *Administrative Science Quarterly,* 39: 439-457 (1994).

47. **Warkentin, M.E., Sayeed, L., and Hightower, R.** Virtual Teams versus Face-to-Face Teams: An Exploratory Study of a Web-Based Conference System. *Decision Sciences,* 28: 975-996 (1997).
48. www.alnresearch.org
49. **Yoo, Y., Kanawattanachai, P., and Citurs, A**. Forging Into the Wired Wilderness: A Case Study of a Technology-Mediated Distributed Discussion-Based Class. *Journal of Management Education*, 26: 139-163 (2002).

V. ACKNOWLEDGEMENTS

The Learning Networks Effectiveness Research project, of which this paper is a part, is supported by the Alfred P. Sloan Foundation.

Many thanks to all of the participants in the workshop, who helped to shape the ideas discussed in this paper: Maryam Alavi, Ben Arbaugh, Raquel Benbunan Fich, John Bourne, Nancy Coppola, Martha Crosby, Donna Dufner, Charles Dzuiban, Ricki Goldman, Linda Harasim, Starr Roxanne Hiltz, Peter Shea, Karen Swan, and Murray Turoff. In addition, several NJIT Ph.D. students who are doing dissertation research related to this topic helped to facilitate the process and participated in the issue formation stage: Hyo Joo Han, Eunhee Kim, David Spencer, and Yi Zhang.

VI. ABOUT THE AUTHORS

Dr. Starr Roxanne Hiltz is Distinguished Professor of Computer and Information Science, New Jersey Institute of Technology, where she also directs the Ph.D. in Information Systems. She received her A.B. from Vassar and her M.A. and Ph.D. from Columbia. She has spent most of the last 20 years engaged in research on applications and social impacts of computer technology. Her research interests include educational applications of computer-mediated communications, human-computer interaction, and computer support for group decision making.   In particular, with major funding from the Corporation for Public Broadcasting and the Alfred P. Sloan Foundation, she created and experimented with a Virtual Classroom® for delivery of college-level courses. This is a teaching and learning environment which is constructed, not of bricks and boards, but of software structures within a computer-mediated communication system.

Her publications include six books and over 150 articles and professional papers. The Network Nation: Human Communication via Computer (with Murray Turoff; 1978, Addison Wesley; 1993 revised ed., MIT Press) is probably the best known. She is the recipient of the Electronic Frontier Foundation's "Pioneer" award, 1994, for "significant and influential contributions to computer-based communications and to the empowerment of individuals in using computers." In 2000, she was named one of "New Jersey's Women of the Millennium" by the Easter Seals Foundation for "creating solutions and changing lives, in the field of educational technology."

Dr. J. B. (Ben) Arbaugh (B.B.A., Marshall University, M.B.A., Wright State University, M.S., Ph.D., The Ohio State University) is an Associate Professor of Strategy and Project Management in the College of Business Administration at the University of Wisconsin Oshkosh. His current research interests include the delivery of education via the internet, international entrepreneurship, project management, and the intersection of spirituality and strategic management research. His recent publications include articles in the Journal of Management Education, the Journal of High Technology Management Research, Management Learning, Frontiers of Entrepreneurship Research, the Blackwell Handbook of Entrepreneurship, Business Communication Quarterly, the Academy of Management's Best Papers Proceedings, and the Academy of Management Learning and Education Journal. Ben's recent research on characteristics of effective ALNs have won the Academy of Management's Best Paper in Management Education in 2001 and 2002, and the 2001 Fritz Roethlisberger Award for the best article in the Journal of Management Education.

Cost Effectiveness

LINKING COST EFFECTIVENESS WITH INSTITUTIONAL GOALS: BEST PRACTICES IN ONLINE EDUCATION

Tana Bishop
University of Maryland University College

- Online programs should ask themselves: What kinds of approaches to online learning will improve the quality of student learning and enhance overall academic productivity?

- Four key practice areas for online cost effectiveness include:
  - curriculum and course redesign
  - student access and support
  - library and information services
  - consortium/collaborations

- Cost effectiveness aligns with different institutional objectives, such as cost control, cost savings, making profit.

- Identifying key institutional goals helps administrators enact leadership roles in higher education.

- Competing priorities for educational dollars and increasingly limited fiscal resources require institutions to identify, project, and control the costs associated with online learning.

I. INTRODUCTION

Cost effectiveness is a topic of considerable interest for today's institutions of higher education. Competing priorities for educational dollars and increasingly limited fiscal resources require institutions to identify, project, and control the costs associated with online learning. While profit-making typically is not the goal of public institutions, there is a growing desire to control costs or to achieve some cost savings. Consequently, both private and public higher education institutions increasingly focus on the role and impact of online education [1].

There also is a growing recognition that quality, access, and cost are inextricably linked issues in the educational environment, and Twigg [2] suggests that information technology provides a means to address these three key areas simultaneously. It is valuable to ask "what kinds of approaches to online learning will improve the quality of student learning?" [2]. Perhaps a more salient question for the academy in the prevailing economic environment is, "What kinds of approaches to online education will improve the quality of student learning, stimulate the intellectual growth of faculty, and enhance overall academic productivity?" In other words, there can and should be value added for the students, the faculty, and the institution. Beaudoin argues that, "A new role for the professoriate in the new century has been recognized, especially as technology-assisted instruction has proliferated and changed the means by which faculty and students interact, as well as the manner in which educational entities must now do business to meet the demands of a digitized society" [3]. Toward this end, a number of institutions have addressed ways to improve the quality of their programs and increase access while controlling their current levels of expenditures or achieving cost savings.

The results of the research findings suggest that online education has moved beyond the "no significant difference phenomenon" that Russell [4] identified in his research on the effectiveness of distance education programs. Research now shows that online offerings can result in significant positive learning outcomes [5]. Much research also offers evidence that online courses can help control institutional costs as well as help reduce costs to students [5].

The cost effectiveness research on online education examines a variety of delivery models – the traditional classroom, the combination or hybrid model that combines some traditional classroom activities with online, and the fully asynchronous approach. However, most of the research compares traditional classroom costs with hybrid models. Only limited research exists on the cost effectiveness of completely asynchronous courses and programs.

Of these studies that examine the various delivery models, the research is in four general areas: curriculum and course redesign, student access and support, library and information services, and consortium/collaborations. While it is logical to separate curriculum and course redesign from student access and support, I found the two areas inextricably linked in the cost effectiveness studies reviewed. Consequently, I collapsed these into just one category for the purposes of this paper. In the next section, I identify and discuss exemplars of the current best practices of cost effectiveness in the digital learning environment. Within each of the key areas, I describe the practice, identify the associated cost effectiveness methodology, present the cost effectiveness aspects of the particular practice, analyze the evidence of the effectiveness, and discuss how the practice relates to the Sloan Consortium (Sloan-C) pillars [6] of learning effectiveness, access, student satisfaction, and faculty satisfaction. In the concluding section of the paper, I summarize the findings and discuss how these studies might be used to inform policy and practice.

II. BEST PRACTICES

Many higher education institutions that offer distance education courses require such offerings to show fiscal viability. The institutions discussed in this paper are exemplars of the current best practices in cost effectiveness. As you will note in the discussion that follows, the institutions represent a range of two- and four-year, private and public higher education institutions. In this section, I also include the best practices of state library systems that provide cost effective e-learning support.

A. Curriculum and Course Redesign/Student Access and Support

Until rather recently, many institutions that offered online education typically replicated the campus experience in their curricular programming [2]. Despite the quality of those offerings, the fact that they resulted in "no significant difference" [7] from the traditional classroom model suggests that the replicative approach perhaps is an inappropriate application. Consequently, some higher education institutions have found new ways to leverage the technologies in order to achieve gains in student learning through curricular and course redesign. At the same time, they manage to control costs effectively.

1. Cost effective Aspects of Online Environment

Many of the institutions that exhibit best practices intentionally targeted large enrollment courses for their redesign efforts. Two such examples include Riverside Community College, which redesigned its Elementary Algebra course that enrolls around 3,600 students annually and Penn State University, which enrolls 2,200 students per year in its Elementary Statistics course at University Park, just one of its many campuses. Other schools involved in similar curricular redesign initiatives, such as the University of Dayton's Introductory Psychology course, have more modest real numbers but nevertheless substantial impact in terms of the percentage of overall student enrollments at the respective campuses. More than 50% of the students at the University of Dayton, for example, enroll in the Introductory Psychology course.

At the University of Southern Maine, the Psychology Department faced serious resource issues with large lecture sections of the Introductory Psychology course and no graduate assistants (since they do not offer a graduate degree in this discipline). The course fulfills a core requirement and, as such, is offered year-round to some 850 students. The department found that their traditional classroom model did not serve students or faculty well because the faculty to student ratio necessarily prohibited a desirable learning environment in which students would receive frequent feedback. Although a significant level of faculty resources were devoted to serving the large introductory course sections, students were not benefiting from a learner-centered environment. And since faculty devoted the majority of their time to these introductory classes, they had less time to spend on developing and revising upper-level course materials. The introduction of online resources provides a way for the department to improve learning opportunities (through more interaction) and save or re-deploy their key resources.

The University of Tennessee, Knoxville focused its redesign efforts on Spanish 150, Intermediate Spanish Transition, since historically it has been an oversubscribed course. The course redesign provides more interactive class time and collaborative learning opportunities since grammar, vocabulary, and listening activities now are part of the online environment instead of face-to-face. In-class time now is spent primarily on such activities as interpretation, the negotiation of meaning, and exchange of information. This mixed delivery model is attentive to improving student learning while, at the same time, decreasing the costs of labor.

The redesign of the Introduction to Sociology course at Indiana University–Purdue University, Indianapolis (IUPUI) allows the institution to increase the number of large course sections and decrease the number of small sections previously offered. It is anticipated that the redesign will result in lowering overall labor costs. Multiple course sections have been redesigned so that all sections have more technology. In addition, some of the Introductory Sociology sections have been linked to Elementary Composition I sections in an effort to aid student learning.

At the University of Iowa, the curriculum redesign targets General Chemistry, a large enrollment course that typically serves the science, engineering, and allied health departments as well as students in pre-professional studies. Since the structure of the course material is hierarchical and the basic concepts and methodology are interdependent, stepping-stone skill-building is critical and should extend throughout the course. Thus, the faculty assign students homework to reinforce the building blocks of learning. With such high-enrollment courses, however, the faculty found that they had to sacrifice either the time required to promote time-on-task activities or the amount of feedback they could provide to students on their assignments. The Chemistry Department determined that by implementing online homework systems they could address this dilemma and, at the same time, provide a richer learning environment for students. The online homework assignments allow students to complete their homework online at any time (24/7) and to receive immediate feedback. Students do not have to wait for feedback on their graded assignments, and the decrease in TA labor decreases costs.

The Introductory Statistics course at Penn State University currently serves more than 2,800 undergraduate students. With the traditional course delivery model, the Statistics Department found that student needs were not well-served, nor was the offering cost effective. The redesigned course addresses pedagogical concerns as well as cost issues. The restructuring involves a reduction from three to one in weekly lectures—to allow faculty more time interacting with students and less time with the preparation and delivery of lectures. Two of the traditional lectures have been replaced with computer-mediated workshops. Faculty and teaching assistants utilize these workshops to provide students with interactive and substantive feedback. In addition, the redesigned course offers a variety of online learning materials as well as computerized testing. With the new testing model, students have more practice time and feedback. The redesigned course provides a more interactive model of student learning and reduces costs, particularly in terms of TA support typically required in large, traditional lecture sections.

Similarly, Virginia Polytechnic University has undertaken the course redesign of Linear Algebra, an introductory course taken by first-year students in engineering, science, and mathematics. The course typically enrolls about 2,000 students annually divided into 40 students per section. The simultaneous goals of the redesign have been to retain the individual focus of these small sections and to reduce costs. The redesigned course is entirely online, with personal support provided by a staff of peer tutors and faculty who manage the innovative Math Emporium, a large 24/7 learning laboratory that is adjacent to campus. Students receive their lectures, participate in interactive learning modules, and take their tests online. By strategically utilizing the existing space and equipment, the Math Department is able to reduce their annual operating costs and to provide a more consistent level of support to students.

Drexel University has combined two computer courses (Introductory Computer Programming and Computer Programming I) in its curricular redesign efforts. The new modular design allows students to progress through the course at their own pace. This restructuring acknowledges the diversity of students and their entry points for the course. The new design further promotes a learner-centered environment that combines presentations with hands-on, highly interactive Web-based activities. Since the new course also accommodates differences in the learning goals of students with different majors (for example, computer engineering majors versus information systems majors), students are able to work on the aspects of modules that are relevant to their particular fields of study. The modularized and online formatting allows the department to deploy its resources more efficiently and effectively.

Riverside Community College undertook its redesign effort in hopes of improving student learning outcomes. With an original student success rate of only 50% and a repeat rate of 30% in the Elementary Algebra course, resources were deployed to redesign the course to try and improve the pass rate. The new course design includes: (1) replacing the traditional lecture format with an interactive software model; (2) creating a Math Collaboratory with tutors and various learning technologies to support different student learning styles; (3) decreasing the number of course sections but increasing interaction between student and instructor; and (4) implementing a flexible asynchronous learning model. This course redesign thus allows the institution essentially to substitute technology "capital" for some of the traditional teaching "labor." Some of the instructional components associated with the traditional Elementary Algebra course have been replaced with the interactive computer-mediated model. This results in a direct reduction in faculty salary costs. In addition, Riverside CC also has determined that there are savings to students with this new model, such as transportation costs, the time previously utilized to get to the traditional classroom, and child care.

The course redesign piloted at Rio Salado College utilized one faculty member to teach four different math courses concurrently, thus reducing staffing costs. This effort took full advantage of the academic strengths of the faculty and the capacity of the technological infrastructure. With a 20-year history in distance education, and more than three years of experience with online education in particular, the College was well-positioned to undertake such an unique initiative. Central to the redesign project was the addition of a course assistant who monitored student progress and served as the troubleshooter for technology issues. This allowed the faculty member to devote his full attention to the curricula and focus on pedagogy.

The University at Buffalo (SUNY) initiated two redesign strategies for their Computer Literacy course in the hope that this would result in cost savings. Faculty selected this particular course for redesign for several reasons: (1) it serves a large number of students (currently around 1,000 freshmen enroll in this course for non-majors); (2) they expect the enrollments to increase even more when the course becomes a General Education requirement; and (3) students are required to have computer access. One redesign strategy (Plan A) was to keep enrollments at the original level, reduce faculty lecture time by replacing some lectures with more interactive online material, and employ undergraduate learning assistants rather than graduate assistants for technical help. The other redesign strategy (Plan B) applied the same academic plan but raised course enrollment and correspondingly increased faculty and learning assistant time a bit more to accommodate the increase in students. They found that both plans yielded cost savings.

By substituting a primarily asynchronous learning model for the traditional classroom model in their American National Government course, the University of Central Florida is able to reduce classroom space and achieve some cost savings. Faced with a burgeoning student body that has created a 40% shortage in classroom space, efficiency is of critical concern to the University. The course redesign addresses their critical space issue and helps with cost containment.

The University of Dayton anticipates that it will be able to control costs through a course redesign that is a mixed delivery model. The targeted Introductory Psychology course is a combination of on-site and online instruction. Cost savings are expected to be achieved primarily through a reduction in faculty staffing and student "seat time" in the traditional classroom setting. The redesigned course features a combination of face-to-face meetings with interactive asynchronous collaborative activities.

2. Cost effectiveness Methodology

"Cost effectiveness is a technique for measuring the relationship between the total inputs, or costs, of a project or activity, and its outputs or objectives" [8]. Typically, there are two approaches to this analysis. One way is to compare "alternative ways of achieving the same objective," while the other is to compare two or more products to determine "… which achieves the highest level of output or results" [8]. Each of these two approaches involves activity-based costing or the detailing of "cost ingredients" – a concept introduced by Henry Levin and widely used in cost analyses today [9, 10]. Each of the "best practices" of institutions discussed in this paper applied this type of methodology to examine the cost effectiveness of the redesigned curriculum. In all of the analyses, the examination involved the comparison of the "old" course with the redesigned curriculum to determine if and where there might be any cost savings.

3. Evidence (or plan to obtain evidence)

The reallocation of resources is an efficient and cost effective means for achieving a more learning-centered environment. The features of the course redesign at the University of Southern Maine include: a reduction in lecture time by 50% (replaced with a variety of interactive computer activities in which students receive timely feedback); more interaction between students themselves and between students and faculty/faculty assistants, as well as more personalized attention (through online resources); the development of a standard curricula with common materials that are shared across the multiple course sections; an increase in course section size from 75 to 125; and the introduction of asynchronous learning materials.

At the University of Tennessee, Knoxville, the Spanish Department plans to reduce costs by increasing class size and decreasing instructor grading time by placing previously hand-graded activities online. In addition, employing teaching assistants to help with some of the assignments is a further attempt to achieve cost savings while providing a teaching/mentoring opportunity for first-semester master's students.

IUPUI estimates that the overall cost savings they will achieve with the redesign of the Introductory Sociology courses will be around 20% overall in the cost-per-student. That reduction would amount to nearly $26,000 annually. In addition, IUPUI expects there will be some cost recovery from the anticipated decrease in the drop-fail-withdrawal rate of the "old" course.

Virginia Tech expects annual cost savings of approximately $130,000 after netting out all of the operating costs that are directly related to the course, as well as a share of the Math Emporium tutors' time. Additional savings accrue with the elimination of traditional class meetings on campus, thus freeing some of the regular classroom space during the busy daytime hours.

Since many of the instructional tasks associated with the traditional Elementary Statistics course have been replaced with the interactive computer-mediated model, there is a direct reduction in the costs for faculty and teaching assistants at Penn State. PSU estimates an overall 30% reduction in cost-per-student, from approximately $176 to $123. Annually, this means a projected savings of more than $115,000. Similarly, at Rio Salado College, the Math Department expects to achieve a 37% overall cost savings. By reducing faculty staffing, adding a course assistant, and increasing class size, Rio Salado anticipates that the cost-per-student will decrease from $49 to $31. At the same time, the redesign allows the College to use faculty expertise more efficiently and productively by keeping them close to the course content.

Drexel's curricular redesign of its introductory programming course achieves efficiency through its modular design. The modular approach not only utilizes faculty time more productively, but the redesign provides students with a more individualized curriculum. The redesigned course allows students to change majors and still receive credit for the particular modular work they have completed. This redesign will result in some cost recovery (faculty and TA resources) since students will not have to repeat the modules that they have mastered already.

The University of Central Florida found that the traditional 100-student course section costs the University around $1,200 for classroom space. UCF anticipates that their mixed model American National Government course redesign (mostly asynchronous) will yield annual savings of nearly $70,000 in terms of classroom space. The Psychology Department at the University of Dayton also expects to achieve cost savings resulting from less demand for classroom space. The redesign includes reducing the number of course sections annually from 12 to 6 which, in turn, results in a reduction in faculty staffing and classroom space. Even with the addition of teaching assistants to support the redesign, cost savings accrue.

4. Estimated Costs Associated with the Practice

As noted above in the section on cost effectiveness methodology, all of the institutions discussed in this paper applied similar activity-based costing measures to examine all of the direct expenses associated with their respective online offerings. Each of the institutions itemized the costs for both the "old" and redesigned courses. As expected, the itemization for the traditional courses included the costs associated with physical classroom space requirements. The new courses had unique expenses resulting from the technology software and support that is integral to the course redesign. The labor (faculty and teaching assistant time) required to develop and deliver the courses also reflected the particular effort for the respective delivery modes (synchronous, asynchronous, and mixed model). In each of the institutional practices presented here, the results show lower costs for online education than the traditional classroom format.

5. Relation to Other Pillars

The growing body of research on cost effectiveness in online education suggests that institutions not only can operate efficiently but that they also can improve upon the quality of their programs, show positive learning outcomes, increase student access, and foster an intellectually-stimulating environment for students and faculty alike. The primary goal of each of the institutions discussed in this paper was not to achieve cost savings but to find new ways to create and sustain learning-centered environments; the secondary goal was to find ways to control costs. Consequently, each of the redesigned courses addresses one or more of the other four pillars of online education.

Penn State redesigned the Introductory Statistics course to address specific academic concerns, such as poor student performance. In a traditional lecture and recitation format, differing student learning styles were not acknowledged. The interactive approach of the mixed delivery model provides students with the opportunity to: "understand and apply basic concepts of statistics (for example, variables, inferences, probability); actively participate in data analysis and design; critically evaluate reports containing statistical analyses of surveys and experiments; and actively engage with course materials and other students" [11]. This course redesign particularly relates to learning effectiveness and student satisfaction—as well as cost effectiveness. The interactive approach of the mixed delivery model helps to improve the curriculum by focusing squarely on learner needs.

At the University of Southern Maine, the Psychology Department addressed similar concerns of other institutions: creating and sustaining learning-centered environments. The old course structure typically realized a 30% failure rate. The intended aims of the redesign were meant to: increase access (by making the course accessible to students with geographical and/or physical constraints); increase student retention (student satisfaction); and improve learning effectiveness (by offering a more learning-centered model). The University of Tennessee, Knoxville also seeks to create a more learning-centered environment with their redesigned Spanish course. Specifically, the faculty would like the redesign to improve the language competency and performance currently observed in the traditional course offering.

Rio Salado College wanted to increase student access with their online math courses, and at the same time, improve their student retention rate in the four math courses that underwent redesign. The College addressed both goals simultaneously while also controlling costs. At the University of Iowa, the Chemistry Department undertook the redesign to create a more active learning environment, but this meant a pedagogical shift. With continuous improvements routinely emerging in the technology software, the new learning environment reflects better matches between the texts and the homework content—resulting in a more cohesive curriculum.

At Virginia Tech, the math faculty found that the redesigned Linear Algebra course contributes to student satisfaction. In 2001, they replaced their optional live lectures with online video lectures and found that student usage of the lectures increased from 43% to 84%. The faculty also have found generally favorable response rates (range of 70%-85%) to their main computer presentations and Math Emporium staff support.

The intent of the redesign primarily was to improve student success rates in the Elementary Algebra course at Riverside Community College, with the secondary objective to achieve some cost savings in the process. By linking student achievement goals with efficiency, the college created a truly cost effective model. A by-product of this redesign is the newly-mined data that they gathered on the amount of time students spend on homework assignments. Specifically, the faculty found that students spend considerably less time (average of two hours per week) on their homework than the six hours recommended by faculty.

The two redesign strategies employed at the University at Buffalo (SUNY) relate well to learning effectiveness and student satisfaction. In addition to achieving a cost savings, the new design resulted in improved learning outcomes. The University used four measures to compare learning in the traditional classroom with the redesigned structure (amount of material covered, course grade, pre-test and post-test scores, and attitudinal surveys). Overall, the results showed that students in the redesigned courses outperformed the students in the traditional course model.

At the University of Dayton, the primary objective of their redesign effort in Introductory Psychology is to create a richer learning environment for the students through the development of a common syllabus with common objectives and assessment tools. The replacement of some of the lecture format with a more interactive and collaborative learning model is intended to increase student satisfaction and retention. In addition, faculty have the opportunity to grow professionally through the application of new technologies that enhance the learning environment.

B. Library and Information Services

The asynchronous learning environment has altered the library and information services model as well as the traditional classroom. Students in online courses and programs need 24/7 services if they are to be served effectively. Since there are costs associated with the provision of these additional services, some institutions have found consortial arrangements to be cost effective. For example, the University System of Maryland institutions have joined together in purchasing electronic information resource databases, thus lowering the costs for individual schools. University of Maryland University College (UMUC), a leading provider of online education, is able to maximize its fixed library and information resources budget by participating in this consortium. This cost effective arrangement allows UMUC to purchase more than 100 electronic databases and, at the same time, to provide critical support for online classes through tutorials, online classroom instruction (undergraduate- and graduate-level courses) in information retrieval, and assistance with searches, interlibrary loans, etc. The Virtual Library of Virginia provides a good example of the cost effectiveness of these kinds of arrangements.

1. Cost effective Aspects of Online Environment

The 39 state-supported colleges and universities in the Commonwealth of Virginia formed a consortium, known as the Virtual Library of Virginia (VIVA), to utilize technology as a way of improving faculty and staff productivity while, at the same time, enhancing student learning and lowering costs. Group purchase and sharing of online library resources has achieved cost savings and, at the same time, improved library services and expanded the holdings of the individual institutions.

2. Evidence

Over an eight-year period (1994–2002), the consortium of libraries in Virginia (VIVA) has been able to achieve around $74.5 million in cost avoidance by coordinating and sharing online library resources throughout the Commonwealth of Virginia. In other words, if the 39 state-supported colleges and universities had to obtain the same level of resources independently of one another, the costs would have increased by more than $74 million. This practice of cooperatively purchasing electronic resources has resulted in cost savings from 8–79% of list prices.

3. Estimated Costs Associated with the Practice

Funding for the VIVA initiative comes primarily from the Virginia General Assembly, with additional monies derived from local college/university library budgets and grants. For the two-year period 2000–2002, the total funding was $10.7 million.

4. Relation to Other Pillars

Both traditional classroom and online courses need adequate library and information resources to deliver high-quality learning opportunities both to students and faculty. The electronic library widens access far beyond the traditional campus geography. In addition, students and faculty are able to retrieve information anytime through the e-databases. This 24/7 information service increases both student and faculty satisfaction. While there are observable benefits of the electronic library in terms of cost effectiveness, access, student and faculty satisfaction, the relationship between the e-library and learning effectiveness remains to be researched.

C. Consortium/Collaborations

In addition to the consortial arrangements that some state university and college systems have entered, others have pursued collaborative activities to expand their online programming and control costs. This can work well when the institutions have similar goals and strategies for achieving their objectives.

1. Cost effective Aspects of Online Environment

The Center for Distance Education at Carl von Ossietzky University of Oldenburg (Germany) has partnered with the University of Maryland University College (UMUC) on the development and delivery of the Master of Distance Education (MDE) program. Both institutions have committed resources to this effort, and each receives the tuitions from their respective students. Without the resources of both institutions, it is unlikely the program would have run successfully at either institution since the relationship is highly synergistic. For example, the faculties at the Germany and Maryland campuses offer different academic strengths in this discipline. Together, they have the bench strength needed to produce a high-quality MDE program.

2. Cost effectiveness Methodology

Like the other institutions discussed in this paper, the University of Oldenburg is applying an activity-based costing model to examine the cost effectiveness of this program. Specifically, the University has identified the following areas for their cost analysis: direct and indirect committed costs that include the costs of course development, costs of course presentation, course and program management, and marketing.

3. Evidence (or plans to obtain evidence)

The detailed cost analysis will determine whether or not the MDE is a fiscally viable program. The research is in progress as of this writing, and the study is expected to be completed in December, 2002.

4. Estimated Costs Associated with the Practice

While the cost analysis is a work-in-progress, the University of Oldenburg has benchmark figures on course development, course presentation and course maintenance. The course development costs range between $15,000 and $25,000, and course instruction costs from $7,000 to $10,000. The cost variability is attributable to the specific course content. The final study will provide further explication of the associated costs.

5. Relation to Other Pillars

The University of Oldenburg/UMUC collaboration directly relates to most of the other pillars of quality education. Without such a partnership, it is unlikely that the MDE program would have been realized. Through the collaborative arrangement, students around the globe have access to an innovative programmatic area. The partnership has fostered the intellectual growth and satisfaction of the faculty and contributed to student satisfaction with the program.

III. CONCLUSION

The key institutional goals expressed in the research include increasing access, improving the quality of student learning, stimulating the intellectual growth of faculty, and enhancing the overall productivity of the institution. According to Levin & McEwan [10], attaining a certain level of effectiveness at a minimal cost is the essence of cost effectiveness. As the research on online education shows, institutions can achieve their institutional goals while also controlling costs. The findings from the studies discussed in this paper demonstrate that online education not only is as effective as traditional classroom programs, but in many instances is more effective [5]. The studies also demonstrate the importance of linking the individual institution's core goals with effective practices.

For example, Virginia Tech found in their redesigned Linear Algebra course a clear increase in student retention and completion rates over the traditional classroom format. At the University of Iowa, faculty in the online General Chemistry course have a cost effective model and one that adds to faculty satisfaction. The introduction of online homework software provides timely, accessible, and detailed information to the instructor. In the traditional course model, faculty typically do not have this type of rich compilation of data since TAs usually assist with grading assignments. Consequently, faculty in the online course sections are able to examine correlations between student completion rates, homework grades, and performance on exams.

Findings from the University of Tennessee, Knoxville also show that online education has moved beyond the "no significant difference" phenomenon. One goal of the redesigned Spanish 150 course was to examine the effectiveness of online instruction and to identify any significant differences between the online and traditional classroom formats of the course. In particular, the examination focused on language competency and performance. The measures used to compare the traditional and redesigned online courses included: pre- and post-test placement scores, midterm and final grades, satisfaction questionnaires, and oral interviews. The preliminary results from the study suggest there is no significant difference in proficiency, but that students who participated in the redesigned course outperformed their peers in language competency (achievement). A compilation of the final results of the full implementation of the redesign (Fall 2002) will be available in Spring 2003.

Indiana University–Purdue University, Indianapolis (IUPUI) provides additional evidence that online education can make a significant difference in learning outcomes. The faculty piloted their redesigned Introduction to Sociology course over three terms and found very positive results both in terms of student learning and cost savings. Students in the redesigned sections performed as well as, or better than, students in the traditional courses in terms of understanding key sociological concepts. When comparing final grades for the differently formatted courses, the faculty found that students in the redesigned course had significantly higher grades in at least two of the three terms (the third term grades were not yet available). As for the drop-failure-withdrawal (DFW) rate, the research showed that the overall DFW rate continued to decline in the redesigned course over the three terms. This is an important finding that suggests an improvement in student learning; historically, large sections of the course had very high DFW rates.

"Over a number of years the cost effectiveness of using technology to support, or in some cases supplant, conventional higher education teaching and learning has been hotly debated" [12]. The results from the best practices presented in this paper show that online education can be both cost effective and an effective learning model for students. Consequently, the policy discussions relating to the "academic cost/quality struggle" [13] have lost some of their salience. Higher education institutions now need to examine cost effectiveness systematically and routinely for all delivery models—whether traditional, hybrid or fully online—and determine how to leverage the available technologies to improve all student learning.

IV.   REFERENCES

1. Throughout this paper, I use the terms "online education," "distance education," and "online learning" interchangeably.

2. **Twigg, C.,** *Innovations in Online Learning: Moving Beyond No Significant Difference.* Troy, NY: Center for Academic Transformation, Rennsselaer Polytechnic Institute, 2001.

3. **Beaudoin, M.,** Distance Education Leadership: An Essential Role for the New Century. *Journal of Leadership Studies, 8,* 131-145, 2002.

4. **Russell, T.,** *The No Significant Difference Phenomenon.* Montgomery, AL: International Distance Education Certification Center, 2000.

5. **Center for Academic Transformation,** *The Pew Grant Program in Course Redesign,* 2002. http://www.center.rpi.edu/PewGrant

6. The Sloan Consortium framework for quality online education is built upon five pillars: learning effectiveness, access, cost effectiveness, student satisfaction, and faculty satisfaction. The framework serves as a heuristic tool for the examination and application of quality in web-based programs and courses.

7. Thomas Russell reviewed 355 research studies to compare the effectiveness of traditional classroom instruction with distance education courses. He concluded that, "There is so much research on this matter that I find it incomprehensible that any reasonable, knowledgeable, unbiased, and professional person could deny the fact that technology can deliver instruction as well as traditional modes – at least when we look at student populations as large groups" (Russell, quoted in *The Chronicle of Higher Education,* "Scholar Concludes that Distance Ed Is as Effective as Traditional Instruction," February 10, 2000).

8. **Woodhall, M.,** Cost effectiveness Analysis in Education. In G. Psacharopoulous (ed.), *Economics of Education,* Oxford, United Kingdom: Pergamon, 1987.

9. **Levin, H.,** Cost Analysis. In N.L. Smith (ed.), *New Methods for Evaluation,* Beverly Hills, CA: Sage, 1983.

10. **Levin, H. and P. McEwan,** *Cost-Effectiveness Analysis, 2nd ed.* Thousand Oaks, CA: Sage, 2001.

11. **Center for Academic Transformation,** *The Pew Grant Program in Course Redesign,* 2002. http://www.center.rpi.edu/PewGrant/rd1award/PSU.html

12. **Ash, C.,** Towards a New Cost-Aware Evaluation Framework. *Educational Technology & Society, 3*(4), 2000. http://ifets.ieee.org/periodical/vol_4_2000/ash.html

V.   ABOUT THE AUTHOR

Tana Bishop is the Associate Dean for Administration in the Graduate School at the University of Maryland University College (UMUC). Prior to that, she was Assistant Director for the United Kingdom and Iceland with UMUC's European Division. She also worked in Japan as the Executive Director of the Navy Relief Society, a non-profit financial institution. Other professional experience includes many years as an educator. She spent more than a decade living and working outside the continental United States. That international experience has influenced her interest in offering asynchronous courses and degree programs to diverse student populations. She holds a master's degree in Japanese Studies from the University of Hawaii and a Ph.D. in Education Policy and Leadership from the University of Maryland, College Park. Her areas of specialization include the economics of education, educational leadership, and international teaching and learning. She is the Immediate Past President of the Maryland Association of Higher Education.

THE COSTS OF LEARNER-CENTERED ONLINE LEARNING: AN EXPLORATORY CASE STUDY

Christine Geith
MSU Global Online Connection

- Characteristics of learner-centered education include elements of instructional delivery, instructional practices, services, and assessment:
    - Emphasis is on the student's competence and proficiency.
    - Competency-based assessment is an integral part of the system.
    - The environment supports individual rates of learning and decouples credit hours and time in the classroom.

- Different approaches, such as lectures or group projects, can significantly impact how faculty spend time developing and teaching courses, how much up-front media production is required, and the technology features needed to support the course.

- Technology can redirect faculty time from covering content and toward facilitating student learning.

- Online learning can enable the learner to control the time, place, content, and outcomes of instruction rather than being organized by the provider's scheduling and resource needs.

- Institutions can create cost effective learning experiences by leveraging existing resources, such as experienced faculty, learning and assessment activities enabled by the available media and communication channels, off-the-shelf courseware with built-in ability to customize individual content "paths and instructional delivery focused on coaching.

I. INTRODUCTION

Most cost studies of online learning make distinctions between the different technologies used in course delivery. Few differentiate, however, among different pedagogies used in online courses. Different approaches, such as lectures or group projects, can have significant impacts on how faculty spend their time developing and teaching a course, on how much up-front media production is required, and on the technology features needed to support the course.

The literature identifies the need to examine the pedagogy of online learning in order to make meaningful comparisons for research including costs and effectiveness. Reeves [1] in his critique of empirical research on educational technology argues that useful evaluation of educational technology must "reveal the relevant pedagogical dimensions… if evaluations are to be meaningful and have utility." Piccoli [2] states that to compare different web-based learning environments, research needs to "explicitly acknowledge the role of the learning model" and either control for it or evaluate its effects. Most cost analysis does not differentiate or compare the costs of different pedagogical approaches.

With the change in faculty role described in learner-centered approaches, it appears that a key driver of cost – faculty time – could be much different in courses using these models. When faculty in Communication Arts and Sciences and MSU Global developed this custom program in the winter of 2001-2002, the project provided an opportunity to investigate the costs of a learner-centered approach.

II. BACKGROUND

A. MSU Global Online Connection

Three years ago, MSU's continuing education unit initiated a strategic review to reinvent itself as a financially self-sufficient provider of online degrees, certificates and services to working professionals in Michigan, the United States and around the world.

MSU's continuing education activities were small in the context of total campus enrollment (43,000), continuing education's general budget allocation was facing cuts, and other units in the University were encroaching on its core business and establishing independent online learning activities.

With the creation of MSU Global, strategic decisions and operating procedures were established to reposition continuing education as the driver of MSU's continuing online education activities and a central component of Michigan State University's 21st Century learning vision.

Six action steps were critical to achieving operational success:

1. Creation of a University-wide online learning committee to ensure faculty buy in and support
2. Formulation of strategic objectives consistent with MSU's vision and guiding principles
3. Formatting partnerships with other units and colleges within the University
4. Establishment of distinct lines of business to develop and deliver online educational programs and services
5. Codification and enforcement of internal operating procedures
6. Standard legal documentation to guide external alliances

MSU Global is now in the third year of its initial three-year strategic plan. Support within the University continues to grow, general funds allocation has increased, and the unit's span and scope of responsibility continues to increase. New online programs, enrollments, revenues and external alliances have all far exceeded base line projections.

MSU Global has a full-time staff equivalent of nine and a growing number of part-time experts across the country working on projects. The department supports a variety of MSU's academic units, assisting with their outreach activities that focus on making MSU academic and life enrichment programs accessible for people beyond the MSU campus. The unit reports directly to the Provost of the University and partners with MSU's Virtual University Design and Technology team which produces the majority of the online offerings.

MSU Global has three lines of business. Academic and Professional Programs provides academic business planning and marketing support for more than a dozen degree and certificate programs developed and taught by MSU faculty including an M.S. in Education, M.S. in Packaging, and M.S. in Criminal Justice. The Global Institute creates and markets custom professional development programs and personal enrichment products in partnership with internal academic partners, professional organizations and corporations. The Horticulture Gardening Institute, the Global Community Security Institute, and the Michigan Tourism Virtual Training Academy are among the initiatives of the Global Institute. The third line of business, Global Vista, offers custom strategic consulting services for organizations seeking to use online learning.

B. Learner-Centered Education

1. Foundations

Learner-centered educational practice is a growing movement in education reform at all levels. The foundations of learner-centered approaches are based on the science of learning. In 1991, the American Psychological Association released its first draft of the research-based Learner-Centered Psychological Principles intended to inform the redesign of school systems and curriculum from pre-school through college and life-long learning. Nearly ten years later, in 2000, the National Research Council published *How People Learn* linking the findings of research on the science of learning to the principles of learner-centeredness and to practice in the classroom [3]. These landmark works provide a research-validated framework for enhancing student motivation and achievement.

"Learner-centered education places the student at the center of education...this approach strives to be individualistic, flexible, competency-based, varied in methodology and not always constrained by time and place" [4]. Characteristics of learner-centered education include elements of instructional delivery, instructional practices, services, and assessment (Table 1).

Instructional Delivery	Instructional Practices	Services	Assessment
▪ Learners assume primary responsibility for their choices ▪ Learners have control over their	▪ Collaborative group learning ▪ Individual student research and discovery ▪ Research and	▪ Educational experience involves the whole student outside of the formal learning experience such	▪ Emphasis is on the student's competence and proficiency ▪ Competency-based assessment is an integral part

learning ■ The environment facilitates exploration of meaning and content knowledge through personal and interpersonal discovery ■ The environment meets individual learning styles, special needs, skills, and cultural backgrounds ■ The environment supports individual rates of learning and decouples credit hours and time in the classroom ■ The process uses active involvement by the student	discovery by students and faculty together ■ Problem-based inquiry learning ■ Student-faculty studio and performance activities ■ Service learning activities ■ Hands-on, experiential learning activities ■ On-site field experiences ■ Self-paced tutorials	as counseling, advising and tutoring ■ Services such as child and elder care ■ Co-curricular activities	of the system ■ Competence can be demonstrated and assessed in a variety of ways including: solving real or simulated problems, tests, demonstrations, papers, portfolios, performances, individual or group reports and projects.

Table 1. Learner Centered Education (adapted from the Arizona Board of Regents [4])

Learner-centered approaches to these elements of education differ in the ways they are accomplished compared to teacher-centered approaches. The learner-centered versus teacher-centered dichotomy, while over-simplifying the complex issues of teaching and learning, is a useful tool for facilitating a change in perspective. For example, a teacher or institution-centered perspective focuses on providing the best courses, providing a stimulating environment and extending services. A learner-centered perspective focuses on what students will know and understand, what students will do to learn, and from whom they will need services. These perspectives are not mutually exclusive—they are interdependent.

2. Faculty Roles

One of the primary differences between faculty-centered and learner-centered education is the role of faculty. Guskin [5] describes the difference as moving "from faculty productivity to student productivity; from faculty disciplinary interests to what students need to learn; from faculty teaching styles to student learning styles; from classroom teaching to student learning." Students may spend more time learning independently by themselves and with their peers and more time using interactive technologies. Students may also spend less total time with faculty, but receive more individualized attention.

The shift in focus reflected the "Five Key Changes to Practice" of learner-centered education identified by Weimer [6] and summarized in Table 2.

Key Changes to Practice	Learner Centered	Teacher Centered
1. Balance of Power	Student Control	Faculty Control
2. Function of Content	The Means to Knowledge	Content to Cover
3. Role of Teacher	Learning Facilitation	Knowledge Transmission
4. Responsibility for Learning	Student Self-Directed	Teacher Directed
5. Purpose and Processes of Evaluation	The Means for Learning	The Means for Grades

Table 2. Summary of Weimer's Five Key Changes to Practice [6]

3. Online Learning Characteristics

The characteristics of online learning enable the time, place, content, and outcomes of instruction to be tailored for, and controlled by, the learner rather than organized around the scheduling and resource needs of the provider [7]. These characteristics appear to make online learning inherently learner centered.

In practice, however, online courses are still predominantly faculty centered. Weigel [8] states that, "Nearly all varieties of distance education have failed to bring depth and dimensionality to the experience of learning. With the exception of a few innovative firms like Cognitive Arts and Unext.com, most distance education providers are serving up variants of a "post-a-lecture" and "host-a-discussion" approach." Results of the initial pilot test of the Technology Costing Methodology Project of the Western Cooperative for Educational Telecommunications, suggest that institutions are "not fundamentally reengineering their courses to take advantage of truly effective uses of technology. Instead they appear to be simply putting classroom-based courses on the web [9]."

Technology, particularly asynchronous learning networks, can be used to free up faculty time away from covering content and toward facilitating student learning. At the same time, technology gives students more opportunities for different types of instructional assistance, and greater control over the pacing and sequencing of their learning. "This means more opportunities to engage students in small-group instruction, more opportunities to offer students one-on-one tutoring sessions, and more opportunities to engage in what some cognitive scientists have referred to as scaffolded instruction, including coaching, mentoring and modeling activities [10]."

III. METHODS

During the development and delivery of the program used in this case study, efforts were made to identify and track information useful in developing the study.

- Direct and indirect costs were identified and tracked by the MSU Global project manager (the author).
- The primary faculty member kept a time log during development and instructional delivery.
- During the program, the faculty developed a weekly briefing of activities for MSU Global and the client.

- During the program, the MSU Global project manager and the client program manager had weekly telephone calls to check progress and identify any technical, logistical, program, or participant issues.

- Surveys were developed as part of the program to gather learner self-evaluations of skill levels before and after the program.

- End-of-program evaluations were used to determine learner satisfaction regarding all program components.

- A de-briefing telephone conference was held with the client program manager and the program participants to gain feedback on the program content, program structure, logistical and technical components, and perceived outcomes.

The project cost estimates, budget records, instructor time log, weekly briefings, project management notes, participant pre and post self-evaluation results, end-of-program evaluations and faculty and program manager notes from the telephone de-briefing were used in the development of this case study.

IV. CUSTOM BUSINESS COMMUNICATION PROGRAM

The MSU Global Institute and faculty in MSU's College of Communication Arts and Sciences created a custom non-credit program in business communication for a corporate client. MSU has an outstanding communications program, yet nothing was available online. The client request offered the MSU Global Institute the opportunity to build a brand-new custom solution from the ground up.

A. Program Requirements

The program was designed to client specifications to provide learners who already had a bachelor's degree with knowledge and practical application of business communication skills for personal growth and professional development. The client's primary goal was to enable employees to improve their ability to succeed in their careers, starting with the basics of business communication skills.

Goals for the program were to provide a learning experience with the flexibility to work around participant's unpredictable and constant travel schedules; to focus on interpersonal communication competencies applicable to familial and work settings; and to provide feedback on cognitive and behavioral aspects of learning.

Client requirements included working within a negotiated price point; delivering the program within eight weeks of acceptance of the proposal and on a schedule set by the client; delivering the program initially at a small scale (6 initial participants); building in scalability for increased enrollment after the pilot phase; building contingencies for unpredictable travel schedules and for unknown access to the web.

MSU Global constraints included recovering direct costs and working in partnership with academic faculty. Fortunately, MSU Global was able to identify faculty champions and appropriate instructor expertise. In addition, MSU Global had access to a large library of high-quality commercial courseware that it could license for small-scale applications.

B. Program Design

1. Development Approach

Due to the unique program requirements and constraints of the project, the process for developing the new program needed to be different from the traditional approach used in the development of online courses. The project did not have the resources or time to build curriculum from scratch or convert existing courses to an online format. Not having the resources to produce course content shifted the focus of the development process from the teacher to the learner. Instead of spending time focusing on transforming an existing course to an asynchronous format, the team focused on defining the individual learning outcomes, developing learning assignments for performance feedback, and identifying a library of resources to support specific skill development.

2. Courseware Library

The team explored existing courseware and corporate training models (since one of the primary goals was career development) and decided to build the program around available high-quality "soft skills" multimedia courseware. The depth and breadth of titles available provided an extensive library from which to choose titles that would best fit the learning objectives and provide depth of resources for learners at more advanced levels. In addition, the commercial courseware was customizable to each individual's needs through pre-tests and post-tests of knowledge built in to the courseware and the ability for learners to skip units already mastered.

The availability of an extensive courseware library was a key factor that changed the course development activities from a more traditional faculty-centered approach. Results of the new process included eliminating up-front media production and focusing the role of the instructor on being a personal coach to help each participant improve their personal skills. The change in the course development process is outlined in Table 3. To more clearly describe the process used for the project, a generalized "traditional" process is provided purely for contrast, and the Five Key Changes to Practice are used to illustrate the differences.

	Business Communications Program Development Process	Traditional Development Process
1. Balance of Power	**Student Control**	**Faculty Control**
Development Perspective	"What will help them build their skills?'	"What do I need to cover?"
2. Function of Content	**The Means to Knowledge**	**Content to Cover**
	Started with existing student skills and corporate skill benchmarks	Started with curriculum
	Created participant pre- and post- self-evaluations	
	Identified, evaluated and licensed existing courseware to support the skills desired	Produced new, or repurposed classroom, presentation materials
	Developed assignments for application, practice and feedback on performance	Same

	Designed student/instructor coaching, feedback, and assessment around specific skills; Designed student/student assignments and informal interaction with peers	Designed student/instructor feedback and assessment on assignments; student/student: assignments and topical discussions
3. Role of Teacher	**Learning Facilitation**	**Knowledge Transmission**
	Hired experienced instructor to be a personal tutor and coach for each participant	Hired experienced instructor to teach the class
4. Responsibility for Learning	**Student Self-Directed**	**Teacher Directed**
	Designed for student control and choice over: which program topics to learn based on their self-assessments; which courseware units to learn based on their goals and previous knowledge; when to schedule their weekly session with the instructor; when to do their work within the pacing set by the client	Instructor determines assignments and due dates with flexibility of anytime/anywhere within those limits
5. Purpose and Processes of Evaluation	**The Means for Learning**	**The Means for Grades**
	Created activities for feedback and performance assessment by the instructor	Created assessments of what was covered for grading (for credit courses) or for completing the course (non credit)
	Created skill pre- and post- self-evaluations for participants to reflect on their learning	

Table 3. Comparison of Development Processes Using Weimer's Five Key Changes to Practice [6]

C. Program Curriculum and Structure

To meet the client requirements of a 6-week program and to offer flexibility and learner choice so learners could focus on their skill gaps, a modular program structure was developed.

In weeks 1 & 2, every learner participated in "foundation" topics in Listening, Verbal, and Non-verbal Skills (interpersonal skills with an emphasis on listening and identifying/removing communication barriers). At the end of week 2 the learners completed an assignment evaluated by an MSU instructor.

During weeks 3 & 4, each learner chose either Negotiation or Conflict Management. At the end of Week 4 the learners turned in an assignment. In addition, the learners participated in a role-playing exercise on the telephone with an MSU instructor. Both assignments were evaluated.

During weeks 5 & 6 each learner chose either Effective Presentations or Effective Meetings. At the end of Week 6 learners had to turn in an assignment. The assignment was discussed with the learners and evaluated by an MSU instructor.

D. Program Features

1. Custom Learning Paths

The most productive way for learners to improve their skills is to spend their limited time on only those top-priority skills that need attention. The results of each participant's skill self-assessment, as well as interviews with learners about their own related experiences were used as a basis to provide a suggested customized program for each learner within the curriculum. Each learner had the option to go through all modules or to follow the customized path.

2. MSU Content Expertise

MSU instructors reviewed and recommended resources from the skills library of self-paced modules, developed practice and performance activities, and created and reviewed assessments to achieve the learner's personal learning goals.

3. MSU Instruction

MSU instructors provided personalized feedback and instruction to learners on hands-on practice and performance activities, conducted assessments, and scheduled interaction both individually with each learner as well as scheduled group interaction using the telephone and email.

4. Skills Library

MSU developed a custom library of high-quality self-paced modules specifically for this program from the holdings of MSU business partners. These skill-building modules, delivered on CD-ROM, were selected by MSU instructors to match the requirements of the curriculum and used in conjunction with MSU instruction to achieve the learning objectives for each participant.

5. Certificate of Achievement

Each participant received a non-credit certificate from MSU upon successful completion of the program.

E. Program Implementation

In the Spring of 2002, six adult learners took part in the pilot program. Participants were provided with a laptop computer by the client and a program binder from MSU Global that included CD-ROMs (curriculum/coursework), syllabi for each topic, assignments, and contact information. The program began with a telephone conference orientation meeting with all participants, the client program manager, the participant's direct supervisors, the MSU faculty, and the MSU Global project manager.

Before the orientation meeting, participants completed their skill self-assessments. They used these to choose two out of the four "specialty topics" available for weeks 3 & 4 and 5 & 6 (during weeks 1 & 2 all participants participated in the foundation topics). During the call, each participant scheduled weekly telephone sessions with the MSU instructor to participate in assignments and get personalized feedback on their performance. E-mail was used to send out reminders, send feedback from evaluations, turn in written assignments, and/or reschedule appointments.

Though designed to be an online program supplemented by telephone sessions for feedback on listening and audio communication skills, during the pilot the telephone was the primary mode of communication between participants and the instructor. This was the contingency plan for the unknown level of web access. Though the program was designed for a blended model of web-based resources supplemented by telephone sessions the telephone turned out to have the most convenient access during the pilot. We also determined that participants did have a reasonable level of dial-up access and could be required to use the Internet as part of the program in the future.

F. Program Costs

Detailed cost estimates were developed prior to the contract negotiations with the client. During the development and implementation of the project, MSU Global tracked the costs of the pilot program through its standard program planning, budget tracking and disbursement systems. The costs for this project are summarized in Table 4.

Direct Variable Costs		
Instructional Materials (notebooks, postage, courseware licenses and CD duplication)	4,500	$750 Per Participant, Variable Cost x 6
Instructional Delivery (instructor time, instructor direct expenses (cell phone))	3,300	$550 Per Participant, Variable Cost x 6
Total Direct Variable Costs	7,800	
Direct Fixed Costs		
Instructional Development for five, two-week topics – 10 weeks total (faculty time)	3,300	Fixed Cost
MSU Global Development and Management (client relationship management, contract development, project management and weekly client updates, office support)	3,700	Fixed Cost*
Total Direct Fixed Costs	7,000	
Total Direct Costs	14,800	
Indirect Costs (Standard University Facility and Administration 48.5% of Direct Costs)	7,178	
Total Costs	21,978	
*MSU Global must recoup its base budget costs through revenue. This is accomplished on most projects by calculating a percentage of the direct costs to		

estimate the share of staff time and indirect expenses of the department to support the project		

Table 4. Program Costs

There are two items to point out in the cost data. First, there are no up-front production costs. Instructor time for program development is incurred, but calculation of media production costs or instructor time spent creating media for presentations was not needed due to the use of commercial courseware. Another benefit of courseware is the decrease in licensing costs as volume increases.

Second, due to the small scale of the pilot project (6 participants) a learning management system was not necessary. This decision reduced costs because MSU Global incurs direct cost for technology support of non-credit courses. Future offerings of the program with more participants will use a course management system, and incur the associated costs, to more efficiently handle course logistics and reduce instructor time spent on that element of course delivery.

The university overhead cost of 48.5% of direct cost is the standard overhead rate calculation for grants and contracts. In MSU's accounting system this is disbursed to university administrative offices including the academic college and provost's office. Theoretically a portion of the overhead goes to offset the budget of MSU Global. In reality, MSU Global must be self-sustaining and recoup its costs through project revenue. The MSU Global "Development and Management" fee is therefore listed in this case as a direct cost.

Significant costs in this case were borne by the client. These included providing each participant with a laptop computer and providing technical support for the laptop. The client also paid for the telephone calls for each participant. In addition, the client program manager spent a significant amount of time working with MSU on determining the program goals and requirements, being a champion for the program within the organization, coordinating with IT staff and participant's direct supervisors, and facilitating implementation and evaluation of the program. This client involvement was a large part of the success of the program.

Revenue from the project covered direct costs of the project. MSU deemed this pilot project important enough to forego payback of indirect costs for the pilot offering.

G. Instructor Time

Throughout the project, the lead instructor kept a time log. The tasks and total time are summarized in Table 5.

The instructor's role during program development included structuring the curriculum, developing the participant skill assessments, selecting appropriate courseware titles, going through the courseware and developing review notes to check participants' knowledge, and developing assignments to provide skill application and feedback on skill performance.

The instructor's role during delivery of the program was primarily as a personal coach and tutor to each participant as s/he worked on individual communication skills.

Task	Hours
Instructional Development: For a total of 5 different 2-week courses	
Choosing course content and course modules	5.0
Creating/developing course objectives, syllabus and activities for each course	30.5
Creating welcome page advertisement and opening meeting agenda	1.5
Reviewing and selecting skill assessment evaluation questions	1.5
Preparing phone conference agendas and discussion questions	7.0
Creating program schedule and overview	1.0
Reading and critiquing course modules	70
Preparing weekly reports	3.0
Total Instructional Development Hours	**119.5**
Instructional Delivery: for 6-week program for 6 participants	
Phone conferences: 40 minutes/learner/week (estimated based on 3 learners who called once per week consistently throughout the program, 25 min. low – 55 min. high for evaluations).	24
Assignment evaluations and write-ups: 2.5 hrs/learner total	15
Email correspondence: 1 hr/learner total	6
Total Instructional Delivery Hours	**45**
Grand Total	**164.5**

Table 5. Instructor Time Summary

V. RESULTS

The pilot program using this model was a success as indicated by the satisfaction of the client, the participants, and the instructor. Four of the six participants completed the program. Two that did not finish had work priorities that interfered with their ability to fully participate after the fourth week of the program.

A. Success Factors

Results of program evaluation identified the following success factors:

- Instructor engagement, especially the connection with participants at the start of the program
- Coaching role of instructor
- Focus on competencies
- Participant selection of courseware modules
- Easy-to-use materials
- Timely feedback about performance (instead of just knowledge)
- Emphasis on applying the information and developing skills
- Short-term program length
- Client program champion provided visible, ongoing contact and support for learners

- Program's fit to client goals
- Support of participants' immediate supervisors

B. Future Enhancements

Based on client and participant debriefings and evaluations from the pilot, several things will be adjusted to improve learning, and to increase efficiency for students and the instructor as the program increases in scale. With increased enrollments, course management will increase. Enhancements include using a learning management system to more conveniently support program logistics. Assignments will be required to be submitted online. Scheduling, and rescheduling, telephone sessions will use a more standardized process. Also, in the next offering of the program, a threaded discussion will be implemented to enhance peer-to-peer exchange during the program.

C. Future Cost Issues

A pilot program such as this may not accurately represent what will occur at a larger scale. Given the results of the pilot, costs of the program per person are estimated to remain roughly the same for the second offering of the program and to decline as the number of participants increase.

Increased costs for adding a course management system in the second offering are projected to be offset by reduced costs for faculty program development. Costs for courseware licenses per participant are projected to decrease as the volume increases. Project oversight by MSU Global is expected to remain about the same, as these activities are independent of the number of participants.

Instructor management and quality oversight, however, will increase, as the number of participants increases and more instructors are needed for coaching. While unbundling faculty roles and compensating for development separately from delivery enables scalability, scaling up personalized coaching will require innovative approaches in order to maintain quality and manage costs.

VI. GENERALIZABLE FINDINGS

This case is specific to MSU Global and describes only one example of a learner-centered approach. As such, it is not appropriate to generalize conclusions from its findings. However, it does provide insight and a model, for those who may wish to adapt it and apply it to their own environment.

This case illustrates a method for creating learning experiences by leveraging existing resources. In this case, the key combinations were:

- Experienced faculty
- Design of learning and assessment activities enabled by the available media and communication channels
- Availability of off-the-shelf courseware
- Use of courseware that had the built-in ability to customize the content "path" to individual learner needs
- Instructional delivery focused on coaching for personalized feedback and evaluation

The case also illustrates an instructional approach based on the learner-centered perspective. The program was developed by:

- Focusing on building individual skills and knowledge
- Beginning with an assessment of current skills and tailoring the experience to address skill gaps
- Enabling learner control and choice in content, assessment, time and place
- Providing individualized coaching and personalized feedback
- Using assessments for skill building and self reflection

VII. CONCLUSION

This case study of the development of a new custom program highlights the cost benefits of having robust multimedia courseware readily available and combining it with faculty expertise and a learner-centered approach. This combination, as illustrated by this case example, changes some of the cost elements. Course development, for example, does not include media production of presentation materials. In addition, course delivery reflects a changed instructor role. In this case, instructor time in delivery was primarily spent providing individualized feedback and coaching to each participant. This individualized and personal approach, combined with the individualization inherent in the courseware, was the key to client satisfaction and success of the program. It was also the key to creating a high-quality, brand-new program at a price and timeline set by the client.

VIII. REFERENCES

1. **Reeves, T. C.,** Evaluating what really matters in computer-based education. Open Learning Technology Corporation Ltd., 1996.
   http://www.educationau.edu.au/archives/cp/reeves.htm

2. **Piccoli, G., Ahmad, R., & Ives, B.,** Web-based virtual learning environments: A research framework and preliminary assessment of effectiveness in basic IT skill training. *MIS Quarterly.* 25(4): 401-26 (December 2001).

3. **Bransford, J. D., Brown, A. L., & Cocking, R. R.** (eds.) *How People Learn: Brain, Mind, Experience and School.* Washington, D. C.: National Academy Press, 2000.

4. **Arizona Board of Regents**, Arizona Faculties Council (AFC) definition of learner-centered education. Arizona Board of Regents, 2000.
   http://www.abor.asu.edu/4_special_programs/lce/afc-defined_lce.htm

5. **Guskin, A.,** Learning more, spending less. *About Campus.* (July/August 1997).
   http://www.abor.asu.edu/4_special_programs/lce/guskin.htm

6. **Weimer, M.,** *Learner-centered teaching: Five key changes to practice.* San Francisco: Jossey-Bass, 2002.

7. **Matthews, D.,** The transformation of higher education through information technology: Implications for state higher education finance policy. Western Interstate Commission for Higher Education, 1998.
   http://www.educause.edu/nlii/keydocs/finance.html

8. **Weigel, V. B.,** *Deep learning for the digital age: Technology's untapped potential to enrich higher education.* San Francisco: Jossey-Bass, 2002.

9. **Jones, D.,** TCM project: Project findings. Western Interstate Commission for Higher Education, 2002. http://www.wiche.edu/telecom/projects/tcm/proj-findings.htm

10. **Baker, W., Hale, T., & Gifford, B. R.,** From theory to implementation: The mediated learning approach to computer-mediated instruction, learning and assessment. *Educom Review.* 32(5.) (September/October 1997).

IX. ACKNOWLEDGMENTS

I would like to thank the individuals at Michigan State University and on the MSU Global team whose work informed this study. In particular, I am indebted to our faculty partners in the College of Communication Arts and Sciences.

X. ABOUT THE AUTHOR

Christine Geith has over twelve years of experience in higher education in the areas of instructional technology and distance learning including technical infrastructure, faculty development, marketing, strategy, business and program development, finance, operations and management. She received a Master's in Business Administration from Rochester Institute of Technology and is a doctoral candidate in the PhD program in Higher Education Leadership and Administration at the University of Nebraska, Lincoln.

As director of MSU Global Online Connection's Global Institute, she is responsible for new product development and creating new lines of business, matching client and market needs with the expertise of Michigan State University and its external partners. Prior to joining MSU, she was executive director of Online Learning at Rochester Institute of Technology. She serves on the board of directors for the National University Telecommunications Network (NUTN) and is a founding board member of the Higher Education Knowledge and Technology Exchange (HEKATE).

BALANCING EFFICIENCY AND EFFECTIVENESS IN FIRST YEAR READING AND WRITING

Gregory L. Waddoups
Gary L. Hatch
Samantha Butterworth
Brigham Young University

- Cost effective redesign calls for a systematic plan to use online teaching and learning to provide higher quality and more efficient learning.

- Providing numerous sections taught by graduate instructors causes some problems with the course. Primary among these difficulties are inefficiency and inconsistency across sections.

- This course redesign was intended to enhance course quality by ensuring consistency across sections and increasing the amount of individual attention each student receives.

- In addition to improving student reading and writing, redesign reduced instructional costs by reducing the total hours each instructor spends teaching the course and the hours needed to train and supervise new instructors.

I. INTRODUCTION

Emily is an 18-year-old freshman majoring in chemical engineering at Brigham Young University (BYU). Her parents are paying her tuition and housing, with the understanding that she will complete her degree in four years or less. However, the average graduation time in her program is 9 semesters, including time to fulfill the required hours of General Education credits. Most people in her program have Advanced Placement credits that fulfill the requirements for First-Year Composition, Physical Science, and Math 110, but because Emily's small town high school did not have an AP program, she missed the opportunity to earn college credit in high school.

Emily's aunt, Ms. Pearson, is also attending BYU. After her husband passed away three years ago, she was left without any formal education or means to support her three young daughters. She has come back to school to complete a degree in nursing, but must first take several general-education courses. Working full time, running her children to school and piano lessons, and shuffling day-care, Mrs. Pearson is struggling to keep up her course load and wonders whether she will ever be able to graduate. These hypothetical cases represent the realities of education for many students at BYU, who have to balance work, school, family, and other personal matters to graduate in a timely manner

At BYU, we have attempted to satisfy the needs of students who require flexibility in their schedules. To do this, we have sought to balance their needs with those of the institution, which requires increased capacity and efficiency. The solution we have chosen is to implement a systematic plan to use online teaching and learning to provide higher quality and more efficient learning for BYU students Waddoups and Howell, 2002 (7); Campbell, 2002 (2). For example, by redesigning many of the General Education courses to integrate technology, BYU hopes to provide students with both efficient and high-quality learning opportunities. This paper analyzes one such course, English 115: College Writing and Reading, the standard first-year composition course for BYU. This course was redesigned to integrate multi-media course modules to teach certain aspects of the course content, and to use Blackboard as a communication portal. In the future, we hope to extend this course from a hybrid model to one that could be administered entirely off-site as part of BYU's large program in Independent Study. In all cases, students are able to self-select which version of the course they wish to take. However, in the future fewer and fewer traditional sections will be offered, limiting the number of students who can enroll in the traditional version of the course. A $200,000.00 grant awarded by the Center for Academic Transformation and the PEW charitable trust funded the redesign of this course. This grant was created to fund curriculum-redesign projects that incorporate online learning with the goal of improving quality and efficiency.

This research takes place within the debate concerning the effectiveness of using online technologies to provide efficient and effective learning opportunities for college students. Some have argued that online education is of poorer quality than traditional education, and that it represents the incursion of corporate interests and "logics" into higher education Noble, 1997 (5). In contrast, others argue that, if used properly, these technologies can potentially provide robust learning environments Levin, Levin, and Waddoups, 1999 (4); Hiltz, Zhang, and Turoff, 2002 (3).

II. HISTORICAL BACKGROUND

David O. McKay, an early church leader, described BYU as a religious institution established for the purpose of associating science, art, literature, and philosophy with religious instruction Richards, 1997 (6). This idea, reflected in the University's mission statement, is to provide a spiritually enriched learning environment for all members of The Church of Jesus Christ of Latter-day Saints. This desire to provide a combination of sacred and secular learning to all members of the Church presents two challenges. First, the rapid growth in church membership has compromised BYU's ability to serve a significant proportion of the church membership on campus. Second, the University has placed a cap on enrollments. To address these challenges, BYU sponsors the use of technology to bridge the gap between increased membership and enrollment caps. This goal is the primary impetus for online learning at BYU.

The current president of BYU, Dr. Merrill Bateman, supported faculty teams interested in creating online courses that had the potential to (1) create efficiencies by substituting capital for labor and (2) improve teaching and learning through strategic uses of technology. Among other things, the Center for Instructional Design (CID) was created to support large-scale course design and development efforts to meet these goals. English 115 is one course that has been redesigned to improve cost effectiveness and learning effectiveness Bateman, 1998 (1).

English 115, BYU's primary first-year writing course, introduces students to the fundamental processes of critical reading and writing, library research, and information literacy and knowledge of academic genres and conventions. The course enrolls approximately 3,300 students each academic year in 87 sections per semester with 20 students per section. The course traditionally meets three hours a week and is taught primarily by graduate instructors in the English department MA program, who have full responsibility for the course.

Providing numerous sections taught by graduate instructors causes some problems with the course. Primary among these difficulties are inefficiency and inconsistency across sections. Few of these instructors have ever taught before, and most never took a first-year writing course because they fulfilled the requirement with Advanced Placement examination scores. Because of their inexperience, the English department devotes significant resources to training and supervising these instructors. Much of this training involves simply acquainting the instructors with the course itself. The instructors' inexperience also leads them to spend a significant amount of time preparing for classes, often duplicating the efforts of other instructors.

In addition to inefficiency (or perhaps because of it), English 115 suffers from inconsistency across sections. Presently, graduate instructors aim to achieve course objectives in a multitude of ways, and despite the efforts of full-time faculty to train and supervise these graduate instructors, student evaluations reveal a wide range of quality. In addition, graduate instructors teach only two years, so the department cannot benefit much from the experience they gain in the program. Because space on campus constrains the number of sections that can be offered at times that students demand, English 115 is also inefficient in meeting the students' scheduling demands. Although there are usually enough seats in English 115 for all new students, constraints of space limit how many courses can be offered at popular times (such as MWF between 9:00 and 11:00).

This course redesign was intended to enhance course quality by ensuring consistency across sections and increasing the amount of individual attention each student receives. The redesigned course reduces the amount of time students spend in the classroom from three hours to one hour a week, allowing the faculty to spend more time in one-on-one student consultations. A series of interactive multimedia lessons and additional peer-to-peer sessions replace the time students previously spent in class. These lessons were designed to standardize the curriculum across all sections of the first-year writing course, provide students with a more consistent experience, and reduce the time graduate instructors spent preparing and presenting in the classroom. Because the department can use these lessons to acquaint instructors with the course before they ever teach, they help reduce the amount of time needed to train new instructors. Finally, the course was redesigned to allow students spend more time one-on-one with faculty and with tutors in BYU's Writing Center, thus increasing the amount of feedback they receive on their work in progress, and improving students' academic reading and writing.

In addition to improving student reading and writing, the redesigned course was intended to reduce instructional costs by reducing the total hours each instructor spends teaching the course and by reducing the hours needed to train and supervise new instructors. By reducing these hours, we could in theory teach the same number of students with fewer instructors (increasing class size from 20 to 25), allowing us to improve the overall quality of instructors because we could be more selective in the hiring of new instructors. The question guiding this research is whether the course redesign of English 115 effectively improved course quality while decreasing costs.

III. METHODS

To measure whether the course redesign increased course quality while decreasing instructional costs, we developed a research study comparing student satisfaction and learning in both the traditional and redesigned versions of English 115. We are particularly interested in whether there is a mutually exclusive relationship between making courses more cost effective and maintaining or increasing student satisfaction and learning. What elements of the online course would students be most satisfied with, and where are their areas of concern? We collected data in three online and three traditional courses, including pre and post student surveys, instructor time surveys, instructor interviews, feedback from student focus groups, completion rates and grades, and student writing samples. The following paragraphs briefly outline the type of data we collected.

A. Pre-Survey

A survey was administered by the research team via email at the beginning of the course to students enrolled in both the online and traditional sections. This survey aimed to ascertain students' expectations of the online learning experience, as well as sample demographic information such as year in school and technological experience. The research team also administered an exit survey via the Internet to all students enrolled in the targeted sections. This survey collected students' feedback about their actual experience in the course.

B. Instructor Time Survey

We distributed a weekly time log survey to instructors of the 6 sections under evaluation. This survey prompted them to record how many minutes they spent each week in the following areas: preparation, instruction, grading, office hours, email, and development. In the category "preparation," instructors logged the time they spent preparing lectures for class, posting to their Blackboard site, and preparing for student conferences. "Instruction" denoted how much time instructors spent face-to-face with their students in a classroom environment. Instructors also logged the time they spent grading both small online exercises and larger writing assignments. Only the instructors of traditional sections were required to hold office hours; this category reflects the time they spent holding scheduled office hours. Additionally, instructors tracked how much time they spent writing emails and responding to student emails. Finally, instructors logged how much time they spent in developmental activities such as staff meeting, Blackboard training, attending professional conferences. Completion of this survey was voluntary, but we contacted instructors on a weekly basis and followed up with those who had not yet completed the survey.

C. Focus Groups

An outside evaluator conducted two focus groups in the middle of the semester, one for students enrolled in the traditional course and one for those in the online course. Participation was voluntary and confidential. The research team contacted students via email or telephone to ascertain their willingness to participate. Two internal evaluators and Gail Hawisher, our external evaluator, also attended the sessions. Questions focused on student satisfaction with their experience in the course.

D. Completion Rates and Grades

The research team collected unobtrusive data from each course under evaluation regarding overall completion rates and grades.

E. Portfolio Analysis

In addition to the above instruments, English 115 students enrolled in the three online sections of the course, along with students enrolled in three randomly selected traditional sections of the course, were asked to submit portfolios of their work during the semester. Each portfolio included four papers: a narrative, a textual analysis, a research paper, and a negotiation proposal. These portfolios were assessed anonymously by a panel of readers chosen from the ranks of English 115 instructors. Each paper was read a minimum of three times, and a standard rubric was used for all readings.

F. Instructor Interviews

In addition to the portfolios and the above evaluation instruments, the instructors of the six target English 115 courses were asked to participate in two interviews during the course of the semester. Questions focused on instructor satisfaction with their experience in the course.

IV. RESULTS

A. Cost Savings

One of the objectives of the English 115 redesign was to reduce the cost of teaching by making capital for labor substitutions. More specifically, we hoped to take advantage of online multi-media modules that teach students key concepts about reading and writing rather than rely on the time instructors spent preparing and teaching the traditional class. We further hoped that as a consequence of the increased efficiency, we could increase the number of students enrolled in each section. To measure this hypothesized reduction in instructor time, we prepared and distributed a weekly time-log survey to the instructors of the traditional and online courses. This survey asked the instructors to log how much time they spent each week in the following categories: (1) preparation, (2) instruction, (3) grading, (4) office hours, (5) email, and (6) teacher development. During our instructor interviews, we also asked how they managed their time.

Table 1: Instructor Time Log

Category	Online	Traditional
Preparation	101.9 min/week	117.56 min/week
Instruction	38.5 min/week	132.82 min/week
Grading	146.25 min/week	164.87 min/week
Office Hours	0 min/week	147.69 min/week
Email	110.38 min/week	17.31 min/week
Conferencing	75.63 min/week	73.08 min/week
Development	27.38 min/week	39.49 min/week
Total	500 min/week	692.82 min/week

Our analysis showed an overall 25% time savings in the redesigned course versus the traditional course. Generally, we saw time savings where we expected to see it: in instruction, because the online class met only once a week; and in office hours, because online instructors did not hold regular office hours. Although online instructors spent more time emailing their students, the reduction of office hours compensated for the emailing time. Instructors said they used email much like office hours to answer student questions about assignments and to provide feedback on student work. Instructors in traditional courses said students rarely visited them during office hours and instead preferred meeting during scheduled conferences. The online instructors' increased use of email created more flexibility for both instructors and the students. However, online instructors did not take full advantage of asynchronous discussion boards for student-instructor and student-student communication. The three instructors did not feel comfortable using the asynchronous discussion because they felt overwhelmed with learning the new technology.

When we view the line graph of the average number of instructor minutes spent per week in each version of the course (see Appendix 1), the peaks in the graph roughly correspond with the end of each of the four major units: (1) the narrative, (2) textual analysis, (3) research, and (4) negotiation units. The large amount of time the instructors expended in grading each of the four major papers explains these peaks. Overall, grading is the most time-consuming activity for all instructors. Grading time was slightly less in the online course, possibly because instructors read more interim drafts of students' papers. Because grading required such a significant amount of instructor time, we are planning grading workshops to increase our instructors' efficiency in reading and grading student papers. We may also use the standard rubric developed for the portfolio analysis to provide instructors with more direction for grading. We hope that this rubric, along with grading workshops, will improve the efficiency of instructor grading.

One area in which we had projected a savings in time was in preparation; however, we did not realize the expected results. In fact, during the first several weeks, the online instructors spent *more* time preparing than the traditional instructors; in weeks 2 and 5 they spent almost double the time preparing (see Appendix 2).

From our interviews with the online instructors we learned that they spent "preparation time" learning to use Blackboard, fixing technical problems, posting quizzes, and creating their Blackboard site. In other words, their preparation time was spent *administering* the course, rather than preparing lesson materials. To alleviate this situation, we developed more extensive training that focused on using the Blackboard course-delivery system and taught them to more effectively implement the course modules. Areas for improvement included how to best use asynchronous conferencing software, how to best use weekly class time, and how to best structure writing conferences.

The question for many involved in this project is how the course redesign influenced students' satisfaction with their experience in the course and whether the redesigned course produced better writers. In short, did we sacrifice quality of learning and student satisfaction for cost effectiveness?

B. Student Satisfaction

Through the surveys and focus groups, we measured overall student satisfaction in the online versus the traditional course. From our analysis, the students rated the quality of the traditional and online version of the course almost identically. The response rate to both the pre and post surveys was fairly high. 69% of student enrolled in the online course responded to the pre survey, while 100% of students in the traditional course responded. 64% of students enrolled in the online course responded to the post survey, compared to 87% of students in the traditional course.

Table 2: Overall Course Quality

Question	Traditional	Online
Rate the overall quality of the course. (Scale: Poor = 1 — Excellent = 7) No significant difference at 95% confidence interval.	Mean= 5.18 SD=1.08	Mean= 4.88 SD=1.20

We asked additional questions about the quality of the assignments and the clarity of the course objectives students rated both lower in the online version of the course. However, only assignment quality was statistically significant when we used a one-way analysis of variance (ANOVA).

Table 3: Course Quality Variables

Question	Traditional	Online
The assignments helped me apply what I learned. (Scale: Strongly Disagree = 1 — Strongly Agree = 7) Significant difference at 95% confidence interval.	Mean=5.29 SD=1.33	Mean=4.47 SD=1.24
The course objectives were clear. (Scale: Strongly Disagree = 1 — Strongly Agree = 7) No significant difference at 95% confidence interval.	Mean=5.76 SD=1.69	Mean=4.97 SD=1.45

From our instructor interviews, we found that instructors assigned all the online reading and assessments from the online course modules. These were assignments that they did not write, probably didn't understand, and for which they felt little ownership. According to one instructor, it was "difficult for a student to see the purpose of an assignment when that purpose is unclear to the instructor." There are a few ways to mitigate this: instructors could be free to design all of their own activities in the online course, or they could receive a more in-depth introduction to the course material, so that they know what is there and what they are assigning.

We also asked students whether the course increased their interest in writing, increased their understanding of writing, and improved their writing skills. In all instances, the traditional students rated their experience higher. However, the only question found to be significantly higher was whether the course increased their interest in the subject matter. In response to this finding, we wondered whether students who were less confident with their writing skills "self-selected" into the online course. From our analysis of the presurvey, we found that 33% of *online students* reported that they were confident in their writing versus 51% of *traditional students*. The lower confidence of students in the online course may have influenced their response to this question. However, we are concerned that many online students reported lower interest in writing and are exploring reasons for their response. In particular, we need to carefully consider ways to help the online instructors communicate the importance of writing and help increase students' confidence in their writing ability and their interest in writing generally. We think better use of one-on-one conferences will help increase students' writing self-confidence by having the instructor focus on students' strengths and weaknesses.

Table 4: Self Report of Student Learning

Question	Traditional	Online
The course increased my interest in the subject area. (Scale: Strongly Disagree=1 — Strongly Agree=7) Significant difference at 95% confidence interval.	Mean=4.39 SD=1.26	Mean=3.55 SD=1.56
The course increased my understanding of writing. (Scale: Strongly Disagree=1 — Strongly Agree=7) No significant difference at 95% confidence interval.	Mean=5.45 SD=1.28	Mean=4.65 SD=1.69
The course improved my writing skills. (Scale: Strongly Disagree=1 — Strongly Agree=7) No significant difference at 95% confidence interval.	Mean=5.55 SD=1.40	Mean=4.71 SD=1.55

Students were generally very satisfied with the level and quality of the student/instructor interaction. When we asked whether the students would like more instructor interaction, the mean for the online course (on a 7-point scale) was 4.59, versus only 4.20 in the traditional course.

Table 5: Interaction Comparison

Question	Traditional	Online
In this course I would have liked more interaction with the instructor. (Scale: Strongly Disagree = 1 — Strongly Agree = 7) No significant difference at 95% confidence interval.	Mean=4.20 SD=1.55	Mean=3.85 SD=1.35
In this course, I would have liked more interaction with other students. (Scale: Strongly Disagre e= 1 — Strongly Agree = 7) No significant difference at 95% confidence interval.	Mean=4.00 SD=1.43	Mean=3.85 SD=1.35

When we asked whether the students would like more peer interaction the mean in the online course was 3.85, versus 4.00 in the traditional course. It seems that students are satisfied with the amount of peer interaction in both types of courses.

Online students made it clear that face-to-face instructor conferences were a must. Students said that a purely online self-paced version of the course would be very difficult. They were pleased with how accessible their instructors were, letting students call them at home and responding to their emails promptly. Indeed, students in both versions of the course rated the level of instructor feedback highly: 6.12 in the traditional version and 6.03 in the online version.

Table 6: Interaction Quality Comparison

Question	Traditional	Online
The instructor gave prompt feedback. (Strongly Disagree = 1 — Strongly Agree = 7)	Mean=6.22 SD=1.17	Mean=6.00 SD=1.30
The instructor gave constructive feedback on assignments and tests. (Strongly Disagree = 1 — Strongly Agree = 7)	Mean=6.12 SD=1.50	Mean=6.00 SD=1.29

Despite the lack of regular face-to-face interaction, every online student who participated in the focus group felt that the instructor cared for them as individuals and that the instructors were genuinely concerned with their progress in the course.

Students from both the online and the traditional courses were asked to identify the courses' strengths and weaknesses. From the analysis of their open-ended responses, we found that online students liked the flexibility and convenience of the course, appreciated the quality of the multi-media course material, and felt the course improved their writing skills. One student said, "It was nice to have all the info I needed anytime I needed it. The instructor made it easier because she was always quick to answer questions and help me out when I had a problem." Another said: "The online website—it helped me to understand the concepts of the course, and it was easy to refer to if I needed to. Blackboard was a nice thing to have for taking quizzes and immediate feedback. The writing assignments were a good test of what I have learned and what I need to work on. The opportunity I had to work at my own pace and only having class once a week."

The students in the traditional sections also made positive comments about the course. They said the course improved their writing (33%). And they identified the instructor (27%) and the course material (23%) as strengths. One student said: "I like the way the course is presented. I enjoyed a lot working on most of the papers. The teacher was awesome and not only helped me understand the importance of the course, but she was friendly and open to my ideas."

When asked to identify course weaknesses, 45% of the online students said technology problems were a weakness. During this semester, we had significant problems with the Blackboard system, which functioned as the course portal. Online students also pointed to lack of interaction (15%) and poor organization (12%) as weaknesses. It is clear from our research that some students are not comfortable with a more independent learning style and depend on more frequent course meetings to pace them through the course. In contrast, the traditional students disliked the midterm (28%) and grammar assignments (23%). They also felt that the workload was too heavy (21%) for the credit they received.

From our analysis of student satisfaction data, the Winter 2002 pilot demonstrated that through our course redesign efforts we were able to maintain student satisfaction while implementing cost savings techniques. Indeed, students were equally satisfied with the overall effectiveness of the instruction and the course quality. From our research, we have learned that instructors need training to clarify course and assignment objectives. We are concerned that students may not be using the course modules to complete their readings and assignments, and we are considering ways to increase students' use of these modules. We are also designing training for the instructors that will help them use their class time and student/teacher conferences more effectively to increase students' interest in writing.

C. Learning Effectiveness

We also measured the learning effectiveness of this course by collecting a portfolio of writing from students in the online and traditional English 115 courses. We conducted a comparative analysis on student portfolios to determine the extent to which course type affected the quality of student writing.

1. Study Background

Throughout the winter 2002 semester, English 115 students prepared four papers: (1) personal narrative, (2) textual analysis, (3) research paper, and (4) argumentative synthesis group paper. The instructor graded these papers and placed them into a student portfolio. Several copies of each portfolio were created for our evaluation purposes. A numeric identifier was assigned to each paper stripping out all identification of the author and whether they were in the traditional or online version of the course. The purpose of the portfolio-analysis portion was to compare student writing in the three traditional courses and the three online courses. To evaluate student writing, we developed a detailed rubric to provide raters with a common reference to judge the quality of student writing.

2. Study design

Two generalizability studies were conducted during the Winter 2002 pilot. The first was a nested study in which three raters read each student portfolio. Sixteen readers participated in the nested study with each reader rating a total of 30 papers. The second study involved a fully crossed design. In this study, we had five readers read the same 16 portfolios, and we compared their ratings. These sixteen portfolios were randomly selected from each of the traditional and online sections; eight students came from the traditional sections and eight students from the online sections. Unlike the nested study, all readers were required to read all portfolios in the sample. As a result, all five readers read a total of 48 papers

Prior to receiving the student portfolios, all readers attended a training session. During the session, the study designers explained the scoring rubric and how to assign points to each portion. The rubric included five categories: (1) introductions and conclusions; (2) focus and organization; (3) development and detail; (4) sentence structure and word choice; and (5) adherence to convention. Each category was assessed on a scale from 1 to 10, with 10 being the highest score possible. The raw scores were then weighted, so that focus and organization, and development and detail, each accounted for 30% of the composite score. Sentence structure and word choice accounted for 20% of the composite score, and the final two categories accounted for 10% each of the composite score. The instructions to the readers said that they were to rate each section on its own merits against the rubric.

To retain the holistic evaluation present in English composition courses, the readers had the flexibility of assigning points within a range. This rubric gave the readers the scaffolding they needed to increase the likelihood of quantitative consistency between grades while also allowing the readers to follow their own instinct about the quality of the paper.

During the training session, all readers received the same paper and had 30 minutes to grade the paper using the rubric. They returned the grade sheets and we compiled the results. We showed readers how their ratings compared to those of other readers and gave them the opportunity to evaluate their own rating consistency and determine what corrective action, if any, they needed to bring their ratings in line with other readers. The objectives of this exercise were to familiarize the readers with the rubric and to give them an opportunity to see whether they were "easy" or "hard" graders.

The readers then received their packets with either ten or sixteen student portfolios. The readers shuffled all papers in the packet, so that all papers for all students were randomly graded and two papers from the same student would not be graded back to back. Anonymous, shuffled papers reduced the chance of the halo effect.

When all papers had been graded and returned, the score sheets were entered into a spreadsheet. To ensure accuracy, each sheet was entered twice into two different spreadsheets, and the two sheets were compared. Any differences were corrected by reviewing the original score sheets a third time.

3. Portfolio analysis findings

The preliminary results showed that 3% of the variance is caused by the paper effect. The student effect accounted for almost 50% of the total variance. Readers accounted for approximately 15% of the variance. The interpretation of the data is that readers are not consistent with each other: some readers are easy graders, while others are hard graders. This inconsistency resulted in an inconsistency in students' relative ranking, depending on the reader who read the paper. Yet, each reader was fairly consistent with him or herself. In other words, easy raters tended to be easy on all students and difficult raters tended to be hard on all students.

Overall, the papers in the online sections had a significantly higher average score than those in the traditional sections, with a p value of .055. In other words, at a 94% confidence interval, the scores from the online course were higher than the traditional course. Scores from the traditional sections tended to vary the most, while scores from the online sections were more consistent and uniform. Since we hoped that standardizing instruction would result in less variability in student writing quality, these results may indicate that we were successful in achieving this objective. of the course redesign.

We also compared student writing according to the five categories in the rubric. In the fully crossed study, we found that raters graded the papers in the online course significantly higher in (1) the quality of the introductions and conclusions (99% confidence interval) and (2) focus and organization (94% confidence interval). There were no significant differences in the other three categories: (development and detail, sentence structure and word choice, and adherence to convention). Additionally, in the nested design, we found no significant differences in any of the rubric categories. The nested study is less precise and is especially open to errors related to the variance related to inconsistency among the raters.

Based on our initial pilot we are encouraged that overall paper quality is higher in the online versus the traditional version of the course. We are also encouraged that there was a significantly higher rating for the introductions and conclusions, and focus and organization. Because these are global writing skills that were a focus in the online modules we developed, we feel the online portions of the course helped improve student writing. To further assess quality in writing, we will conduct a similar analysis during the Fall 2002 implementation. During this analysis, we will provide more extensive training for our raters to increase their inter-rater reliability.

V. SUMMARY AND CONCLUSION

What can we conclude from this research about the nature of efficiency and learning effectiveness in online education? What can we learn about the relationship between cost effectiveness to student learning and satisfaction? In this study, we found that implementing cost-effectiveness measures did not decrease overall student satisfaction and learning effectiveness. In this limited implementation of the English 115 course, we demonstrated a 25% reduction in instructor time. In our Fall 2002 implementation, we plan to increase the number of students in 10 online sections while keeping the number of students constant in 10 online sections, with the intent to study the effects of class size on time savings. We are also taking measures to improve training so instructors spend less time learning to use the technology and administering the course and more time interacting with their students.

The next important question is the extent to which the course redesign affected student satisfaction and learning effectiveness. Indeed, does redesigning a course to be more cost efficient lead to a decrease in student satisfaction and learning? We found that generally student satisfaction with the course quality, instructor, and instructional interactions were not significantly different in the traditional and redesigned course. However, we did find that students rated the redesigned course significantly lower in the quality of assignments. The online students also rated their interest in the subject matter as significantly lower than those in the traditional sections. In addition to the self-selection of less confident writers in the online course, we feel that instructors did not effectively use the student conferences and weekly class meetings to communicate the course and assignment objectives. Rather, they used precious class-time to manage technical problems and course administration issues, instead of focusing on helping students understand the course assignments. We hope that through training instructors and students to use the individual conferences and in-class time more wisely, both will develop a better understanding of the assignments and develop a greater appreciation for writing. Additionally, we hope that through training the instructors to use the Blackboard course system they can more effectively and efficiently communicate with their students.

As we have stated previously, student writing in the online course was found to be significantly better than in the traditional course. In particular, we found that student introductions and conclusions and focus and organization improved in the online course. This makes intuitive sense given that these are the areas in writing that are most easily taught online.

In sum, the results of our research demonstrate that there is a delicate balance between cost effectiveness, student satisfaction, and learning effectiveness. Through our research, we have demonstrated that systematic course redesign, including the integration of technology, can create efficiencies while maintaining the quality and effectiveness of the course.

VI. REFERENCES

1. **Bateman, M. B.** University conference address given to campus faculty and staff. (August, 1998).
2. **Campbell, J.O.** Factors in ALN Cost Effectiveness at BYU. In Bourne, J. and Moore, J.C. (Eds.), *Elements of Quality Online Education,* Sloan-C, Volume 2, 59-70.
3. **Hiltz, R. Zhang, Y. and Turoff, M**. Studies of Effectiveness of Learning Networks. In Bourne, J. and Moore, J.C. (Eds.), *Elements of Quality Online Education,* Sloan-C, Volume 2, 15-44.
4. **Levin, J.A., Levin, S.R, & Waddoups, G.L.**. Multiplicity in learning and teaching: A framework for developing innovative online education. *Journal of Research on Computing in Education*, 32 (2), 256-269. (1999)
5. **Noble, D.** Digital diploma mills: The automation of higher education. *First Monday, 3 (*1), 1-16. (1997).
6. **Richards, L. A.** What I Now Believe About a BYU Education That I Wish I Had Believed When I First Came [Online]. Available: http://speeches.byu.edu.devo/96-97/RichardsW97.html . 1997.
7. **Waddoups, G.L. & Howell, S**. Bringing Online Learning to Campus: The Hybridization of Teaching and Learning at Brigham Young University. *International Review of Research in Open and Distance Learning*, 2(2): 1-15 (2002).

VII ABOUT THE AUTHORS

Gregory L. Waddoups has an interest in online and distance education and program evaluation. For the past five years, Dr. Waddoups has conducted evaluations in Web-based learning environments with a particular interest in using formative evaluation to help faculty and instructional designers construct effective Web-based learning environments. Prior to joining Brigham Young University (BYU), He has conducted extensive evaluations of two online Master degree programs at the University of Illinois. He has presented numerous papers at professional conferences and his research has been published in several scholarly journals. Dr. Waddoups is currently responsible for evaluating the effectiveness of Web-based courses at BYU as well as courses at the University's satellite campuses in Idaho and Hawaii. Additionally, he has taught First-Year Writing at BYU and the University of Illinois.

Gary L. Hatch is the Writing Program Administrator for the English Department at BYU and the Associate Chair for Rhetoric and Composition. Along with Nichole Van Valkenburgh, he developed the content for the English 115 course and teaches the Independent Study version of the course. He trains and supervises all of the graduate instructors in the English Composition program. He is the primary investigator for the grant in course redesign given to BYU from the Center for Academic Transformation.

Samantha Butterworth is a graduate student in Comparative Literature at Brigham Young University. She has also taught English 115 for the English Department. As an evaluator for the Center for Instructional Design, she has studied the success of online learning for the last three years.

APPENDIX 1

Total Instructor Time

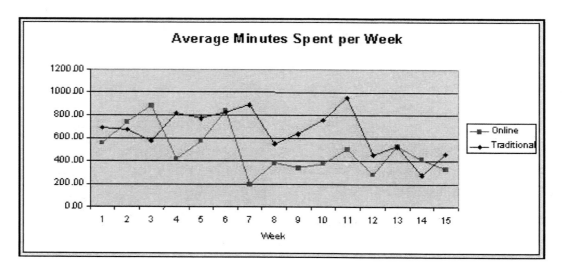

APPENDIX 2:

Instructor Preparation Time

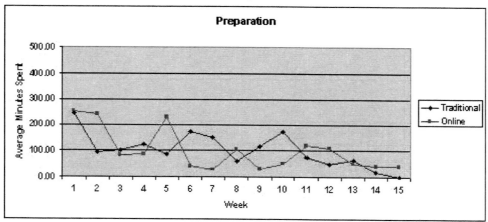

Access

IMPROVING ACCESS TO ONLINE LEARNING: CURRENT ISSUES, PRACTICES, & DIRECTIONS

John Sener
Sener Learning Services
Sloan Center for OnLine Education

- Improving access involves building new channels and tearing down barriers; neither activity by itself is sufficient as a strategy for improving access.

- Online learning providers need to identify the access issues of the specific learner groups they serve.

- Gaining the attention of prospective online learners is *the* foundational access issue.

- Serving populations for which motivation is an issue raises additional access issues.

- Some assessment instruments appear to be designed to 'screen out' learners who are perceived to be less likely to succeed in an online learning course. A more promising approach may be to build courses and self-assessment resources which offer students a "buffet" of learning opportunities.

I. INTRODUCTION

Several papers in the Sloan-C Online Education quality series have dealt more or less indirectly with the issue of access, and this one focuses exclusively and explicitly on access as a pillar of effective online learning. The topic of providing and improving access to online learning is an appropriate one with which to conclude this volume, as it brings the discussion full circle, returning to the core vision of the Sloan-C asynchronous learning networks (ALN) initiative.

Because access to online learning opportunities is such a vast issue, a comprehensive critical review of work related to improving access is not attempted here. Instead, this paper provides a fairly comprehensive map of access-related issues from several frames of reference. It also provides representative examples of the current state of practice, in particular, those exemplified by effective practices which appear on the Sloan-C effective practices website (http://www.sloan-c.org/effective). In addition, this paper will discuss and suggest some likely directions for improving access.

A. What is Access?

Three frames of reference are useful in defining access to online learning: (1) scope and domain, (2) strategies for improving access, and (3) areas of effective practice.

Defining scope and domain: Although it has evolved since its inception in 1993, the core vision of the Sloan-C ALN initiative contains several key elements: enabling qualified and motivated learners to succeed and complete a course, degree, or program through online access to U.S. higher learning in their chosen discipline, at a place and time of their choosing, and at affordable cost (Figure 1).

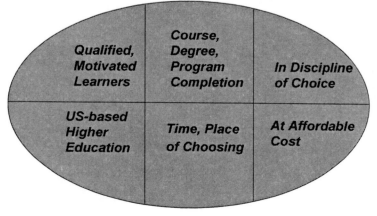

**What Is Access?
Scope of Sloan-C Initiative**

| Qualified, Motivated Learners | Course, Degree, Program Completion | In Discipline of Choice |
| US-based Higher Education | Time, Place of Choosing | At Affordable Cost |

Figure 1. Scope of Sloan-C ALN Initiative

These criteria reflect the specific focus of the Sloan-C ALN initiative. For each of these parameters, it is possible to take a more comprehensive view of access-related issues by expanding the domain of issues. Figure 2 reflects some of the major areas of interest; some of these are outside the scope of the Sloan-C initiative, and others have emerged as issues within the initiative as online education itself has evolved.

Audience: The Sloan-C ALN initiative has focused primarily on serving qualified and motivated learners. Serving populations for which motivation is an issue, such as at-risk youth or "2nd chance" learners attempting higher education after an earlier unpleasant experience with formal education, raises additional access issues. An area that falls between these two is the extent to which access barriers, for instance insufficient computer skills, prevent otherwise qualified and motivated learners from accessing online education.

Course/Degree/Program Completion: The Sloan-C initiative has also focused on enabling degree and program completion in a variety of ways, for instance by funding the development of nearly 100 degree and certificate programs. More attention is being devoted to providing access to learning in smaller chunks, for instance the online learning resources being collected under the MERLOT (Multimedia Educational Resource for Online Learning and Teaching) project (www.merlot.org) or the "enhanced learning objects" developed under MarylandOnline's Project Synergy [1]. Access also includes lifelong learning opportunities not related to degree completion, for instance the host of mini-courses, workshops, seminars, and online conferences offered for professional certification, continuing education, or enrichment.

Discipline of Choice: Closely coupled with the emphasis on degree and program completion has been an effort to make as many subject disciplines available as possible. Beyond the structure of academic disciplines, the Internet has made a plethora of informal and incidental learning opportunities and resources accessible—listservs, newsgroups, and special interest websites among others. Even five years ago, using a search engine to access information on a topic of interest was a relatively uncertain proposition; today, the chances of finding information and even knowledge on a topic of interest using a standard Internet search engine are relatively high.

U.S.-based Higher Education: The Sloan-C ALN initiative has also focused primarily on American higher education institutions, although it has also made some valuable international connections with higher education institutions abroad through its annual conferences, and it has also been involved in efforts to promote online learning in certain industries (e.g., telecommunications) through linkages with higher education institutions. Overall, however, online learning in international higher education, corporate training, and K-12 are largely separate worlds, each with their own specific sets of access-related issues.

Affordable Cost: In recent years, the Sloan-C ALN initiative has put increased attention and emphasis on assuring that online learning is affordable, both for students to pursue and for institutions to develop and sustain, since affordability is a major access issue for most online education programs. However, there have been online programs for which high cost has apparently been less of an issue because of a desire to reach a high-end clientele (and thus deliberately restrict access to those who can pay), government subsidies, greater emphasis on software or multimedia development, and other reasons.

What Is Access?
An Expanded Scope

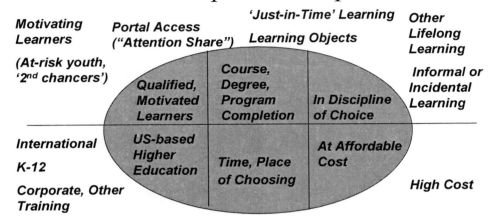

Figure 2. Expanded Scope of Access Domain

Strategies for improving access: Strategies primarily involve *expanding* opportunities and/or reducing barriers. These two strategies are closely linked and often inseparable. The distinction is useful in reminding us that improving access involves both building (e.g., reaching existing learner populations or new ones; providing more resources better, faster, and more cheaply) and tearing down barriers, and neither by itself is sufficient as a strategy for improving access. Building new programs has failed to increase access in some cases, for instance where a "field of dreams" approach to program development was employed; programs were built but the anticipated learners didn't come.

The core emphasis on removing place, time, and cost barriers is still important, but evolving practice has identified numerous other barriers—technology, program and course entry, motivational or readiness levels, and many others. Some access barriers, for instance poor course navigation design, impose a 'cognitive load' on online learners, i.e., additional mental burdens caused not only by the task of organizing and comprehending information during the learning process [2] but also by the 'meta-tasks' of figuring out how to access information to engage in the learning process. Other barriers simply prevent prospective learners from embarking on the learning process in the first place.

To describe what improved access is, it is necessary to describe what limitations on access are appropriate. Although now-commonplace phrases such as "anywhere, anytime learning" may suggest vistas of unlimited access to boundless learning opportunities, appropriate access has boundaries. "Anywhere, anytime learning" in practice must be defined operationally in terms of place, time, and interface—in the office? On a mountaintop? A military barracks in a foreign country? A foxhole? At 3 a.m. in a dorm room? On a laptop in a hotel room? A wireless setup in an RV traveling down an interstate? A mobile phone? A web browser wired into one's eyeglasses [3]?

Limitations and boundaries come in a variety of forms—practical, cultural, technological, economic, psychological. Efforts to remove current limitations and create new opportunities, including those external to the domain of online learning development, are worth keeping an eye on, even some of the more seemingly outlandish ones. Will voice recognition technology finally mature to the point where keyboard interfaces are no longer needed? Will the U.S. develop a wireless network that enables students to use wireless devices to access learning opportunities from anywhere in the country as is already being done in Finland (see Promising New Directions section below)? Will scientists perfect current development on a pill that reduces or eliminates the need for sleep? How will these developments create new opportunities to improve access? What new barriers or problems will they create? A strategic approach to improving access requires considering such issues.

Areas of Effective Practice: The Sloan-C Quality Framework is a tool designed to enable continuous quality improvement by measuring progress towards goals in each of the five pillars. The categories used to identify areas of effective practices related to access (Figure 3, following page) are based on the work performed to develop the Sloan-C quality framework. With a couple of notable exceptions, these categories capture the most important aspects of a student's experience relative to access issues— programs, courses, learning resources, academic and administrative services, and technical infrastructure. There is also a category for faculty support services, recognizing that faculty also have access issues. The ultimate intent for the Sloan-C Effective Practices website is to obtain at least one effective practice related to each of the sub-areas listed in Figure 3.

Program Access (General, Comprehensive, Other)
Basic Program Information
Marketing
Quantity, Variety of Available Program Options
Niche or Pioneer Programs
Course Access (General, Comprehensive, Other)
Course Information
Readiness Assessment
Navigability/Ease of Use
Scheduling (Frequency, Quantity, Variety)
Learning Resources (General, Comprehensive, Other)
Faculty/Instructor
Other Students
Other Learning Participants
Learning Community Formation/Involvement
Support Content
Self-Assessment Resources
Academic and Administrative Services (comprehensive)
Academic Services (comprehensive)
Basic Program Information
Readiness Assessment
Orientation to Online Learning
Academic Advising
Counseling
Tutoring
Library Services
Bookstore Services
Testing Services
Administrative Services (comprehensive)
Admissions/Registration
Tuition Billing/Payment
Financial Aid
Disability Support
Career Services
Transfer/Articulation Services
Commencement Services
Alumni Services
Technical Infrastructure (General, Comprehensive, Other)
Server/Portal Reliability, Uptime
Technical Support
Faculty Support Services
Other (describe)

Figure 3. Sloan-C Categories Used to Identify Effective Access Practices

II. ACCESS ISSUES AND THE CURRENT STATE OF PRACTICE

A. Market Share and 'Attention Share'

One way to look at relative degree of access to online learning opportunities is to look at its "market share," i.e., the percentage of learners in higher education and elsewhere who are engaged in online learning relative to the total number of learners. While the relative market share of online learning is still somewhat small and likely to remain so—for instance, a recent Pew study of 1,027 learners reported that only 6% of respondents had taken online courses [4] —online learning's market share is growing rapidly. The number of students taking online courses in U.S. postsecondary institutions tripled from 1999-2001 to approximately two million students and is expected to nearly triple again in the next five years to around five million [5]. Another more recent survey of 75 college distance learning programs reported a mean annual enrollment growth rate of 41% [6]. Statistics measuring access to blended online learning are much harder to come by, but some figures suggest a very rapid adoption. For instance, Kenneth Green's 2001 Campus Computing Survey found that approximately one-fifth (20.6 percent) of all college courses now use course management tools, an increase of over 40 percent from the previous year [7]. Although many of these courses no doubt use the course management system to post syllabi or assignments rather than for blended learning, this figure still suggests that there are hundreds of thousands, if not millions, of learners in online blended learning courses.

In terms of improving access, a more relevant measure might be termed "attention share." A recent (pre-Enron) advertisement campaign by Arthur Andersen captured this new reality: the most precious commodity in the online world is no longer financial cost, time cost, or even 'eyeballs' —it's attention. Gaining the attention of prospective online learners is *the* foundational access issue—prospective learners can't access what they don't know or care about. Attention share does not appear on the Sloan-C list of effective practices criteria (Figure 3) because it is a very big-picture issue, larger than individual institutions or even consortia. The most basic issue related to attention share is awareness— how do prospective learners learn of the existence of programs in the first place? However, getting prospective learner's attention is only the first step; holding their attention by adequately informing them of availability (What are my range of choices?), relevance (What relates to me?), and quality (Is it good (enough) for me?) is also essential to gain attention share for online education.

Based on these criteria, it is a safe guess to say that online learning has not yet caught the attention of most of its prospective users. Although many portals (Peterson's, America's Learning Exchange {ALX}, Sloan-C, et al.) have emerged to inform learners of available opportunities, each of them has significant weaknesses to go with their individual strengths (Figure 4), and they are still relatively unknown to most prospective learners. Most of these portals also fall short of adequately informing prospective students of the availability, relevance, and quality of listed programs.

There is some anecdotal evidence to suggest that online learning is doing a pretty good job of attracting 'repeat business' —students who take other online courses based on their experience in their first one or as part of an online degree or certificate program—or referrals. For instance, in a Spring 2001 student survey at Rochester Institute of Technology, 20% of students taking their first online course indicated that they found out about RIT through a co-worker's recommendation, and 11% found out about RIT from a friend or family member. On the other hand, although there has been an increase in positive articles about online learning which is helping to raise awareness, online learning is still often portrayed in the academic and mainstream media as a niche, novelty, or gnarly product.

Portal	Strengths	Weaknesses
Peterson's	Name recognition from print publications; easily searchable program listing; comprehensive range of programs available, institutions listed	Delivery mode selection criteria; detailed descriptions provided only for 'paying' programs
Sloan-C	Clear and focused lists of degree programs and related courses	Not a comprehensive list of available programs
Electronic Campus	Comprehensive list of degree programs and courses in Southeastern US	Limited in geographical reach (SE U.S.)
America's Learning Exchange (ALX)	Very comprehensive list of program providers	Lists non-academic and non-accredited providers; search results are often large because of wide range of included providers
TeleCampus	Lists thousands of online courses from around the world	Lists courses only
World Lecture Hall	Lists thousands of courses in a wide variety of subjects	Lists any course with a web presence (syllabus, course notes, etc.)

Figure 4: Selected Higher Education Portals: Strengths and Weaknesses

Access to blended learning opportunities, on the other hand, is a very different story. In one sense, attention share is not at all an issue for blended learning environments: the vast majority of college students (86% according to a recent Pew Internet & American Life Project Survey of over 1,000 college students) have gone online, and a large percentage of them are using the Internet for academic purposes. Nearly three-quarters (73%) say they use the Internet more than the library for information searching; almost half (48%) say they are required to use the Internet to contact other students for course work; two-thirds reported subscribing to academic-oriented mailing lists and using these lists for course-related discussions; and nearly one-fifth of students said that they communicate more with their professors via e-mail than via face-to-face [4]. Although some of these measures pertain more to online communication or resource access than to online learning directly, they clearly indicate that the Internet has already gotten college students' attention and is well on its way to being a seamlessly integrated part of the academic experience. While it is difficult to say to what extent the Internet is being used as a learning medium in addition to a communications and resource access medium, one can infer from this level of adoption that there must be a significant level of online learning activity occurring as well.

B. Program Access

Program access refers to accessing individual degree, certificate, or certification programs at the institutional level. Depending on the type of institution and learner's career path, program access issues may be encountered before or after learners enroll in specific courses. The core vision of the Sloan-C initiative within its specific parameters has been to make a full menu of program options available. Ten years ago, no such online programs existed; at present, hundreds of programs now exist, primarily career-oriented degree and certificate programs at the associate, bachelor's, and master's levels. However, there are still few programs or courses available in some market sectors, for instance, fully online bachelor degree programs in 'arts and sciences' disciplines [8].

Some strategies for improving program access have focused on reaching existing learners in new and better ways. For instance, the University of Illinois at Urbana-Champaign (UIUC) and the University of Vermont have offered online courses in the summer specifically to maintain students' connection to the school throughout the year [9, 10]. Forming partnerships with industry and professional associations is another effective practice. For instance, in addition to the now well-known NACTEL project operated through Pace University, Stevens Institute of Technology and several other universities are partnering with the Institute of Electronic and Electrical Engineers (IEEE) to offer several online engineering certificate programs designed to help engineers keep up with their rapidly evolving fields [11].

Several institutions have also enacted effective strategies for reaching new learner populations. For instance, UIUC pioneered a graduate (hybrid) online degree program in library science after research indicated a need for such a program. Penn State launched its World Campus with programs that were among the university's historical strengths, such as geographic information systems and turf grass management [12] and has subsequently developed additional such programs (e.g., noise control engineering, logistics and supply chain management) as one of its key strategies for continued growth. In another project sponsored by the Monroe County (NY) Health Alert Network and offered through Rochester Institute of Technology (RIT), instructor-led online learning has proven to be an effective way to provide access for 'non-traditional responders' to public health emergencies. Besides demonstrating the power of online learning courses to provide access for a widely geographically dispersed audience—one of the courses included participants from a dozen different states and seventeen different agencies, for instance—student comments indicate that the online learning format was the only way to enable these busy working professionals to access the course. As one student noted, "You would not get the wide audience if you didn't have something like this" [13].

Doing the basics well, such as providing basic program information with a minimum of barriers, can also be an effective access strategy. For instance, the Penn State World Campus website was redesigned to help users quickly identify the best path for them in their roles as prospective/current students, corporate decision-makers, or faculty/distance education professionals and to navigate the site effectively based on their roles [11]. And anyone who lives in the metropolitan Washington, DC area must surely be well aware by now of the University of Maryland University College's existence; UMUC conducts a broad, ongoing multimedia marketing campaign including print mailings, Web banner ads and sponsorship of education-related websites, radio, and television.

Another closely related issue is identifying and accommodating the access needs of specific learner groups. Just as commercial marketers generally identify and target specific sub-groups rather than treat their audience as a monolithic one, online learning providers need to identify the access issues of the specific learner sub-groups they serve. Many online learning programs have at least a basic level of knowledge about the characteristics of the learners they serve. For instance, many online learning programs report that a disproportionate share of the learners they serve are women, or employed (full-time, part-time, or both, depending on the program), or older (mean age often in late 20s or early 30s), or with prior educational degrees. A few universities, perhaps most notably the University of Phoenix, have identified and targeted a learner population with a specific set of characteristics. However, there are a variety of important ways to categorize online learners into sub-groups in terms of the related access issues each sub-group is likely to face. In addition to the more common ones such as gender, age, race, or socioeconomic status, there are also several other significant categories to consider—for instance, non-traditional vs. traditional, adult vs. college age, degree-seeking vs. enrichment-seeking, first-timers vs. experienced online learners, etc.

C. Course Access

Depending on the type of institution and learner's career path, course access issues are encountered before or after those related to program access. The most basic course access issue is providing accurate and complete course information to current and prospective students, and institutions have developed a variety of effective practices for providing this service. For example, each of RIT Online's courses has a customized course page with course-specific information such as course materials and courseware used, as well as general course information common to all RIT courses. Noteworthy features include easily accessible online ordering of course materials, course-specific library reserve materials, and a printable preparation checklist to help students get ready for the course. Northern Virginia Community College (NVCC) uses several strategies to provide access to course information for prospective students in Web-based and distance learning courses offered by its Extended Learning Institute (ELI). These strategies include a website with multiple navigational paths, a detailed course information page enabling prospective students to get information prior to enrollment, and an iconic guide to course delivery modes in the print and online NVCC Schedule of Classes [11].

A few institutions such as Rio Salado College and NVCC offer 'continuous' or 'rolling' enrollments which allow students to enroll in online courses at their convenience rather than waiting several weeks or an entire semester to enroll. Although both institutions have enabled such scheduling flexibility for many years, this practice remains relatively rare, perhaps because of the considerable logistical effort required. Another strategy for increasing access to courses is radical course redesign. Although other reasons (e.g., improving cost effectiveness or student retention) are often the primary purpose of most such efforts underway to date, improving access by increasing learner flexibility is a by-product of such efforts. For instance, Brigham Young University has redesigned its Freshman Composition course in part to satisfy students' needs for schedule flexibility while also improving course quality and efficiency [22].

Effective practices can also improve course access once a student is in a course. For instance, plug-ins (i.e., online software such as Adobe Acrobat, Real Player, etc. that are required to access certain types of documents, video clips, or other files) have long been a bane for many online learners who have difficulty with using them effectively. The University of Illinois-Springfield systematically uses a commercial software product (Impatica^{TM}) to convert PowerPoint lectures to digital format; this simple process cuts down on student frustration with plug-ins [11].

D. Access to Learning Resources

While the quality and availability of learning resources is closely related to learning effectiveness and student satisfaction, it is worth considering separately as an access issue. In part, this mirrors what traditional place-based programs have done for decades, i.e., look at 'input' measures such as the availability and quality of the physical learning resource infrastructure from library books to lab equipment to computers. Beyond these traditional measures, however, it is useful to consider whether and how students are provided access to the learning resources that are deemed essential for success in online learning—appropriate interaction with faculty, other learners, and other learning participants; appropriate level of learning community formation and involvement; availability of support content; and learning self-assessment resources.

A variety of approaches are being developed to provide access to learning resources. Access can be provided systematically on a large scale, as exemplified by the SUNY Learning Network (SLN)'s university system-wide approach to offering online learning opportunities. SLN's course development approach emphasizes the importance of required, frequent student-faculty and student-student interaction which fosters the creation of online learning communities while providing increased, flexible access to learning [11]. For faculty interested in discipline-specific learning resources, the MERLOT website (www.merlot.org) offers a large number and variety of learning resources categorized by subject area. MarylandOnline's Project Synergy has focused on six discipline areas, three general (Liberal Arts, Science, Allied Health) and three specific (Information Technology, Mathematics, Teacher Education). Project faculty in related disciplines have enhanced dozens of online learning objects by adding assignments, assessments, and instructions for use; the ultimate goal is to encourage faculty in related disciplines to incorporate these "enhanced learning objects" in both online and classroom courses [1].

Learning resources that are less commonly used at present also illustrate effective practices related to learning resource access. For instance, inviting virtual guest speakers or experts into a graduate course through web-based conferencing provides students with the ability to interact with guests in new ways by expressing individual concerns and discussing them without time and place constraints [14]. Providing support content in new ways is another strategy; for instance, Stanford University is currently developing "courselets," self-contained, integrated sets of learning materials designed as custom tutorials and offered online in support of Stanford engineering, science and engineering management courses. Courselets cover small sets of concepts for students who need to review, brush up, or fill gaps in prior knowledge. They index content and guide students to learning activities and materials they need, and include course evaluation tools for continuing improvement and innovation [11].

Approaches designed to meet the needs of adult learners in continuing education programs are also being developed. For instance, Michigan State University's Global Online Connection (MSU Global) is developing what it calls "event-centered, online-supported learning communities," in which programs for adult learners are built around in-person learning events, and subsequent learning is supported by online assignments and activities [21].

E. Learning Self-Assessment Resources

This is an emerging area. Increasingly, online learners are being provided with opportunities to access learning self-assessment resources. On a more elementary level, there are now dozens of varieties of "Is Online Learning for Me?" pre-course questionnaires available online, most of which appear to be voluntary. Some of these instruments appear to be designed to 'screen out' learners who are perceived to be less likely to succeed in an online learning course. A more promising approach may be to build courses and self-assessment resources which offer students a "buffet" of learning opportunities, as Ohio State University has done with its introductory statistical course. Along with the wide array of learning options, students also complete learning styles and study skills assessments which they can use to build online course contracts which specify how they plan to complete their coursework [15].

Learning self-assessment resources are also often embedded within courses themselves. For instance, the Stanford courselets offer self-tests to enable students to assess their level of knowledge on an ongoing basis [11]. Course management systems such as Blackboard and WebCT allow course designers to embed surveys, mastery checks, and other learning self-assessment tools within lessons. Certainly these tools are being used, but it is difficult to know to what extent.

F. Access to Administrative and Academic Services

The state of practice in this area is advancing fairly rapidly, becoming more comprehensive as more institutions become more proficient in practice. A few institutions, for instance UMUC and Rio Salado, have undertaken a comprehensive, whole systems approach to providing online academic and administrative services [16, 15]. Other institutions such as Pace University focus on providing effective access to student support services in several key areas, in Pace's case upfront technical support and orientation to the online learning process, student access to student information, and math tutoring services [17].

A variety of effective practices have also emerged in many specific service areas. For instance, many institutions have reported success using commercial tutoring services such as SMARTHINKING (www.smarthinking.com), although others have reported that using such services was not worthwhile because not enough of their students used them. Other institutions have developed their own methods for providing tutoring services. For instance, Rio Salado's "Beep-A-Tutor" program uses pagers to provide rapid on-demand student access to a tutor (response time of one to two hours, 14 hours/day, seven days a week) [18]. Mercy College uses "course wizards" as online teaching assistants for tutoring students, facilitating discussion and modeling the role of a successful student [19]. Several institutions, including UMUC, now offer online electronic delivery of journals and book chapters, a service which is far more convenient than having to visit campus or wait for the mail. Saint Leo University (FL), which serves a substantial number of active duty military personnel, has developed a Rapid Transfer Credit Reporting capability. Their tracking and evaluation system provides rapid responses to applicants, and creates program outlines for degree completion that include thousands of sources of equivalent transfer credit [11]. These examples illustrate that institutions are demonstrating considerable creativity in developing effective practices in student services provision.

A support service area which deserves special attention, indeed the one which many people most commonly associate with access-related issues, is the area of disability support services. Despite recent legislation requiring higher education institutions to offer at least an adequate level of access for learners with disabilities, it is difficult to know how many institutions are offering disability services and to what degree they are adequate. Some institutions offer a relatively broad array of disability support services; for instance, UMUC has made extensive efforts to make its web pages more accessible, offers a variety of support services for online students with disabilities, and has even begun implementing a grant-funded program called Implementing Distance Education Access (IDEA) designed to promote online learning environments that provide better access for students with disabilities [16]. However, it is also likely that at least some institutions are lagging in their efforts to provide the necessary level of disability services.

G. Technical Infrastructure

Technical infrastructure issues are singled out for special attention because they affect access in each of the other areas. Institutions are confronted with a variety of access-related issues, for example server and portal reliability, help desk, and other technical support functions.

One apparent leader in this area is the University of South Queensland (USQ), which is undertaking a strategically planned, systematically integrated, and institutionally comprehensive implementation of information and communication technologies (ICTs) called the e-University Project. Key elements of the project include incorporating the use of automated response systems and intelligent object databases in the context of Internet-based delivery. This project will enable USQ to use technology to automate certain aspects of interaction with students, increasing access to higher education on a global scale [11].

There are also some identifiable trends in this area. For instance, there is a trend toward standardizing on a single course management system. According to Green's 2001 Campus Computing Survey, roughly three-fourths (73.2 percent) of institutional respondents report having established a "single product" standard for course management software, up from 57.8 percent in 2000. Another discernible trend identified in Green's survey is that campuses are "going wireless:" one-fourth of respondents have a strategic plan for wireless networks, with another third having a strategic plan in development. Technological advances in other areas—for instance, voice over IP or implementation of ERP (Enterprise Resource Planning) systems—indicate that technical infrastructure development continues to contribute to improving access in many ways, while perhaps also creating new barriers in other ways due to increasing complexity or unanticipated consequences.

In addition, some 'micro-level' effective practices are beginning to emerge. For instance, the University of Illinois-Springfield uses an animated gif screen capture program (GifgIfgiF) to facilitate better student support by helping students when they are having trouble finding something online, logging on, or performing a function in a course management system. Anecdotal evidence to date suggests that this practice reduces technology barriers by decreasing related help desk calls [11].

H. Faculty Access to Support Services

Faculty need access too, to professional development opportunities, support services, and reward structures which enable them to participate in online learning delivery and development effectively. Substantive professional development opportunities and support services are now available for many faculty both at the institutional and larger-scale (e.g., consortial or state system) level, as illustrated by substantive faculty training programs such as those offered by the Illinois Online Network, Maryland Faculty Online, Michigan Virtual University, and SUNY Learning Network. However, the availability of these opportunities is far from universal in the U.S. By contrast, the Finnish Virtual University has launched a comprehensive, university system-wide in-service training program in university pedagogy for all of Finland's university-level teachers in each of its educational institutes. The aim of the program is that by the end of 2004, every teacher will achieve basic level skills, 50% of the teachers will have intermediate level skills and about 10% will have advanced level skills. Thus far, the project is on schedule to meet its goals for basic and intermediate level training [11].

Faculty promotion and rewards policies relative to online learning, especially at research and doctoral universities, are a difficult and unresolved issue in most instances.

III. PROMISING FUTURE DIRECTIONS AND NEEDED DEVELOPMENTS

A. Gaining Attention Share

There is a need for truly effective portals that have name recognition and garner attention share in all of its aspects (awareness, availability, relevance, quality) so that prospective learners know where to find programs they may be interested in. The level of attention share for online learning does seem to be rising overall, and it is difficult to see how its future direction could be anything but up.   Inclusive portals (e.g., Peterson's, ALX, etc.) continue to grow in size and quality, while exclusive portals (i.e., those which serve a specifically defined population) such as eArmyU, Virtual Historically Black Colleges University (V-HBCU), or the many statewide consortia portals, are successfully reaching targeted populations and learning valuable lessons about what works and doesn't work in the process. Whether these portals are collectively sufficient, or whether some sort of 'mega-portal' for higher education would achieve a critical level of name recognition, remains to be seen.

The academic and mainstream media coverage of online learning seems to be increasingly positive, which is also a significant factor in achieving greater attention share. However, more positive media coverage is needed; as the recent Pew Internet & American Life survey [4] illustrates, there are still too many studies and articles which are missing the point, focusing on trivial or non-existent issues such as whether online learning will replace traditional classroom instruction or whether one is better than the other.

In addition, there is room for improvement, as studies remind us that online learners are far from a monolithic population, and different sub-groups (non-traditional vs. traditional, adult vs. college age, degree-seeking vs. enrichment-seeking, first-timers vs. experienced online learners, and so on) may be more satisfied by different course designs, learning communities, student services, and other factors.

B. Program and Course Access

The rise of blended learning offers the prospect of making learning opportunities available in a full array of blends to accommodate different learning styles, convenience and flexibility needs, and preferences for interaction and learning community involvement levels.   Many institutions are consciously beginning to offer courses in multiple delivery formats. Ideally, the same course or other learning opportunity will be made available in several 'blends or delivery options. This strategy may be most applicable to the 'top 25' or 'top 50' largest courses, which at most institutions constitute a sizable percentage of total student enrollment.   Fully online courses will serve learners who need maximum convenience and flexibility or who prefer them; blends will serve learners who want or need some 'in-person' learning experiences.

However, a greater emphasis on using the Internet as a medium for learning design in addition to being a communications and resource access medium is needed in blended learning courses.   Using communication tools and utilizing online resources such as listservs, newsgroups, MERLOT, and others. is good, but using these resources in a structured, intentional, thoughtful manner is preferable. There are an eclectic mix of developments in this direction, such as WebQuests, enhanced learning objects, utilization of course development teams, and faculty training opportunities for learning how to teach online, among others.

As the Ohio State's Introductory Statistics course illustrates, attempts to design learning environments that accommodate as many different kinds of learners as possible is an encouraging direction. The Ohio State statistics course, which gives students the option to sign up for one to five course credits, also illustrates another promising direction: providing access to learning at the modular level. Programs and even most courses are often a larger learning chunk than many learners need. The growing use of reusable learning objects (RLOs) and other developments hold promise for the eventual creation of a learning infrastructure that supports learning experiences at a higher degree of granularity.

A growing number of institutions are becoming adept at providing more comprehensive advance information about programs and courses, including specific topics and assignments, delivery media, level of required interaction or collaboration with other course participants, and rubrics. However, these practices need to become much more common; some programs provide some of this information, but very few if any provide all of it at present.

C. Technological Advances

Although technological advances also mean dealing with new barriers caused by increased complexity, on the whole there are many promising future directions in this area. The drop in the prices of personal computers in recent years suggests that there is likely to be a continued decrease in the cost of technology required to access courses, including both hardware and software. For instance, there is a high likelihood that multiple and cheaper devices (such as PDAs) will be used to access future online learning opportunities. Some particularly intriguing initiatives in this area include pilot projects at the University of Helsinki which demonstrate the potential of mobile learning to increase access to learning opportunities and resources. The LIVE (Learning in a Virtual Environment) project and the UniWap project undertaken in connection with personnel training both demonstrated that mobile learning can allow students to establish a connection to an information network, define their own learning and guidance needs, and support learning at their own convenience. The results of these projects offer a glimpse of a vision in which all academic students may be said to have a university in their pocket [11].

There appears to be no end in the continued development of products that steadily lower barriers to access. For instance, a recently released product called VmailTalk enables people to send video messages over e-mail [20] without requiring any special software to open and observe the "videograms." Although this almost certainly means enduring an impending proliferation of "v-spam," the potential for increasing access to visual content is obvious. On the more distant horizon is affordable videoconferencing with full multimedia capabilities; however, utilizing video, audio, and high-resolution graphic materials on the Internet is still severely hampered by lack of bandwidth. Internet 2 is touted as a solution to this problem; but a related problem is providing faster *and* more ubiquitous Internet access. Improved access in rural areas is particularly needed. High-speed broadband connections such as ISDN, (A) DSL and wireless have become much more accessible in most U.S. metropolitan areas in the past two years or so. However, such connections are still very difficult, expensive, or impossible to obtain in large areas of the country, even in some areas relatively close (< 100 miles) to major population centers.

Another needed development is for improved interfaces with computers and other devices. Despite its widespread usage, keyboard input is still a cumbersome and daunting barrier for many people. Voice recognition technology continues to make steady improvement in quality and accuracy and may be coming of age, but its use in learning environments is not yet common or transparent. Just as the Dvorak keyboard has not supplanted the traditional QWERTY keyboard because it has failed to demonstrate a sufficient margin of superiority, voice recognition will have to be either sufficiently superior to keyboarding to gain converts, or find a way to attract new customers.

Another related issue that needs more thorough attention is multi-platform infrastructure support for faculty and students. The technical infrastructure on the vast majority of college campuses is designed to support an installed base of Windows computers; as a result, Macintosh computer users often face many significant barriers related to file sharing, firewalls, video and audio files, functionality of applications designed for Microsoft Windows, among others [23].

D. Online Student Support Services

A promising direction in this area is more comprehensive and focused provision of online student support services, as more and more providers realize that such services support all of an institution's learners, not just those in online courses. At the same time, an emerging question is whether it is necessary to replicate the same level of service for online courses as is provided for on-campus courses. Some institutions are starting to find ways of providing services in a focused, more 'just-in-time' manner.

In place-bound learning environments, instruction and student services have historically been physically separated for reasons of necessity and convenience. There is no comparable need for such separation in online environments, however. As online student support services mature, integrating these services directly and seamlessly with courses is feasible and a promising direction. Course management systems allow online testing to be integrated with the course; many online courses have links to online libraries or tutoring services. Further progress in this area would be a powerful way of improving online instruction and services. Imagine, for example, an online mini-course on basic library skills or Internet research (both of which already exist at some institutions). Students needing a quick review of library skills for a research project could access the library skills mini-course directly from their other courses; if all that was needed were information or self-assessment checks, students could access these directly on the mini-course without requiring any intervention from an instructor. For students who need to interact with an instructor, the course would include a course registration link that would allow the student to sign up for the course on demand, pay for the course online, and begin the course immediately.

IV. CONCLUSION

Widening access to learning opportunities was the original impetus for the Sloan-C ALN initiative and a prime motive for the development of online learning. Online learning has evolved from an emphasis on providing access to courses and instruction to recognition that access is an enterprise-wide issue. Fundamental issues include enabling prospective learners to be aware of the learning opportunities available to them and to assess the potential worth of these opportunities. As practices for providing access continue to evolve, useful ways to measure the level of quality of access may be developed to help practitioners better determine how best to improve access for the learners they serve. In the meantime, access remains the foundational issue in the evolution of online learning, and dealing with access issues will remain essential for the continued success of online education.

V. REFERENCES

1. Maryland Faculty Online's website (http://www.mdfaconline.org/grantsinfo.html) has more information about MarylandOnline's Project Synergy.

2. **Oren, T.** Cognitive Load in Hypermedia: Designing for the Exploratory Learner. In Macron, S. and Hooper, K. (Eds.), "Learning with Interactive Multimedia: Developing and Using Multimedia Tools in Education." Redmond, WA: Microsoft Press/Apple Computer, Inc., 1990.

3. **Brown, J.S.** Growing Up Digital: How the Web Changes Work, Education, and the Ways People Learn. *Change*, 10-20, March/April 2000.

4. **Jones, S.** The Internet Goes to College: How Students Are Living in the Future with Today's Technology. Pew Internet & American Life Project. September 15, 2002.
   http://www.pewinternet.org/reports/toc.asp?Report=71

5. Giving It the Old Online Try. *Business Week Online*, December 3, 2001.
   http://www.businessweek.com/magazine/content/01_49/b3760072.htm

6. The Survey of Distance & Cyberlearning Programs in Higher Education, 2002 Edition. *Distance Educator*, August 27, 2002.

7. **Green, K. C.** The 2001 Campus Computing Survey Summary.
   http://www.campuscomputing.net/

8. **Sener, J.** Why Are There So Few Fully Online BA/BS Programs In Traditional 'Arts and Sciences' Disciplines? *On the Horizon.* 10(1), 2002.

9. **Wang, X. C., Hinn, D. M., Arvan, L.** Stretching the Boundaries: Using ALN to Reach On-Campus Students during an Off-Campus Summer Session. *Journal of Asynchronous Learning Networks.* 5(1), June 2001.

10. **Rudavasky, S.** UVM Prospers with Summers Online. *Boston Globe*, August 25, 2002.

11. Detailed descriptions of effective practices featured in this paper can be found at the Sloan-C Effective Practices web site, http://www.sloan-c.org/effective/SortByAccess.asp

12. **Turgeon, A., DiBiase, D., and Miller, G.** Introducing the Penn State World Campus Through Certificate Programs in Turfgrass Management and Geographic Information Systems. In Bourne, J. (Ed.), Online Education: Learning Effectiveness and Faculty Satisfaction, Volume 1. Needham, MA: Sloan Center for OnLine Education, 273-286, 2000.

13. **Vignare, K. and Sener, J.** Fighting Bioterrorism with Instructor-Led Online Learning. Presented at the 8th Annual International Conference on Asynchronous Learning Networks, Orlando, FL, November 2002.

14. **Kumari, D.S.** Connecting Graduate Students to Virtual Guests through Asynchronous Discussions—Analysis of an Experience. *Journal of Asynchronous Learning Networks.* 5 (2), September 2001.

15. **Twigg, C.** Innovations in Online Learning: Moving Beyond No Significant Difference. Troy, NY: Center for Academic Transformation, 2001, 14.

16. **Stover, M.** Access Issues and the Current State of Practice at the University of Maryland University College. Proceedings of the 2002 Summer Workshop on Asynchronous Learning Networks.

17. **Sachs, D. and Hale, N.** Pace University's Focus on Student Satisfaction with Student Services in Online Education. In: Bourne, J. and Moore, J. (Eds.), Elements of Quality Online

Education. Needham, MA: Sloan Center for OnLine Education, 127-144, 2002.

18. **Twigg, C.** Innovations in Online Learning: Moving Beyond No Significant Difference. Troy, NY: Center for Academic Transformation, 2001, 10.

19. **Sax, B.** New Roles for Tutors in an Online Classroom: Report of a Program at Mercy College. To be published in the *Journal of College Reading and Learning*, 2002.

20. **Richtel, M.** Invited or Not, Get Ready for Video by E-Mail. *New York Times*, August 19, 2002.

21. **Geith, C.** The Costs of Learner-Centered Online Learning: An Exploratory Case Study. Proceedings of the 2002 Summer Workshop on Asynchronous Learning Networks.

22. **Waddoups, G. L., Hatch, G. L., and Butterworth, S.** Balancing Efficiency and Effectiveness in First Year Reading and Writing. Proceedings of the 2002 Summer Workshop on Asynchronous Learning Networks.

23. **Joan McMahon** at Towson University articulated this issue in detail during the Sloan-C Elements of Quality Online Education Summer Online Workshop, August 2002.

VI. ABOUT THE AUTHOR

John Sener is a consultant whose private practice focuses on supporting the evolution of online and other learning environments in higher education institutions and consortia, government agencies, and non-profit organizations. He currently serves as Project Evaluator for Maryland Faculty Online's Project Synergy and for a joint pilot project by the Rochester Institute of Technology and Monroe County (NY) to teach bioterrorism courses using instructor-led online learning. He also currently leads a project to survey online student services provision in Maryland higher education institutions for MarylandOnline (http://www.marylandonline.org). During his seven years at Northern Virginia Community College's Extended Learning Institute, Mr. Sener directed development of associate degrees in engineering, information systems technology, public management, and business management, available through home study and on-line distance education. Mr. Sener's career in education and training over the past twenty-three years includes directing a number of foundation and federally funded projects; he has also been a trainer, teacher, administrator, instructional designer, and tutor in the areas of adult literacy, basic skills, information systems, and English as a Second Language. He holds a M.S. degree in Education from Johns Hopkins University and a B.A. in Psychology from Oberlin College.

ACCESS ISSUES AND THE CURRENT STATE OF PRACTICE AT THE UNIVERSITY OF MARYLAND UNIVERSITY COLLEGE

Merrily Stover, Ph.D.
University of Maryland University College

- The Sloan-C vision is to provide affordable programs and comprehensive services so that qualified and motivated students may successfully complete studies in their chosen fields.

- Distance learning requires both scalability and excellent personal service.

- UMUC's comprehensive website contains the full range of academic, administrative, and career planning information in its 10,000 searchable pages.

  - The orientation site provides examples of student and faculty participation, assigned readings, individual and group assignments. It also links to library resources, and to proctored examination registration.

  - Sample syllabuses for each course are online and accessible at any time, and titles of textbooks and materials for the class are available online four to six weeks in advance of the start of the class.

  - Personal advising and counseling opportunities are available to the online student, as are the full range of administrative and academic supports, including textbook purchasing, tutoring, and technology support.

I. INTRODUCTION

The concept of access is at the core of the Sloan asynchronous learning network (ALN) initiative to provide academic options for students and faculty without restrictions of time and space. The Sloan-C vision is to provide affordable programs and comprehensive services so that qualified and motivated students may successfully complete degree programs and certificates in their chosen fields [1].

This paper presents a case study of an institution that has developed successful ways of serving students and faculty online around the globe. By focusing on Sloan-C's range of access factors, this paper shows how one institution has been able to increase access for students and faculty. It is hoped that the discussion will be of help to others also involved in serving online students and faculty and become part of an ongoing exchange of ideas on best practices and policies.

A. Background

The University of Maryland University College (UMUC) is a global university, headquartered in Adelphi, Maryland. Established in 1947 originally to serve the military in Europe and Asia, UMUC is now known for high-quality academic programs and student services in the State of Maryland, across the U.S., and around the world. UMUC has as its central mission providing access to university opportunities for adult part-time students worldwide through innovative programs using a variety of delivery formats and scheduling options. UMUC has four academic divisions: the School of Undergraduate Studies and the Graduate School, both housed in Adelphi, Maryland; and two overseas divisions in Europe and Asia, headquartered in Germany and Japan, respectively [2].

Online learning is a central strategy for UMUC in serving students, faculty, and society. In the past year, UMUC had over 87,000 enrollments with 32,787 students taking online classes: 15,757 students were enrolled in the School of Undergraduate Studies; 7,483 in the Graduate School; and 9,547 in overseas divisions [3]. Classes are offered through WebTycho, UMUC's proprietary course management system.

B. Philosophy of Access for Online Learners

As an institution, UMUC works to ensure that no student is disadvantaged by his or her choice of delivery format, and that all students, wherever they be, have seamless access to the UMUC experience. UMUC is committed to offering the full range of student services at a distance as well as on site. This includes admission, registration, student advising, information and library services, career planning, and testing, among other services. Providing full access to higher education for online students takes the combined efforts of all departments in the University working together.

As much as possible, UMUC provides full information online for students so that they can make informed decisions about their academic careers. UMUC's comprehensive website contains the full range of academic, administrative, and career planning information in its 10,000 searchable pages. The web site includes a live chat feature enabling students to ask questions and get immediate answers. The web pages also provide secured, interactive sites where students may access personal information regarding registration, class records, and financial aid, among other reports. UMUC uses technology to provide the efficient ways to help students online through ISIS (Interactive Student Information System) or by phone through IRIS (Interactive Registration and Information System.)

Distance learning requires both scalability and excellent personal service. This paper accents both practices. While the online environment provides the opportunity for students and faculty to retrieve and act on information on their own, other services require one-on-one interaction. Institutions must decide how to best to offer these personalized services: whether to use their own personnel or to contract with outsider vendors to provide personalized service. UMUC has followed both routes to create an environment that promotes learning success.

II. PROGRAM ACCESS

A. Schedule of Classes and Catalogues

Students and others may find basic program information in many places, in multiple formats. *The Schedule of Classes, Online Schedule of Classes, UMUC Catal*ogue, brochures and other marketing materials are all available in print and online. All students are sent a catalogue upon admission to UMUC. The print schedule of classes is sent automatically to all students and faculty each term. Print catalogues and schedules are sent to students upon request and may be picked up in person at the UMUC Information desk in Adelphi. UMUC's web site also contains the schedule of classes, the UMUC catalogue, and academic and administrative information. Basic program information in the website includes the academic calendar for the current, past, and upcoming years with term dates, holidays, registration dates; graduation and commencement dates including details for each of ten sites around the globe where the ceremonies take place [4].

B. Student Success Center

UMUC has contracted with a call center to handle student questions 24/7. A single toll-free number serves students nationwide, and for a toll, students globally. Service representatives handle any question that can also be answered through information from UMUC's web site. Representatives help students navigate the web, fill out forms, and use their PINs to access personal records. The call center provides directory information only; representatives do not have access to student records. However, representatives are trained to teach students how to access their records themselves.

The call center also answers e-mail in a 24-hour turn-around and has Web Chat capacity 24/7. Representatives "push" web pages to the students so that students may directly view specific pages. The transcript of the chat is saved and sent to the student for reference. Students are encouraged to give feedback on the service of the Student Success Center through a satisfaction survey accessed through the website.

C. Orientations

Through the UMUC website, students have opportunities to learn in advance about WebTycho classes and about online learning.

1. Distance Education Orientation Site

The UMUC web site offers a basic orientation to distance education, including the elements of an online class and of asynchronous instruction. The orientation site provides examples of student and faculty participation, assigned readings, individual and group assignments. It also links to library resources, and to proctored examination registration [5].

To help prepare students for online instruction, the orientation site informs students about the qualities that lead to success. These qualities include self-discipline, strong writing skills, and the ability to learn without face-to-face interaction. The orientation site details the technical requirements necessary to take an online class. These requirements include an Internet service provider, an active e-mail account, and a Netscape 4.5 or better, or Internet Explorer 5 web browser. Students are notified that some courses, e.g., business, finance, and accounting, sometimes require spreadsheet or other software programs. Students are reminded that they are responsible for their own Internet access costs.

The site links to sample classes in a variety of disciplines so that students may get a sampling of what an online class would be like, e.g., Cost Accounting, Introductory Programming in C++, Discrete Mathematics for Computing, Language in Social Contexts, Learning Analysis and Planning, Software and Hardware Concepts, Bankruptcy Law for Paralegals are the undergraduate courses included. Students may enter the classes and explore. However, all active links to classes actually in progress have been disabled.

2. WebTycho Virtual Tour and Tour 101

To further prepare students for online instruction and for WebTycho, learners may take a virtual tour of a WebTycho class which presents a series of twenty screen images as guides. Students are taken page by page through a WebTycho class. At the end of the tour, students are encouraged to take a self-assessment test to determine whether they would feel comfortable taking an online course and learning at a distance [5].

Students are also invited to visit a live WebTycho site. Visitors are given a guest ID and password to enter Tour 101. The format of this class is exactly like a normal UMUC online classroom, with announcements, syllabus, conferences for questions and feedback, assignment folder, bios, etc. Tour 101 is intended to be interactive so WebTycho support staff members oversee the conference and reply to submissions [6].

3. Peck Virtual Library Classroom

From the WebTycho orientation site visitors may also enter the Virtual Library Classroom. This library classroom is housed as a regular online class so that students are given practice in navigating a WebTycho class as well as learning about UMUC's extensive virtual library. The conferences are live so students may pose questions and take part in discussions moderated by one of UMUC's librarians. The class links to several guides including Library Handbook, Research Skills Tutorial, Guide to General Academic Research, and Using the Web For Academic Research. [7].

4. Self-assessment Quiz: Is Distance Education for Me?

Students may take an interactive self-assessment quiz to determine whether distance learning is appropriate for them [5]. Students are asked to consider their ability to concentrate, and to understand and remember what they read. They are asked to consider strategies for addressing course materials and to assess self-discipline, time-management, and reading and writing skills needed to be successful in a distance learning environment. Students are also asked to review their technological skills, their computer access for e-mail, and their experience and comfort in using a Web browser for accessing resources on the World Wide Web, and in downloading and installing software from the Internet. The quiz is automatically evaluated when the quiz is submitted.

The self-assessment test determines readiness for online learning in four areas: learning self-awareness, self-discipline, writing and language skills, technology readiness, all qualities of learners who are successful in the online environment. While the self-assessment test is not compulsory, students are strongly encouraged to take it and to heed evaluation results before enrolling in online classes.

III. ACCESS TO A VARIETY OF PROGRAMS

Following the vision of the Sloan-C initiative, UMUC is committed to having the full-degree programs available online across all disciplines. UMUC's undergraduate school currently has 17 majors and 20 minors that can be completed online. All general education requirements, electives, and required courses for these degrees are available online. Not every course is online but every program has a sufficient number of courses online so that students may complete these degrees totally online. UMUC's graduate school also has 17 degree programs online, with numerous tracks, and more than 30 certificates online [8].

A. Making the Full Menu Available

1. The Liberal Arts

UMUC has offered traditional liberal arts classes at a distance since the 1980s when it provided print-based through its former Open Learning program. This program originally brought in from the British Open University courses supporting specializations in the humanities and behavioral and social sciences. The courses had voice mail interactivity, supplemented by video and audiotapes. When UMUC made the commitment to go online in the 1996, these specializations were poised for development.

In 2001, UMUC transformed its curriculum from specializations within the General Studies degree, to majors. The resulting online majors in the liberal arts are History, English (to be completed in Spring 2003), Humanities with tracks in General Humanities and American Studies, Communication Studies, Psychology, and Social Science. Journalism and gerontology are offered as minors online [9]. Liberal Arts online certificates include Workplace Spanish, Workplace Communications, and Gerontology [10].

2. Business and Computing

Among the majors available fully online in the areas of business and computing are Accounting, Business Administration, Computer and Information Science, Computer Studies, Environmental Management, Human Resource Management, Information Systems Management, Management Studies, and Marketing [9].

Online certificates in the business area include Intermediate and Advanced Accounting, E-Commerce Management, Environmental and Occupational Health and Safety Management, Human Resource Management, Management Foundations, and Technology and Management. Certificates in the computer area include Applications Database Management, Information Management, Internet Technologies, Object Oriented Design and Programming, Project Management for IT Professionals, and Visual Basic Programming [10].

B. Pioneer and Niche Programs

UMUC also offers two uncommon online majors: Fire Science and Legal Studies.

1. Fire Science

The Fire Science online major is one of the very few in the nation. The Fire Science program serves all levels of fire service professionals to help advance them to leadership and executive positions. Volunteers and career firefighters as well as managers and administrators are served by the curriculum which covers knowledge in fire, life safety, and emergency services. UMUC partnered with the National Fire Academy of the Federal Emergency Management Agency helped develop the program. Students may earn an academic major, minor, or certificate in Fire science. Certificates include: Public Fire-Protection management and administration; Systems Approach to Fire Safety; National Fire Academy Certificate of Completion; Certificate in Volunteer Fire Service Management. All UMUC fire science course are online [11].

With grant funds, the Fire Science program has developed a CD-ROM and companion website to market the fire science program at UMUC. UMUC is a member, with five other institutions, of the Degrees-at-a-Distance Consortium at the National Fire Academy. While some other members of the consortium have online courses, only UMUC has an entire degree program online.

2. Legal Studies

The online major in Legal Studies is also one of a few. Students may take all of their required courses online with enough courses for choice in completing the major, minor, or certificate. Students may also get credit for law office internships through the Co-op program. The Legal Studies program is one of the majors available to students in the Navy College Program Distance Learning Partnership [12].

C. Flexible Programs

UMUC provides increased access through flexible programs including cooperative education and prior learning.

1. Cooperative Education

Through cooperative education, students earn gain college credit while gaining professional experience. Each academic discipline at UMUC offers a co-op course that combines career-related work with the student's field of study. The work may be in a new position or in the student's current employment. Co-op session lasts 15 weeks and may begin at any time. Each student works closely with a faculty member who evaluates the student's progress. Students may complete the course online, in a classroom, or through one-on-one consultation.

UMUC's co-op web site features an interactive learning proposal guideline with pop-up examples to help students think through and write their proposals. Students may also download an outline to follow while writing their proposals. In such cases, the completed proposal may be mailed to the university. UMUC co-op staff members are available to answer questions via e-mail, telephone, in person, or by mail. The co-op website articulates eligibility requirements and transfer credit options [13].

2. Prior Learning

The Prior Learning program provides students with the opportunity to receive college credit for learning from life experiences including employment, volunteer work, or hobbies. The Prior Learning program helps students translate that knowledge into college credit.

Two paths are available to students to earn college credit for previous learning. Through Course Challenge, students may take the final exam for a course and get credit for the class. Through EXCEL students may prepare a written portfolio that documents college-level learning obtained through work experience. The portfolio is evaluated by faculty for possible credit.   Students may take EXCEL classes online or in a traditional classroom.

Prior Learning helps students complete their degree programs more quickly and to save money in tuition and course materials. Students may earn up to 30 credits towards a bachelor's degree and up to 50% of the credits required for a certificate. Any UMUC student who is working on his or her first or second undergraduate degree may participate in the Prior Learning program. Students may begin a prior learning program at any point in their curricula [14].

3. Standardized Tests

UMUC students are able to earn credit towards a Bachelor's degree through standardized tests including College Level Examination Program (CLEP), DANTES Subject Standardization Test (SST), and Excelsior Examination (formerly ACT/PEP). Credit gained through these tests help move students closer to degree completion [15].

D. Expanding Access for the Working Poor

In 2000, in partnership with Goodwill Industries of the Chesapeake, UMUC began the Better Opportunities through Online Education program to help low income workers access higher education and achieve economic self-sufficiency. The program provides scholarship admission to UMUC, a computer, a printer, assistance in arranging for internet service, an introductory online study skills course, and student services including advising, financial aid assistance, and career counseling.

Twenty-one community-based organizations, primarily in the Washington, D.C., and Baltimore areas, participate in the Better Opportunities through Education Scholarship Program. Recently the program expanded to include students from Delaware and New Jersey through funding from the Morgan Stanley Foundation.   Seventy -five students enrolled in the program for Fall 2002. Each student is sponsored by a community-based organization which provides the student with vocational evaluation, mentoring, case management services, and job-placement assistance.

Students in the program may earn certificates in Introductory Accounting, General Computer Applications, General Management Studies, and Workplace Communications. Students must register for at least 3 semester hours in both fall and spring semesters and maintain a minimum of 2.0 GPA. They must also complete 100% of their coursework each semester and apply for federal financial aid to supplement scholarship funds. This program addresses the "Digital Divide" issue, opening up higher education to those who would not otherwise be included [16].

IV. COURSE ACCESS

A. Course access and information

Students access their online courses through WebTycho, UMUC's course management system. Students may enter their online classes one week prior to the start of the term. Students thus have early access to their class syllabus and beginning conferences.

However, students also have access to course information before this time. Titles of textbooks and materials for the class are available online four to six weeks in advance of the start of the class. Sample syllabuses for each course are online and accessible at any time. Course descriptions through online catalogues, from 1998 through to the most recent edition, are also easily accessible.

With the interactive schedule of classes online, students may get up-to-date information about class availability through the web at any time. Information includes the number of seats in a class and the instructor's name. Students may search for classes by location, areas of study, format, and session. Each class in the schedule is linked to the course description, class availability, location of class, course materials, and options for purchasing course materials, including a link to the Virtual Book Store. The interactive schedule is available for both frames browsers and all other browsers. Through the web site, students may also request a print Schedule of Classes be mailed to them [17].

B. WebTycho and WebTycho-Enhanced Classes

Each online class has its own web site with all the information students and faculty need to navigate the course. Information includes the course description, course introduction, course goals/objectives, course materials, grading information, project descriptions, course schedule, and academic policies. A print version of the syllabus may be downloaded from the site. Included also is a detailed course description with specific suggestions for how to successfully approach the course, ground rules for online participation, and designated credits. The course content (equivalent to lecture), provides the core subject matter of the course through a series of modules. Each module contains an overview, detailed objectives, comprehensive commentary, and relevant URLs. The modules, developed by a team of content experts, instructional designers, and editors, are the same for all sections of a given course. The syllabus and conference topics may be modified by the individual instructors.

Each WebTycho class also provides direct links to final exam registration, required of all students, and to UMUC's writing resources. The Writing Resources link gives students easy access to "The Guide to Writing and Research," required for use in all undergraduate courses where another guide to writing and research is not already in use. Students may access the "Online Guide to Writing and Research" with instructions for printing it. Details on how to access the Online Writing Center and the face-to-face writing center are also provided. The class links to the plagiarism self-help tutorial developed by the UMUC's Effective Writing Program and the Center for the Virtual University. Online classrooms also include reserved readings, study groups, webliographies, grade books, work books, and other features of the WebTycho platform.

As of Fall 2002, all face-to-face classes are WebTycho-enhanced. This means that all UMUC students, through WebTycho, have ready access to the class syllabus and to UMUC's policies and writing resources.

V. READINESS ASSESSMENT

A. Writing and Math Placement

All incoming students who require lower-level math and English composition courses must take a placement test in writing and math. UMUC uses Accuplacer, an online proctored test, to place students into their appropriate classes. The testing is computerized and students receive their placement results at the time of the test. Students may take their tests at the testing center in Adelphi, at a UMUC regional site, or with an approved proctor.

B. Research and Documentation Assessment

Both undergraduate and graduate programs require that all students complete a course in information literacy skills that addresses how to design a research project, access material online, and accurately cite references. Students are instructed in methods for retrieving information through online sources, and are introduced to UMUC's library databases, both proprietary and open. Students are assessed on their knowledge of research writing and documentation. This introductory class, taken in the first semester of the student's career at UMUC, prepares students for online research and learning. The class also alerts to problems of plagiarism and how to avoid it.

C. Online Learning Readiness

Students have several avenues for orientation to online learning and developing learning readiness. As discussed above, the Orientation to Online learning includes access to a WebTycho class where students may practice using the class features. Students are also encouraged to take the self-guided mini-course, WebTycho 101, which introduces students to an online class. Again, as discussed above, because all face-to-face classes at UMUC are WebTycho enhanced, all students are introduced to WebTycho and to asynchronous learning. Each section has its own WebTycho class where faculty members post syllabuses and handouts, and students may interact via the conferencing tool. WebTycho enhancements are compulsory for the class, but are used in a supplementary manner. The mild introduction to WebTycho serves to acquaint students with the features of the online class.

Students may also orient themselves to online learning through online open house. Using the chat function during appointed hours, students may address questions to advisors and representatives of the academic units.

VI. EXPANDING ACCESS TO LEARNING RESOURCES

UMUC works to see that online as well as face-to-face students have full access to learning resources, including access to faculty, other students, the library, and writing and math tutoring, and all student services. Online classes are limited to 30 students for most classes (fewer for intensive writing classes) to encourage and support student and faculty interaction.

A. Faculty as learning resource

Faculty members are available to online students through their WebTycho classes. UMUC undergraduate faculty guidelines request that faculty respond to all electronic communication within 48 hours. Most faculty members are online daily and respond immediately to student inquiries. All faculty members have completed training for teaching on WebTycho.

Online computing, foreign language, and other classes have teaching assistants available to students as learning resources. Large enrollment classes also have graders to help both the instructors and the students. T.A.'s and graders' names and e-mails are listed in WebTycho classes so that students may send messages to them with just a click.

B. Other Students as learning resource

Online students have access to their fellow students in many ways. WebTycho classes are structured so that student names and e-mails addresses are available to all. A basic part of each online class is the interactive conference area in which all students participate. WebTycho has a study group section, where instructors may divide students for small group activity. Many instructors provide a "student lounge" within the WebTycho conference area where students may freely exchange ideas.

History and English students may join online clubs in their disciplines. Those students with declared majors in these areas are rostered into the WebTycho site. Here, students may interact with other students with similar interests. These active clubs invite guest speakers, professionals in the field, who are online for a given period to share knowledge with students and answer questions.

C. Content Support

Students find content support through their WebTycho classes. All undergraduate classes are designed with substantive materials included. As discussed above, each course is comprised of several modules which cover the content of the course including overview, content commentary or lecture, follow-up questions, suggestions for activities, and URL links to relevant resources.

UMUC's library staff members are available to assist students in researching writing projects. Librarians may be invited into an online class as guest lecturers to help students with research topics. Librarians may post special exercises to guide students in their work and are available to answer individual questions.

D. Tutoring

Free tutoring is available for UMUC undergraduate students in math and writing.

Writing Tutoring Through UMUC's Online Writing Center, students may submit writing assignments via e-mail for advice from trained writing advisors. Responses have a 24-hour turnaround. Writing assignments are returned to students within 48 hours with guidance and questions to help the students. The papers are not edited: comments guide the students to review and improve their writing. Students may access handouts on a variety of writing topics through the Online Writing Center [18].

Math Tutoring Through a pilot project supported by a grant from Maryland Online, students were offered free math and statistics tutoring through Smartthinking.com for the 2001-2002 academic year. Students in business statistics, college algebra, calculus, psychological statistics, elementary statistics and probability, and all natural science courses offered free tutoring. UMUC is in the process of contracting directly with Smartthinking.com to continue to provide online tutoring opportunity in math and statistics.

VII. INCREASED ACCESS THROUGH ACADEMIC SERVICES

A. Basic Program Information through UMUC's Web Site

UMUC website gives high priority to providing information about academic services. A comprehensive "Frequently asked Questions" site addresses a full-range of issues. Basic questions address transfer credit, degree requirements, and how to get credit for work experience. Admission questions address how to apply to UMUC, and explain what terms mean, such as "regular" student, and "provisional" student, conditions of academic probation, registration payment and procedures. Students may access detailed guidance on financial aid and veterans benefits, including how to apply, deadlines, types of aid, and reward limits, discussed in more detail below [19].

B. Student Success Center

The Student Success Center provides special support to new and prospective students to assist them at every step through graduation. Telephone representatives are available all day, every day, to answer general questions and to help students navigate Web site. Prospective students may request to be on the mailing list for upcoming class schedules, open house invitations, and other announcements [20].

Through the Student Success Center, students may receive assistance from enrollment specialists in applying for admission, gathering financial aid information, planning curriculum, and in registering for first semester classes. Prospective students may have potential transfer credits assessed using Curriculum Planning Worksheets available through the UMUC website [21]. The worksheets help students determine degree requirements based on coursework already completed. Registered students are assigned a personal academic advisor to support them through to graduation. Advisors and enrollment specialists are available via telephone, fax, e-mail, or in-person.

Technology is enabling advisors to proactively reach out to students. Through use of the software, Goldmine, a customer relationship management tool, advisors track students' progress and contact them with reminders and concerns. Goldmine stores advising information and tracks interactions with students. E-mail messages are automatically stored; telephone interactions may be manually inputted. Multiple advisors thus have access to the students' information in Goldmine and may intelligently assist and advise students. The goal of the Student Success Center is to have a single advisor responsible to seeing a student from admission to graduation, with interaction and proactive contact along the way.

All students wishing to see an advisor or enrollment specialist in person are strongly advised to schedule an appointment via telephone or e-mail. Enrollment specialists and advisors are at Adelphi (UMUC Headquarters) and at ten regional sites in the State of Maryland.

C. Access through Interactive Systems

UMUC's Interactive Registration and Information System (IRIS), enables students to access student services via touchtone telephone. With their Student Identification (SID) and Personal Identification Number (PIN), students may obtain grades from the current semester or previous semesters, the name of their assigned resource team, and financial aid status. Through IRIS, students may register for courses, change registration, or get on a waiting list and change registration. The telephone number is toll free.

UMUC's Student Interactive Information System (ISIS) gives students online access to their personal UMUC electronic records. Students need their student identifications, and person identification numbers to access ISIS. ISIS enables students to change contact information, (home address, e-mail, telephone, etc.), retrieve personal class schedules, grade reports, statement of accounts, and unofficial transcript audit. Students may also register for classes online through ISIS. If students loose their PINs, they may retrieve them online [22].

D. Other Online Opportunities

1. Scenario for Success

While personal academic advising is available to all students, students may also seek "generic" advising from UMUC's website. One such area, Scenario for Success takes students from application form to graduation in simple story form. Beginning with a UMUC open house, either in person or online, the scenario follows the process of admission completion, course selection, and official evaluation of transfer credit. The scenario also introduces students to sources of non-traditional credit including Prior Learning and Credit by Exam, the advising process, career opportunities, and the degree completion process. The scenario links to important sites and documents, such as the curriculum planning worksheet for all majors and minors, course planning guides for new students, registering for classes using the IRIS system, important dates, and frequently asked questions about academics [23].

2. Forms

Almost every form required for university operations is online. Student may submit required forms interactively online, or download them and submit by fax or mail. These include admissions forms, applications for diploma or certificate, FERPA release forms, name change requests, and official evaluation requests. The form to request a transcript from another institution must be downloaded and printed.

3. Library Services

The full range of library services is available online for students. UMUC's Information and Library Services (ILS) offers access to over 100 databases; nearly fifty percent of the databases provide full-text resources including articles, e-books and statistical information. These databases cover a wide range of topics including computer science, medicine, business, management, and the humanities. In addition, students and faculty have access to over nine million volumes via the University System of Maryland online catalog. No password is needed to search, but users need a UMUC ID with barcode to check out books.

Users may request that books be delivered to any University System of Maryland campus or a UMUC circulation site nearest their home for convenient pickup. For materials not available with full-text online, ILS provides the full-text of the requested item via desktop, in paper, or via email; most items are delivered within 48 hours of receipt of the request. ILS also provides home delivery of books to students and faculty throughout the continental United States. An electronic reserve service is available in every online classroom. At the request of the faculty member, ILS will scan and load any materials needed by the faculty member for his/her class. The reference services ILS provides are comprehensive, including synchronous chat with a research librarian, e-mail, telephone, face-to-face, and computer-based conferencing assistance to help students and faculty with any questions.

ILS provides an extensive array of instructional services for the face-to-face or online classroom. The Virtual Library Classroom (discussed above) enables students and faculty to receive one-on-one help, take a short course, or access tutorials, guides, and the library handbook. A UMUC librarian facilitates a conference area for discussion and questions. The Virtual Library Classroom is available from the library's Web page and within WebTycho [24].

4. Bookstore Services

Books and other materials: Students may buy and sell books and published materials, including CD ROMs, through UMUC's Virtual bookstore, contracted through MBS. The virtual bookstore is linked to every WebTycho class and to the UMUC website. Students may order textbooks and other course materials online, by fax, through the US postal service or by telephone through an 800 number with extended hours weekdays and weekends. The Virtual Book Store (MBS Direct) ships order within 24 hours. Payment is by credit card, personal check, or money order. Orders may be shipped internationally.

All privileges that are available through the regular bookstore are available through the virtual bookstore. Students may receive full refund for books if they are still in new condition, should the student withdraw from a class or should a class be cancelled. At the end of the term, students may also sell their books back to the vendor. Two weeks before the end of the classes, the virtual bookstore sends a quote by mail or e-mail to students giving them the buyback value of their textbooks. A prepaid shipping label is enclosed so students may easily send their used books back to the company. Students may also get quotes by telephoning the 800 number. Telephone service is available 7 days a week, with published hours [25].

Videos and Lab Materials: Videotapes and lab kits are distributed through UMUC's Learning Market Place. Students may download the order form from the UMUC web site and mail or fax their orders. A deposit is returned to the students upon return of the videos at the end of the term.

5. Testing Services

UMUC provides testing services in two primary areas: proctored exams for online students, and placement testing [26].

Final Exams: All classes, no matter the format, are required to have a proctored, graded, activity. For most classes, this activity is the final exam. Online students must register for their final exam, declaring where they will take the exam. Students may take their exams at one of several UMUC sites in the State of Maryland or may choose a proctor which must be submitted approval. Students register for proctored exams online on ISIS using their PINs and student ID numbers. Students may access the exam registration site through their WebTycho classes or through the UMUC web site.

Placement exams: All incoming UMUC students who require lower-level math and English courses must take the Accuplacer placement exam. This proctored exam may be taken at UMUC's regional sites or through arrangement with an approved proctor.

VIII. INCREASED ACCESS THROUGH ADMINISTRATIVE SERVICES

A. Admissions/Registration

1. Admissions

UMUC's comprehensive website provides all the information needed to apply for admission. The site details admission criteria for new and prospective students, for students transferring from Overseas Divisions, for former UMUC Students with a two year break in enrollment, for dismissed or suspended students, for non-citizens and foreign educated students, for high school seniors, for students from UMUC's Graduate School, students from other USM Institutions, and senior citizens. The site details policy on residency determination for tuition and marks different pathways for those with social security numbers and those without. Students may apply for admission online.

Most applicants who have a high school diploma or the equivalent may be admitted and register for undergraduate courses. UMUC generally does not require transcripts nor test scores at the time of admission. These may be submitted at the end of the first semester. Students who have attended other regionally accredited colleges and universities must have a cumulative grade-point average of 2.0 or better on all college-level classes. Graduates of U.S. colleges or universities automatically qualify for admission. Students must submit a completed and signed application, along with admission fee [27].

2. Registration

Once admitted to the University, students may register for all classes online, via touch-tone telephone, or in person. From the UMUC web site, students may download an instructional worksheet to assist the process [28].

B. Military

UMUC has had a special relationship with the military, providing educational opportunities for active duty service personnel and their family members around the world. In the Maryland, Virginia, and Washington, DC, area, classes are offered at nine military bases in a variety of formats including evenings and weekends. Military students may combine these face-to-face classes with online courses. ITV classes are available at smaller bases in the State of Maryland. UMUC offers reduced tuition for undergraduate courses to active-duty military personnel and their spouses regardless of where they live in the US. UMUC's web pages provide detailed guidance for applying for Veteran's Benefits [29].

Special pages provide information to US active duty military personnel stationed anywhere in the world [30]. The pages provide step-by-step instructions on getting started, with details of course options for Maryland, Europe, Asia, and distance education options. UMUC is a member of the Navy College Program Distance Learning Partnership (NCPDLP), a Navy initiative to provide an educational path from Navy "A" school to a bachelor's degree in Management Studies, Computer Studies and Legal Studies [31]. UMUC is also a participant in the e-army initiative, providing access to majors in business administration and computer science.

C. Tuition Billing/Payment

Students have a variety of ways to pay for their tuition. The amounts and procedures for paying tuition and fees are detailed on the UMUC web site. In addition to credit card, check, cash, loans, employer assistance programs, financial aid, veterans' benefits, and scholarships, students may choose a monthly payment plan. UMUC's plan is administered through an outside contractor whose interactive and secured site is linked to the UMUC web site. Installments are interest-free. The company provides free guidance through the program web pages as well as workshops in determining payment plan. The company provides toll-free telephone customer service 8 a.m. to 10:00 (ET) [32]. Policies regarding schedule adjustments, withdrawals, and refund policy are clearly linked on UMUC's tuition web page.

D. Financial Aid

Students may find all the information they need online to apply for financial aid and may apply online, as well. Federal aid information, financial aid web resources, UMUC's financial aid procedures, and all application forms are included on UMUC's web site. Deadlines, eligibility requirements, steps for application, student's responsibilities, and the awarding process are all clearly presented. Online scholarship applications are in HTML and PDF form. Students may check the status of their financial aid application through IRIS. Telephone numbers and e-mail addresses of financial aid advisors are provided online [33].

E. Disability Support

1. Making UMUC Web Pages Accessible

UMUC is committed to ensuring that all individuals, including persons with disabilities, have equal access to programs, facilities, and admission [34]. Of primary importance is accessibility to information on online sources. UMUC, through its Webmaster, designs the web pages so that they can be navigated by screen readers for people with vision problems. Frames are avoided as these interfere with screen readers. UMUC's web pages are designed to be in compliance with Section 508 of Rehabilitation Act of 1998 so all information technology is accessible to people with disabilities. The UMUC Webmaster is redesigning pages to be read in a more linear fashion. Pages are coded so that screen readers read the navigation menu first but can also skip the menu and go from page to page. Each page has text-only equivalent pages. The colors on UMUC's web pages are selected with care so that colorblind persons can easily read the pages. The philosophy of design from the beginning has been that simpler is better. UMUC's 10,000 web pages are being evaluated now, both with consultants and with tools.

UMUC's web pages also are designed with few plug-ins and so that the graphics may be turned off for faster loading. Students need not have high-end equipment to view the pages. Pages are designed to be loaded within six seconds and with a minimum size so that individuals may view them without scrolling. Users are given the option of PDF or HTML forms. UMUC's designers are aware of their international audience where Internet users are charged by the minute so fast loading and easy viewing are essential. The web site is structured so that pages are accessible with minimum number of clicks.

2. Support for Online Students with Disabilities

UMUC's Office of Disabilities assists all students with disabilities who have registered with its office. Students, whether in online or in face-to-face classes, must document their disabilities and impacts on their learning. The Office notifies the students' instructors of the accommodations to be made. The most frequent request for accommodation for online students concerns learning disabilities that require increased time for assignments and tests. Classroom access for the physically handicapped is seldom a factor except for examinations. The Office of Disabilities works with the students' proctors to ensure accommodation [35].

3. Implementing Distance Education Access (IDEA)

UMUC has recently received a grant from Verizon Foundation and NEC Foundation of America to help faculty members and others in online learning understand accessibility standards and to include all learners in instruction. The program, Implementing Distance Education Access (IDEA), will promote better access to online learning for people with disabilities. Through the IDEA Project, a web site will provide examples of well-designed materials, and tutorials for faculty members and others to learn the mechanics of incorporating good design into online learning. The IDEA Project also includes a training program and handbook. The project hopes to enable the online environment to meet the needs of all learners. Faculty, staff, and students with disabilities are invited to test the materials to determine the effectiveness of the IDEA project [36].

F. Career Services

Students and alumni have access to a range of free and fee-based career services through the Career and Cooperative Education Center. Free services include online job search tools and the UMUC mentor network. Through the program, CareerQuest, students and alums can post their resumes and look for job announcements [37]. Students may explore career options through a self-guided academic and career management tool sponsored by a joint project with the Department of Labor and the Public Broadcasting Service. This online tool enables students to examine educational options, assess their skills, plan their financial futures, research careers possibilities, and create portfolios.

The Career Center sponsors the UMUC Mentor Network which brings together students, alumni and employer partners of UMUC to share expertise in career fields. Through this volunteer network, students may find a mentor to help with career development. Students may also get free advice on improving job search skills through the Career Center's web pages on current trends, preparing for a job interview, resources for finding a job, successfully planning a career, résumé writing and resources including writing electronic résumés with key words, career planning for those with disabilities, and hints on how to jumpstart careers from college. The Center also sponsors a listserv with notices of jobs and internships and other events.

The Career Center's fee-based services include job development seminars, résumé reviews, mock interview sessions, career planning counseling, career transition counseling, Myers-Briggs Type Indicator assessments, and follow-up career counseling. The Myers-Briggs Type Indicator assessment is administered online. Clients receive an individual counseling session and customized career report [38].

The job development seminar helps students learn skills needed for the job search. The seminar includes self-assessment, résumé writing, interview preparation, and networking techniques. The seminar includes a follow-up résumé review and mock interview. In the interview, a staff member takes the client through a mock interview and, if face-to-face, will videotape the session. The job development seminar is opened to all UMUC students and alumni via e-mail, telephone, or face to face. Registration is online through ISIS.

Students may request additional personal career planning counseling by telephone, e-mail, or face-to-face. Career transition counseling combines personality self-assessment through the Myers-Briggs Type Indicator with two career-counseling sessions. Follow-up counseling is provided those who request it. These one-on-one 45-minute sessions may be by telephone or in-person.

Personal counseling by a licensed psychologist and counselor is available to students, alumni, and the general public by appointment through telephone, e-mail, or face-to-face. Appointments may be made online through interactive registration form. UMUC's career and cooperative learning website is linked to CounselorFind, a service of the National Board of Certificated Counselors website to help clients find professional counselors nation-wide. The site is searchable by name, location and type of need.

G. Transfer/Articulation Services

About 80 to 90% of all students come to UMUC with transfer credit. Students may transfer up to 90 semester hours of credit from four-year regionally accredited colleges to help complete the 120 semesters hours required to graduate from UMUC. A maximum of 60 semester hours may be transferred from community colleges. Students may also transfer credits from military and other non-traditional sources.

To help transfer students, and other potential students in course planning, coursework planning worksheets, including a self-assessment tool, are available online. The worksheets show the degree requirements for each major and enable students to determine their own requirements based on coursework already completed. All admitted students are also assigned an advising team to help with course planning. Students may request an official evaluation through the web. Instructions for international credit evaluations may be downloaded. Students may also download a form to request official transcripts from another institution [39].

1. Alliances

UMUC has established alliance programs with seven community colleges within the State of Maryland and with Honolulu Community College. The alliance with the Maryland colleges supports dual admission and simultaneous enrollment. One application form admits students both to their allied community college and to UMUC. Students may take classes at the same time at UMUC and their community college, and may also go back and forth between the two institutions from one term to the next. The alliance with Honolulu Community College offers students easy transfer of up to 60 credit hours towards their Bachelor's degree with UMUC. Students may complete their degree through online courses at UMUC. The curriculum is seamless for alliance students [40].

H. Accelerated Scheduling

Students with associate's degrees (or 60 semester hours of appropriate credit) may complete bachelor's degrees in specific disciplines within two years through accelerated degree programs using both face-to-face and online options. The accelerated programs currently offered are Business Administration, Information Systems Management, and Criminal Justice. Face-to-face classes run half as long (seven weeks) as the standard semester and are offered at specific locations around the State of Maryland [41].

IX. ACCESS THROUGH TECHNOLOGY SUPPORT

A. Software and Computer Support

All UMUC students and faculty need to be able to use and have access to computers. Telephone and in-person help desk support is available for all during business hours. Homework lab space is provided 7 days a week from 9 a.m. to 11:00 p.m. so that all local students and faculty have free access to the

Internet. Faculty may check out laptop computers, for home use and travel, for the duration of a semester. UMUC's servers support e-mail and web-hosting for all students and faculty.

Local students in computer programming classes have access to software language assistance, a service available online starting in spring 2003. Most online classes in computing have a teaching assistant to provide technical assistance to students. UMUC's Information Technology web pages provide host computer information including steps for creating a web page, for using Unix accounts including C++ programming, for forwarding e-mail, and more [42].

B. WebTycho Support

Help-desk tech support for all WebTycho users is provided 24/7 through an outside technology support call center. Technology representatives respond to both telephone and e-mail requests. Level II WebTycho support is provided in-house through telephone and e-mail responses. UMUC's website supports an extensive, searchable WebTycho users' guide. An additional detailed guide for faculty takes the user through every part of the class. Detailed information helps users set up and get started in WebTycho, and introduces enabling features [43]. The WebTycho Tour 101, described above, orients new users to the system [7].

X. INCREASED ACCESS FOR FACULTY

UMUC is committed to providing its faculty with strong professional development opportunities, support services, and reward structures. This commitment extends equally to online and to face-to-face instructors. UMUC relies on adjunct faculty for much of its teaching commitments.

A. New Faculty Orientation and General Faculty Meetings

All new faculty are required to attend the New Faculty Orientation, a three-hour session introducing UMUC, its services, and its policies. A CD-ROM is available for those outside the area. All faculty are asked to attend general faculty meetings, held in Fall and Spring semesters each year. Graduate and Undergraduate Studies hold separate meetings. The sessions are usually three hours in length, including a meal and a professional development event [44].

B. WebTycho Training

In order to teach online, each faculty member is required to successfully complete a five-week training course in WebTycho. This course covers both the techniques and pedagogy required to be successful in online instruction. Instruction is online and includes faculty from around the globe. As part of the training, faculty observe existing classes. Each new faculty member is also assigned a peer mentor who works with the new instructor for a year.

All face-to-face faculty members are given training in the use of WebTycho for enhancement of their classroom-based courses. This is a single session, usually lasting two hours. Faculty may request further sessions if they wish [45].

C. Professional Development

UMUC's faculty development office offers a wide range of workshops, both face-to-face and online. These workshops cover both technology and pedagogical issues. The workshops are given free of charge. Twice a year, a full day is devoted to technology training where faculty may take part in workshops covering a wide range of skills, both elementary and advanced.

Faculty members are provided the opportunity of taking LIBS 150 Information Literacy and Research Methods. This is a required course of all UMUC undergraduate students that teaches the use of the online library, and documentation and research. By taking the course, faculty not only learn what they can expect from students regarding knowledge of documentation, plagiarism, and online databases, but their familiarity in these areas are enhanced as well. All faculty teaching LIBS 150 have access to a comprehensive online Faculty Primer which includes details of WebTycho classroom, creating learning activities, and UMUC policies.

UMUC offers its faculty, whether online or face-to-face, small grants for research and for travel. UMUC also sponsors annual two-week online symposia, drawing together faculty from around the world [44].

D. Teaching Support

Faculty members receive support for their teaching through a variety of avenues. Their supervisors and support staff in their academic units are available by telephone and e-mail during working hours. The office of Faculty and Distance Education Services oversees desk copies and text books, parking, photocopying, faculty ID, final exam registration distribution for distance courses. Almost all faculty services may be carried out electronically or through interactive sites accessed through UMUC's web site. Through Interactive Faculty Information Services (IFIS), with password and ID, faculty may post and change grades electronically [26].

Many departments sponsor sites within WebTycho (WebTycho 999) where faculty can take part in asynchronous discussions on topics of concern to them and their colleagues within their specific disciplines. Staff members from UMUC's Center for Teaching and Learning are also available to work individually with faculty who may encounter trouble in their teaching.

Faculty members have access to the Virtual Resource Site for Teaching with Technology developed at UMUC through a grant from Bell Atlantic. The site features examples of online teaching from across the disciplines, tutorials on Web-based technologies, and video interviews with practitioners on strategies for effective online learning. The Chronicle of Higher Education, Technology Source and the Scout Report have commended the site [46].

E. Incentives for online teaching

UMUC provides a number of incentives to encourage faculty to teach online. Faculty members are given a one-time bonus when they teach their first online class after successfully completing their five-week training course. To show that the university recognizes and values the additional time needed to teach in WebTycho, faculty are given increased pay for teaching online. All considerations for promotion include online teaching.

XI. CURRENT INITIATIVES

UMUC's success is built on continuous innovation. Included here are some current initiatives.

Faculty Media Lab

UMUC's Center for the Virtual University (CVU) is exploring and piloting technological advances to be used in online courses. Through the Faculty Media Lab, faculty, staff, and course designers may develop multimedia enhancements for courses, create CD-ROMs, develop videoconferencing with multimedia capability. Faculty are also assisted in the use of whiteboard in synchronous learning, in designing multimedia tutorials as well as developing streaming audio and streaming video among other features [47].

Course Design

UMUC is piloting the use of reusable learning objects (RLO) in course design. For example, modules on the scientific method and reference tools have been designed and are being used in multiple science courses. UMUC faculty and staff have been active participants in Project Synergy, a project supported by Maryland Online. RLO are identified for the liberal arts, sciences, computing, and business areas [48].

Proctored Online Testing

A call for proposals is in process for providing proctored exams for online testing. UMUC plans to provide online students around the world the opportunity to take their final exams online in a proctored situation.

Writing Assessment

UMUC is working to ensure that students have the necessary writing skills to be successful in their studies and careers. Initiatives are in process to assess student writing at the lower, intermediate, and upper levels of English composition as well as to increase the assessment of writing across the curriculum.

Faculty Training

UMUC's Center for Teaching and Learning is designing supplemental tutorials that build on the WebTycho training. These tutorials will be offered to faculty who need additional help with necessary skills. The training modules will be self-paced and self-administered.

XI. CONCLUSIONS

Successful online education requires that access for students and faculty be both personal and scalable. This paper has reviewed areas of practice that successfully support such access at the University of Maryland University College. Through comprehensive well-designed web pages, including interactive technology, students are able to access information needed to make sound decisions for their academic careers. Students may access their personal records and update information on their own. Interactive technology further provides personal access for faculty to services, including desk copies, ID, library access, and grade submission. These practices enable UMUC's growing number of students and faculty to keep current without taxing staff. Personal advising and counseling opportunities are available to the online student, as are the full range of administrative and academic supports, including textbook purchasing, tutoring, and technology support. Such services are manageable through contracts and partnerships with specialized providers and through advanced technology.

Online instruction itself is supported by a robust proprietary learning platform, WebTycho, which provides course content as well as interactivity among students and faculty. Courses are designed to be scalable so that additional sections can be easily added as enrollments increase. At the same time, online class sizes are limited so that students may receive personal attention from faculty members and active involvement in online discussions. Through its practices, UMUC has been able to support extraordinary growth in online enrollments. The University continually reviews its service in order to provide the best possible experience for its students and faculty throughout the State of Maryland, the nation, and beyond.

The field of online learning is quickly changing, however. As technologies are introduced, and as the numbers of enrollments increase, new ways of operating need to be explored to ensure the practice is both satisfactory for students and faculty and cost effective for the institution. To a large extent, UMUC has been successful because its leadership has been committed to making online learning effective for students and faculty. As a result, the institution is open to new ways of organizing itself and of doing business to better serve the growing numbers of online students and the faculty who teach them.

It is hoped that some of the practices here may help others as they serve students and faculty. It is also hoped that this paper will be part of an ongoing exchange of experiences of providing access in this pioneer environment.

XII. REFERENCES

1. **Sener, J.**, Improving Access to Online Learning: Current Issues, Practices, and Directions. This volume.
2. UMUC at a glance http://www.umuc.edu/gen/about.html
3. University of Maryland University Office of Institutional Planning, personal communication.
4. University of Maryland University College http://www.umuc.edu
5. Orientation to distance learning http://www.umuc.edu/distance/de_orien/
6. WebTycho Overview http://www.umuc.edu/distance/de_orien/tour_course/start_tour.html
7. Peck Virtual Library Classroom http://www.umuc.edu/library/vlc.html
8. Online degree programs http://www.umuc.edu/grad/online/degrees.shtml#Online Degree Programs
9. Online majors and minors http://www.umuc.edu/prog/ugp/mjr_chart_online.shtml
10. Online certificates http://www.umuc.edu/prog/ugp/certificates/cert_online.shtml
11. Fire science http://polaris.umuc.edu/firesci
12. Navy College program in legal studies http://www.umuc.edu/navy/bs_plgl_req.html
13. Cooperative education http://www.umuc.edu/prog/ugp/coop/coop_welcome.html
14. Prior learning http://www.umuc.edu/priorlearning/whatispl.html
15. Alternative options for earning credit http://www.umuc.edu/ugp/catalog00_01/page68.shtml
16. Crossing the digital divide http://www.umuc.edu/events/press/news47.html
17. Schedule of classes http://www.umuc.edu/studserv/isis/schedule/
18. Writing Center http://www.umuc.edu/writingcenter/
19. Application: Frequently asked questions http://www.umuc.edu/prog/ugp/asp/faq.html
20. Student Success Center http://www.umuc.edu/studserv/ugp_ss/teams.html
21. Curriculum planning worksheet http://www.umuc.edu/worksheet
22. Student services http://www.umuc.edu/studserv
23. Scenario for success http://www.umuc.edu/studserv/ugp_ss/scenario.html
24. Library http://www.umuc.edu/library/library.html

25. Bookstore http://www.mbsdirect.net/UMUC
26. Faculty and distance education services http://www.umuc.edu/prog/ugp/fdes/fdes.html
27. Admissions http://www.umuc.edu/students/admissions.html
28. Registration http://www.umuc.edu/students/registration.html
29. Veterans benefits http://www.umuc.edu/studserv/va/programs.html
30. Military http://www.umuc.edu/mil/mil.html
31. Navy http://www.umuc.edu/navy/ncpp.html
32. Tuition payment http://www.TuitionPay.com
33. Financial services
    http://www.umuc.edu/studserv/financial/financial_aid/2002-2003/2002-2003_home.shtml
34. Diversity initiatives http://www.umuc.edu/diversity
35. Disability services http://www.umuc.edu/studserv/dss.html
36. Implementing Distance Education Access (IDEA) http://www.umuc.edu/press/news129.html
37. Career and Cooperative Education Center http://www.umuc.edu/careercenter
38. Career Quest http://www.umuc.edu/careercenter/ccec.html
39. Transfer students http://www.umuc.edu/studentaffairs/transfer.html
40. Community College alliances http://www.umuc.edu/alliances/alliances.html
41. Accelerated programs http://www.umuc.edu/acceleratedprograms/
42. Computing resources http://www.umuc.edu/suppserv/it/
43. WebTycho help http://tychousa.umuc.edu/help.nsf
44. Center for Teaching and Learning http://www.umuc.edu/distance/odell/ctla/
45. Faculty training and certification http://www.umuc.edu/distance/odell/ctla/training.html
46. Virtual resources for teaching with technology http://www.umuc.edu/virtualteaching/vt_home.html
47. Faculty staff newsletter http://www.umuc.edu/fyionline/july_02/fyionline4.html
48. Maryland Faculty Online http://www.umuc.edu/mdfaconline/ps_admin_contacts.htm

XIII. ABOUT THE AUTHOR

Mary Liana (Merrily) Stover is Professor and Immediate Past Assistant Dean, School of Undergraduate Studies, at the University of Maryland University College (UMUC). A leader in distance learning in postsecondary education, Dr. Stover helped guide nationally recognized undergraduate distance learning programs through periods of rapid growth. At UMUC, she guided the online development of History, English, Communication Studies and Humanities majors, as well as the design and development of UMUC's award winning Online Writing Center. Previously, as Director of the Extended Learning Institute, Northern Virginia Community College, she helped bring associates degree programs online across the curriculum. Dr. Stover has presented numerous papers on distance and online learning to national and international audiences. An anthropologist by training, Dr. Stover previously taught at the British Open University, the University of London Birkbeck College, Monterey Institute of International Studies, and the University of Hawaii. She currently teaches online for UMUC in the Graduate School and School of Undergraduate Studies. Address: 45 Cabana Drive, Oroville, CA 95965. Email: mstover@polaris.umuc.edu. Phone: 530-533-9465.

REMOVING BARRIERS TO ACCESS: POLICY INITIATIVES TO MAKE DISTANCE LEARNING ACCESSIBLE, AFFORDABLE AND AVAILABLE TO ALL LEARNERS

Bruce N. Chaloux
Southern Regional Education Board

- The *Electronic Campus* was built on principles of quality, reducing barriers, reaching the underserved, and providing services on a regional basis that a single institution, or even a single state, could not provide.

- Most available data suggest that distance learning is reaching, by far, a population of traditional students, rather than underserved population.

- Despite extraordinary growth in online programs, there are many fields in which online courses are not available or programs are not complete.

- With concerted efforts at the national, regional, state and institutional levels, policies can successfully address pricing, financial aid for part-time distance learners, and more equitable, fair and just credit transfer and articulation arrangements.

- Technology should be treated as a "core resource" of the state or educational system and financed accordingly.

I. INTRODUCTION

Distance learning has been heralded as a vehicle for increasing access to higher education, reaching under-prepared and underserved populations, and making the lifelong learning a reality. However, data suggest that distance learning is reaching a market that is, by far, a population of traditional students and those who are not underserved. One major barrier to technology-mediated learning is the digital divide, which is real and growing, particularly in the South. Differences in computer ownership and Internet access across racial, geographic, and income groups are larger in the South than in the rest of the nation. While most campuses and elementary and secondary schools are wired, technology has yet to reach the majority of low-income homes and is of little use to those who cannot use it effectively. How can distance learning become a true vehicle for reaching these individuals and groups? Can the technology be made available in rural areas, large urban areas, and other technology-challenged locations? Can a state, a region, or the nation target this goal and realistically achieve it? How can access to powerful information and learning tools, and awareness of the opportunity they can provide, extend to all citizens?

These and other questions are the focus of an ongoing effort by the Southern Regional Education Board (SREB) and its Distance Learning Policy Laboratory (DLPL). This paper outlines the challenges, particularly in the South (but applicable to most regions in the United States), reports on the rating of more than 70 recommendations during a September, 2002 national town meeting, and describes the next steps in the ongoing effort by SREB to utilize distance learning to increase access to higher education.

A. Setting a Context: The Southern Regional Education Board and the Electronic Campus

Effective educational policy makes a difference. The Southern Regional Education Board's 54 year history provides ample evidence of the difference a vibrant policy environment can make in a state, a region, and a nation.

Some 60 years ago, the South was the Nation's number one economic problem, a situation outlined in a report to President Franklin D. Roosevelt from his National Emergency Council. Leaders in the South saw the development of a strong educational system as a central, indeed critical, part of the solution. Ten years after the report, the region's governors formed the Southern Regional Education Board. SREB was the nation's first interstate compact, established with the objective of fostering interstate cooperation, sharing resources, and expanding access to higher education for the betterment of the region. In subsequent years SREB has established a record of service to its member states, tackling difficult issues, and seeking longer-term solutions to educational challenges. SREB programs combine long-term emphases and adjustments for new situations; collecting, compiling, and reporting on these situations; establishing demonstration programs that help lead by example; and then working with governors, legislators and educational leaders in the states to implement change.

In keeping with the traditions of SREB, the growing use of technology in education in member states during the early part of the 1990's dictated adding technology-related activities to the regional agenda. The growing interest in creating new learning environments that permit students to learn at any time and at any place, and the concerns for quality, fit with previous SREB efforts. Responding to these activities, SREB established the Educational Technology Cooperative in 1995 and began to focus attention on technology issues and challenges. Among the initial efforts of the Cooperative was the development of quality guidelines—the Principles of Good Practice for Electronically-Delivered Programs—which would become the centerpiece of quality efforts across the SREB states.

SREB's *Electronic Campus* initiative was designed to provide a regional approach to expanding access, and it was launched in January 1998. The basic concept of the *Electronic Campus* was a simple one: create an "electronic marketplace" of courses, programs and services available electronically from colleges and universities in the 16 member states, thereby increasing opportunities for learners from within and outside the region. Beginning in January 1998 with a modest number of courses from a small number of colleges and universities (104 courses from 40 institutions), the *Electronic Campus* has grown to include over 8000 credit courses, more than 300 degree programs, and over 325 colleges and universities from all 16 member states.

The *Electronic Campus* was built on principles of quality, reducing barriers, reaching the underserved, and providing services on a regional basis that a single institution, or even a single state, could not provide by itself. These principles build on SREB's 50+ year history to share resources among member states, to extend resources from one state across many, and to use interstate agreements and relationships to meet the needs of citizens in the region. The practice of developing innovative state arrangements—a hallmark of the Southern Regional Education Board's long history of serving political, legislative, and educational leaders on educational policies and practices—has already been integrated into the *Electronic Campus*. Courses and programs submitted to the *Electronic Campus* have been reviewed and certified by each state against a number of quality indicators. The Principles are a critical element of the *Electronic Campus* initiative and are used by each member state and participating college or university. Further, each of the 16 member states has agreed to recognize the certification of other states, creating, in effect, a free trade zone in the region. This recognition and quality assurance process is vital for students and participating colleges and universities and is evidence of the regional cooperation and coordination that this proposal is built on.

From its inception, SREB leadership envisioned the *Electronic Campus* as a "laboratory" for policy development. In fact, what quickly emerged in early months of the *Electronic Campus* was a growing awareness that many current policies created real barriers to student access. In large measure, student inquiries to the *Electronic Campus* raised questions about tuition (particularly the differential between in-state and out-of-state rates), the acceptability of credit earned in distance learning courses, the availability of financial aid, and the quality and legitimacy of offerings. Thus, the policy laboratory took on increased importance as barriers to distance learning continued to emerge and to threaten the interstate opportunities for a broad and open "electronic marketplace." Policy change and a vehicle for driving changes were new priorities: SREB acted quickly to address these needs.

B. The Distance Learning Policy Laboratory

At its June, 1999, meeting, the Southern Regional Education Board approved the establishment of the SREB Distance Learning Policy Laboratory with the charge to assess current barriers to distance learning and to suggest policy directions to reduce or eliminate these barriers. Work in the Policy Laboratory was arrayed under three broad areas: *access, quality,* and *cost*. More specifically, the Policy Laboratory's main objectives were to:

- Assess educational policy issues that are identified as barriers;
- Establish policy baselines of current practices, procedures and strategies;
- Assist states and institutions to develop ways to use technology to improve quality, expand

access, and reduce costs;

- Establish trial or pilot efforts with State Partners to test new distance learning approaches or strategies;

- Promote state-level policy changes via existing SREB organizational arrangements and agreements;

- Develop and test agreements among institutions and states;

- Utilize the Policy Laboratory as a clearinghouse for states and institutions to discuss policy issues and concerns; and

- Measure the implementation of policy changes in the SREB states and widely disseminate the results.

The initial work of the Policy Laboratory was supported by a grant from the Fund for the Improvement of Postsecondary Education's Learning Anytime, Anywhere Partnership program. Additional funding was supplied by the Stranahan Foundation. The result of this first phase of the Policy Laboratory's work was the completion of seven reports in SREB states.

1. Establishing the Policy Laboratory Agenda

Through formal and informal surveying with State Partners in each of the higher education systems in the member states and through research conducted by the Policy Laboratory staff, an initial set of issues was developed. Those issues included:

- Tuition policies, particularly in-state and out-of-state charges for the distance learner;

- The lack of an effective solution to provide federal Title IV financial aid for the distance learner;

- The continuation of historic state and campus budgeting and allocation practices and laws which need modification for technology and distance learning programs;

- The continuation of traditional academic terms with start and end dates that do not provide the flexibility that many persons need;

- Regional accreditation, in particular in the Southern Regional Education Board region, where three regional accrediting bodies operate;

- Consumer protection and concerns relating to the quality of distance education offerings;

- The creation of new indicators for measuring productivity in distance education (e.g. workloads, Full Time Equivalent measures);

- Transfer credit policies which may need to be rethought for electronic courses and degree programs;

- The challenges of providing an array of services for the distance learning, including:
  - Academic advising,
  - "Credit banking" that helps students build meaningful collections of credits,
  - Access to library resources and services,
  - A variety of security issues, involving students in distance education; and
  - Defining new relationships between independent colleges, universities and the states.

The issues were subsequently presented to the Policy Laboratory's Leadership Group and a set of seven areas of study were outlined for the first phase of work. Subcommittees were formed around each of the following major policy areas [Note that Executive Summaries and Recommendations from the reports, with the exception of the Universal Access report presented below, are included in Appendix A].

1. Credit Transfer and Articulation
2. Finance Policy
3. Reaching the Underserved
4. Faculty
5. Student Services
6. Financial Aid
7. Quality Assurance

In 2001-2002, the seven issues subcommittees met in person and by conference call to complete an analysis of current policy challenges and to prepare reports and recommendations from their research and deliberations. Members of the subcommittees represented state policy, distance learning, and higher education leaders from state agencies, institutions and other organizations and agencies inside and outside the region. Each of the subcommittees focused attention on developing four specific products:

1. Guiding Principles. The guiding principles build upon or expand the *Electronic Campus* "Principles of Good Practice" in the specific policy areas addressed by each subcommittee. These principles will be shared with colleges and universities in the SREB region to help shape quality distance learning programs, student services, and faculty support.

2. Policy Goals/Actions. Policy goals and actions are recommendations that the Policy Laboratory can present to its Leadership Group, the SREB Board, and state policy makers. These actions will lead to specific changes in educational policy.

3. Illustrative Practices. Illustrative or promising practices are documented policies and programs that colleges, universities, and/or states are using successfully to address barriers to distance learning. These practices and case studies have been analyzed by the subcommittees to determine common themes and underlying factors that ultimately contribute to a program's success. Successful factors can then be used to establish guiding principles, policy goals, and/or pilot programs.

4. Pilot Projects. These are new cooperative agreements or innovative programs that the Policy Laboratory may initiate either alone or with another organization/agency. These initiatives will vary from topic to topic. Depending on focus, some groups may work towards specific pilot projects, and others will not.

C. Access: The Central and Underlying Theme of the Policy Laboratory Efforts

The Underserved Learners Subcommittee report entitled "Universal Access to Technology and Support: An Achievable Goal for the South. A Report of the SREB Distance Learning Policy Laboratory Underserved Learners Subcommittee," December 2001 is the source for information in this section.

No area of the country is more challenged by educational disparity than the South, where only 22.5 percent of adults over the age of 25 have attained a baccalaureate degree (Marks, 2001). SREB states remain about four percent below the national average of higher education degrees earned, and this gap is even greater in some SREB states that fall about 10 percent below the national rates. Many who have not earned degrees have encountered barriers of fixed schedules, high tuition rates, and great distances to higher education institutions. Because distance learning programs are independent of time and location, they hold much promise in extending postsecondary education to previously underserved citizens, such as working adults and rural populations.

Rapid innovation in information and communications technology is transforming the way citizens work, interact, learn, and live. New technology enables instant, easy and efficient global communications that expand resources and widen access to a potentially limitless network of information. Technological innovations have also had a dramatic impact on the economy, which is becoming increasingly global and reliant on information exchange. Successful transformation to the new knowledge economy will depend not only on the technological infrastructure but also on the ability of individuals to access and utilize the enormous wealth of information that the technology provides. The consequences of being unable to adapt to this change are no less, and potentially greater than previous technological revolutions.

In fact, there is strong evidence that advances in technology are aggravating the social and economic divisions that already exist regionally, nationally, and globally. This division, often referred to as the digital divide, results from a complex interaction of factors that have continually worked to depress the quality of life of certain populations time and time again. While rooted primarily in economic disparity, the divide also stems from longstanding differences in educational access and socio-cultural traditions. Given the power and opportunity that technology can provide, unequal access to digital material and differences in technical skill will allow the "haves" to increasingly outpace the "have nots" in quality of life. Access to powerful information and learning tools and awareness of the opportunities they can provide must extend to all citizens.

Three interrelated issues must be addressed. First and of particular concern is the rate of computer ownership and Internet access in the SREB states, which is lower than the rest of the nation. More alarming are data that show the South is divided to an even greater degree than the rest of the nation in terms of differences in computer ownership and Internet access across racial, geographic, and income groups (Bohland, Papadakis, & Worrall, 2000).

Secondly, merely providing equitable infrastructure is not enough to solve the problem. In fact, there is ample evidence that existing infrastructure is not being utilized because of a lack of requisite abilities, available training and support, and relevant digital content. Even in areas where the gap in Internet access seems to be declining, differences exist in how people use and understand information.

Despite extraordinary growth in programs, courses and programs are unavailable or incomplete in many fields. States need to provide direct subsidies in the form of start-up and continuing funding to address these market shortcomings, particularly in the following areas: (1) instructor training for adult literacy programs; (2) workforce training programs aimed at underserved populations (for example, manufacturing technologies, information technologies, health care, and criminal justice); (3) teacher training programs for employed teachers who need certification or upgrading of skills; and (4) allied health programs.

Finally, even when technology access is provided for free or at low cost, students at the lowest income levels still face significant barriers to higher education due to a fundamental lack of financial resources. Distance learning can relieve the transportation and childcare costs associated with education, but rising tuition remains a significant obstacle and is a growing concern. Changes in federal financial aid will help, but states should also encourage employers to expand and extend their tuition reimbursement programs and tax incentive programs.

Because increasing access is such a complex problem, one short-term solution is the use of public access facilities, which may include public libraries, local schools, or community organizations such as Boys and Girls Clubs. The successful Community Technology Centers program provides access to technology and support services. It is recommended that these centers expand services by partnering with colleges and universities to offer continuing and for-credit basic education courses for adult learners.

D. A Vision of Universal Access

No one initiative alone will solve the problem of the digital divide. Rather, an interrelated set of goals must be pursued in an integrated, cooperative effort among all major sectors of society. While the financial cost of doing so will indeed be great, the long-term impact of ignoring the issue is infinitely greater. Failure to mitigate opportunity differences may create irrecoverable disparity, ultimately leading to financial decay of the economy. Therefore, aspirations must not be limited by either short-term financial considerations or more intractable sociopolitical barriers. In the next decade, businesses, governments, and citizens are called to work together to achieve the following:

- Ubiquitous access to technology infrastructure and low-cost broadband services to all citizens;

- Widespread or universal computer ownership or low-cost access to networked computers;

- Free or low-cost access to digital information resources by all learners and citizens through local public outlets such as community centers, libraries, workplaces, and schools--elementary, secondary, and postsecondary institutions;

- Provision of technology training and support for all citizens; and

- Equal opportunity among students and faculty in all institutions and academic programs for using technology tools to optimize teaching and learning.

1. The Subcommittee's Recommendations

In order to achieve these goals, SREB, the states, and institutions in the region will need to improve access in three main areas: (1) access to equipment, networks, and end-user support, (2) access to programs and appropriate digital content, and (3) access to financial aid and tuition reimbursement. To these ends, the Subcommittee made the following recommendations:

1. SREB and state policymakers should support efforts to extend broadband access to homes, libraries, and community organizations, especially in rural areas of the South. SREB and policymakers should also work to extend high-speed access to primary, secondary, and

postsecondary institutions, particularly colleges and universities with a mission of serving minority populations.

2. SREB states and postsecondary institutions should work cooperatively with local organizations to extend or create training programs for populations who are unprepared to use technology to access information.

3. SREB and state higher education executive officers in the South should work to increase access to digital content and programming, particularly in fields with critical personnel shortages and fields not well-served by competitive markets such as teacher education and allied health services. SREB, through the *Electronic Campus*, should play an active brokering role in this process.

4. SREB and the states should support programs that provide financial aid to distance learners and should encourage employers to implement tuition reimbursement programs.

5. States, businesses, and higher education leaders in the South should expand the number of opportunities for learning at the worksite.

6. SREB and its member states should coordinate a region-wide campaign to promote lifelong learning and reduce the educational divide between geographic regions and ethnic/racial populations.

While the Underserved Learners report has a clear focus on access, and specifically on technology infrastructure, many of the Policy Laboratory reports deal with other facets of access. Those of a financial nature are addressed in the Financial Aid report, specifically assistance for adult, part-time learners. Those of an academic nature are addressed in the Credit Transfer report, specifically credit acceptance and transfer. Those of a service nature are addressed in the Student Services report, specifically providing a host of needed services. In all, the category of "access" includes 21 recommendations. Recommendations made in reports other than the Underserved Report are presented below.

- Promote increased financial assistance to part-time distance learners. (Financial Aid #1);
- Promote new state level policies and initiatives that provide incentives to learners in disciplines and workforce areas of significant need. (Financial Aid #6);
- Support and promote SREB's "electronic tuition rate" initiative as a means for increasing access to distance learning. (Financial Aid #7);
- States should identify one or more highly visible institutions or consortia to act as "degree completers" to aid students by forming the various credits earned from multiple institutions into a complete degree program. Degree-completing institutions should accept lower-division general education credits of letter grades "C" or higher from any regionally accredited institution in the region as credit towards the general education requirements. (Credit #4);
- Institutions should ensure that all students have comparable and adequate access to needed services whether they are traditional, non-degree, part-time, distance, disabled, or "home" students of the institution. (Student Services #1);

- Institutions should develop a mentor program for distance learning to motivate students; to model appropriate behavior; to tutor academic needs; and to provide academic advising and support. (Student Services #4);

- SREB is encouraged to pursue its efforts to establish a regional learning network of support services to provide increased levels of service for students as well as financial benefits to states and institutions. The regional gateway should focus on those services that provide advantages that a single institution or state could not achieve on its own while leveling the playing field by sharing resources across the region. (Student Services #10);

- Promote strategies for greater flexibility in financial aid for the distance learner and financial aid providers, including assessing the practicality, efficiency, and effectiveness of shifting financial aid disbursement from an institution-based process to a student-based process. (Financial Aid #2);

- Promote and support changes in existing federal financial aid statues and regulations that are tied to time and place, specifically the:
    - Two "50% rules"
    - "12 hour rule"
    - redefining academic learning periods (standard term, nonstandard term and non-term), and
    - allowing institutions (and thus students) to use overlapping terms, self-paced learning, short and sequential course enrollment, and multiple- and rolling-start dates. (Financial Aid #3);

- Develop procedures that permit specific distance learning expenses to be included in the cost of attendance and need calculations. (Financial Aid #4);

- Promote and support these (Financial Aid #3) changes in the upcoming Reauthorization of the Higher Education Act—and do so in as unified a voice as can be created. (Financial Aid #5);

- Promote and expand working relationships between the state agencies and the regional accrediting bodies to ensure quality. (Financial Aid #8);

- Evaluate the potential of a regional financial aid clearinghouse through SREB, designed to facilitate financial aid efforts that are multi-state and multi-institutional. (Financial Aid #9);

- States and institutions should accelerate their work to include outcome measures in their accountability mechanisms for both traditional and distance learning programs. (Quality Assurance #6);

- Institutions should work to develop a learning community through a centralized Web portal designed specifically for distance learning students. (Student Services #5), and

- SREB should extend and formalize its current "free trade zone" concept in the Electronic Campus, establishing a system of institutional and program reciprocity where approval under agreed-upon standards in one jurisdiction is extended to and accepted by others in the South. (Quality Assurance #4).

E. Setting Policy Priorities: A National "Town Meeting"

In September, 2002, the Distance Learning Policy Laboratory conducted a national "town meeting" to review the policy reports and to participate in an exercise to rate and rank recommendations in the three broader categories—access, quality and cost. Participants were arrayed in small groups of 10 for facilitated discussion and were tasked to select and rank the five most important recommendations in six categories, to suggest specific actions for achieving/implementing the ranked policy recommendation, and finally to address issues that were missed, not properly represented in the reports, or areas that needed further study.

The access category was divided into two sub-categories:

- Policies and Strategies to Reach Underprepared, Underserved and Other Distance Learning Populations, and
- Policies and Strategies to Increase Financial Assistance and Support for Part-time and Distance Learners.

Here are the results (top 5 rankings) from each of the Access sub-category rankings:

Policies and Strategies to Reach Under-prepared, Underserved and Other Distance Learning Populations

- SREB and state policymakers should support efforts to extend (85) broadband access to homes, libraries, and community organizations, especially in rural areas of the South. SREB and policymakers should also work to extend high-speed access to primary, secondary, and postsecondary institutions, particularly colleges and universities with a mission of serving minority populations. *(Universal Access #1)*

- SREB states and postsecondary institutions should work (75) cooperatively with local organizations to extend or create training programs for populations who are unprepared to use technology to access information. *(Universal Access # 2)*

- Institutions should ensure that all students have comparable and (45) adequate access to needed services whether they are traditional, non-degree, part-time, distance, disabled, or "home" students of the institution. *(Student Services #1)*

- SREB and state higher education executive officers in the South (40) should work to increase access to digital content and programming, particularly in fields with critical personnel shortages and fields not well-served by competitive markets such as teacher education and allied health services. SREB, through the Electronic Campus, should play an active "brokering" role in this process. *(Universal Access #3)*

- SREB and the states should support programs that provide (18) financial aid to distance learners and encourage employers to implement tuition reimbursement programs. *(Universal Access #4)*

Policies and Strategies to Increase Financial Assistance and Support for Part-time and Distance Learners

- Promote and support changes in existing federal financial aid (80) statues and regulations that are tied to time and place, specifically the:

- The two "50 percent rules;"
- The "12 hour rule;"
- Redefining academic learning periods (standard term, nonstandard term and non-term); and
- Allowing institutions (and thus students) to use overlapping terms, self-paced learning, short and sequential course enrollment, and multiple and rolling start-dates. *(Financial Aid #3)*

☐ Promote and support these changes in the upcoming (50)
Reauthorization of the Higher Education Act — and do so in as unified a voice as can be created. *(Financial Aid #5)*.

☐ SREB and the states should support programs that provide (30)
financial aid to distance learners and encourage employers to implement tuition reimbursement programs. *(Universal Access #4)*

☐ Promote increased financial assistance to part-time distance (27)
learners. *(Financial Aid #1)*

☐ Promote strategies that provide greater flexibility in financial aid (27)
for the distance learner and financial aid providers, including assessing the practicality, efficiency, and effectiveness of shifting financial aid disbursement from an institution-based process to a student-based process. *(Financial Aid #2)*

F. Next Steps

Armed with a broad set of policy recommendations, 175 participants in the "town meeting" suggested policy priorities, targeted recommendations, and suggested actions for pursuing policy change. The Policy Laboratory leadership will move the agenda forward by placing the suggested actions on to the broader agenda of the Southern Regional Education Board, and proposing an agenda for SREB's Legislative Advisory Council, the Executive Committee of the Board, and finally the full Board. In taking this "conversion" step from Policy Laboratory reports/recommendations to SREB's "action" agenda, the recommendations targeted for action will have the full force of SREB and enter state policy agendas in the coming year.

Policy Laboratory staff will pursue an action agenda to develop appropriate pilot projects and to launch these projects with selected states and institutions. This will help to establish a second phase of the policy effort—those actions that will require some demonstration to support policy changes.

Finally, the Leadership Group of the Policy Laboratory, utilizing the results of the "town meeting" and staff analysis, will develop the next round of policy areas to be studied. This work will continue to focus on access and reducing policy barriers to distance learning.

II. CONCLUSION

Distance learning can ensure greater access to learning. It is "hamstrung" by a myriad of policies and practices that, while effective for a traditional-aged population studying full-time on traditional classrooms, are barriers to access. While the goal of universal access through the development of an accessible, affordable, ubiquitous technical infrastructure will take many years, concerted efforts at the national, regional, state and institutional levels can attach and overcome policy barriers. Policies for pricing, financial aid for part-time distance learners, and more equitable, fair and just credit transfer and articulation arrangements can be successfully transformed. SREB will play a leading role in making the case for change—others in the broader academic and policy communities will need to join forces to help make effect change. The hard work is about to begin.

III. ABOUT THE AUTHOR

Bruce Chaloux directs the Electronic Campus program and Distance Learning Policy Laboratory for the Southern Regional Education Board. Prior to joining SREB in 1998, Dr. Chaloux was at Virginia Tech for 13 years, serving as Associate Dean for Extended Campus Programs in the Graduate School and earlier directing VT's Northern Virginia Graduate Campus. He served on the staff of the State Council of Higher Education for Virginia for five years; and he was a faculty member in Business and Assistant, Associate and Interim Dean for Academic Affairs at Castleton State College (Vermont). He directed a national project on distance learning (Project ALLTEL), has chaired distance learning committees or task forces for the Southern Association of Colleges and Schools and Council of Graduate Schools, and serves on numerous advisory boards and committees, including the Council for Academic Management (CAM) for the eArmyU project. He holds degrees from Florida State University (Ph.D. in Higher Education Administration), the University of Florida (Master's degree) and Castleton State College (B.S. in Business Administration) in his native state of Vermont.

IV. APPENDIX A

A COMPILATION OF EXECUTIVE SUMMARIES OF DLPL REPORTS

Using Finance Policy to Reduce Barriers to Distance Learning

Executive Summary

The purpose of this paper is to examine the ways in which state and system financing policies can more effectively advance the utilization of distance learning technologies and the goals outlined in other committee reports prepared by the Distance Learning Policy Laboratory.

Despite its pervasiveness, states, colleges and universities still treat technology as a "special" category and fund it accordingly through special "one-time" appropriations. States and institutions have yet to establish information technology (IT) as a core budget item or embrace business models that utilize technology to reduce costs and increase productivity in the same way the private businesses have, especially in instruction.

The subcommittee on finance approached its task by establishing a framework for examining financing issues that included the following:

- Tuition, Fees and Charges: In many situations of technology-based instruction, traditional methods of charging based on "seat time" may be inappropriate or even unworkable. Out-of-state tuition, for example, may be a barrier to competitive marketing and in achieving an economic level of enrollment in certain courses or programs.

- Funding Methods: "Life-cycle" funding for technology is critical if it is to become a core resource. Technology funding often is not clearly correlated with important objectives, and definite accountability reporting is not established. Funding methods should also incorporate incentives to support the change process necessary for effective technology utilization.

- Costs and Resource Management: Good information regarding the costs of technology-based instruction is often not available. "Cost accounting" methods are not typically used in educational institutions, and the traditional methods and standards of cost estimation don't usually work well for technology-based instruction.

- Education as eCommerce: Increasingly, fundamental business processes of education are handled electronically. Education is moving in the direction of eCommerce for core functionalities, and yet many of its administrative practices and business policies are not designed to enable this move.

To examine these issues more closely, the subcommittee conducted four cases studies that represented different governance approaches (Centralized, Decentralized, Mixed and Free-standing). The cases were: The University of North Carolina System, The Kentucky Virtual University, the University System of Georgia and the University of Maryland University College (UMUC).

An overarching observation regarding all of the policy issues is the primacy of a state's educational objectives and purpose for using educational technology. Institutions and systems will differ in their goals for distance learning and technology-based instruction; therefore, finance policies will need to follow from those objectives and strategies. States, for example, primarily concerned with expanding access and convenience are likely to put more emphasis on infrastructure and program development. Those concerned with improving the cost-effectiveness of services may emphasize central utilities or outsourcing; while those primarily concerned with on-campus qualitative improvements may emphasize faculty training and course redesign.

Moreover, it is apparent the primary cost factors driving technology initiatives can be found in the people costs, not hardware or software.

The Finance subcommittee proposes the following general principles for financial policy for educational technology:

- Plans for distance learning and technology-based instruction should emanate from the overall strategic educational and business plans of the state, system and institution; and finance plans to implement these goals should an integral part of such planning.

- Technology should be treated as a "core resource" of the state or educational system and financed accordingly.

- Technology policy should move to a more overtly rational and explicit basis; inconsistencies and variations to "regular" finance policies should be minimized.

- Fundamental to the establishment and effective use of technology in higher education is support for, preparation of, and continued development of human capital or "personnel infrastructure."

Subcommittee Recommendations

Specifically, the subcommittee makes the following recommendations:

1. State finance policies should be adjusted to recognize the need for up-front and long-term investments to sustain technology-based instructional programs.

2. States and institutions should make "e-business plans and transactions" a high priority.

3. State or system financing policy should promote and provide incentives for multi-institutional collaborative programs including cost and revenue sharing.

4. To gain economies-of-scale, states, systems and voluntary consortia should pursue centralized services spanning multiple institutions.

5. State and system financing policy should accommodate new staffing patterns that are emerging in technology-based instruction.

6. States and institutions require good technology cost information for decision-making and must establish appropriate means for collecting and comparing this information.

7. State policy should provide institutions the flexibility to make pricing decisions based on a business plan and reflective of purpose, market and knowledge of cost implications.

8. Accountability should be a specific aspect of the plan for technology implementation and incorporated in the request for funding. Technology funding must be seen as an ongoing investment.

9. SREB, through the Educational Technology Cooperative and Distance Learning Policy Laboratory, should continue the work of the case studies by undertaking a formal, in-depth analysis of how each state in the region finances technology, support and technology-based instruction and should report and update these findings on a regular basis.

Creating Financial Aid Programs That Work for Distance Learners

Executive Summary

The emergence of technology and distance learning in higher education during the past decade has created for many individuals greater access and new pathways to colleges and universities. No longer is geographic proximity to a campus or one's work or family commitments a deterrent to acquiring needed skills or to pursuing a credential. As more "adult" students seek to utilize the convenience of distance learning and pursue study in alternative modes, as part-time students, or even as non-degree "coursetakers," more of them are facing real financial burdens. These learners are often the neediest as they work to balance work, family and education. While billions of dollars of financial aid is made available from federal and state governments annually, little of this is available to the distance learner. Financial aid mechanisms, established over the past 40 years and designed to expand access, often limit aid for students who are not traditional-aged, full-time, and learning on-campus. Structures, policies, procedures and practice have become real barriers to getting aid to the fastest growing population of students in U.S. higher education. These barriers, many engrained in federal, state and institutional policy must be removed.

This report outlines and defines the problem, traces the historical record of aid programs, describes real barriers for distance learners, and suggests alternative strategies that might be considered by policymakers at the federal, state and institutional levels to address aid issues. A number of alternative state approaches are discussed that might serve as models for other states. Finally, a regional financial aid "clearinghouse" concept is proposed and described in some detail.

The Distance Learning Policy Laboratory has adopted the following principles for financial aid to support distance learners. Further, the principles guide the recommendations that follow.

- The broader and fundamental goal of financial aid systems at all levels is to make higher education available to all who can benefit and to remove or lessen financial hurdles to such access.

- Any financial aid system must be fair and reasonable to all learners. Financial aid policy should encompass a broader definition of "student learner" than the current traditional classifications.

- Learning is not confined to a campus setting in face-to-face classrooms or in defined blocks of time.

- Students are increasingly learning in part-time, extended and contracted time formats and these new learning arrangements should not penalize or exclude participating learners from access to financial aid.

- Financial aid systems must become more student-centric and responsive to how, where, and when students learn.

- Appropriate accountability mechanisms to prevent fraud and abuse must be maintained.

Subcommittee Recommendations

1. Promote increased financial assistance to part-time distance learners.

2. Promote strategies that provide greater flexibility in financial aid for the distance learner and financial aid providers, including assessing the practicality, efficiency and effectiveness of shifting financial aid disbursement from an institutional-based process to a student-based process.

3. Promote and support changes in existing federal financial aid statues and regulations that are tied to time and place, specifically the:
   Two "50% rules"
   "12 hour rule"
   redefining academic learning periods (standard term, nonstandard term and non-term), and
   allowing institutions (and thus students) to use overlapping terms, self-paced learning, short and sequential course enrollment, and multiple- and rolling-start dates.

4. Develop procedures that permit specific distance learning expenses to be included in the cost of attendance and need calculations.

5. Promote new state level policies and initiatives that provide incentives to learners in disciplines/workforce areas of significant need.

6. Support and promote SREB's "electronic tuition rate" initiative as a means for increasing access to distance learning

7. Promote and expand working relationships between the state agencies and the regional accrediting bodies to ensure quality.

8. Promote and support these changes in the upcoming Reauthorization of the Higher Education Act—and do so in as unified a voice as can be created.

9. Evaluate the potential of a regional financial aid "clearinghouse" through SREB, designed to facilitate financial aid efforts that are multi-state and multi-institutional.

Supporting Faculty in the Use of Technology: A Guide to Principles, Policies, and Implementation Strategies

Executive Summary

The relationship between student and teacher is fundamental to the learning process. That relationship in a technology-rich environment will change, but it becomes no less important. In fact, as retrieval, dissemination and communication of information become automated, the role of faculty member as "teacher" becomes even more critical. To sustain our progress we must learn from the successes of others and accelerate investments in the "human capital" side of technology. Faculty, instructional designers, technical support staff, information specialists and librarians, tutors, and students all need continuous training and development to keep abreast of information technology developments.

The work of the Distance Learning Faculty Issues subcommittee has been aimed at achieving three broad goals:

* To use technology to improve the effectiveness of the teaching and learning process;

* To support new roles for faculty in an e-learning environment and to develop appropriate compensation and incentive structures to accompany those new roles; and

* To establish equitable policies that allow widespread access to information resources while sustaining the traditional rights of content owners to their intellectual property.

Subcommittee Recommendations

The subcommittee has made ten recommendations to SREB, states and institutions to achieve these goals:

1. Faculty need and should expect state and institutional commitment to development and support

structures that improve their productivity and effectiveness as teachers.

2. Institutions and systems should incorporate technology into teaching in both traditional classroom settings and distance learning programs.

3. Evaluation activities at the state and institutional levels need to be strengthened. Further, recent efforts to formulate more effective guidelines for accrediting processes need refinement to address and support emerging e-learning structures.

4. States and SREB should encourage cooperative activities that will achieve both economies of scale and qualitative improvements.

5. Institutions and states should encourage team approaches to curriculum development. This, in turn, will require changes in contracts, workload and compensation policies.

6. Contributions to the scholarship of teaching, the creation of digital learning materials and the effective use of those materials should be honored and rewarded in the hiring, promotion, and tenure and review processes.

7. New structures that are market-responsive and capable of managing change are needed to develop, deliver and sustain e-learning.

8. All institutions need established policies that address questions of ownership of course and course materials. Rewards from the commercialization of course materials should extend to all contributors to the process.

Distance Learning and the Transfer of Academic Credit

Executive Summary

Distance learning increases access to higher education by making it possible for students to fit education into work and family schedules and by providing a greater programmatic choice of courses. Distance learning allows "multiple-institution students" to simultaneously enroll in more than one institution in order to achieve their particular learning goals in a more timely manner. Each institution involved, however, typically maintains a different set of general education, prerequisite, academic major and institutional requirements.

The growth of distance learning, like any major technological innovation, changes the very nature of education—how it is administered, delivered, supported and monitored. As larger numbers of students take advantage of the benefits of "anytime/anywhere learning," more students will encounter difficulties in credit transfer. While transfer disagreements between institutions have existed for many years, the distance learning environment aggravates preexisting transfer problems because of the numerous institutions that can be involved in the education of a single student. Disagreements over credit transfer and degree requirements mean higher costs and more time for students to reach their education goals, whether they are courses, certificates or degrees. Rather than increasing the availability and flexibility of higher education, the promise of learning via technology is undermined when students are required to repeat certain courses or enroll in a single university in order to meet degree requirements.

While it is important that transfer principles be recognized and adopted first on the state level, state systems of higher education can no longer work in isolation if the full potential of distance learning is to be realized. Because distance learning is independent of physical "place" and is not contained by state boundaries, the same principles should be adopted regionally and, eventually, nationally. Just as state systems have adopted statewide policies on articulation and transfer, it is time for the consideration of regional and/or national transfer policies, including major field requirements and residency requirements. The needs of and interests of the learner—not the institution—should be paramount.

We are an increasingly mobile society, and it is in the best interest of both the student and the institution to accommodate movement across states and among different institutions. Students should have the option to change programs and take courses that meet their educational needs, whether the courses are offered by one or several institutions. States seeking to increase access and better serve students should consider designating one or two institutions to act as "degree completers" for the state. Degree-completing institutions would provide an important service to distance learning students by taking various course credits and integrating them into a meaningful, coherent degree. As a credit aggregator, the institution would better utilize their own resources, grow enrollments and receive greater FTE credit.

In addition, as more adult learners demand "just in time learning," the traditional structure of two- and four-year degree programs composed of semester-long courses will no longer suffice. Mechanisms need to be developed to translate various forms of modularized education and competency-based certifications into "credit equivalencies."

In order to facilitate the transfer of credits earned from multiple institutions in multiple states, there must be a consensus among institutions in different states on the elements of degree programs. To foster development of this consensus, it is recommended that SREB, its member states and SREB's *Electronic Campus* adopt the following policies to facilitate articulation and transfer of academic credits. SREB should seek to establish formal state commitments, through a voluntary multi-state compact or other appropriate instrument, to the following policies and practices.

Subcommittee Recommendations
1. States should develop policy statements outlining the responsibilities of students and institutions in the transfer process and clearly communicate these policies to all parties. Information about degree requirements and transfer policies should be featured predominantly and clearly described on institution web sites.
2. A transfer coordinator should be identified at every institution to specifically advise distance learning students. Coordinators should have sufficient authority to resolve transfer issues for students in an expeditious manner.
3. States should establish common methods for calculating the number and percentage of students who are simultaneously enrolled or who migrate from institution to institution on an annual basis and report their findings to the SREB Data Exchange. SREB should use this data to evaluate the effectiveness of transfer policies over time.

4. States should identify one or more highly visible institutions or consortia to act as "degree completers" to aid students by forming the various credits earned from multiple institutions into a complete degree program. Degree-completing institutions should accept lower-division general education credits of letter grades "C" or higher from any regionally accredited institution in the region as credit towards the general education requirements.

5. SREB should appoint a Regional Transfer and Articulation Committee (RTAC), with membership from all SREB states, to follow trends in student transfer activity, including regional policies, compacts, and agreements, and offer advice concerning questions, issues or disputes among states and institutions. Initially, the RTAC should be appointed for a three-year period.

6. SREB should encourage and support activities that bring together community college, technical college, and four-year faculty from various disciplines to discuss and agree upon the content and core curricula that associate and baccalaureate programs should contain, as well as the skill competencies that students should be able to display as a result of course or program completion.

7. SREB should utilize its existing compact agreements to establish a voluntary, mutually reciprocal interstate credit-transfer agreement that would ensure that students earning an Associate of Arts or Associate of Science degree is fully transferable to any public four-year institution in the compact if: 1) sufficient credits are earned from any accredited community or junior college and 2) the student has maintained the appropriate minimum grade point average. General education credits earned in a regionally accredited AA or AS program should be accepted *as a block of credits* without a course-by-course review.

8. All SREB states should participate in the development of an "electronic regional transfer crosswalk," which would allow students to pre-determine the graduation requirements and potential transferability of courses from one public institution to another public institution in any participating state. This "crosswalk" should take the form of a database, accessible through the *Electronic Campus* portal, and should describe the transferability of courses from one accredited institution in the region to any other institution in the region.

9. SREB should initiate a discussion among higher education leaders and accrediting bodies about the purpose and relevance of residency requirements in distance learning degree programs. These discussions should yield a recommended standard on the percentage of degree credits that must be earned at the degree-granting institution, when they should be earned relative to degree completion, and the percentage that may be earned from any other institution(s).

10. SREB should convene the regional accrediting bodies serving in SREB states to discuss the implications of these recommendations for their policies and practices.

SREB should facilitate discussions between the several national and regional accrediting commissions and the United States Department of Education about the implications of these recommendations for national educational policy

Anytime, Anyplace Services for the 21st Century Student

Executive Summary

Student services play a direct, critical role in student success, including students' academic performance, psychosocial growth, and program or certificate completion. While colleges and universities have moved rapidly in the past decade to develop courses, even complete degree programs that are independent of time and place, equal effort and financial commitment have not been given to the development or licensing of support services that accompany those courses. Services should be available at the same times that academic courses are, yet very few institutions provide a full array of academic and administrative services that can be accessed at anytime from anyplace.

Furthermore, evidence is mounting that services designed to serve distance learners also better serve students who live on or near the campus. Institutions must move towards a model in which services are designed around the needs of the student, not the institution. Institutions that can provide quality, convenient services that are available at all times and in alternative formats are more likely to distinguish themselves from their peers and to grow their enrollments.

Therefore, a variety of traditional campus-based services, such as business office functions (including tuition, fee, and other payments), bookstore purchases, financial aid, admission, registration, library, advising, career counseling, and testing need to be modified for learners whose work schedules or physical distance impede them from traveling to campus. The growing use of technology in both on- and-off campus education demands new student services (such as technology training) as well as new delivery formats (such as the Internet) for all students.

In addition, the distance learning environment may be associated with unique learner needs that demand the development of new services. Findings from the Policy Laboratory survey show that students typically report a higher satisfaction with the active, self-directed learning required by distance courses. However, some students are unprepared for the self-discipline required or have unrealistic expectations as to the time, effort and skills necessary to succeed. Distance learning is not appropriate for all students and learning styles. Because distance learning places a greater responsibility for learning on the student, it may require specialized services to support the learning process.

The Distance Learning Policy Laboratory has adopted four guiding principles surrounding Student Services for distance learners:

- The distance learning environment, which places a greater responsibility for learning on the student, requires specialized services to support the learning process.

- The provision of flexible services benefits both on- and off-campus students, as well as institutional efficiency.

- Collaboration pools resources, saves costs and reduces duplication to provide a greater depth and breadth of services. Collaboration on both state and regional levels can achieve economies of scale that no single institution could maintain alone.

- A learner-centered Customer Relationship Management model is fundamental to ensuring that instructional activities and support services truly meet student needs.

Subcommittee Recommendations

Within these guiding principles, the Student Services subcommittee offers the following recommendations for consideration by the Distance Learning Policy Laboratory Leadership Group,

SREB and institutions in its member states.

1. Institutions should ensure that all students have comparable and adequate access to needed services whether they are traditional, non-degree, part-time, distance, disabled, or "home" students of the institution.

2. Institutions should develop and provide realistic previews of the distance learning experience for potential students during the recruitment process.

3. Institutions should provide orientation for all distance learners that adequately prepares them to use technology, manage their time, and regulate their learning. Orientation should inform students about all institutional policies and available student services.

4. Institutions should develop a mentor program for distance learning to motivate students, model appropriate behavior, tutor academic needs, and provide academic advising/support.

5. Institutions should work to develop a learning community through a centralized Web portal designed specifically for distance learning students.

6. Institutional leaders should be encouraged to develop new and innovative funding models, such as unbundling and fee packaging, to meet varying student needs.

7. Institutions should consider outsourcing services to other institutions, consortia, or outside vendors to provide services where appropriate. Partnerships with third-party providers may be very beneficial in terms of financial savings realized by the institution, as well as in the breadth and quality of services available to students.

8. Multiple institutions should seek to collaborate with one another, in consortial or similar arrangements, to offer services and achieve economies of scale wherever possible.

9. The *Electronic Campus* should develop greater capacity within its Web site to provide students with robust evaluative tools for comparing courses, programs and institutional requirements.

10. SREB is encouraged to pursue its efforts to establish a regional "learning network" of support services to provide increased levels of service for students as well as financial benefits to states and institutions. The regional "gateway" should focus on those services that provide advantages that a single institution or state could not achieve on its own while "leveling the playing field" by sharing resources across the region.

11. SREB and its member states should work with the Southeastern Library Network (SOLINET) to assess the feasibility of creating a virtual regional library network that would link the various state library initiatives together through a common Web portal.

The Challenges of Quality Assurance in a Distance Learning Environment

Executive Summary

The purpose of the Quality Assurance subcommittee is to examine the challenges to state and system quality review processes posed by distance learning and to recommend needed changes. The recommendations are directed at state and system leadership and staff, but have implications for other quality assurance bodies and institutions.

Traditional regulatory approaches to quality assurance are severely tested in the distance learning environment. Most of our accountability structures, for example, are tied to political and geographic boundaries and to traditional standards of excellence, based on the presence of physical and intellectual resources onsite. In contrast, distance learning, driven by the global reach of the Internet, has not only evolved beyond these geographic boundaries but is embracing new standards of quality. State and system boards are struggling to balance the goals of student access and innovation with traditional consumer protection functions. National providers, both public and private, are finding it difficult to operate in the maze of federal, state, and accreditation oversight that currently exists.

The emergence of voluntary "best practice" standards is encouraging, however, and many states in the South have adopted national and regional standards. In our survey of state quality assurance initiatives, we also discovered a number of other promising actions, including the development of state and institutional strategic planning in distance learning.

States will continue to be challenged by the changing marketplace, and our report calls attention to such issues as evaluation of consortia and non-educational vendors, evaluation of courses and modules, and dealing with "blended programs."

The Distance Learning Policy Laboratory of SREB, as well as many states and regional organizations, are coming to a consensus on the principles and goals that should shape our distance learning policies. In the case of quality assurance, we believe there are four guiding principles that states should follow:

- States should take advantage of statewide, regional and national networks for sharing high quality offerings, and reciprocity should be maximized.

- States should demonstrate a commitment to innovation and a desire to move the best of these practices into mainstream activities.

- State quality assurance policies should focus on the needs of the student.

- State policies should be shaped with the understanding that "distance" is not a defining characteristic of learning processes; rather it is one among many factors to take into account in designing effective programs.

Subcommittee Recommendations

Within these guiding principles, the quality assurance subcommittee submits the following recommendations for consideration by the Distance Learning Policy Leadership Group and SREB.

1. States should review their current oversight policies to see if they meet the test of: a) taking advantage of regional and national assets; b) promoting innovation; and c) being student-centered. This review should take place in the context of the principles described in this report, namely toward the goals of developing a "regional free-market" in the South and encouraging innovation. As a regional convening body, SREB can greatly aid in this process of review.

2. States and institutions should consider adopting the "best practices" highlighted in this report, particularly those which use peer-review approaches. Our survey of states turned up a number of encouraging practices and guidelines that are likely to improve the quality of distance learning opportunities.

3. States should encourage their institutions to develop more effective evaluative mechanisms to learn student views concerning the quality of distance learning offerings. Regional organizations like SREB, along with state and system-level virtual universities, should encourage states to include easily accessible student evaluations in their information systems and web sites. The recommendations made by the Pew Learning and Technology program for course evaluation systems are a good starting point for designing these evaluation systems.

4. SREB should extend and formalize its current "free trade zone" concept in the *Electronic Campus*, establishing a system of institutional and program reciprocity where approval under agreed-upon standards in one jurisdiction is extended to and accepted by others in the South. While we do not expect that SREB alone can sort out the complexity of overlapping and conflicting standards described in this report, we do believe its leadership can establish a precedent that may inspire all parties toward better cooperation and more open access to all legitimate providers. States and regional accrediting bodies have a special obligation to coordinate their licensing and review activities and to establish ongoing structures for dialogue regarding acceptable standards in the field of distance learning.

5. State agencies with responsibilities for oversight of distance learning activities have an obligation to work toward consistent, coordinated, unbiased, and non-duplicative reviews. Again, we do not expect states to be able to sort out all of the issues raised by entities outside of their control (such as the Federal government), but we do believe that much progress can be made in quality assurance through communication and the development of a greater consensus within the standards-setting community operating in a state.

6. States and institutions should accelerate their work to include outcome measures in their accountability mechanisms for both traditional and distance learning programs. We are encouraged by the development of competency-based measures and exams in higher education as well as the emphasis placed upon outcome measures by accrediting bodies. Many of these efforts are aimed at developing better institutional outcome measures; but as was clearly apparent in recent national efforts to "grade" the states on student learning, there is a pressing need for more and better indicators.

7. SREB, through the *Electronic Campus* and Data Exchange initiatives, should work to establish common definitions and state data reporting mechanisms for technology-mediated learning activities in the region. A continuing challenge for states is the lack of common data collection techniques and even common definitions of the range of technology-mediated activity. SREB can build upon the work already underway to establish workable procedures to aid in assessment activities.

Electronic Tuition Rates

In addition to the reports noted above, SREB, through the Distance Learning Policy Laboratory, has promoted the adoption of "electronic tuition rates." This effort was supported initially by the Leadership Group, which moved quickly to address the traditional in-state/out-of-state tuition policy, which creates a barrier to many learners, particularly in this electronic era where the technology knows no boundaries. The pricing of courses and programs based on residence erects a new barrier in place of the one that technology can lessen, actually adding a cost of unused capacity. The proposed "electronic tuition rates" policy would create additional access, utilize unused capacity, and increase tuition revenue for colleges and universities. The policy would enable colleges and universities to establish an appropriate "market" tuition rate for courses and programs delivered electronically, a rate independent of the student's residency. The benefits for all participants are significant:

For Students
- Increase real access and multiply the opportunities and choices.
- Reduce or remove the out-of-state tuition barrier to distance learning.

For Colleges and Universities
- Expand "markets" for courses and programs that can increase revenues and increase operating efficiency.
- Utilize available capacity, which also can increase revenues and efficiency.
- Reduce expensive duplication of courses.

For SREB States
- Establish distance learning as a regional economic development resource.
- Build upon institutional, state and regional (Electronic Campus) distance learning initiatives.
- Continue the long tradition of SREB states to share educational resources.

A number of SREB states and an increasing number of colleges and universities have acted to establish a single rate policy for distance learning activities. West Virginia allows its institutions to set a single rate for their distance learning courses, and colleges and universities from Alabama, Arkansas, Delaware, Georgia, Florida, Kentucky, Louisiana, Mississippi, Oklahoma, Tennessee, Texas, Virginia, and West Virginia are offering selected courses in the Electronic Campus at a single rate. Almost 20 percent of the courses currently available in the Electronic Campus are offered at a single rate. Recently, the Georgia Board of Regents took action to permit its colleges and universities to request and offer a single rate for distance learning courses regardless of residency.

A variety of short-term and long-term objectives have been defined to establish the policy in the region. During the 2000-2001 academic year, a pilot initiative was launched which "married" the Electronic Campus with a longstanding SREB program, the Academic Common Market (ACM). For over 25 years, the ACM has provided opportunities for students in one SREB state to undertake study in selected programs in another SREB state at in-state tuition rates. However, the ACM historically restricted "electronically delivered" programs from inclusion, and students were required to physically relocate to the out-of-state college or university for their education. With the growth and development of distance learning and the emergence of the Electronic Campus, the Southern Regional Education Board moved to make selected distance learning programs available to out-of-state students at in-state tuition rates as part of the ACM. The success of the pilot led to an adoption of the ACM/Electronic Campus as a full-fledged program in 2002. Today, programs may be included in the ACM if they are not available in the student's state of residence or the delivery method is not available in the student's state of residence

V. APPENDIX B: BACKGROUND SOURCES

1. Association of College and Research Libraries (2001). Objectives for information literacy instruction: A model statement for academic librarians. *College & Research Libraries News, 62* (4), 416-419.
2. Atkinson, R. D., Cort, R.H., & Ward, J. M. (1999). The new state economy index: Benchmarking economic transformation in the states. Progressive Policy Institute.
    http://www.ppi.org/ppi_ci.cfm?knlgAreaID=107&subsecID=294&contentID=1283
3. Barfield, M. A., & Beaulieu (1999). The changing nature of work in the South: The polarization of tomorrow's workforce. Southern Rural Development Center. Mississippi State University. http://ext.msstate.edu/srdc/publications/rdissues.htm
4. Batista, E. (2001; August 28). Wireless village waits to connect. *Wired News.*
5. http://www.wired.com/news/business/0,1367,46050,00.html
6. Beaulieu, L. J., & Barfield, M. (2000). Human capital endowments and labor force experience of Southerners: A ten-year perspective. Southern Rural Development Center. Mississippi State University. http://ext.msstate.edu/srdc/publications/series.htm
7. Bohland, J. Papadakis, M., & Worrall, R. (2000). Creating the CyberSouth. Paper presented at Telecom South II: One South Digitally Divided, North Carolina. Institute for the Social Assessment of Information Technology. http://www.isait.vt.edu
8. Brownstein, A. (2001, October 24). Tuition increases at public and private colleges are largest in years, survey reports. *The Chronicle of Higher Education, 48.*
9. Brownstein, A. (2000, October 27). Tuition rises faster than inflation, and faster than in previous year. *The Chronicle of Higher Education, 47.*
10. Bureau of Labor Statistics. (2001). 2000-2010 Employment Projections.
    http://stats.bls.gov/news.release/ecopro.toc.htm
11. Carnevale, D. (2001, June 15). Some American institutions offer courses in Spanish as well as English. *The Chronicle of Higher Education, 47.*
12. Carnevale, D. (1999, October 29). Colleges strive to give disabled students access to on-line courses. *The Chronicle of Higher Education, 46.*
13. Carr, S. (2000, October 13). Black Colleges lag behind in offering students computer access. *The Chronicle of Higher Education, 47.*
14. Carvin, A. (2000, November/December). More than just access: fitting literacy and content into the digital divide equation. *Educause Review,* 38-47.

15. Cascio, W. F. (1995). Whither an Industrial and Organizational Psychologist in the changing world of work? *American Psychologist, 50* (11), 928-939.

16. The Children's Partnership (2000, March). content for low-income and underserved Americans: The digital divide's new frontier. Santa Monica, California.

17. Chow, C., Ellis, J., Mark, J., & Wise, B. (1998). Impact of CTCNet Affiliates: Findings from a National Survey of Users of Community Technology Centers. Education Development Center, Inc.

18. Chow, C., Ellis, J., Walker, G., & Wise, B. (2000). Who goes there? Longitudinal case studies of twelve users of community technology centers. Education Development Center, Inc.

19. Collins, T., & Dewees, S. (2000). Distance education: Taking classes to the students. *The Rural South: Preparing for the Challenges of the 21st Century*, No. 17. The Southern Rural Development Center. http://ext.msstate.edu/srdc/publications/millennium.htm

20. Committee on Information Technology Literacy. (1999). Being fluent with information technology. National Research Council. Washington, D.C.: National Academic Press. http://www.nap.edu/catalog/6482.html

21. Cornett, L. (2001). Teacher Supply and Demand in Tennessee. Southern Regional Education Board. http://www.sreb.org/main/Publications/catalog/catalog2001/statepolicies.asp

22. Crandall, R. W. (2001). Bridging the digital divide—naturally. *The Brookings Review, 19* (1), 38-43.

23. Dickinson, M. (2000). Giving undergraduates managerial experience. *Education and Training, 42* (3), 159-170.

24. Digital Opportunity Initiative (2001). Global bridges: digital opportunities.

25. Duncan, B., & Culver, V. (2000). The potential impact of e-commerce on the rural south: Will it equalize or deepen the digital divide? *The rural south: Preparing for the challenges of the 21st century*. Mississippi State.

26. Technology Counts (2001). The new divides. *Education Week.* http://www.edweek.org/sreports/

27. Golonka, S. (2001). Opening doors: Expanding educational opportunities for low-income workers. *National Governors Association Center for Best Practices*. Manpower Demonstration Research Corporation.

28. Goo, S. K. (2001, July 24). Despite boom, many families struggling. *The Washington Post*. Section A, page 6.

Faculty Satisfaction

FACULTY SATISFACTION IN THE ONLINE TEACHING-LEARNING ENVIRONMENT

Melody M. Thompson
Penn State World Campus

- Faculty commitment over the long term depends on institutional support, professional rewards, and personal satisfaction.

- The potential of online instruction to generate high student achievement is an important factor in faculty satisfaction.

- Being able to teach on schedules and in locations of their own choosing is a major source of faculty satisfaction.

- Ensuring that plans and policies are *mutually* beneficial and sustainable depends on ongoing faculty involvement and leadership in change planning and implementation.

I. INTRODUCTION: WHAT MAKES ONLINE TEACHING SATISFYING?

A growing body of literature portrays the online teaching and learning environment as a personally rewarding and satisfying one for many faculty members [1, 2, 3, 4]. Specific positive factors reported by faculty include:

Increased access to/by students. Many faculty members report that increasing *students' access to higher education* is one source of satisfaction. Increasing their *program's or institution's access to students* is a related but different cause for satisfaction. A recent update to the National Education Association's national survey of distance education faculty reported that increased access "was by far the most frequently mentioned positive thought about distance education" [5].

Increased opportunities for high-quality interaction with students. Faculty members report being pleasantly surprised to find that online teaching in many cases offers opportunities for more and better interaction with individual students and groups of students, as well as among the students themselves [5, 6, 7, 8].

Flexibility and convenience of teaching and learning. Faculty members appreciate the additional flexibility offered by online learning environments both for themselves and for their students. Being able to teach on schedules and in locations of their own choosing is a major source of faculty satisfaction [3, 5].

Increased knowledge of and experience with educational technologies. Instructional technologies support pedagogical innovations that increase faculty effectiveness and, therefore, satisfaction. Faculty report that this benefit extends beyond their online teaching into their face-to-face classes [1, 4, 9].

Opportunities for research and professional recognition. Faculty members are under considerable pressure to conduct research and publish in their fields. Online teaching is providing new opportunities for faculty members to meet this professional expectation [3, 7, 10].

Positive student outcomes. The potential of online instruction to generate high student achievement is an important factor in faculty satisfaction. The reported experiences of an increasing number of faculty members who teach online reflect high levels of faculty satisfaction with student learning outcomes [2, 4, 8].

The above list reflects specific sources of satisfaction identified by faculty members who teach online. Each element listed above depends on the existence of an institutional context that facilitates these benefits. What are the necessary characteristics of such an environment?

II. FACTORS CONTRIBUTING TO SATISFACTION

Reports from faculty members indicate that institutional support, professional recognition, and personal rewards are all necessary for them to do their jobs well and to feel positive about what they do. These, then, are the necessary conditions for satisfaction with the online teaching-learning experience. Equally important is effective institutional management of the entire change process involved in introducing online teaching and learning into the higher education enterprise. These interrelated and necessary conditions for faculty satisfaction will be briefly introduced below and then discussed more fully in "Major Issues Relating to Faculty Satisfaction."

A. Institutional Support

Institutional support takes a variety of forms, such as technical, policy, and—by no means the least important—"moral" support. For any individual faculty member the relative importance of any one of these types of support will vary, but research consistently suggests that these elements are significant contributors to faculty satisfaction in the online environment.

1. Technical Support

Technical support is reflected in several ways: in technical infrastructure that supports interaction between/among students, faculty, and the institution; in support for course development; and in training and ongoing assistance for delivery of online courses. According to a national survey of higher education faculty teaching online courses, "the level of technical support is the most important determinant of overall feelings toward distance learning" [5].

Studies of institutional factors related to both program quality and faculty satisfaction also report that provision of technical support ranks consistently high, if not first [2, 7, 11]. There is general agreement among practitioners, administrators, professional organizations, and regulatory agencies that faculty members making the transition to the online environment need a robust and reliable technical infrastructure that supports interaction between and among students, faculty, and the institution; up-front support in designing courses appropriate for the online environment and student population; training in new skills to teach successfully online; and ongoing technical support during the delivery of their courses. Conversely, inadequate support in any of these areas lowers faculty satisfaction.

a. Robust and Reliable Infrastructure

For faculty teaching online, the technical infrastructure includes classroom and means of communication with students. Just as faculty need physical classrooms to be in good repair and unlocked so that a class can occur, they also need the technical infrastructure of the online classroom to support that class meeting. And since their primary, if not only, means of communication with their students is through the technical infrastructure, they need to be assured that that line of communication is always open. As Chizmar and Williams [12] point out,

> Nothing frustrates students, especially technophobes, more than instructional technology that doesn't work. When a server is down, e-mail isn't accessible, or the help desk provides an inappropriate answer, they blame the faculty member....Nothing frustrates faculty more than to assign a Web-based quiz, for example, and then discover that the server is down or that its performance has slowed to a snail's pace.

> When catastrophes strike, trust between student and instructor fades and confidence in instructional technology declines. Faculty desire a network and technical infrastructure that never calls attention to itself, one that doesn't create barriers to entry for wary faculty and students...(22).

b. Support in Designing, Developing, and Delivering Courses

Most faculty members do not begin their careers knowing how to design and develop courses for online delivery, nor, to date, have most had the inclination or need to learn how to do so. However, as online programs proliferate and more and more faculty members become involved in online teaching, support in this area becomes crucial to ensuring the quality and success of online programs and the satisfaction of the faculty members teaching in them. Several models of support appear in the literature. On one end of the spectrum are those that offer faculty training in the skills necessary to ultimately take responsibility for design and development; on the other end are those that provide the centralized support services of a team of experts who provide the expertise necessary to transform faculty-developed content into online courses. The existence of support, more than the model for provision of support, is a key component of faculty satisfaction [1, 3, 4].

Similarly, faculty members need guidance in developing the skills necessary for effective delivery of instruction in the online environment. Although some skills and attitudes transfer readily to this new environment, new and different skills are needed as well. Particularly important are skills for the development of a "social presence" that is apparent to students separated from the faculty member by time and distance and the skills to create a learning community among individuals who may never meet face to face. The literature consistently documents the high value faculty members place on relationships and interactions with students. Without institutional support for developing the skills for building and maintaining pedagogic relationships online, faculty satisfaction with this form of teaching will be compromised [7, 13].

c. Ongoing Technical Support for Students and Faculty

Equally important to up-front technical support is the provision of ongoing technical support to students and faculty. Hartman, Dziuban, and Moskal [8] note that

> . . . a major issue affecting faculty satisfaction is the support of students in the ALN environment. Without an institutional response to this issue, faculty must take valuable course and personal time to grapple with the myriad technical challenges and information gaps that face students taking an on-line course. (7)

Faculty members also need the ongoing support of a help desk or similar service that ensures consistent availability of course content and communication with students. The online environment takes the control of these elements out of the hands of the faculty members; faculty members will not be satisfied with this alternative environment in the absence of institutional support in this area.

2. Policy Support

Faculty policies related to online teaching need to address workload, compensation, intellectual property, professional advancement, and governance and quality control issues. As online teaching becomes an expectation for increasing numbers of faculty members, institutional policies can ensure that faculty are appropriately supported in, rather than penalized for, their participation in online teaching and learning.

a. Workload, Compensation, and Institutional Rewards/Advancement

With few exceptions (see, for example, DiBiase [14]), the literature reports that online course development and teaching is more time intensive than is face-to-face teaching [2, 3, 4, 10, 15, 16]. Although some authors distinguish between the workload in developing courses and in teaching courses, others claim that both aspects of instruction are more labor intensive. The perceived heavier workload is reported to be a major deterrent to participation by those faculty members who can "opt out," and an inhibitor to satisfaction among those who have no choice or who choose to teach online [7, 9, 17]. To build faculty satisfaction and commitment, institutions need to study the workload demands of online teaching and develop informed policies that protect faculty from workload inequities.

Closely related to workload are questions of compensation. Although most faculty members believe that their online courses take more effort, many report that their institutions do not compensate them for the extra effort in development or instruction [2, 12]. For some, this situation is a deterrent to participation

[16]; for those who do participate, it is a source of dissatisfaction. Conversely, several studies have reported that extra compensation for the increased workload of online teaching motivates participation [10] and increases faculty satisfaction [7]. This significant factor argues for the development of institutional policy to ensure equity of compensation.

Rewards and advancement in higher education are dependent upon meeting institutional expectations for productivity. Tenure-track faculty members have multiple demands on their time, particularly research/publication, teaching, and service. In most institutions, tenure and promotion depend primarily on research and publication performance. Faculty members who are expected to spend the extra time involved in developing and teaching online courses need to have institutional support in the form of a reward system that recognizes them, rather than penalizes them, for this activity. The absence of such a reward system has been identified by some faculty members as a deterrent to participation in online teaching [18].

b. Intellectual Property

In "Developing a Distance Education Policy for 21st Century Learning" the American Council on Education suggests that one of the first steps an institution should take when developing online programming is to review and, in most cases, revise its existing intellectual property policies [19]. Key points to be covered by such policies are ownership of, use of, and compensation for Web-based courses [20]. Noting a "current climate of distrust and uncertainty" in this area, Twigg [21], in a report for the Pew Learning and Technology Program, argues that developing a clear statement of policy is not enough; policies must also effectively "encourage faculty members to be engaged in online learning" (2).

c. Governance and Control of Academic Quality

Eaton [22] identifies shared governance and the academic authority of the faculty as elements of "a small set of core academic values...central to the history and tradition of higher education." These values are even more directly central to faculty members' sense of professional identity and responsibility, and most institutions have policies that explicitly reflect these values. Although, as Eaton further notes, "distance learning...challenges these values," it is by no means a "given" that faculty have accepted this challenge uncontested. Faculty members' satisfaction with the institutional adoption of and their participation in online learning is closely related to their maintaining responsibility for academic policy making and quality control [5, 7, 13, 23].

3. "Moral" Support (i.e., support that involves respect, approval, and/or sympathy without action)

Not all of the institutional support needed by faculty involves specific actions of the types noted above. Faculty members—even dissenting faculty members—need to believe that they are viewed and respected by the administrative leadership of their institutions as knowledgeable professionals with expertise and values they express in their professional roles. They also need the respect and encouragement of peers in their own departments. This type of support from both administrators and peers is an important factor in faculty satisfaction [9, 16].

B. Professional Recognition

Faculty members are a part of an academic community that includes peers both in and beyond their home institutions. Earning the recognition and respect of their discipline-specific colleagues in this community through research and publication is a compelling goal for most faculty members. Online teaching experiences that move toward this goal through opportunities for discipline-based research and publication contribute to faculty satisfaction. A developing higher education environment that is beginning to recognize and value the "scholarship of teaching" across disciplines may provide this opportunity to a growing number of faculty members [3, 24].

C. Personal Rewards

Faculty members need to find personal satisfaction, as well as professional recognition, in their roles. Although we speak easily and frequently of student "needs" related to teaching-learning environments, it is important to remember that faculty have equally legitimate personal needs and motivations. The 2000 American Faculty Poll reported that, for higher education faculty, "one of the most important factors…in their decision to pursue an academic career was the enjoyment of working with students" [13]. Satisfaction with teaching in the online environment is directly related to the extent to which it allows faculty members enjoy it, and a growing body of literature offers evidence of the potential for this type of reward. Several recent studies have reported that faculty members are gratified to be able to reach and work with underserved, often highly motivated populations of students. Other studies of motivating factors in online teaching have reported additional personal rewards, such as "self-gratification," "fulfilling a personal desire to teach" [9], fulfilling a "personal motivation to use technology," and "overall job satisfaction" [16].

D. Effective Institutional Management of Change

This factor is arguably the most important contributor to faculty satisfaction in that it provides the context within which the other factors have developed and are being addressed. As students of organizational change know well, the success of innovation is dependent not only on the characteristics of the change itself but, at least as importantly, on how the change is introduced and implemented.

Focusing particularly on the innovation of online higher education, Jaffee [25] notes,

> New and emerging information and instructional technologies represent one of the most significant institutional challenges facing higher education. Advocates of instructional technology have argued that changing social and economic conditions demand new educational delivery modes and the application and incorporation of these technologies. (21)

These "demands" are presumed to translate directly into a variety of organizational changes: changes in roles and responsibilities, changes in relationships with students and other stakeholders, and changes in institutional structures and operations [25]. Noblitt [26] reinforces this idea, arguing that the current emphasis on technology masks what he calls the "mythology dominating technology management": the idea that "it is all about technical issues. It can be argued that it's all about managing change – technical, social, pedagogical, political, and financial" (4).

In discussing trends in higher education, Kezar [27] reports "particular concern [related to] faculty participation in the restructuring that affects their lives" (p. 4). She identifies faculty participation in the planning stages of major organizational changes as an important factor in motivation for and acceptance of these changes. How institutions manage the changes brought about by the introduction of educational technologies will have a direct impact on faculty satisfaction with online teaching.

194

III. MAJOR ISSUES RELATING TO FACULTY SATISFACTION

While the list of satisfying elements presented at the beginning of this paper offers an optimistic assessment of faculty satisfaction, the benefits reported and the conditions necessary for their attainment are neither universal nor assured. Similarly, the contributing factors discussed in the section above represent goals to work toward rather than "standard operating procedure" in many higher education contexts.

Currently, institutions vary in the level of support they offer to faculty members in these areas. Thus, many of the factors in and conditions for satisfaction need to be recast as "issues," that is, points or questions still to be debated or decided. In some cases, at issue will be lack of agreement on the need for action or on implementation strategies, while in others it will be failure to follow through on decisions already made. As Turoff points out, the resolution of these issues offers the potential for either "desirable futures" or a "darkside" [28] to faculty participation in online education. Within any institution, it is not only the actual decision made on these issues, but also how and by whom they are discussed and resolved that will ultimately determine which result we see.

A. Institutional Support Issues

1. Technical Support

Although the importance of technical support for faculty seems to be widely understood and accepted, evidence indicates that the provision of such support is by no means universal. A 1998 National Center for Educational Statistics (NCES) report indicated that 40% of faculty teaching at a distance receive no training for that role [13]. A more recent report based on a National Education Association survey noted that overall, 30% of distance teaching faculty receive no training. While this overall proportion may seem low (and may be decreasing), it actually masks the wide variability of training availability, which can be much lower for smaller institutions, rural institutions, and those at which distance teaching is not regulated by collective bargaining agreements [2].

Not only is the actual provision of support problematic, but also the way in which the support is delivered: issues of timing, relevance, and source all influence faculty satisfaction with the support they receive [5, 12, 29]. Faculty members want technical support that respects their time and their particular needs. Therefore, workshops scheduled without regard to faculty convenience or teaching schedules (such as those offered far in advance of need) or with a "one-size-fits-all" focus not particularly relevant to individual pedagogical needs detract from faculty members' satisfaction with technical support [12]. Additionally, some faculty members have concerns about the source of support. Faculty are not satisfied with support provided by those whose only expertise is technical; rather, they desire assistance from someone who also understands the curriculum, who knows what it means to teach, and who knows the best ways to use technology to reach pedagogical goals [29]. For many faculty members, mentoring and/or demonstration by an experienced online faculty member is in important factor in making a satisfying transition to the online environment [5,12].

Institutions understand the importance of technical support to faculty satisfaction; for the past five years, the Campus Computing Project's annual survey of senior information technology officers has ranked helping faculty members integrate technology into instruction as their highest priority task. However, at issue is not the need for support, but rather the level and type of support that is reasonable and possible. Those same information-technology officers "complained that faculty members have unreasonable expectations about the technological support they should receive" [30]. How institutions sort out this difference in perception will have a definite impact on their faculty members' satisfaction with online teaching.

2. Policy

Although the policy *areas* relevant to online teaching and learning are becoming more clearly understood and articulated [31, 32, 33], the *issues* surrounding such policies are often unclear and sometimes contentious. The policy categories discussed below involve issues that have persisted as unresolved concerns over the last several years.

a. Workload, Compensation, and Institutional Rewards/Advancement

Workload, compensation, and institutional rewards/advancement are closely related policy areas. At issue here is how to assess and recognize a faculty member's contribution in the online environment relative to traditional face-to-face instruction and institutional expectations. The wide variety of practices in these areas is reflected in varying levels of faculty satisfaction with their online experiences.

Perhaps the most pressing issue relating to workload is reflected in the questions "Just how real is the perceived increase in workload in the online environment? Is it truly more work or does it seem like more work because it's unfamiliar?" Some reports suggest that while the workload involved in *development* is admittedly greater for online instruction, the *delivery* of instruction, after an initial learning period, is comparable to or, perhaps, even less labor intensive than face-to-face instruction [14]. Other reports reflect a perception among some faculty members of increased delivery workload (due primarily to expectations for interaction and course-administration demands) and of concomitant lower levels of faculty satisfaction or resistance to participation [16, 17]. However, as the American Association of University Professors points out, the "common wisdom" related to workload is based almost exclusively on anecdotal evidence. Although AAUP recommends taking this evidence into account when establishing workload policy, it further recommends that institutions conduct institution-specific research to establish a more solid base for future decision-making [34].

Compensation in cases of documented heavier workloads will need to be a focus for planning and policy development. Should a heavier workload necessarily translate into increased compensation, particularly given expectations for increased institutional productivity or a better "bottom line?" Should other responsibilities be shifted to equalize the workload? Although some argue for the development of standard practices in this area, others suggest that it is more appropriate that, within broad common guidelines, solutions specific to institutional cultures be developed [35].

On the basis of her survey of 212 distance education faculty members in 45 higher education institutions, Shifter [36] reports a wide variety of compensation and incentive practices. She suggests that while compensation and other incentives are more common for faculty members developing a course than for those teaching a course, there are no common standards for compensation or incentives; tangible incentives may range from a stipend to release time accompanied by other non monetary incentives such as a computer, travel support, or support for a teaching assistant. She further notes that inadequate compensation has been a major barrier to faculty participation in distance education initiatives.

Somewhat different results were reported from Rockwell and associates' [9] more-narrowly focused study of 207 faculty members' and 30 administrators' perceptions of teaching via distance education at two campuses of a single land-grant university. Results from this study indicated that for most faculty members, monetary rewards were viewed as neither an incentive nor obstacle. However, administrators were more likely than teaching faculty members to see monetary awards as an incentive. A similar discrepancy between George Washington University faculty members' and administrators' perceptions of incentives for participation was reported earlier by Betts [17].

As with workload issues, compensation issues are anything but uniform and straightforward. While a substantial body of literature suggests a close connection between compensation practices and faculty satisfaction, other equally compelling reports call such a conclusion into question. Clearly, additional research, including institutionally specific studies, is needed as the basis for informed decision-making in this area, as well.

The common wisdom in the area of institutional rewards/advancement is that participation in online learning is counterproductive to professional advancement, particularly for junior faculty members, since the relative value of any kind of teaching—but most particularly online teaching—within formal university reward structures is low and because online teaching, relatively labor intensive, takes time away from other faculty activities that are more highly valued by the institution. This view is articulated in the report of a research study by Wolcott [18], who makes a clear case for the marginality of distance education—and by association participating faculty members—based on its pedigree as the offspring of outreach and technological innovation, neither of which have been highly valued by the academy in the past.

Several more-recent studies report less clear-cut results. Betts' [17] study of faculty members and deans at George Washington University found that although deans identified credit toward tenure and promotion as a motivating factor, faculty members did not. However, faculty members still working toward tenure were less likely to participate in online teaching than were already-tenured faculty members. Another study of incentives for and obstacles to participating in distance programming found that while 30% of the distance teaching faculty viewed their work as an obstacle to promotion and tenure, 40% reported it as a benefit [9]. Hartman and Truman-Davis [3], in their study of faculty satisfaction at the University of Central Florida, found that the institutional reward system did not inhibit faculty participation.

In cases where inequitable reward structures do exist, they represent an obvious barrier to the growth and success of online learning programs and the integration of such programs into the mainstream of higher education. Institutional reward systems that discourage participation by those able and willing to engage in innovative pedagogy will hamper the efforts of institutions to compete effectively in a changing higher education environment. However, the less clear-cut—and to that extent more promising—results of recent research, may reflect a trend toward increasing acceptance of and recognition for faculty participation in outreach, technological innovation, and the online approach to teaching which draws the two together. Given the recent calls for increased engagement and a reassessment of scholarship, such a change seems likely, however disappointingly slow the pace of change may be at times. Two examples of institutions that have changed their reward structure related to online teaching are presented below in "Promising Directions for Practice."

Still at issue, even given an institution's intent to implement a more equitable or inclusive reward structure, is the development of guidelines for review and the availability of knowledgeable and experienced peers to review a faculty member's online contributions. As Twigg [21] points out, "There are so few 'peers'" in this arena.

b. Intellectual Property

Werry [37] notes that "loss of control over the product of academic labor" is one of the most important issues resulting from the "digitization of education." According to a recent NEA study [5], "Faculty were clearly more concerned about controlling how their intellectual property was used than the amount of money they might get for that property."

Ubell [20] identifies three categories of issues related to academic intellectual property: ownership, use, and compensation. Ownership issues focus on questions of rights to externally marketed/distributed e-courses and copyright ownership by either the faculty course developer or the institution (or both). Issues of use include the "unbundling" of development and teaching, licensing of courses to third parties, and the legitimacy of faculty members taking their e-courses with them when they leave an institution. Compensation issues relate to whether to pay faculty members on an overload basis to teach e-courses, to compensate for externally licensed courses, and to compensate to the developer for courses taught by another faculty member.

A survey of higher-education institutions offering online courses found that about half had intellectual property policies specifically related to Web courses. Approximately one fourth of these granted all ownership rights to the institution; about a tenth granted ownership rights to faculty; and about a third shared ownership [20].

In terms of faculty satisfaction, neither the existence of intellectual property policies nor the clarity of those policies is the issue, although some of the more overly general quality guidelines seem to miss this point. What is important is that such policies encourage rather than discourage faculty participation in online programming. When faculty members believe that their institution views them as little more than hired hands, or when they believe that the institution intends to "rob" them of the intellectual capital that they have spent years developing, their commitment to helping that same institution forward online programs will be understandably low. As one faculty member recounts,

> When our university began to outsource Web-based courses, intellectual property was a big issue. In our case, anything placed on the company's Web site belonged to the university. In response, many people did not put anything on the Web site that they had developed themselves or planned to use in research or a textbook. Instead, they would send this material to students via email. As teachers, if we don't own the material that we produce for our courses, what do we own as professionals? [37]

Symposium participants of a Pew Learning and Technology Program focused on intellectual property issues concluded that, given the long and strong tradition of faculty ownership of intellectual property in higher education, the best way for institutions to encourage faculty to participate in the development and delivery of online courses was to proceed cautiously in asserting ownership rights, doing so only when the institution has made a substantial contribution to creation of material [38].

The Southern Regional Education Board's (SREB) Distance Learning Policy Laboratory report [39] on faculty issues further asserts that intellectual property policies need not be uniform across institutions, stating that "circumstances and cultures are too varied in higher education" to justify uniform approaches to this issue. This report offers several representative examples of institutional approaches to intellectual property issues.

c. Governance and Control of Academic Quality

As noted earlier in this paper, the concepts of shared governance and academic authority have long been core values in higher education. A major source of faculty resistance to and dissatisfaction with online teaching and learning is that, in many cases, the way this innovation is being promoted and implemented not only challenges these values, but actually supplants them with those of corporate management models. And, faculty fear that with this change in values comes others:

Advocates of a top-down management style who want to transform faculty from professionals into "employees" and students into "consumers" tend to see liberal education as a waste of time and resources, because they fail to see the immediate "payoff" of the liberal and fine arts and because they are willing to allow the "market" to determine who should and should not be taught [40, (3)].

An interesting aspect of this issue is that it seems to be represented exclusively in articles written by faculty members. Administrators seem not to know that the problem exists, choose not to write about it, or view it as a "non-issue," that is, a matter which has already been resolved and needs no further attention. Yet for faculty members, governance and academic authority issues arguably represent the most potent barriers to acceptance of the changes going on within higher education. To the extent that technologically based pedagogical innovation is associated with these issues, faculty can be expected to resist rather than cooperate.

Thankfully, this seems not to be the either/or proposition: "Either you let us continue with business as usual, or we'll do our best to scuttle the whole change process through passive or active resistance." Although many faculty members are sounding a warning note regarding what they see as a dangerous drift in leadership practice, they are also suggesting that faculty have a responsibility to step forward—rather than "opt out"—to guide change appropriately.

For example, Feenberg [41] might seem to be throwing down the gauntlet when he begins his article "Distance Learning: Promise or Threat?" with the following statement: "Proposals for a radical "retooling" of the university emanating from these sources [i.e., politicians, university administration and computer and telecommunications companies] are guaranteed to provoke instant faculty hostility." However, he follows the statement with a reasoned argument for significant faculty involvement in online learning, reasonably noting that the faculty's lack of interest and involvement has been an important factor in the shift in leadership roles.

Other faculty members are issuing equally strong calls for leadership involvement in online learning, particularly in relation to the development of the policies that will guide it. Werry, [37] for example, chastises faculty members who do nothing more than sit on the sidelines and criticize rather than thinking about how they can harness the changes to improve what they do:

Too much of the debate between faculty and administrators reflects thinking of technology primarily as a delivery mechanism for teaching, rather than a new environment. And it does not make the case that academics ought to have a significant role in shaping that environment....We need to offer alternatives as well as critique. (18)

Faculty members do not need to have their traditional responsibilities taken away from them; to do so would not only decimate faculty satisfaction, but also seriously compromise the ultimate success of online teaching and learning as truly "higher education." On the contrary, what faculty members need is "affirmative authority to shape the environment in which they carry out their responsibilities," which is increasingly an online environment [40, p. 2].

Governance and quality control are closely related to issues of institutional change and change management. This relationship will be discussed further in the section "Management of Institutional Change," below.

3. Moral Support

Moral support might seem an odd addition to a scholarly study of faculty satisfaction. However, a troubling aspect of the literature is language signaling, and reports that suggest a lack of respect between administrators and faculty on the one hand and participating and non-participating faculty in the same department on the other. In the former case this issue relates to (primarily) administrative and executive leadership responses to and depictions of faculty who do not wholeheartedly embrace proposed changes such as those represented by the introduction of educational technologies into the mainstream of the academy. As Noblitt [25] suggests, "Academics are trained to be critical (in the best sense of the word) and may be expected to make demands for justification" of changes to their roles and practices. Yet faculty members believe that when they perform this critical function, administrators view them as "recalcitrant Luddites" [13] or as "obstacles to be swept along by the inevitable momentum of progress" [41].

From the faculty perspective, a similar lack of respect for and understanding of faculty members' very real sense of "calling" and professional identity is signaled by blithe suggestions that the faculty role must be "disaggregated" or "unbundled" in the online environment. This language of deprofessionalization leaves faculty members feeling that their function as scholars and teachers has been "downplayed and demeaned" [42].

A rift between faculty members in the same department results when those teaching online believe that their participation has lost them the respect and support of their peers. In one study, "lack of support and encouragement from departmental colleagues" ranked 4th in a list of 17 factors inhibiting participation in online teaching [15]. This potential for divisiveness has caused some faculty members to avoid asking for appropriate support in the face of the potential "friction and division that could emerge within the faculty group as a result of distance learning faculty members being given special treatment" [5].

B. Professional Recognition

An increasing number of higher education institutions are recognizing and rewarding, through faculty tenure and promotion decisions, those online activities, including research related to effective course design and online pedagogy that reflect true academic scholarship. However, a faculty member's institutional affiliation is only one of several professional community ties. For many if not most faculty members, their disciplinary community, often national or international in scope, exercises a more potent influence on their research and publication scholarship than does their home institution. Within a particular discipline, professional recognition tends to be awarded for research that adds to the knowledge base rather than for research, publication, or other activities that advance the teaching of that disciplinary knowledge. While this is generally less of an issue for faculty members in fields such as education and communication, in which disciplinary content and online pedagogy overlap, faculty members in other fields often experience a conflict when they consider applying time and energy to enhancing their disciplinary teaching. The current traditional professional culture, which awards considerable acclaim for advances in knowledge but little recognition for advances in effectively communicating that knowledge to students rather than peers, can be an effective barrier to increased involvement and commitment to online teaching.

C. Personal Rewards

Although many faculty members report benefits that lead to satisfaction, others indicate that they struggle with the differences between the online experience and their traditional environment. Some continue to have reservations about program quality and the level and type of personal interaction with students, while others suggest that although comparable quality is theoretically possible, it might not be worth the extra workload, cost, and loss of faculty identity [5, 10].

To faculty members who identify the interpersonal or structural benefits of teaching with factors specific to the face-to-face environment, online teaching is an unsatisfying experience:

"Invariably, I come to the end and I'm feeling totally depressed because...you don't see any light bulbs over people's heads, you don't see any flash of recognition...it's very impersonal" [33].

"...this change in the pattern of my working day...has reduced and decentered intellectual tasks to competency and generic skill" [42].

Jaffee [25] suggests that faculty dissatisfaction of the type illustrated in the above comments results not just because a new organizational practice—such as online teaching—threatens a valued practice, but more importantly because it challenges one's core professional identity: "When identity is defined and reinforced through particular forms of social action...then proposals that advocate alternative actions will be met with significant resistance."

However, a faculty member's professional identity comes not only from his or her public, classroom presentation of ideas (the valued practice), but also from concern with effective and innovative teaching techniques. Jaffee promotes the use of what he calls "pedagogical hooks," discussions about pedagogical techniques and outcomes, as a way to open dialogue about how the online environment does not threaten cherished values and goals, but on the contrary can help faculty members be more effective in reaching them.

D. Management of Institutional Change

The convergence of online learning and traditional higher education is one of the educational community's most exciting possibilities and one of its biggest challenges. The excitement comes from the potential to extend universities' knowledge and teaching resources to new populations of students while at the same time revitalizing and enhancing those resources through new technology-enabled pedagogical approaches. The challenge comes in effectively managing a change process that seamlessly melds an innovative, rapidly changing area of practice with a university culture reflected in complex and firmly established norms and structures founded on traditional institutional touchstones of quality—and doing so in ways that release online learning's positive "force" rather than its "darkside" [28], its "promise" rather than its "threat" [41].

Faced with this challenge, institutions are finding that introducing online learning into the academy does not simply represent one more way to deliver instruction; rather, the introduction of online learning into higher education is at least on some levels transformative rather than additive. What, exactly, is being—or should be—transformed, is still the subject of often-heated debate. However, it is clear that the effectiveness with which institutions manage this debate and subsequent change, particularly in relation to their faculty, will be a major determinate of the ultimate success of online higher education.

Realizing that the idea and reality of organizational change management is not only exceptionally complex but also variously understood, I will try here to give merely a brief introduction to some of the key issues at the intersection of faculty satisfaction and change management.

A number of questions related to faculty satisfaction with online teaching are relevant to this issue. For example, will (or should) institutional change

Incrementally or fundamentally change faculty roles and responsibilities?

Be legitimate (i.e., congruent with the institutional mission) or illegitimate? [43]

Be gradual or revolutionary?

Be initiated and managed from the top down or the bottom up?

However, arguably the most important question, the answer to which may determine the ultimate benefit of any of these changes, is "Who gets to decide on the questions and who provides the answers?" That is, "Who *is* the 'top' and who the 'bottom'?"

This last question is being asked and will need to be answered in the context of the competing subcultures—particularly those of the faculty and the administration—that make up a university community. Although to those on the outside the university community might look relatively unified, the concept of institutional subcultures is not unfamiliar to students of and actors in the higher education context. Well before the current issue of technology-based teaching and learning appeared in this context, Adams [44, (15-16)] discussed the subcultures of the university in terms of "academic tribes," focusing particularly on the faculty and the administration and on these tribes' differing views on university governance. Specifically he posited two sets of "antinomies," contradictory yet true principles or laws related to university culture as perceived by those in these two subcultures:

"Antinomy the first: The faculty is the university; the faculty are the employees of the university." (That is, idea that the faculty is the "top" as opposed to the belief that the faculty is the "bottom.")

"Antinomy the Second: The administration is the master of the faculty; the administration is the servant of the faculty. (That is, the idea that the administration is the "top" as opposed to the idea that the administration is the "bottom.")

Although Adams' antinomies were intentionally presented as extreme views seldom (thankfully) seen in their pure form, they are yet clearly recognizable and familiar to those who currently inhabit higher education territory. And, over twenty-five years later, these cultural antinomies are being played out around the institutional change represented by the introduction of online teaching and learning into the academy. As Twigg [21] noted recently in a Pew Learning and Technology report,

> Discussion about…distance education is taking place amid tremendous turmoil on our campuses, is a result of the changing nature of higher education. Faculty and administrators are locking horns over organizational issues such as part-time faculty, governance, and commercialization (8).

This observation supports Feenberg's [41] view that "the distance learning debate polarizes around two hostile positions that usually correspond to the different roles of administration and faculty" (3) and Noblitt's [26] somewhat more understated suggestion that "the dialogue between faculty and administration concerning the use of information technology for teaching and research is not always civil" (1).

Within the university, the faculty and administrative subcultures often exhibit different assumptions, beliefs, and values that seem valid to their own members, but often not to members of the other subculture. This lack of coherence across cultures can become a barrier to successful change management. As Bunn [33] notes, "In recent years, the organizational behavior literature showed that organizations fail to learn or to diffuse innovations because of competing subcultures" (64-65). In the case of the introduction of online teaching and learning, inter-group differences in assumptions and perceptions can result in tensions and conflicts that compromise faculty satisfaction and, ultimately, inhibit the success of the online teaching and learning enterprise.

The conflict and incivility noted above results not only from the change represented by the introduction of an innovation, but also from a perceived change in how things are decided within the university. Faculty and administrative observers of the higher education environment tend to comment on the situation in different terms, as could be expected in light of the antinomies presented above. In general, faculty commentators *decry* while administrators *argue for* a shift from an emphasis on faculty control to greater administrative control, a shift that has been and continues to be accelerated in the current "digitized" higher education environment. Newson, for example, characterizes this shift as an "inversion" of leadership roles, with "more and more policy…formulated in and by the expanded and increasingly professional/executive offices of senior administrators, with the faculty bodies acting as ratifiers, rather than originators of these policies" (cited in [23 (18)] Allen and Fifield [45] suggest that "any restructuring of the organization is likely to be viewed as an encroachment" by faculty, who do not recognize "managerial hierarchies" (14). Administrators, however, tend to see themselves and their peers as the logical "decision makers," and the faculty as the recipients and implementers of those decisions.

At least as significant as the cultural conflict over governance is faculty concern over perceived changes in values and goals. As Prebble [46] points out, in dual mode institutions online programming forces an uneasy alliance between an academic culture that emphasizes the intrinsic value of a broad, "higher," education and an industrial/bureaucratic culture that emphasizes efficiency, market responsiveness, and "bottom-line" profitability [47].

Some faculty members, alarmed by what they view as an imposition of corporate/bureaucratic values into the academic arena, have drawn back from the fray, choosing passive resistance over active engagement, through non-participation in online teaching and learning. However, such non-participation is counter-productive since it not only ignores the potential benefit and inevitability of *some* change, but ultimately allows the direction and extent of that change to be determined by the institution's non-faculty leaders. Werry [37] sees "withdrawal from the sphere of online education" as a less-responsible alternative to taking control of change, to engaging in "ways of contesting and reconfiguring online education that are more amenable to the interests of academics" (12). Feenberg [41] concurs, noting that realizing "the ideal of educational community to which faculty are attached by their culture and traditions" (3) in the online environment depends on faculty moving "beyond defensive contempt for this significant education innovation" (7) to an acceptance of responsibility for shaping distance teaching and learning.

Others cast the resolution of this conflict in broader terms, seeing the issue not as that of protecting the rights, privileges, and/or responsibilities of one internal subculture against another, but rather as that of protecting the future of the non-profit higher education enterprise itself. From this perspective, the best aspects of traditional academic culture offer institutions not only an objective good in themselves, but also a competitive advantage in the marketplace [45]. However, in an increasingly competitive environment this advantage cannot be realized without a creative melding of an institution's academic traditions with an appropriate level of attention to its place in that market [48]. From this perspective, one result of a decision by faculty to opt out in the hope of protecting the purity of academic values from "crass commercialization" will be to rob the university of strategic input in the face of threats from a for-profit sector with often quite different values and goals.

Given the inherent complexities of this situation, what principles will maximize the chances for successful change management, particularly in terms of faculty satisfaction? The literature offers several general suggestions that reflect a belief that change will be successful only in a context of mutual understanding and shared responsibility.

First, both faculty and administration must become better at recognizing the legitimate concerns and needs of the "other" subculture. This recognition must be reflected first and foremost in the rhetoric surrounding the change process. Kusmierek [49] notes a paradox: "Change depends on rhetoric, but rhetoric makes change less likely" (7). In the case of online higher education, neither the "revolutionary fervor" that causes administrators to view faculty members as obstructions to progress nor faculty references to administrative creation of "electronic sweatshops" [37] reflect the cross-cultural understanding necessary to support effective institutional change.

What logically follows from increased mutual understanding will be recognition of the importance of focused and ongoing dialogue between and among all change stakeholders, but most particularly between mixed groups of administrators and faculty. As Noblitt [26] points out, intra-group dialogue alone will do nothing more than confirm already-held perspectives: "Stratified discussions...only serve to harden rehearsed positions and create converts to the legions of the chronically aggrieved" (6). Werry [37] further suggests the need to develop a rhetoric of online education with shared criteria and meanings as the basis for dialogue and decision making.

Finally, higher education institutions must use institutional planning and policy development to create first their unique visions for change and then policy/procedure frameworks to support it. As Olcott [50] argues, institutions need to develop and sustain an environment that reflects "a mutual commitment to an education process that is driven by quality, access, integrity, responsiveness and the central role of faculty" (p. 27). Of particular concern to the faculty will be plans that reflect critical examination of the effects of change and policies that address concerns about professional rewards and core educational and pedagogical values. Ensuring that plans and policies are indeed *mutually* beneficial and sustainable will depend on ongoing faculty involvement and leadership in change planning and implementation [13].

IV. PROMISING DIRECTIONS FOR PRACTICE

Recognizing the importance of a committed faculty to fulfilling the promise of online teaching and learning, higher education institutions are implementing innovative practices to enhance faculty satisfaction. Similarly, professional organizations and other communities of practice have developed guidelines and recommendations related to faculty support. Following is a representative review of some promising trends and effective practices in this area. More complete descriptions of most of these and other practices related to faculty satisfaction are available on the Sloan-C Effective Practices site at http://www.sloan-c.org/effective/index.asp.

A. Comprehensive Faculty Support

Some institutions have committed high levels of centralized support to faculty who design for and/or teach in the online environment. This approach ensures equitable support and consistency of services.

The SUNY Learning Network (SLN), for example, developed a research-based, scalable faculty development and course design process. The four stages in the faculty development process are "Get connected and online;" "Conceptualize your course;" Develop your course;" and "Pilot your course." Elements of the process include an online faculty resource and information gateway; asynchronous conference for course developers; asynchronous faculty orientation; workshops for new faculty; instructional design sessions for continuing faculty; comprehensive course developer's handbook; course template; faculty help desk; opportunities to evaluate SLN services; and assigned instructional design partner [51].

The Monroe Model, developed at Monroe Community College (part of the SUNY Learning Network), combines centralized the SLN support described above with a campus-based resource for faculty teaching online. This framework provides immediate on-site guidance and customized support in six areas: academic support, training, instructional design, library support, technical support, and student services. The approach is "team based, collaborative, comprehensive, action-oriented and non-hierarchical" [52].

The University of Washington's Catalyst web site is part of a multi-dimensional faculty and student support service that includes elements such as a workshop series, custom workshops for academic departments, face-to-face consultation services, and outreach activities. The Catalyst site increases faculty satisfaction by taking the "mystery" out of online teaching through the provision of tools, guidance, and resources needed to develop, deliver, and evaluate online courses [53].

Boise State University has developed a "graduated model" of faculty development that extends over three to five semesters. Within this model, teams of faculty members learn the skills they need to develop and teach online through collaboration on the development of a targeted general education course. Participants move from training to practice to full development and delivery of online courses. Additional program support elements that contribute to faculty satisfaction include incentive stipends of $3500 to $5500 per team member; technical support, including a student technology assistant; a laptop computer; and formal recognition from the University and expression of appreciation from the provost [54].

B. Peer Review of Courses and Teaching

Initial faculty unfamiliarity with online learning and/or resistance to the institutional adoption of online initiatives has sometimes meant that administrators, rather than faculty, develop and implement quality standards for online programs. Recognizing both the need for such standards and legitimate faculty concerns related to oversight, some institutions and professional communities of practice are extending the traditional peer review process to online courses and programs.

The MERLOT peer review process for evaluating teaching-learning materials consists of a national network of online discipline communities. Within each discipline, faculty expert reviewers have formed panels that select and evaluate the learning materials. Each panel develops professional standards for online materials; engages in peer review processes similar to those used for scholarly works; and provides a mechanism to validate and share high-quality work. This project offers two benefits related to faculty satisfaction: having their online work viewed as serious scholarship and having a source for high-quality online materials and resources that meet quality standards of their disciplines [55].

An important component of the Web Initiative in Teaching (WIT) program of the University System of Maryland is the process of peer review. This element of the initiative was implemented to address three prevalent concerns related to teaching in the online environment: recognition in promotion and tenure decisions for faculty who develop and teach online courses; promotion of the concept of a scholarship of online teaching; and increasing awareness among skeptical faculty of the nature and potential high quality of web-based learning. The peer review model calls for both internal and external peer review of technical and content aspects of the course. Reviewers, who are selected by a course team, focus their initial review on course goals, navigation, and adequacy of orientation to learning approach and roles. A mid-course review focuses on dynamic interactivity, and the end-of-course review targets the overall design and delivery of the course. The WIT peer review process is an effective tool for increasing program quality; it also contributes significantly to faculty satisfaction by providing a basis for formal academic recognition and peer validation of scholarship [56].

C. Institutional Support for Innovation

Faculty commitment and satisfaction are enhanced by institutional support for innovation. Some universities have implemented large-scale intra-institutional grant programs that signal institutional support not just for the idea of online learning, but, more importantly, support for their own faculty in the development and delivery high-quality online programs and resources. A good example of such programs is that developed by North Carolina State University.

NCSU has implemented the DELTA (Distance Education and Learning Technology Applications) RFP Program to support faculty innovation in online teaching and learning. This competitive program is intended to empower faculty to meet the challenges of and shape the new online environment. Financial grants support faculty in the planning, design, and development of distance education programs, and allow them to realize the personal and professional rewards inherent in forwarding educational transformation at their institution. This program contributes to faculty satisfaction by ensuring that the growth and innovation of distance education programs remains appropriately in the hands of the faculty [57].

D. Revision of Institutional Reward Structures

Traditionally, institutional-rewards decisions have focused on faculty members' research scholarship. Some institutions are beginning to re-examine and expand their approach to more adequately reward scholarship related to teaching and service. Specifically, they are recognizing the possibilities and opportunities offered by new online environments and are developing approaches for including scholarly work related to online programming in the faculty review process.

Indiana University-Purdue University/Indianapolis (IUPUI) recognizes that learning to use and teach with technology is a major time commitment for faculty members who have multiple, high priority demands on their time. It is clear from the literature that for many faculty members, teaching online becomes a low priority if institutional reward systems recognize, value, and reward other activities more highly. IUPUI signals the value of online teaching and related scholarship in several ways. High-level administrators model institutional expectations by teaching occasional technology based classes. Promotion and tenure decisions are based on scholarship, and currently about half such decisions are based on teaching and service scholarship, often related to technology. As Boschmann [58] notes, when the reward system recognizes faculty members with promotion, tenure, sabbatical, salary increases, and release time for technology-focused scholarship, then improved faculty satisfaction naturally follows.

Penn State University has developed the UniSCOPE (University Scholarship and Criteria for Outreach and Performance Evaluation) model for evaluating and recognizing multiple forms of teaching, research, and service scholarship and has formally implemented it into the university's multi-tiered promotion and tenure review process [59]. Although not focused exclusively on online teaching, this practice will have a major impact by removing a potent barrier to participation as well as providing a formal structure for rewarding it.

E. Ongoing Research Related to the Faculty Experience

To date, much of the information about the faculty experience in online teaching has been anecdotal and situation specific. Some institutions are conducting or supporting cross-discipline studies of the faculty experience to identify commonalities, establish guidelines for practice, and provide the basis for informed planning and decision making.

Penn State's World Campus has initiated a Faculty Self-Study Grant Program. Through an intra-university RFP process, the World Campus identifies faculty members to study particular aspects of the faculty experience in the online teaching-learning environment. The focus of the studies awarded funding for the 2002-2003 academic year is comparative workload between resident and online teaching environment and the impact of workload in this new environment on faculty members' other professional responsibilities. These modest grants ($4000-5000) offer faculty members opportunities not only for the research and publication important to professional advancement, but also for contributing to the very sparse research and knowledge base in this area [60].

The Greater Detroit Area Partnership for Training (GDAPFT) is a regional interdisciplinary educational program to prepare nurse practitioners. Believing that a clear understanding of the faculty experience is necessary to foster satisfaction and long-term commitment to online teaching, GDAPFT is using research as the basis for development and ongoing enhancement of faculty performance and support standards. Faculty concerns including workload, quality issues, intellectual property issues, student assessment, and training for online teaching were identified through an initial faculty satisfaction survey. The results of the survey were then used to guide development of a faculty support and development program that includes one-on-one training, instructional design support, workshops, improvements to library services, rewards for increased workload, interdisciplinary collaboration, sharing of course content and best practices, and incentives to use support services. Future research will be used to guide new support strategies. GDAPFT's commitment to ongoing research is paying off in more faculty members agreeing to teach online and a resultant expansion of programming [61].

F. Guidelines and Norms of Practice

Many institutions and faculty members are new to online programming and are uncertain about what constitutes good practice in this environment. Guidelines that identify necessary elements of good online teaching or that provide benchmarks for instructional effectiveness are a useful support for faculty in this new environment and thus contribute to satisfaction.

The Indiana Partnership for Statewide Education has developed a set of guiding principles that define good practice and offer clear benchmarks specifically from the faculty perspective in the areas of instructional performance and institutional support. Specific faculty elements include course design; assessment of student outcomes; faculty development; course evaluation; copyright issues; ownership of course materials; and delivery methods. The types and levels of support for which the institution is responsible are also delineated, and additional resource links are provided [62].

An additional set of guidelines for institutions that focuses specifically on faculty issues is provided in the report recently released by the Distance Learning Policy Laboratory of the Southern Region Education Board (SREB). "Supporting Faculty in the Use of Technology: A Guide to Principles, Policies, and Implementation Strategies" [39] lists three broad goals:

To use technology to improve the effectiveness of the teaching and learning process;

To support new roles for faculty in an e-learning environment and to develop appropriate compensation and incentive structures for those new roles; and

To establish equitable policies that allow widespread access to information resources while sustaining the traditional rights of content owners to their intellectual property.

The report offers ten recommendations that provide the basis for policy development related to faculty issues in online teaching and learning. It also includes a useful appendix of "illustrative practices" in various areas of faculty support.

V. CONCLUSIONS

A wide variety of factors contribute to faculty satisfaction in the online teaching-learning environment. Because a growing and committed group of faculty members is crucial to the success of online higher education, institutions need to understand these factors and address them in their policies and practices. Successful change—that is, change that is both widely beneficial and widely supported by the multiple stakeholders in the academic enterprise—will depend not only on successfully targeting areas for change, but also on implementing changes in a respectful, participatory manner.

VI. REFERENCES

1. **Frederickson, E., A. Pickett, K. Swan, W. Pelz, and P. Shea.** Factors Influencing Faculty Satisfaction with Asynchronous Teaching and Learning in the SUNY Learning Network. Sloan-C, Needham, MA, 2000.

2. **National Education Association.** A Survey of Traditional and Distance Learning Higher Education Members. Washington: NEA, 2000.

3. **Hartman, J., and B. Truman-Davis.** Factors Relating to the Satisfaction of Faculty Teaching Online Courses at the University of Central Florida. In *Online Education Volume 2: Learning Effectiveness, Faculty Satisfaction, and Cost Effectiveness*, Sloan-C, Needham, MA, 109-128, 2001.

4. **Thompson, M.** Faculty Satisfaction in Penn State's World Campus. In *Online Education Volume 2: Learning Effectiveness, Faculty Satisfaction, and Cost Effectiveness,* Sloan-C, Needham, MA, 129-144, 2001.

5. **National Education Association.** Focus on Distance Education. Update 7(2), (March 2001).

6. **Kashy, E., M. Thoennessen, G. Albertelli, and Y. Tsai.** Implementing a Large On-Campus ALN: Faculty Perspective. *JALN* 4(3), (September 2000) http://www.sloan-c.org/publications/jaln/v4n3/v4n3_kashy.asp

7. **Smith, L.** Faculty Satisfaction in LEEP: A Web-based Graduate Degree Program in Library and Information Science. In *Online Education Volume 2: Learning Effectiveness, Faculty Satisfaction, and Cost Effectiveness,* Sloan-C, Needham, MA, 87-108, 2001.

8. **Hartman, J., C. Dziuban, and P. Moskal.** Faculty Satisfaction in ALNs: A Dependent or Independent Variable. *JALN* 4(3), (September 2000). http://www.sloan-c.org/publications/jaln/v4n3/v4n3_hartman.asp

9. **Rockwell, S.K., J. Schauer, S. Fritz, S. Marx.** Incentives and Obstacles Influencing Higher Education Faculty and Administrators to Teach. *Online Journal of Distance Learning Administration,* 3(4), (Winter 1999). http://www.westga.edu/~distance/rockwell24.html

10. **Hislop, G., and M. Atwood.** ALN Teaching as Routine Faculty Workload. *JALN* 4(3), (September 2000) http://www.sloan-c.org/publications/jaln/v4n3/v4n3_hislop.asp

11. **Husman, D., and M. Miller.** Improving Distance Education: Perceptions of Program Administrators. *Online Journal of Distance Learning Administration,* 4(3), (Fall 2001). http://www.westga.edu/~distance/ojdla/fall43/husmann43.html

12. **Chizmar, J., and D. Williams.** What Do Faculty Want? *Educause Quarterly,* Number 1: 18-24, 2001.

13. **Bower, B.** Distance Education: Facing the Faculty Challenge. *Online Journal of Distance Learning Administration,* 4(2) (Summer 2001). http://www.westga.edu/~distance/ojdla/summer42/bower42.htm

14. **DiBiase, D.** Is Distance Teaching More Work or Less Work? *The American Journal of Distance Education,* 14(3):6-20 (Fall 2000).

15. **Clay, M.** Development of Training and Support Programs for Distance Education Instructors. *Online Journal of Distance Learning Administration,* 2(3) (Fall 1999). http://www.westga.edu/~distance/clay23.html

16. **Schifter, C.** Perception Differences about Participating in Distance Education. *Online Journal of Distance Learning Administration,* 5(1) (Spring 2002). http://www.westga.edu/~distance/ojdla/spring51/schifter51.html

17. **Betts, K.** An Institutional Overview: Factors Influencing Faculty Participation in Distance Education in Postsecondary Education in the United States: An Institutional Study. *Online Journal of Distance Learning Administration,* 1(3) (Fall 1998). http://www.westga.edu/~distance/Betts13.html

18. **Wolcott, L.** Tenure, Promotion, and Distance Education: Examining the Culture of Faculty Rewards. *The American Journal of Distance Education,* 11(2): 3-18 (Summer 1997)

19. **American Council on Education.** Developing a Distance Education Policy for 21st Century Learning. Washington: Division of Government and Public Affairs, ACE. http://www.acenet.edu/Washington/distance_ed/2000/03march/distance_ed.html

20. **Ubell, R.** Who Owns What? Unbundling Web Course Property Rights. *Educause Quarterly,* No. 1 (2001).

21. **Twigg, C.** *Quality Assurance for Whom?* Troy, NY: Center for Academic Transformation, Rensselaer Polytechnic Institute, 2001.

22. **Eaton, J.** *Core Academic Values, Quality, and Regional Accreditation: The Challenge of Distance Learning.* CHEA Monograph Series. Washington, DC: Council for Higher Education Accreditation.

23. **Teaching at an Internet Distance:** The Pedagogy of Online Teaching and Learning. The Report of a 1998-1999 University of Illinois Faculty Seminar. Champaign, IL: University of Illinois, 1999.

24. **Bass, R.** The Scholarship of Teaching: What's the Problem? *Inventio* 1(1), February 1999. http://www.doit.gmu.edu/Archives/feb98/works_cited.htm

25. **Jaffee, D.** Institutionalized resistance to asynchronous learning networks. JALN 2(2) (September 1998) http://www.sloan-c.org/publications/jaln/v2n2/v2n2_jaffee.asp

26. **Noblitt, J.** Making Ends Meet: A Faculty Perspective on Computing and Scholarship. *Educom Review,* 32(3), (May/June 1997). http://www.educause.edu/pub/er/review/reviewArticles/32338.html

27. **Kezar, A**. Higher Education Trends (1997-1999). Policy and governance. ERIC Clearinghouse on Higher Education (n.d.) http://www.eriche.org/trends/policy.html

28. **Turoff, M.** Alternative Futures for Distance Learning: The Force and the Darkside. http://www.westga.edu/~distance/turoff11.html

29. **Irani, T. and Telg, R.** Building It So They Will Come: Assessing Universities' Distance Education Faculty Training and Development Programs. *Journal of Distance Education* 17(1): 36-46 (Spring 2002).

30. **Lynch, D.** Professors Should Embrace Technology in Courses. The Chronicle of Higher Education, in the issue dated January 18, 2002.

31. **Gellman-Danley, B., and M. Fetzner.** Asking the Really Tough Questions: Policy Issues for Distance Learning. *Online Journal of Distance Learning Administration,* 1(3), (Spring 1998). http://www.westga.edu/~distance/danley11.html

32. **King, J., G. Nugent, E. Russell, J. Eich, and D. Lacy.** Policy Frameworks for Distance Education: Implications for Decision Makers. *Online Journal of Distance Learning Administration,* 3(2), (Spring 2000). http://www.westga.edu/~distance/King32.html

33. **Bunn, M.** Timeless and Timely Issues in Distance Education Planning. *The American Journal of Distance Education,* 15(1): 55-68.

34. **American Association of University Professors.** Suggestions and Guidelines: Sample Language for Institutional Policies and Contract Language. http://www.aaup.org/Issues/DistanceEd/Archives/speccmt/ipguide.htm

35. **Faculty Workload and Compensation:** Key Insights. *Distance Education Report* 6(13): 5, (July 2002).

36. **Schifter, C.** Compensation Models in Distance Education. *Online Journal of Distance Learning Administration,* 3(1), (Spring 2000). http://www.westga.edu/~distance/schifter31.html

37. **Werry, C.** The Work of Education in the Age of E-College. *First Monday* 6(5). http://firstmonday.org/issues/issue6_5/werry/index.html

38. **Twigg, C.** *Who Owns Online Courses and Course Materials? Intellectual Property Policies for a New Learning Environment.* Troy, NY: Center for Academic Transformation, Rensselaer Polytechnic Institute, 2000. http://www.center.rpi.edu/PewSym/mono2.html

39. Southern Regional Education Board. *Supporting Faculty in the Use of Technology: A Guide to Principles, Policies, and Implementation Strategies.* SREB, 2001.

40. Gerber, L. "Inextricably Linked": Shared Governance and Academic Freedom. *Academe,* May/June, 2001. http://www.aaup.org/publications/Academe/01mj/mj01gerb.htm.

41. **Feenberg, A.** Distance Learning: Promise or Threat? 1999.
http://www-rohan.sdsu.edu/faculty/feenberg/index.html

42. **Brabazon, T.** Internet Teaching and the Administration of Knowledge. *First Monday,* 6(6), (June 2001). http://www.firstmonday.dk/issues/issue6_6/brabazon/

43. **Kraatz, M. and Zajac, E.** Exploring the Limits of the New Institutionalism: The Causes and Consequences of Illegitimate Organizational Change. *American Sociological Review,* 61:812-836 (October 1996).

44. **Adams, H.** *The Academic Tribes.* Urbana and Chicago: University of Illinois Press, 1976.

45. **Allen, D. & Fifield, N.** Re-Engineering Change in Higher Education. *Information Research,* 4(3), (February 1999). http://www.informationr.net/ir/4-3/paper56.html

46. **Prebble, T.** Holding the Decision Makers Accountable: Relocating the Locus of Financial Accountability within a Dual-Mode Institution. In Indira Gandhi National Open University, *Structure and Management of Open Learning Systems.* Proceedings of the Eighth Annual Conference of the Asian Association of Open Universities, New Delhi, February 20-22, 1995. Vol. 1, pp. 1-7. http://www.globaldistancelearning.com/Management/Operations/bud-01.html

47. **Tait, A.** The Convergence of Distance and Conventional Education. In: A. Tait and R. Mills (eds.) *The Convergence of Distance & Traditional Education,* pp. 141-160. New York: Routledge. (1999)

48. **Knight Higher Education Collaborative.** Inside Out. *Policy Perspectives* 10(1), (March 2001). http://www.irhe.upenn.edu/cgi-bin/cat.pl

49. **Kusmierek, K.** Understanding and Addressing Resistance to Organizational Change. Ann Arbor, MI: Managing Institutional Change and Transformation Project Center, University of Michigan, (2001).
http://www-personal.umich.edu/~marvp/facultynetwork/whitepapers/kusmierekresistance.html

50. **Olcott, D.** Aligning Distance Education Practice and Academic Policy: A Framework for Institutional Change. Continuing Higher Education Review, 60(1): 27-41 (Spring 1996).

51. **Pickett, A.** Faculty Development Process.
http://www.sloan-c.org/effective/SortByFacultySat.asp

52. **Fetzner, M.** Online Support for Online Faculty: The Monroe Model.
http://www.sloan-c.org/effective/SortByFacultySat.asp

53. **Thompson, M.** Online Faculty Guide to Distance Teaching.
http://www.sloan-c.org/effective/SortByFacultySat.asp

54. **Hambleton, B.** CoreOnline@Boise State Project.
http://www.sloan-c.org/effective/SortByFacultySat.asp

55. **Thompson, M.** Peer Review of Online Teaching-Learning Materials.
http://www.sloan-c.org/effective/SortByFacultySat.asp

56. **Braha, H.** Challenge of Peer Review. Presentation at the 7th Annual Sloan-C International Conference on Asynchronous Learning Networks, Orlando, FL, November, 2001.

57. **Thompson, M.** North Carolina State University Distance Education and Learning Technology Applications (DELTA) RFP Program. http://www.sloan-c.org/effective/SortByFacultySat.asp

58. **Boschmann, E.** Including Technology Scholarship in the Faculty Reward Structure.
http://www.sloan-c.org/effective/SortByFacultySat.asp

59. **Thompson, M.** Faculty Self-Study Grant Program.
http://www.sloan-c.org/effective/SortByFacultySat.asp

60. **Thompson, M.** Multidimensional Model for Review of Scholarly Activity.
http://www.sloan-c.org/effective/SortByFacultySat.asp

61. **Thompson, M.** Analysis of faculty experience and initial identification of standards of excellence. http://www.sloan-c.org/effective/SortByFacultySat.asp
62. **Indiana Partnership for Statewide Education.** Guiding Principles for Faculty in Distance Learning, 2001. http://www.ihets.org/learntech/facprinc.html

VII. ABOUT THE AUTHOR

Melody M. Thompson is assistant professor of education and Director of Quality and Planning for Penn State's World Campus. Her primary responsibilities include strategic planning, policy development, process improvement, and research coordination for the World Campus. She has designed and taught graduate courses in the Penn State Adult Education Program, including Introduction to Adult Education, Course Design in Distance Education, and Women and Minorities in Adult Education. Her current research interests focus on institutional policy related to distance education and the faculty experience in the online environment. Prior to her role with the World Campus, she was the publications editor of the American Center for the Study of Distance Education (ACSDE) and the editor of DEOS (Distance Education Online Symposium). She has written a number of peer-reviewed articles and several book chapters about distance education; with Alan Chute and Burton Hancock she co-authored the 1997 *McGraw-Hill Handbook of Distance Education*. She has served as book review editor for *The American Journal of Distance Education* and currently serves as the Sloan-C Effective Practices editor for faculty satisfaction and on the editorial board of *JALN* (Journal of Asynchronous Learning Networks). She received her B.A. degree in English from Bryn Mawr College and her M.Ed. and D.Ed. degrees in Adult Education from Penn State University.

THE IUPUI STORY OF CHANGE

Erwin Boschmann
Indiana University Purdue University Indianapolis

- Technology promises transformative challenges for faculty and administration.

- Faculty are generally motivated by intellectual challenge and by reward structures

- At IUPUI, the Promotion and Tenure Review Form is available to committee members on paper or as a secure Web site, and includes spaces for judging:
    - External peer evaluation of materials
    - Mentee/alumni comments
    - Effective use of technology
    - Student outcome results
    - Plans for future teaching effectiveness

- Four principles are generalizable to ensure faculty satisfaction in various contexts: strong advocacy; ongoing policy and training updates; faculty involvement; and faculty support.

I. INTRODUCTION

What drives most faculty? They are generally propelled by two motivations: intellectual challenge and the reward structure. If these are attended to, faculty will stay, be productive, and be happy. An article in The Chronicle of Higher Education, "Ever So Slowly, Colleges Start to Count Work With Technology in Tenure Decisions" [1], indicates that accepting technology in promotion and tenure decisions is a growing movement that includes peer review of Web sites and online teaching materials. IUPUI (Indiana University Purdue University Indianapolis) has promoted and tenured some professors primarily on their scholarship of technology, and IUPUI has made an increasing number of positive decisions about the use of technology as one of several emerging forms of scholarship. IUPUI is a national success story of an urban campus excelling in many areas, one of which is the general satisfaction of its faculty. One reason for that satisfaction, namely the successful infusion of information technology (IT) into the fabric of IUPUI, is the topic of this paper. The story begins in 1987; first, here is some evidence of faculty satisfaction.

II. SURVEYS

IUPUI conducts a bi-annual survey of faculty life on campus, and the surveys show that collegiality, quality of life at work, the work environment, technology access, technology support and technology training are positive, and are increasing among faculty.

Specifically, the 1994 survey indicates that the instructional use of software, simulations, e-mail, multi media, and CD-ROMs were already in use, and faculty indicated that they would like to use more of these in the near future. The table below shows the faculty's desire to acquire new skills.

1994 Faculty Survey

Instructional Use	Now Use	Would like to use
Software	21.4%	12.6%
Simulations	7.6%	17.8%
E-Mail	7.0%	13.1%
Multi media	6.5%	12.2%
CD-ROMs	2.8%	12.0%

The 1996 survey indicated that faculty morale, as measured by leadership in the department, job satisfaction, and competence of colleagues, was 47.4%, compared to 39.6% at Carnegie Research I institutions nationwide.

The 1998 survey indicated that IT use steadily increased from 1994 through 1998; e-mail from 7% to 35%; multimedia from 7% to 22%; and internet use from 3% to 23%. National data gathered annually by Kenneth C. Green [2] mirror the IUPUI findings.

1998 Faculty Survey

IT use	'94	'96	'98

214

E-mail	7%	17%	35%
Multimedia	7%	12%	22%
Internet	3%	17%	23%

The 2000 survey produced these results in faculty satisfaction with technology access (82%), with support (68%), and with training (57%). 73% of the faculty were satisfied or very satisfied with the availability of IT equipment in the classroom; 69% were satisfied with its quality. Faculty also indicated their definite plan to increase active learning, and they displayed a positive change in attitude toward campus IT presence. This latter item is likely a reflection of the life cycle for funding that the institution implemented.

Finally, the 2002 survey indicates continued growth in the use of Oncourse, the IUPUI course management system (CMS). The numbers of active courses, by year, are: 1999: 200; 2000: 610; 2001: 1254; and 2002: 1767. Furthermore, students' reported learning gains in use of technology are slightly better than those reported in the National Survey of Student Engagement. The same is true for the use of technology to complete assignments and to communicate with the instructor. Results measuring faculty satisfaction with technology for teaching activities were: 50%, 60%, and 71%, for 1998, 2000, and 2002. Results measuring faculty satisfaction with technology for student classroom use were: 41%, 48%, and 61%, for the same years.

III. CONSEQUENCES OF SATISFIED FACULTY

A satisfied faculty is a more stable faculty. At IUPUI there is a high level of collegiality among the faculty, which has become a primary reason why faculty do stay. Well over 80 percent of the faculty indicate that the main reason they continue to stay at IUPUI is the collegiality they sense among colleagues with whom they work every day. Another aspect leading directly to a satisfied faculty is consistent, long-term leadership at the top. IUPUI's Chancellor and the Dean of the Faculties have been leading the institution for some 16 years. When the University President saw the very positive third 5-year review of the Chancellor, he commented: "Everyone ought to see a good report like this once in a lifetime." [The chancellor, who has announced his retirement, was recently asked by the trustees to become the Interim President of Indiana University.]

IUPUI's annual faculty loss to other institutions is relatively light. IUPUI's 'balance of trade' shows very positive numbers between those faculty who leave, and those who come from other institutions. For instance, during the year 2000, thirteen colleagues left to go to places like the University of Michigan, Texas A&M, Rutger's University, Duke University, Vanderbilt, and others. However, 35 faculty members were recruited from institutions like University of Pittsburgh, University of Connecticut, California State University, University of North Carolina, University of Cincinnati, Cornell University, University of Southern California, University of Kansas, University of Florida, and the University of Texas, among others.

However, a most interesting phenomenon that has taken place is a shift in promotion and tenure decisions. In 1988 the percentage of positive promotion and tenure decisions based on excellence in teaching/service was 35, while that for research was 65. (The total number of faculty being considered each year varies between 80 and 120.) Nine years later, in 1996 these numbers had essential reversed to 62 percent promoted on excellence in teaching/service, and 38 percent on excellence in research. The years since then have stabilized at about fifty percent for each. What has happened? First and foremost, the campus understands that faculty are promoted on the scholarship of teaching, service, or research, and that scholarship is to be interpreted in an ever-changing manner. (About 20% of the faculty are promoted on excellence in two areas.) This emphasis will be treated throughout this paper.

IV. BEGINNING IN 1987

A new leadership team, installed in 1987, produced a development plan for IUPUI in early 1988. The plan and the fact that the same leadership team is still in place (with great faculty approval) are reasons for the high faculty satisfaction on the IUPUI campus, despite the fact that IUPUI has undergone more changes than perhaps most other places. Faculty don't like change, but this is a story of change that has brought the faculty along, and at the same time has developed a very positive faculty/administration relationship.

Prior to 1987, promotion and tenure decisions in teaching were based on student evaluations, courses taught, teaching awards, letters from colleagues, offices held, workshops attended, and talks given. Then a new plan was written, and was soon billed as "innovative, far-seeing, and experimental." It asked "Can students receive more individual attention through technology?" And it claimed that "computers match the learning styles … where students, faculty, and learning resources are not always in the same place at the same time." The plan announced that IUPUI expected to be at the forefront of learning in the electronic age.

In a bold leap, the plan envisioned that "the library will become a learning center where students, faculty and citizens gain access not only to materials, but to each other. This concept of learning community will guide the creation of a new type of a library suitable for a new century."

> *Reform the environment; stop trying to reform the people. They will reform themselves if the environment is right.*
> *—Buckminster Fuller*

V. EXPECT CHANGES

Very quickly the faculty became used to the idea that the new leadership team did mean business, and that the business meant change. The Dean of the Faculties sent annual letters to the deans of the various schools announcing new expectations to be implemented in the promotion and tenure (P&T) process a year or two down the road. Topics brought to the attention of the campus using such letters have included:

- Post-tenure review
- Assessment
- Inclusion of librarians in P&T
- Inclusion of clinical faculty in P&T
- Peer review of teaching
- Mentorship of students through research participation, co-authorship of papers, and independent study
- Service learning

- Professional service
- Teaching with technology
- Teaching vs. student learning
- Economic development
- Increase student retention
- Collegiality
- Teaching awards, added to base.

Some specific examples of the Dean of Faculties' letters to the school deans follow.

Peer Review of Teaching (1998). "… students can evaluate the effectiveness of classroom teaching, and peers are most effective in evaluating other teaching activities, including learning outcomes. Most schools have effectively sought external evaluation of course design and materials as a part of their review of teaching accomplishments, especially when excellence in teaching is a basis for advancement. This type of evaluation may be especially helpful in considering materials prepared for use with the new technologies (e.g. internet, multimedia, videos, computer simulations, data bases, software) or in incorporating service learning as a part of courses."

Personal Statement (1998) ". . . the personal statement is an opportunity for reflection and integration. It is the one place where a candidate can speak directly to reviewers. The personal statement is very important and brevity is as appreciated as clarity."

Advising Students (1998): "Advising and student mentoring is a special form of teaching and faculty who have developed competency in advising or who have been actively involved in mentoring students should document this work and report it."

Teaching and Professional Service (2002). "Over the past several years, expectations for peer review of teaching and professional service – to match that expected for research – have been increasing. Some evidence of peer review is expected for all candidates, but it is required for those who intend to document excellence. While peer review need not be conducted in every course every semester, for example, there should be a systematic and continuing review of teaching by peers and appropriate teaching materials; results should be assessed by external peers when a case for excellence is being made."

Collegiality (2002). "Collegiality is not a criterion, but as a form of mutual respect, it is expected, and there are adequate statements in the 'Code of Academic Ethics' that set forth clear expectations. Collegiality has also been construed to cover the responsibility of faculty to engage in a satisfactory level of service to the university."

Thus, for instance, clinical faculty and librarians were now to be included in the faculty review process; and professional service meant service to students, to the institution, to the discipline or profession, and to the community. Soon after the Dean of the Faculties' letter, the Annual Report for faculty and librarians changed in appearance – as it has every year since then. The major change was its content in the teaching and service areas. These sections now contain three pages, whereas research has just one page. The new technology items included in the teaching section are:

- Nature of teaching: electronic interaction

- Publications: multimedia software, videos
- Revisions: learning technologies (interactive video, network communication)
- New Uses: technology to enhance student learning; increase teaching effectiveness

Prior to beginning of the P&T process, the campus committee is called into session for an extensive half-day orientation process devoted to topics such as professional service, the evolving nature of scholarship, the meaning of peer review, or scholarship of assessment.

For example, the Dean of the Faculties makes this statement:

> "Results of teaching, research, or professional service disseminated through electronic media are as valuable as results published in print media. The same care and concern for objective assessment should be observed when reviewing such electronic publications."

Thus, all review now includes software, multimedia presentations, films or videos; all aspects of electronic course design; and, of course, peer review, whether in print or electronic forms.

The P&T Review Form is made available to committee members either in paper form or as a secure Web site, and includes spaces for judging:

- External peer evaluation of materials
- Mentee/Alumni comments
- Effective use of technology
- Student outcome results
- Plans for future teaching effectiveness

As a special demonstration of the power of the re-interpretation of scholarship, IU held a conference in April, 2000 on "New Times, New Technology, New Scholarship: Evolving Faculty Rewards" [3]. Invited were Brian Copola, University of Michigan, and Randy Bass, Georgetown University, both of whom established tenure for themselves in very different ways by documenting their scholarship using the Web. Jack Wilson, former Dean of the Faculties of Rensselaer Polytechnic Institute, spoke from the evaluation side based on his experience with studio courses.

VI. ASSISTANCE TO FACULTY

There are many, many ways in which faculty are being assisted in their efforts to improve their teaching, especially with technology [4].

First, new faculty are invited to an all day orientation session during which the Chancellor and Dean of Faculties give brief talks, followed by a keynote address, lunch, open fair, and a series of academic workshops. Among the talks given are, for example:

"Twenty Survival Tips for New Faculty"

"An Agenda for the First 100 Days"

"Documenting Professional Development"

Second, the process of faculty evaluation, which years ago was secretive, is now open, with the faculty member being informed at every step as to the progress of the deliberations. In addition, good faculty documents are made public (with all the proper permissions) and occasional mock promotion and tenure sessions are held. These are held soon after the actual P&T process is finished, when about six of the committee members are asked to serve on the mock session. With proper permissions, three of the best P&T documents of that year are assembled, then three additional ones are prepared, all fictitious, but with many flaws seen that year in the P&T process. Some are borderline cases, and some would receive definite negative votes. All of these documents are then distributed to the participants with the instruction to read and evaluate. At the actual mock sessions the process is kept very much as in the actual meeting with a primary reader reporting, a secondary reader making additional comments, followed by an open discussion among the committee. After evaluating the pros and cons a vote is taken. Only after the vote is in, is the audience invited to address the committee with its questions. This is one of the most popular workshops, and it provides a good opportunity to talk about new requirements, and new views and interpretations of scholarship.

Third, every year the Dean of the Faculties, along with other administrators, holds a luncheon with newly tenured faculty members in small groups of perhaps five at a time. This is a good opportunity not only to congratulate faculty for achievements and invite the faculty to talk about their specific work, but it also is an opportunity to give the message that the future of the university lies in their hands. It is a way of telling the newly tenured faculty members that it is up to them to lead the university, to carry its image into the world, and to make sure they understand that the prestige of the institution rests on their shoulders.

Fourth, the Network for Excellence in Teaching, the oldest grant system at IUPUI, with a history of more than twenty-five years, has always adapted its emphasis to the current academic agendas. Thus, for a number of years each applicant had to demonstrate how the proposed work would enhance student learning through the use of technology.

Fifth, four centers have become essential in the work of the faculty. These are

Center for Teaching and Learning

Center for Service and Learning

Center for Research and Learning

Copyright Management Center

Sixth, IUPUI currently works on an e-Portfolio, an electronic template that enables students to demonstrate their work, and their improvement in learning, particularly in relation to the IUPUI Principles of Undergraduate Learning. There is a section where students can demonstrate who they are, not only as learners at IUPUI, but also as citizens, individuals and family members. Students can create multi-media presentations to demonstrate any aspect of their learning and their creativity. The e-Portfolio can be used to qualify for further courses, for independent study, for graduate school, or for a job. Faculty can thus easily determine the learning accomplishments of students, and thereby shape the learning environment in their classrooms.

Seventh, a great assistance to the faculty of all IU campuses is the creation and adoption of Oncourse, the IUPUI-created course management system. All eight campuses, 2621 courses, 3012 faculty, and 54,598 students employed Oncourse in the spring of 2002. For IUPUI a quarter of its courses use Oncourse, which translates into 79% of the students and 71% of the faculty.

One of the early lessons learned by the faculty is that time may be synchronous or asynchronous, located in the same or different places. The Web lends itself to all options.

Eighth, the campus has the oldest Teaching Learning Technology Roundtable, first initiated by Steve Gilbert of AAHE. Over the years IUPUI has learned to include many offices and brought together under one umbrella most aspects of IT in teaching and learning. For Fall 2002, IUPUI has instituted a series of talks to stimulate faculty thinking. For instance, the CEO of e.Lilly discussed the development of technological innovations intended to reshape basic and operational practices of Eli Lilly and Company. An EDUCAUSE officer discussed the research on student learning in the IT environment, and two former executives of Unext/Cardean University and U.S. Open University discussed reasons why ventures fail.

Ninth, several documents have been prepared for faculty to use. The Dean of the Faculties published an article entitled "Future Work: Faculty Time in the 21st Century" [5]. "Technology Success Stories" is a booklet featuring some 50 faculty members who make innovative use of IT tools. "General Policies" is a document prepared by an all-university committee on guidelines to follow. (Where does a distance education student belong? What tuition does a student pay? What about non-credit work?) And "Practical Tips" is a compendium of best practices on how to develop a Web-based course. It is abstracted from national organizations that have a DE component.

The "Toolkit" is a checklist for documenting and evaluating faculty scholarly activities in information technology. There are guidelines for faculty, departments, deans, and P&T committees to follow to successfully complete documents for promotion and tenure decisions. Thus, for faculty the "Toolkit" suggests ways to

- Devise a plan,
- Consult with chair,
- Produce scholarly IT works,
- Publish in peer-reviewed media,
- Assemble a teaching portfolio,
- Stay tuned to policies,
- Attend/organize conferences,
- Insist on peer review.

For departments it recommends how to

- Hold orientation,
- Distribute P&T policies,
- Do P&T workshops,
- Have advisory committees,
- Provide incentives,
- Hold 3rd year reviews.

And for deans and P&T committees it recommends how to

- Familiarize with current trends,
- Sponsor mock P&T session,

- Sponsor orientations and public discussion,
- Display successful dossiers,
- Evaluate handbook language.

The website, "Distributed Education Resources." includes these documents at http://it.iu.edu/deresources.

Tenth, the Copyright Management Center is working with the Library to obtain copyright clearance for faculty use of electronic resources.

VII. A CASE IN POINT

The School of Nursing is a good example of how cultural change at the university has affected cultural change within a school. As the largest School of Nursing in the country, change may not come easily, yet because they have all the right ingredients in place, the faculty have accepted and adapted to change.

Over the years the school has had the highest percentage of faculty who applied for, and received, university grants and fellowships. This is a testimony, in part, to the leadership and a very strong faculty development office. Today, over 90% of the faculty use information technology in their teaching. Some 50 of the school's classes are totally online, and 80 classes have an online component.

Again, good practices support these numbers. The school Dean's office makes available school teaching awards that are well promoted, announced, and celebrated. Every year there are merit bonuses, and there is summer support for faculty who develop courses for Oncourse delivery. Furthermore, the Dean has created a Center for Teaching and Lifelong Learning, an Online Orientation, and a Certificate Program for Teaching Online; the latter is available to its faculty at no cost. Classes on teaching and learning are also available to the faculty. For instance, different uses of technology are studied varying from its shallow use with a narrow impact on people (one unit using e-mail, for instance), to its deep use with a wide impact on most learners (multimedia use by all units, for instance).

The resident expert on assessment has developed RILO, the Readiness Index for Learning Online, and has worked with other institutions to create national standards for teaching and learning online courses, now widely used by institutions outside IUPUI.

All this is possible because the Dean has a real interest in the faculty, and has been in office for over 12 years.

VIII. WHAT IS IUPUI

Known as Indiana University Purdue University Indianapolis, the campus is located in the state capital and allows students to earn either Purdue or Indiana University degrees. It is the state's most comprehensive institution serving over 29,000 students, and it is one of two core campuses of an eight campus system. With 1,763 full time, 849 part time faculty members, and 21 academic schools, it includes the state's only medical and dental schools. Its operating budget is 832.6 million per year, and the annual revenues generated from external grants accounted for 204.5 million last year. This is larger than what either IU Bloomington or Purdue West Lafayette takes in. Its state-of-the-art library houses not only books and journals, but, more importantly, it is one of the country's best libraries in electronic information systems. IUPUI runs a NCAA Division I athletics program.

IX. THE PEDAGOGY OF IT USE

Much has been written about pedagogy of teaching and learning, especially with the use of technology [6-20]. There is a difference between the scholarly use of technology and the scholarship of technology. The former applies the research findings of the literature, whereas the latter refers to conducting the research and publishing its findings. Thus, to teach using technology as a tool only means to use it to deliver material to students in a new way, whereas if it is used as scholarship then it may call for the development of a new course, investigate new research methods, undergo peer review, publish the work, obtain grants, present before conferences, and generally make sure that students become engaged with the material.

Broadly seen, information technologies can be divided into two categories: delivery technologies and engagement technologies. Delivery technologies substitute for lectures, books, notes, and are exemplified by videos, television, and CD-ROMs. The impact on student learning of these technologies is generally neutral with no advantage or disadvantage to lectures, for instance. Many studies have been conducted to verify these findings. Among them are Chu [20], Schramm [21], Johnson [22], and Johnston [23].

Engagement technologies, on the other hand, call for student involvement and are illustrated by interactive computer programs, the Web, and e-mail. The impact on learning, where studied, is quite positive. The positive learning outcomes, though, are not due to the technology *per se*, but instead, are due to the sound pedagogy being promoted. Researchers like the Kuliks [24, 25] found that interactive computer aided instruction improves learning outcomes and speed, that computer based instruction results in significantly higher achievement and more positive attitude, and Abbott [26] found that computer modeling improves student exam performance. Stanley Smith, University of Illinois, found that chemistry laboratory scores improve by some 20% with the use of interactive video discs; and quizzes improve from 3.9 to 4.8 points out of seven points.

Derek Bok, President Emeritus of Harvard University, said:

> *"The most apparent need is to change the emphasis of instruction away from transmitting bodies of information toward preparing students to engage…"*

Likewise, Pascarella and Terenzini [27] have said:

> *"Simply put, the greater the student's involvement in academic work, the greater his or her level of knowledge acquisition…"*

One might thus conclude that learning takes place best when the students are engaged, and we may further suggest that IT is a good tool to foster student engagement. The delivery technologies tend to display these features: faculty control, teaching centered, passive student, active faculty, promoting recall, focus on the individual, compartmentalization, and holding to one teaching style. On the other hand, the engagement technologies emphasize student control, learning centeredness, with active students and active faculty, require understanding, and foster group work. Engagement technology is ongoing and seamless, and it includes many learning styles.

Bloom's taxonomy [28] ranks learning from knowledge acquisition to comprehension, application, analysis, synthesis, and at the top, evaluation. Practicing the Socratic Method, Problem Based Learning, or class discussion tends to promote the higher orders of the taxonomy; whereas the lecture promotes the lower ranks. Similarly, on the taxonomy scale, the Web, e-mail, and interactive computer programs also tend to promote the higher orders of learning, whereas television, video, and CD-ROMs promote the lower levels.

X. REPLICATION

The most common question and suggestion made about this paper is how can other institutions replicate what IUPUI has done. Are there generalizations that go beyond any one institution and hence are adaptable by others? At the risk of sounding elitist, the following four key principles are offered.

A. Strong Advocacy

It is absolutely imperative that there be an advocate office occupied by a person who carries campus-wide respect, and who can champion the cause. Such a person can be an administrator, which will make it a top-down process, thus calling for extreme sensitivity to include the faculty at all steps, to avoid even the appearance that the process is mandated. Or, the advocate may be a faculty member, widely recognized on campus, perhaps elected by the faculty, who will then have the challenge of making sure that the administration resonates with the wishes of the faculty. In either case, the key person must make sure s/he is surrounded by a strong personal support group, by an official advisory committee, and colleagues who will serve as an honest sounding board.

B. Ongoing Update

Higher education is constantly changing, with new initiatives appearing yearly. The advocate must be plugged into the national fora where such emerging issues are being exposed and discussed. Based on these national discussions, and in consultation with support groups and advisory committees, the home campus agenda will have to be balanced against the national issues, and then implementation proposed where appropriate.

C. Faculty Involvement

Faculty do want to be part of the decision making formula—even when the issue is not of direct academic concern. It is one thing for the advocate to come before the faculty and explain in great detail why a decision was made. But it is quite another to include the faculty in the decision making process by saying: here is the decision we have to make; here are the issues as I understand them, what is your counsel? While this approach cannot be used all the time, it is the best way to build trust, which once received, will allow the advocate to make decisions even without faculty input.

D. Supporting the Faculty

If it is true that faculty are driven by two motives, intellectual challenge and rewards, then it becomes the advocate's responsibility to support the faculty with rewards in multiple manners. Such support includes tangible and in-kind assistance. For instance, monetary awards, achievement awards both on and off campus, trips to conferences, salary increases, and key committee appointments, access to experts, equipment, centers, and publications are all important. Still more important is the atmosphere of mutual trust that must be created in order for the more tangible assistance to have meaning. Create an open and inclusive environment about academic issues, about promotion and tenure, about salary concerns, and so on. Generally, the rule is that it is better to ask for permission rather than forgiveness.

XI. THE FUTURE

It is difficult to know what the future will bring; for example, Tom Watson, Chairman of IBM, said in 1943 that there might be a world market of maybe five computers. Nevertheless, clear signs of the future include ubiquity, inter-institutional and international exchange, student-centered learning services and outsourcing:

- Ubiquitous computing is the wave of the future. The mainframe computers are being phased out, and while the use of the stand-alone desktop computers has risen dramatically, it is plateauing off. On the other hand, the personal computer connected to the Web, and thereby to many computers, is clearly the future.

- Trend watchers [29] have observed that the distance education land rush is over, and that the pace of faculty adoption of IT is slowing. They point to the inability to control costs and that on most campuses distance education has gone from the #1 issue to #6. They also claim that it is not being integrated into education.

- We see additional important trends. The largest mega-universities are not in the Western world, but are, among others, in China [30] and Turkey. Relating to these countries could bring vast and heretofore unknown changes for our traditional institutions.

- Islamic Studies [31] and Arabic languages are developing major interests among the American public; and students appear quite eager to obtain these studies via Web courses.

- India is a country to watch for major impact on the shape of IT development. India has English as a strong second language, has a large population base including citizens who are very well trained and very bright, and India can produce work using Ph.D.s for a fraction of costs in the U.S. and Europe.

- Spanish is an emerging environment deserving attention in the Western Hemisphere. Hispanics are the fastest growing population in this country. For Hispanics living in this country, courses and programs can simply be translated into Spanish. There is no academic reason this cannot be done. A degree is content rather than language sensitive. For those living in Latin countries the translation of U.S. materials needs to be carefully adapted to local nuances, traditions, and flavors.

- The electronic student portfolio is now being developed and will soon be part of what students will demand in the very near future. It is an electronic template that enables students to demonstrate their work, and their improvement in learning.

- Finally, much of what is being done in-house today will soon be outsourced, as the telephone and electricity were outsourced long ago, and as, more recently, the bookstore, the dining hall, and student housing are being outsourced on many campuses. IT outsourcing likely will include not only hardware and software development, but tutoring and some programs and courses as well. It is just too expensive for every institution to develop good courses in every field.

Whatever the future brings, there are some quality indicators to heed for online courses. An emphasis on animation over text, the uses of data bases, and the hands-on nature of courses will be constant challenges. It must be clear the course being developed has a team behind it and that evaluation is important.

XII. CHALLENGES

As we embark on this new phenomenon of technology-mediated higher education, a number of issues are important to keep in mind:

- Will technology we choose serve students better, or will it just serve them differently? We must, on the one hand, constantly push the limits of technology to exploit all possible advantages, and at the same time we must know its limitations. Unless technology serves students better, with the promise of greater student learning outcomes, there is little reason to implement it.

- We must constantly remind ourselves that the message molds the medium. For example, when students wanted live broadcasts of classes, we resorted to what we thought was a somewhat lower level of delivery: pre-taped videos. The quality of the taped videos was better than live broadcasts, and students were happier.

- We must learn to be adaptable and learn to work in teams. Faculty have always been independent individuals who have developed an 'in-charge' approach to all they do. Working in the IT environment means that faculty will have to learn to be members of a team of instructional designers, technology personnel, librarians, and assessment experts.

- For many traditional institutions it is a challenge to accept the fact that distance education is a new sun rising over the horizon of higher education, one that should be embraced. As Sir John S. Daniel [32] put it: "The great contribution of the United States to the advancement of humankind has been to stress the importance of the individual. Why, in distance education, are you so fixated on the collectivity of the classroom?"

- We must be willing to be patient. This applies to the student evaluations which likely will diminish when a change is implemented, as well as to student outcomes. The invention of the printed book had little impact on education for about a century since most people could not read and there was no mass distribution system.

- It is imperative to be visionary. The overhead projector was invented in the 1876, but it was not used until the 1930s when the bowling alleys did finally apply it to keep score. And it was some thirty years later that educators finally saw some application for the classroom. We must ask ourselves what new uses, thus far not thought of, does the internet, e-mail, the digital camera, and others have?

- Of great concern to universities is the reward structure for its faculty. Will those who sit on promotion and tenure committees who came through the system the 'old way,' be willing to visualize new ways to interpret scholarship? Does the Web allow a faculty member to publish and then get reviewed, rather than the other way around as print media require?

- Congress issues copyright and fair use legislation, which currently is general and vague, and hence open to interpretation. Will these issues become more explicit so as to be of real help to the faculties?

- We must answer these and other questions regarding residency requirements, tuition, who does a student belong to, and who is the degree provider. And, we must answer the question: "What will technology not be used for?"

XIII. CONCLUSION

The longevity and insight of administrative leadership, the openness of the faculty review process, the expectation of constant change, the liberal award structure, the constant emphasis on using technology not just in research, but in teaching and learning as well, and the stress on true scholarship, especially in the use of technology, have contributed to a faculty satisfaction with academic life at IUPUI. Others can replicate these practices.

XIV. REFERENCES

1. **Young, J. R.** Ever So Slowly, Colleges Start to Count Work With Technology in Tenure Decisions. *The Chronicle of Higher Education.* XLVII (24): A25-A37 (February 22, 2002).
2. **Green, K. C.** The Campus Computing Project, 2002. http://www.campuscomputing.net
3. "New Times, New Technology, New Scholarship: Evolving Faculty Rewards." http://www.indiana.edu/~ovpit/rewards/
4. **Boschmann, Erwin,** Moving Toward a More Inclusive Reward Structure. The Technology Source, October, 1998, Faculty and Staff Development. http://ts.mivu.org/default.asp?show=article&id=7
5. **Plater, W. M.** Future Work: Faculty Time in the 21st Century. *Change: The Magazine for Higher Learning.* 27(3): 22-33 (May/June 1995).
6. **Abelson, P.H.** Editorial, Evolution of Higher Education. *Science.* 277(8): 747 (August 1997).
7. **Barr, R. B. and J. Tagg.** From Teaching to Learning; A new Paradigm for Undergraduate Education. *Change: The Magazine for Higher Learning.* 27(6): 13 (November/December 1995).
8. **Bollentin, W. R.** Can Information Technology Improve Education? Measuring Voices, Attitudes and Perceptions. *Educom Review.* 33(1): 50 (January/February 1998).
9. **Chachra, V.,** in Erwin Boschmann, ed., *The Electronic Classroom,* Learned Information, Inc., Medford, NJ, 228, 1995.
10. **Chickering, A.W. and Z. F. Gamson.** Seven Principles for Good Practice in Undergraduate Education. *The Wingspread Journal.* 1-4 (June 1987).
11. **Chickering, A.W. and S. C. Ehrmann.** Implementing the Seven Principles; Technology as Lever. *AAHE Bulletin.*3 (October 1996).
12. **Dewey, J.** *Experience and Education,* New York: Collier Books, 1938.
13. **Ewell, P.T.** Organizing for Learning. *AAHE Bulletin.* 50(4): 3 (1997).
14. **Gardner, H.** *Seven Ways of Learning,* Twilight Press, 1991.
15. **Hammonds, K. H. and S. Jackson.** The New University. *Business Week.* 12(22): 96 (1997).
16. **Kennedy, D.** *Academic Duty,* Harvard Press, 1997.
17. **Laurillard, D.** *Rethinking University Teaching: A Framework for the Effective Use of Educational Technology,* London & NY: Routledge, 1993.
18. **Russell, T. L.,** The "No Significant Difference" Phenomenon, North Carolina State University. http://teleeducation.nb.ca/nosignificantdifference/
19. **Schrage, M.** Technology, Silver Bullets and Big Lies. *Educom Review.* 33(1): 32 (January/February 1997).
20. **Twigg, C.** The Changing Definition of Learning. *Educom Review.* 29(4): 23-25 (July/August, 1994). http://www.educause.edu/pub/er/review/reviewArticles/29422.html
21. **Chu, G. and W. Shramm.** Learning from TV: What the Research Says. *Stanford University.* (1967).
22. **Schramm, W.,** *Big Media, Little Media: Tools and Technologies for Instruction,* Sage Publications, 1977.
23. **Johnson, D. and R. Johnson.** Implementing Cooperative Learning. *Contemporary Education.* 63: 173-80 (Spring 1992).

24. **Johnston, J.,** *Electronic Learning: From Audiotape to Videodisc,* Englewood Cliffs, NJ: Lawrence Erlbaum Associates, 1987.
25. **Kulik, J., R. Bangert-Drowns and G. J. Williams.** *Educational Psychology.* 75: 19-26 (1983).
26. **Kulik, C-L. C. and J. A. Kulik.** Effectiveness of Computer-Based Instruction: An Updated Analysis. *Computers in Human Behavior.* VII(1-2): 75 (1991).
27. **Abbott, J.** Quantitative Critical Thinking. *College Teaching.* 41(3): 92-95 (Summer 1993).
28. **Pascarella, E. T. and Terenzini, P. T.,** *How College Affects Students, Insights from Twenty Years of Research*, San Francisco: Jossey-Bass, 1991.
29. **Bloom, B. S.,** *Taxonomy of Educational Objectives: The classification of Educational Goals: Handbook I, Cognitive Domain.* New York, Toronto: Longmans, Green, 1956.
30. **Molenda, M. and M. Sullivan.** Issues and Trends in Instructional Technology: Treading Water. Submitted to *Educational Media and Technology Yearbook 2003.* Englewood, CO: Libraries Unlimited (2003).
31. **Olsen, F.** Chinese Institutions Look Toward Distance Education. *The Chronicle of Higher Education.* XLIX(8): A38 (October 18, 2002), and Chronicle.com/infotech (October 3, 2002).
32. **Read, B.** A New Web Site Offers a Window on Islamic Architecture and Planning. *The Chronicle of Higher Education.* XLIX(8): A38 (October 18, 2002), and Chronicle.com/infotech (October 4, 2002).
33. **Daniel, Sir J. S.** Why Universities Need Technology Strategies. *Change: The Magazine for Higher Learning.* 29(4): 10-17 (July/August 1997).

XV. ACKNOWLEDGEMENTS

I am grateful to the following IUPUI offices for furnishing data used in this paper: Planning and Institutional Improvement, Academic Policies, Dean of the Faculties, Communications and Marketing, Center for Service and Learning, and the School of Nursing.

XVI. ABOUT THE AUTHOR

Erwin Boschmann developed new pedagogical models and instructional delivery methods as Indiana University's Associate Vice President for Distributed Education from December, 1998 through June, 2002. In that capacity he also was "instrumental in defining and implementing a distributed education strategy," with oversight responsibility for developing and enhancing instructional capabilities across all eight campuses. IU's School of Continuing Studies reported to him. Today he serves as Special Assistant to the IUPUI Administration.

From 1988 to 1999 he served as Associate Dean of the Faculties charged with responsibilities for faculty development for the 1500 full time and 800 part time faculty at IUPUI. Duties included administering an internal grants program, organizing workshops, facilitating one-on-one faculty consultations, coordinating all awards, implementing technology into the curriculum, assisting with promotion, tenure, and sabbatical decisions, and supervising a publications program. The offices of the Center for Teaching and Learning, Office for Women, Senior Academy, Minority Faculty, Part Time faculty, were all managed through his Office of Faculty and Senior Staff Development. He has spoken, taught, and consulted widely in this country and overseas.

He received his Ph.D. in Inorganic Chemistry from the University of Colorado, Boulder, Colorado, and has been with IU since 1968, where he is Professor of Chemistry. He has taught chemistry at the undergraduate and graduate levels and served as consultant to chemistry departments in South America and Indonesia. He is the author of several dozen articles and numerous books on research and teaching. He chaired the American Chemical Society's national examination committee for General, Organic,

Biological Chemistry, and has been table leader for the College Board's Educational Testing Service Advance Placement examinations. In 1983 he received Indiana University's statewide H.F. Lieber Award for Distinguished Teaching, and in 1986 he was awarded a Lilly Faculty Open Fellowship. During 1997 he served as chair of the Indiana Section of the American Chemical Society. In 1991 his Chemistry 101 was made available on the local PBS and cable systems, and in 1997 his course became the prototype for the development of what today is Oncourse, Indiana University's course management platform. In 1998 he received the Distinguished Alumnus Award from Bethel College, Kansas.

INSTITUTIONAL SUPPORT FOR ONLINE FACULTY: EXPANDING THE MODEL

Marie J. Fetzner
Monroe Community College

- Institutional support for online faculty is a pivotal point for faculty satisfaction

- The need for faculty support escalates when an institution rapidly expands its online course delivery efforts.

- *The Monroe Model* parallels the best practices of an online learning experience—it is team-based, collaborative, comprehensive, action-oriented, and non-hierarchical.

- Key advantages include a consistent learner interface a standard template, a centralized help desk for students and faculty, a formalized faculty course development and design process, and centralized servers to support the technology infrastructure.

- For effective faculty technology training: Follow general morning sessions with afternoon work teams; foster inter- and intra-institutional collaboration; convene institutes away from most attendees' work environment; and focus on implementing pedagogy as well as technology.

I. INTRODUCTION

For over a decade, the distance learning field has recognized that on-site institutional support is critical to the level of faculty participation in distance learning [1]; [2]; [3]. Schifter suggests that the lack of institutional support for faculty, insufficient technical infrastructure, and course development needs are the top three factors that inhibit faculty participation in ALNs [4].

Rockwell and colleagues take a more individualized approach to faculty satisfaction. They suggest that for faculty to teach successfully in distance education, institutions must consider the wants, needs, interests, and aspirations of the faculty to develop effective distance learning educational models and techniques [5]. Thompson's examination of the literature emphasizes three necessary conditions that promote online faculty satisfaction: institutional support, professional recognition, and personal rewards [6]. Hartman and colleagues note that student outcomes impact online faculty, as well as a "complex pattern of interactions" within colleges, departments and program areas [7]. These writers capture the wide range of systemic, institutional, student, professional, and personal factors related to online faculty satisfaction.

Although many factors contribute to online faculty satisfaction, the level of institutional support for online faculty is a pivotal point for faculty satisfaction. Low levels of institutional support for online faculty can inhibit participation in online teaching, while comprehensive institutional support can encourage online faculty participation and increase satisfaction. Individual faculty and staff support efforts may be able to meet short-term needs, but strategic, long-term online faculty satisfaction can best be sustained through a systemic and comprehensive institutional support. *The Monroe Model* is a campus-based, institutional model of online faculty support coupled with a system-wide, centralized online support framework. This study explores the impact of *The Monroe Model* on online faculty satisfaction.

A. Online Faculty Training and Support

A key component of online faculty satisfaction is the availability of high-quality faculty training and support. Research on institutional faculty training efforts provides useful insights into this area. LeBlanc shares three distance education faculty support lessons learned in the early 1990s at the University of Maine: 1) Find a training balance between the practical and theoretical; 2) Recognize that experienced faculty and staff are the institution's most valuable resource; and 3) Remain open to viewing instructional design as a dynamic, not a linear, process [8].

Following a three-year study on faculty and learning technologies, Bullock and Schomberg offer these practical suggestions for faculty technology training: Have general morning sessions followed by afternoon work teams; foster both inter- and intra-institutional collaboration; convene institutes away from most attendees' work environment; and focus on implementing pedagogy as well as technology [9].

Emphasis on online pedagogy is a key component of faculty training and support; its positive impact on faculty satisfaction cannot be overstated. As Passmore states,

> So much of the current emphasis in design, development, and delivery of web-based instruction focuses on technical issues....So much of what stands for web-based instruction is little more than 'shovel ware,' that is, a migration of a syllabus and yellowed notes, along with

a few visuals and URLs, onto a Web site [10].

Faculty members appreciate well-designed and comprehensive professional development sessions that focus on the quality of the teaching-learning environment. Individual trainers can work well with small numbers of online faculty, but as online programs scale-up, other approaches are required. On-going institutional support for online faculty development enables team approaches to reconceptualizing course design and delivery that move beyond a focus on faculty training [11]; [12]; [13].

Lorenzetti suggests that "support cannot come only from one department or one group. In order for an online faculty member to be successful, the institution as a whole, including the upper levels of administration, must be committed" to support [14].

The need for faculty support escalates when an institution rapidly expands its online course delivery efforts. Institutional response to the need for this support plays a major role in the success of any online learning initiative and in the satisfaction of its online faculty [15]. With support of its senior faculty and administration, Monroe Community College created *The Monroe Model*—a comprehensive, team-based, approach to faculty support. Although some researchers advocate totally online faculty development and support environments [16], MCC chose to use a balanced approach that includes centralized resources provided by State University of New York's SUNY Learning Network (SLN), and on-site, comprehensive, campus-based face-to-face training and support.

B. Background

Monroe Community College (MCC) is a large, upstate New York community college that is part of the SUNY system. The College serves the Rochester and Monroe County vicinity and has an annual headcount enrollment of approximately 30,000. Established in 1962, MCC supports two campuses, four extension sites, and offers more than 70 degree and certificate programs. MCC is one of nineteen board member community colleges in the League for Innovation in the Community College.

MCC supports over 4,000 annual online enrollments (490+ FTE) via the SUNY Learning Network, representing approximately 5% of FTEs generated annually by the College. More than 80 online courses and 100 online sections are offered each semester. Over 70 faculty members have received training to develop, deliver, review, and revise their online courses. This faculty cohort receives support from on-site members of the MCC online support team, and receives centralized support from SLN within *The* Monroe Model framework.

C. Monroe Community College and the SUNY Learning Network (SLN)

In 1997, Monroe Community College joined Phase II of the State University of New York's SUNY Learning Network. MCC was designated as SLN's Western New York training site, and MCC faculty members developed and delivered four online, totally asynchronous courses to thirty-two students (20 FTEs) that year.

Benefits of MCC's participation in SLN were many. Key advantages included a consistent learner interface via the SLN template, a centralized help desk for students and faculty, a formalized faculty course development and design process, and centralized servers to support the SLN technology infrastructure. MCC faculty members worked collaboratively with SLN and MCC staff to develop effective online learning course design and delivery strategies. The majority of MCC's early online faculty adopters reported anecdotally that the online environment was an academically sound vehicle for providing educational access to students. They also indicated that they were transferring some of their online pedagogical activities and strategies into their campus-based courses. These reports indicate that a majority of MCC's early SLN faculty believed that the concept of web-based course delivery was viable.

By Summer 1998, online enrollments and courses had increased ten-fold, and at this juncture the need for comprehensive online faculty and course development support reached a critical point at MCC. The institution recognized the need to address faculty course design, delivery, and training issues, as well as operational details, important scale-up issues, and policy implications for the campus. MCC responded by forming an on-site faculty support team that would work closely with SLN staff members to support MCC's online faculty needs.

The MCC online support team—the precursor to *The Monroe Model*—was developed as a model of shared resources that could meet strategic faculty and program needs. Concurrently, MCC embraced the philosophy that online courses would be conceptualized and supported comparably to campus-based courses. Online courses would be academically sound, be based on the same learning outcomes as their campus-based counterparts, and would involve all areas of MCC. In other words, online learning would not be treated as an enclave, but would be considered as one option in the array of instructional modalities available at MCC.

The Monroe Model is configured in a way that parallels the best practices of an online learning experience—it is team-based, collaborative, comprehensive, action-oriented, and non-hierarchical. The support team coordinates the academic, training coordination, instructional design, library, technical support, and student services aspects of online course development. One team member serves as the liaison to the SUNY Learning Network central office in Albany to ensure that the faculty members' primary concern is the development and delivery of their online courses, not the many other significant but pedagogically tangential details. As enrollments in online courses continue to grow at MCC—in the Fall 2002 semester, online enrollments exceeded 2,000—the level of faculty support and coordination required also increase. Issues related to the impact of program scale-up are addressed in section II.

D. The Monroe Model

The Monroe Model has two main structural components, the SLN (centralized) portion and the MCC (distributed, local, campus-based) portion. Although the focus of this study is on the campus-based part of the model, some background and a brief summary of the centralized components will help to frame the model and present benchmarks for replication of the model outside of the SUNY system.

The State University of New York received a grant in 1994 from the Alfred P. Sloan Foundation to develop an online course delivery system. Unlike other models that reflected a totally asynchronous, online approach, SUNY did not create a virtual university. Instead, SUNY "virtualized" an existing university system. The SUNY Learning Network was conceptualized and developed as an alternative way to deliver courses that could originate from any one of SUNY's sixty-four campuses. It is important to note that SLN is not a separate degree-granting institution and it is not part of any individual campus. SLN is designed to provide a centralized online course development and support infrastructure to participating SUNY institutions, so that each campus does not have to create or reinvent the services on its own.

The centralized support services offered to campuses that participate in the SLN initiative are represented in the top portion of the model. The four key areas of support provided to local campuses by SLN include:

1. Faculty Development Support—Faculty Training and Materials, and On-going, Online Faculty Support
2. Technical Infrastructure Support—Servers, Automated Web Applications and Technical Support
3. Operational Support—Marketing and Promotional Activities, Data Collection/Analysis, Help Desk
4. Administrative Support—Central Inquiry Response Capacity, Student Registration, SUNY Website Development

These core services provided by SUNY are invaluable to SLN institutions because they take a great burden off campus partners as they initiate and sustain their online programs. SLN provides the framework and infrastructure for asynchronous delivery, and the institution focuses on the developmental, instructional, and administrative activities for the local campus. SLN defers to all local campus deadlines and academic calendars so that the online courses parallel the institution's campus-based courses and exam schedules. SLN defines the local campus partner's role in SLN as one that

- Grants the degree

- Designs/develops courses

- Offers courses/degrees

- Provides academic review

- Provides advisement

- Registers students

- Administers financial aid

For institutions outside of the SUNY system, the SLN centralized services included in the model may be used as benchmarks in assessing the support from proprietary online course system partners, "home-grown" systems or both. A graphical representation of *The Monroe Model* follows:

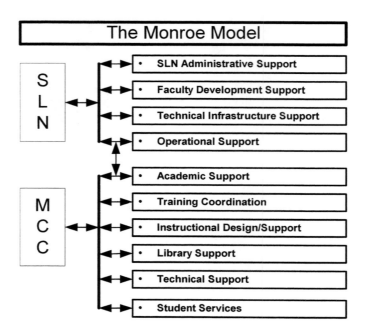

Table 1.0 The Monroe Model

The continuous connection of arrows in the model's graphical representation reflects the complicated nature of the SLN activities, which may or may not be linear in nature. The integrated nature of MCC's program is illustrated by the continuous loop of services provided by SLN and by the campus. The MCC team's role has six components: Academic Support, Training Coordination, Instructional Design/Support, Library Support, Technical Support, and Student Services. Each component is supported by MCC staff members who participate on the SLN team while continuing in their existing (and disparate) roles at the College.

Following are examples of the types of on-site support services provided by *The Monroe Model* team members:

- **Academic Support**—Coordinates the development and Master Schedule listing of online course offerings with department chairs, is the single point of contact for online faculty issues, coordinates SLN promotional efforts, and acts as the MCC liaison to SLN.

- **Training Coordination**—Coordinates Western New York regional training for the SUNY Learning Network, develops MCC's on-campus wrap-around faculty training to enrich the SLN training sessions, conducts research on online learning, and coordinates SLN efforts with the web development team.

- **Instructional Design/Support**—Assists faculty with the course reconceptualization process, conducts design sessions, coordinates on-site graphics/video support, and conducts technical checks of course links.

- **Library Support**—Acts as a resource for faculty in researching and identifying appropriate library materials that are integrated into the design of the course. Specific areas addressed include copyright, fair use, content-related sites and information literacy.

- **Technical Support**—Acts as technical liaison for related hardware and software issues, coordinates faculty access to course templates with SLN, and provides on-site emergency technical support for faculty.

- **Student Services**—Acts as the liaison to MCC student services, such as counseling, advising, testing, financial aid, bookstore, and online student services.

The examples provided for each area above represent the typical functions team members perform. *The Monroe Model* team's general activities typically are not linear in nature—they are issue-oriented and require multiple layers of cooperation between all team members. However, the graphic representation of model is useful in helping to clarify the institutional impact of an online program and in identifying the comprehensive on-site campus support requirements of an online learning initiative.

Blending a centralized support system with available on-site, local campus support provides faculty with multiple layers of scaffolding. This kind of support contributes to their confidence in the online delivery system and to their overall satisfaction with the online teaching process. Centralized services such as the SLN template and SLN help desk ensure that all online faculty and students—not just those faculty and students involved with a mature online program—receive equitable support. The availability of local on-site campus support for online faculty increases the chances that faculty can get issues resolved personally and in a timely manner. Over time, online faculty members build rapport with members of the local support team—especially with staff who work closely with them on the development, design, and revision of their courses. These multiple layers of centralized and local support help to assure the online faculty that their innovative ideas, their course content, and their virtual connection to their students will be supported and maintained at the highest of standards.

Team members work closely with each other and with online faculty members to sustain and expand online programming and to contribute to both student success and faculty satisfaction. A summary of issues directly related to the impact of *The Monroe Model* on faculty satisfaction follows in Section II.

II. THE IMPACT OF PROGRAM MATURITY AND SCALE-UP ON FACULTY SATISFACTION

The Monroe Model was begun as an informal response to rapidly rising online enrollments and program expansion. It now has evolved into a formal resource for addressing and collaboratively resolving online learning issues. The model accommodates the need for general and specialized skills for addressing some thorny problems with online initiatives.

The model also supports cross-divisional perspectives and encourages open communication that can mitigate potential programmatic roadblocks. Often, asynchronous course delivery is viewed as a "stand-alone" project that directly affects only the faculty and students of the online program. *The Monroe Model* team can attest to the fact that MCC's online program now involves coordination with almost every area of the College, and that its work has a direct impact on faculty satisfaction.

A. *The Monroe Model* Team as an Informational Resource

As the SLN program has grown at MCC, the support team has become an easily accessible information source for online MCC faculty. Team members have the opportunity to see the "big picture" in terms of the College's online learning program. Through collective brainstorming, they work with faculty, staff, and administrators to resolve issues. To date, the team has assisted in the development of over 100 online courses, working with twelve faculty-developer cohorts comprising over sixty-five faculty members. Several team members have participated in at least ten online faculty-training sessions each year since 1997. This continuity and the resulting knowledge of the online learning program's history and participants—from the early adopters to the newest faculty developer cohort—lend credibility to the team.

The Monroe Model team members have gained an in-depth knowledge of online learning operations, services, and support at MCC. They know the online faculty members well and can pinpoint the person or expertise needed to address and resolve faculty issues. The team often connects faculty members to other online faculty, both within and outside of their departments. New online faculty members are introduced by team members to experienced online faculty members working on a similar online learning activity in the same and unrelated disciplines. Generally, these peer-to-peer collaborations benefit both participants and lead to other cooperative efforts.

Development is very much a collaborative and mutually supportive endeavor. Online faculty members appreciate the support team's awareness of the time commitment involved with the design and development of an online course. Team members and experienced faculty share tips and best practices with new online developers. The Academic Coordinator works with the administration to ensure that all new developers appear on the developer stipend listing for that semester. Other team members confirm that new faculty developers are registered for training and provide pre-training sessions to respond in advance to any questions and to alleviate any concerns.

Changes to the local campus online faculty training and wrap-around session formats are usually the direct result of online faculty input. The faculty members appreciate the fact that team members accept and respond to feedback, making appropriate revisions within a reasonable timeframe. Online faculty members often comment that they are more willing to provide constructive input into the process since the team has a track record of evaluating and implementing recommended changes on a timely basis. Although the rapid expansion of MCC's online program has challenged the institution's capacity for faculty support, the *The Monroe Model's* on-site support and personal team contact, complemented by SLN's centralized services, has enabled the College to meet the challenge.

B. Contributing Factors to the Success of the Model

One component that significantly contributes to high faculty satisfaction levels is peer-to-peer support in the wrap-around sessions, facilitated by support team members. Faculty members appreciate and benefit from hearing the experiences of colleagues in a face-to-face setting. Typically, the topics of online pedagogy and strategies for improving and sustaining online interactions generate the most discussion in these sessions. The interaction between the faculty members and their willingness to accept comments and suggestions from support team members results in invigorating and engaging sessions. Once the course reconceptualization and pedagogical issues are addressed, then the specifics about the technical portions of the course template are addressed.

As MCC's online program has expanded, creating short-cuts for online faculty has become even more critical. For example, if a faculty member's laptop computer is damaged, the faculty member may be closed out of his or her class. Rather than being added to the normal College equipment repair queue, online faculty members contact the technical support member of the team for assistance. With over 2,500 desktop and laptop computers in use at the College, this service to online faculty is particularly appreciated and increases satisfaction levels.

The costs associated with the implementation of *The Monroe Model* have been kept to a minimum, and this factor has contributed to the overall success of and support for the model. Six of the eight team members subsumed their online faculty-support roles within their existing job responsibilities. Rapid program expansion was addressed through the creation of two new positions: a Technical Specialist/Trainer and a Distance Learning/Collaborative Librarian. A percentage of time for each of these positions is apportioned to the support team efforts. Additionally, an MCC direct cost-benefit model for the online program was developed to monitor and assess cross-divisional expenses associated with the SLN activities. Although this cost model does not directly relate to faculty satisfaction, it assures the faculty and administration that program costs are being monitored and reported.

The on-site support concept has benefited greatly by word-of-mouth support from experienced online faculty. New faculty members are told that their needs will be met if they work directly with the support team members. If online faculty are having difficulties with a particular issue, the team intervenes and assists in the resolution of the problem. Regardless of the online faculty member's need, an on-site support person is available to assist in person, online, or via telephone. Because they understand the comprehensive needs of a maturing and continually expanding online program, faculty members recognize and appreciate the efforts put forth by the team on their behalf.

The team as a whole provides a stable "home base" for information on a wide variety of online learning questions. Over the years, the support team has built credibility with the faculty, staff, and administration, who rely on the team to recommend solutions or to favorably resolve online learning issues. Although there has been some turnover in team personnel, the group retains a collective history of the faculty cohorts, their online courses, and the development of the College's online initiatives.

C. Unanticipated Impacts of The Monroe Model

The expansion and maturity of MCC's online program has brought unplanned and ancillary benefits of the support team concept to the forefront. One of the unanticipated results is the value of the team's historical perspective and their depth and breadth of knowledge of individual online faculty members' teaching styles. Coppola, Hiltz and Rotter describe the major impact of technology on the teaching process and the role changes that occur as professors "change their mode of teaching" [17]. The bonds established between the faculty members and the support team help MCC faculty members as they move through various role changes and stages of online course development, delivery, and revision. Team members follow the progression and development of first-time, online faculty and observe them as they change their teaching processes and bring lessons learned in the online environment to their campus-based classrooms.

Another unanticipated impact of this special connection between online faculty and on-site support team members is reflected in new collaborations between online faculty and team members. Team and faculty members have jointly written proposals and implemented projects and instructional development grants. Faculty members are willing to experiment with pilot projects and beta-tests of other modes of instructional delivery because they now are confident that sufficient institutional support will be available to them.

A third unexpected result of *The Monroe Model* framework relates to faculty recognition. Team members know the level of commitment and effort that online faculty members put forth. The team now publicly recognizes teaching excellence through annual nominations of MCC online faculty for various local, state, and national teaching awards. For the past several years, many of the online faculty members nominated for these awards by the support team have been successful recipients. This type of formal recognition by the support team contributes to the respect and trust between the faculty members and the members of the support team. Faculty members also appreciate the collective strength and credibility of the support team; the number of faculty requests for promotion and tenure advocacy letters from the support team increases each year.

The use of the distributed on-site support team approach at MCC clearly has helped to overcome some of the hurdles involved with the operationalization of a maturing and expanding online program. Online faculty members recognize that the "course is a course" philosophy is now accepted and that the support team has played a major role in promoting the concept and making it work. Members of the support team collect and analyze data on the online program (such as cost-benefit analyses, student retention rates, and course and program offerings) and readily share these data with the online faculty. Several online faculty members regularly present at conferences with support team members and work collaboratively to improve the online teaching-learning process. These events and interactions have evolved over time and mutual respect continues to grow between the support team and the online faculty.

The evolution of the MCC on-site support team demonstrates that on-going coordination with centralized SLN services and other college departments, and direct interaction and support of online faculty plays an important role in the success of online programming. Comprehensive efforts add to the overall quality of the institution's online initiatives and contribute to the satisfaction of online faculty and to the success of students. To obtain empirical data on the impact of *The Monroe Model* on faculty satisfaction, an online faculty survey regarding the initiatives and operations of the support team is under development. The results of this survey will help to inform the expansion of, and revisions to, the model. Section III summarizes the specific areas under consideration for revision.

III. EXPANDING THE MODEL

The highly interactive nature of *The Monroe Model* team facilitates cross-divisional information exchange and allows team members to view the online learning environment from a variety of perspectives. The perspectives come from teaching faculty, student services staff, technology support personnel, librarians, web-designers, registration and records staff, students, and administrators. The team's historical and comprehensive perspective on MCC's online learning program—and requisite faculty needs—provides a good basis for reviewing the current model.

A. Training Issues

Prior to developing a faculty satisfaction survey on the on-site support team's efforts, team members reviewed past and current practices for *The Monroe Model*. This review identified the training coordination area as being the most challenging, and the area that has the most potential for increasing online faculty satisfaction.

One of the major concerns for first-time online faculty (and some experienced faculty) is responding in a timely manner to student questions and appropriately managing the large numbers of discussion postings in an online course. On-site support personnel—and other experienced online faculty members—can model effective practices and suggest ways for faculty to manage these communications without becoming overwhelmed or obsessed with their course 24-hours each day [18]. As the model has evolved, the team has become more proactive in this area. "Niche" sessions—especially for first-time online course developers—on course management strategies is one training approach currently under review for revision. Adding a series of such targeted training opportunities is likely to be one element in the expansion of the training portion of the model.

An unanticipated situation that affects the structure of the model is the increasing stratification of the training and development needs of faculty. After the first semester of online delivery in 1997, SLN and MCC began offering training services to only two groups—experienced online (typically full-time) faculty, and first-time online (typically full-time) faculty. These two cohorts formed the training framework for online faculty members for several semesters. As the program grew, and additional faculty members were developing and delivering online courses, the faculty target audience became more and more stratified while the training curricula generally remained static.

Faculty have asked to receive training specific to their particular needs, and the support team has made efforts to offer MCC faculty more focused training options. Generally, logistics dictate that SLN and MCC training serves a variety of online faculty "categories" within the same training session. The team identified nine potential faculty categories: (1) full time, new faculty, (2) full-time, experienced faculty; (3) first-time, full-time faculty who are teaching an already-developed online course; (4) first-time, adjunct faculty who are teaching an already-developed online course; (6) adjunct faculty who are developing and delivering their first course, (7) co-developers of a new course who may be full-time/adjunct, new/experienced faculty; (8) department chairs who never have taught an online course but need an understanding of online pedagogies and best practices in order to evaluate their online faculty, and (9) faculty who need "just in time" training to take over an existing course mid-semester. It is unclear where the law of diminishing returns takes effect, but the use of niche sessions and peer-to-peer sessions will be evaluated as potential solutions to this training challenge.

These nine newly identified faculty groupings still cannot account for the wide variation in the extent to which the faculty members have had exposure to specific online course challenges. Issues of particular concern to the support team are the following: the culture shift from the instructor as a lecturer to one of facilitator; a general understanding of the course reconceptualization process; the shift from an independent course designer to a team-based course design and delivery process; an understanding of the "course is a course" philosophy (same outcomes, different means of designing activities and assessments for online initiatives); peer mentoring as part of the training process; technical skills and support issues; and the importance of ensuring the consistency of the institution's mission with the online program's plan and goals.

Institutional support for online faculty is a key contributor to faculty satisfaction, to the success of online programming, and to the success of online students. Although emphasis will be placed on faculty feedback and team review of the local training portion of *The Monroe Model*, all campus-based components will be studied in an effort to address the specific, yet broad-based needs of online faculty. In the same way that online services for students are being expanded to accommodate a broader base of learners via a niche services approach, institutional support services for online faculty may also improve faculty satisfaction using a similar strategy.

IV. SUMMARY

The Monroe Model originated as a response to a convergence of issues: faculty course design, development and delivery needs; rapid online program growth; unresolved protocol and communication issues; and the general operational on-site support requirements of a comprehensive online program. The model has evolved as a collaborative, comprehensive, action-oriented, and non-hierarchical team that strives to parallel the best practices of an online learning environment.

MCC's experience suggests that institutions interested in providing quality online programs that support and encourage online faculty participation, faculty satisfaction, and student success should give serious consideration to a blended approach to institutional support for online faculty. Although this case study emphasizes the online faculty support roles of SLN campuses, the model may also be useful as a framework for institutions that utilize proprietary or home-grown technical and course management support systems.

The centralized support provided by the SUNY Learning Network—in particular, the server infrastructure, the help desk support, and the pedagogically sound template—has allowed the local campus to focus on faculty, student, and local process issues. *The Monroe Model* is a successful framework that continues to evolve. It has provided needed online faculty support, and has helped the on-site support team to gain the mutual respect and support of faculty and administrators. This advocacy has encouraged the team to continually seek improvement and to meet the needs of online faculty in an expedited and professional manner. MCC will continue to aggregate SLN faculty satisfaction data to inform its practice. MCC's Fall 2002 online faculty satisfaction survey will provide empirical data with which to assess specific on-site support team initiatives. The results of this survey will play a key role in the expansion and revision of *The Monroe Model*.

V. ACKNOWLEDGEMENTS

I acknowledge the creativity, commitment to high academic standards and the enthusiasm demonstrated by the online faculty members of Monroe Community College. Their willingness to break new ground and to explore innovative instructional methods serves our students well. Special thanks to past and present members of *The Monroe Model* team and to Eric Fredericksen, Alex Pickett and Tammy Mooney, who shared their SLN vision and inspired us all. Finally, I gratefully acknowledge my very first teacher and mentor, Mary J. Morin.

VI. ABOUT THE AUTHOR

Marie J. Fetzner is Assistant to the Vice President of Educational Technology at Monroe Community College in Rochester, NY. She is a founding member of *The Monroe Model* team and is an adjunct instructor in the MCC Transitional Studies Department where she teaches both campus-based and online courses. She is a consultant on online learning and is conducting research on online student retention as part of her Ph.D. program at the Margaret Warner Graduate School of Education and Human Development at the University of Rochester. She earned her Master of Public Administration degree from SUNY College at Brockport, and earned her Bachelor in Music Education degree from the Eastman School of Music at the University of Rochester.

VII. REFERENCES

1. **Dillon, C. and S. Walsh**, Faculty: The Neglected Resource in Distance Education. *The American Journal of Distance Education,* 1992. **6**(3): p. 5-19.

2. **Olcott, D.J. and S.J. Wright**, An Institutional Support Framework for Increasing Faculty Participation in Postsecondary Distance Education. *The American Journal of Distance Education,* 1995. **9**(3): p. 5-17.

3. **Lee, J.,** Instructional Support for Distance Education and Faculty Motivation, Commitment, and Satisfaction. *British Journal of Educational Technology,* 2001. **32**(2): p. 153-60.

4. **Schifter, C.C.,** Faculty Participation in Asynchronous Learning Networks: A Case Study of Motivating and Inhibiting Factors. *Journal of Asynchronous Learning Networks (JALN),* 2000. **4**(1): p. Available online at: http://www.sloan-c.org/publications/jaln/v4n1/v4n1_schifter.asp.

5. **Rockwell, K.,** and colleagues, Faculty Education, Assistance and Support Needed to Deliver Education via Distance. *The Online Journal of Distance Learning Administration,* 2000. **Volume III, Number II** (Spring 2000, State University of West Georgia): p. Available at: http://www.westga.edu/~distance/rockwell32.html.

6. **Thompson, M.** Faculty Satisfaction in the On-line Teaching-Learning Environment. Sloan ALN Workshop 2002. Lake George, NY, Conference Presentation.

7. **Hartman, J., C. Dziuban, and P. Moskal**, Faculty Satisfaction in ALNs: A Dependent or Independent Variable? *Journal of Asynchronous Learning Networks,* 2000. **4**(3). Available at: http://www.sloan-c.org/publications/jaln/v4n3/v4n3_hartman.asp.

8. **LeBlanc, G.,** Bridging the Distance: Supporting Distance Education Faculty and Staff at the University of Maine, in From Vision to Reality: Providing Cost-effective, Quality Distance Education, Eighth Annual Conference on Distance Teaching and Learning. 1992, University of Wisconsin-Madison: Madison, Wisconsin. p. 94-98.

9. **Bullock, C. and S. Schomberg**, Disseminating Learning Technologies Across the Faculty. *International Journal of Educational Technology,* 2000. **2**(1): p. Available at: http://www.outreach.uiuc.edu/ijet/v2n1/bullock/index.html.

10. **Passmore, D.L.,** Impediments to Adoption of Web-Based Course Delivery Among University Faculty. *ALN Magazine,* 2000. **4**(2). Available at: http://www.sloan-c.org/publications/magazine/v4n2/passmore.asp.

11. **Boettcher, J.V. and R.M. Conrad,** *Faculty Guide for Moving Teaching and Learning to the Web.* 1999, League for Innovation in the Community College: Mission Viejo, CA.

12. **Clay, M.,** Development of Training and Support Programs for Distance Education Instructors. *The Online Journal of Distance Learning Administration,* 1999. **Volume II, Number III**(Fall 1999, State University of West Georgia): p. Available at: http://www.westga.edu/~distance/clay23.html.

13. **Robinson, P. and E. Yu Borkowski,** Faculty Development for Web-Based Teaching: Weaving Pedagogy with Skills Training, in *Web-Based Learning and Teaching Technologies: Opportunities and Challenges,* A. Aggarwal, Editor. 2000, Idea Group Publishing: Hershey, Pennsylvania. p. 216-226.

14. **Lorenzetti, J.P.,** Giving Online Faculty a Full Circle of Support, in *Distance Education Report.* 2002. p. 1, 6 March 1, 2002.

15. **Visser, J.A.,** Faculty Work in Developing and Teaching Web-Based Distance Courses: A Case Study of Time and Effort. *The American Journal of Distance Education,* 2000. **14**(3): p. 21-32.

16. **Ko, S. and J. Lieberman,** An Integrated Model of Training and Support for Online Teaching. 2000, *Net*Working* 2000. http://flexiblelearning.net.au/nw2000/talkback/p03.htm.

17. **Coppola, N., S. Hiltz, and N. Rotter.** Becoming a Virtual Professor: Pedagogical Roles and ALN. In the 34th Annual Hawaii International Conference on System Sciences (HICSS-34). 2001. Maui, Hawaii.

18. **Young, J.R.,** The 24-Hour Professor: Online Teaching Redefines Faculty Members' Schedules, Duties, and Relationships with Students, in *The Chronicle of Higher Education,* May 31, 2002. 2002. p. A31-A33.

Student Satisfaction

STUDENT SATISFACTION WITH ONLINE LEARNING: AN EXPANDING UNIVERSE

John Sener
Sener Learning Services
Sloan Center for OnLine Education

Joeann Humbert
Rochester Institute of Technology

- Is there is a fundamental contradiction between maximizing student satisfaction and providing the best possible learning experience?

- For a quality program, development of services must be equal to the development of courses.

- A greater recognition of the student as customer is a welcome reversal of institution-centered, student-unfriendly practices of the past.

- Technical support services and academic services such as academic advising, mentoring and tutoring influence student satisfaction.

- "Immediacy behaviors" such as encouragement, addressing people by name, and humor are positive predictors of student satisfaction.

I. INTRODUCTION

Although student satisfaction has been a frequent topic in the previous three Sloan Consortium's summer workshops on Asynchronous Learning Networks (ALNs), last year's workshop was the first one for which student satisfaction was an explicitly identified topic with several associated invited papers. This overview of student satisfaction builds upon the work presented in the previous volume (*Elements of Quality Online Education*) and attempts to:

- Identify some of the key issues associated with student satisfaction;
- Outline the current state of practice by highlighting some examples where student satisfaction has been attained and measured effectively;
- Speculate about possible future directions in the area of improving and measuring student satisfaction; and
- Suggest some areas where improvements are needed.

In some respects, student satisfaction is a relatively simple variable to evaluate. On many evaluation scales (e.g., Kirkpatrick's 4-level scale or Phillips's 5-level scale), student satisfaction is considered the lowest, most elemental level of evaluation. In fact, many evaluators often deride student satisfaction surveys as "smile tests" that don't reach deeply enough to evaluate what is really important – actual learning and its effect on post-course outcomes such as learners' subsequent performance or return on investment.

Nonetheless, student satisfaction is a vital element in determining the overall quality, success, and evolution of online learning environments. Establishing that students in online courses are comparably satisfied with their courses relative to students in traditional classroom courses helps legitimize online education. Indeed, some observers (e.g. [1]) believe that online education has been held to a higher standard of scrutiny than classroom instruction, and that the resulting greater attention paid to evaluating online education by using such measures as student satisfaction has not only elevated the practice of online learning, but is starting to elevate the practice of traditional education as well. Also, as online education continues to evolve in complexity, the need to evaluate students' satisfaction with their overall learning experiences and with key elements of those experiences grows accordingly.

In other respects, student satisfaction is a complex, multi-faceted, and challenging area of evaluation. As online education evolves, there are a rapidly growing number of elements and related practices to evaluate, as well as an increasing need for evaluation of how the parts work together on the programmatic or systems level. This paper will highlight some examples of evaluating student satisfaction with both individual practices and programs. The volume of student satisfaction evaluation seems to be steadily increasing, and the studies illustrated in this paper represent the tip of an iceberg of evaluation studies, many of which have been conducted internally by institutions and are not readily available to a larger audience. However, the studies highlighted here also illustrate, by implication, vast gaps in knowledge about student satisfaction and the need to learn much more about what satisfies students in online education.

It is also necessary to distinguish between student satisfaction in fully online [2] learning environments and that in hybrid, or blended learning [3] environments. An appropriate analogy might be the difference between wilderness camping and car camping. Wilderness camping, like fully online learning, is essentially a 'self-contained' process that requires the participant to enter the environment equipped with everything needed to negotiate the environment successfully. If something is not adequately provided for, the wilderness camper/online learner is out of luck if s/he cannot find it by foraging locally. By contrast, learners in blended learning environments, like car campers, can rely on a backup resource (the physical campus) which lessens the need to provide every service online. As a result, although the issues related to student satisfaction are similar in both types of environments, the approaches, needs, and current state of practice in each type of learning environment are different in many respects. Another reason the distinction is important is because fully online learning environments are in some ways easier to study and evaluate than blended learning environments. Online learning programs have been seen as the 'new kid on the block' that require special attention to determine their legitimacy; also, they are often located in separate institutional units which out of necessity have evolved significant ongoing experience and expertise in justifying their existence. By contrast, blended learning environments often originate from traditional academic units such as discipline-based departments and are generally not accustomed to even superficial outside scrutiny of their practices; thus, less is currently known about them. For instance, the Maryland Higher Education Commission compiles statewide statistics on higher education distance learning programs, but collecting similar statistics on blended learning programs is at present essentially impossible because of the political and other logistical issues involved.

Student satisfaction can be usefully divided into several areas of inquiry as depicted in Figure 1: student satisfaction with courses, with programs, and with the overall learning experience. At the most basic level, *student satisfaction with individual courses* involves determining whether students are satisfied overall with their online courses and with what they learned in them, or whether they would take other online courses and recommend them to their friends. More in-depth evaluation focuses on one or more specific variables related to courses, such as the instructor (quality, effectiveness, etc.), instruction, interaction level with the instructor, other students, or other learning participants, and/or establishment of learning community. *Student satisfaction with programs* includes measuring basic overall satisfaction with students' programs of study, as well as specific variables that directly impact student satisfaction with programs such as administrative support services (e.g., admissions, registration, career services, etc.) and academic services which students are more likely to associate with programs than with courses (e.g., basic program information provision, placement testing). Several important variables, in particular technical support services and certain academic services such as academic advising, mentoring, or tutoring, tend to influence student satisfaction with both courses and programs. *Student satisfaction with the overall learning experience* may simply involve combining course and program satisfaction, or it may also include considering the effects on student satisfaction of factors over which an institution has some influence but no control, for instance learners' other life demands and responsibilities, students' career goals, perceived reputation of the institution, and many others.

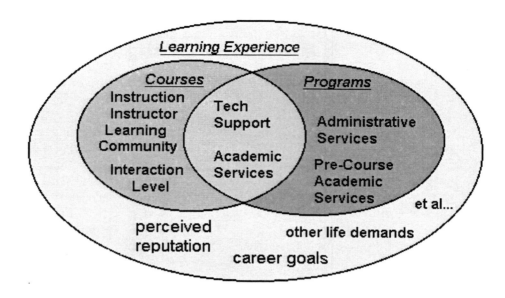

Figure 1: Student Satisfaction: Areas of Inquiry

II. KEY ISSUES AND THE CURRENT STATE OF PRACTICE

A. Basic Satisfaction with Online Learning – Courses, Programs, Overall Learning Experience

1. Key Issue

At the most basic level, verifying basic student satisfaction with their courses is a useful way of establishing and confirming the ongoing effectiveness of online learning. Quasi-experimental or other direct comparisons of student satisfaction with online versus classroom courses have dubious value for establishing which delivery mode is "better" [4, 5]. However, such comparisons are useful for establishing 'ballpark equivalency' and also as a method of identifying possible problem areas with online courses. Thus, continuing to verify student satisfaction with online learning on a basic level is important in supporting the ongoing growth and development of online education. Establishing basic student satisfaction with their overall programs and learning experience, although done somewhat less often, is similarly useful for attaining these purposes.

2. Current State of Practice

As documented in previous volumes in the Sloan-C series, students have reported on many satisfaction surveys at a variety of institutions (e.g., SUNY Learning Network members [6], University of Phoenix [7], Northern Virginia Community College [8]) that they are satisfied with their online courses and with what they learned in them, and that they would take other online courses and recommend them to their friends. Although such measures may seem rather simple or perhaps even insignificant, in fact they reflect some of the positive effects of achieving high levels of student satisfaction. For instance, in a Spring 2001 student survey at Rochester Institute of Technology, 20% of students taking their first online course indicated that they found out about RIT through a co-worker's recommendation, and 11% found out about RIT from a friend or family member. Based on the results of these and other surveys of individual institutions (e.g. [9]) and consortia (e.g. [10]), it seems reasonable to state that attaining high levels of student satisfaction with online courses, programs, and overall learning experiences is now a frequent occurrence, verifying the effectiveness and legitimacy of online learning. While this statement will hardly surprise most practitioners in the field, it is far from common knowledge in higher education, let alone with the general public or the media who report on online learning.

Initial attempts to measure student satisfaction tend to focus on the most basic level of satisfaction with individual courses. Many student evaluation studies have moved beyond this most basic level to focus on other aspects of student satisfaction with a variety of measures related to instruction and the learning experience, for instance:

- Willingness to recommend instructor to other students; degree to which course met expectations; satisfaction with faculty expertise, professional experience, presentation, and effective course management and organization; satisfaction with course assignments and allotted learning time; satisfaction with increased problem-solving skills [7];

- Curriculum content, instructional quality, clarity of objectives, ability to achieve objectives, clarity of requirements [10];

- Amount of knowledge gained; analytical and problem-solving skills developed [11].

Other student evaluation studies have focused on other key issues, in particular the role of interaction among learning participants, primarily instructor-student and student-student, the level of satisfaction with other elements of the learning process such as academic and administrative support services, and the relationship between student satisfaction and other key variables such as learning effectiveness and interaction level.

B. Appropriate Level of Interaction Among Learning Participants

1. Key Issue

The key issue here is matching learners' needs with the level of interaction and learning community involvement.

2. Current State of Practice

Some studies have found that high perceived levels of interaction correlates strongly with high student satisfaction levels. For instance, the SUNY studies reported in previous Sloan-C volumes found that interaction with the instructor is the most significant contributor to perceived learning and that high levels of participation and interaction with other classmates directly related to high levels of perceived learning. Student satisfaction data from many programs such as SUNY [12], New Jersey Institute of Technology [13], and many others suggest that requiring high levels of interaction or collaboration among learners can result in successful courses and viable programs.

At the same time, online courses with required interaction or collaboration with other learners generally have more rigid schedules (e.g., scheduled interactive events, fixed project timeframes). Not surprisingly, anecdotal and other informal evidence suggests that high levels of required interaction or collaboration with other learners can reduce learner flexibility and convenience. This is a significant consideration because many studies indicate that flexibility and convenience are among the most important reasons why students take online courses. For instance, a study of almost 1,000 students at 23 higher education institutions in Connecticut found that almost all students surveyed rated flexibility of time and place as "very important" (90% and 86% respectively) in their choice of online classes [10]. Over 80% of respondents in another study at Frederick (MD) Community College cited convenience and time constraints as their most important reasons for taking an online course [27]. Learners who face severe time and flexibility constraints or prefer more individualized study approaches may find courses with required interaction or collaboration with other learners to be insufficiently flexible to meet their needs. For instance, the eArmyU initiative encourages its education provider partners to offer courses that minimize required interaction or collaboration. This is because soldier-students often experience sudden and severe schedule changes (e.g., relocation, training missions) that interfere with their ability to adhere to more rigid schedules. Geographically dispersed, adult working professionals often have similar constraints. Also, some evidence indicates that the quality of instructor-student interactions, assignments, and activities in online courses contribute more to student satisfaction than do student discussion and student to student contact [14].

Fortunately, other models which rely on interaction between the instructor and individual students are also emerging and have engendered student satisfaction. For instance, instructor-led online learning has proven to be a satisfying way of delivering courses to public health professionals [15]. An online 'tutorial model' of instruction emphasizing feedback between instructor and student has also produced effective and satisfying results in community college courses [8].

Many online courses also include other learning participants – tutors, guest experts or discussants among others – to enhance the learning experience. Although such efforts are still relatively rare, a few efforts have attained positive results in achieving student satisfaction. For instance, Mercy College in New York uses student peers as online teaching assistants or "course wizards" as tutors, discussion facilitators, and role models; survey data indicated increased comfort levels from students in courses that had 'wizards,' as well as a high level of satisfaction from the student 'wizards' themselves [16]. In short, it appears that finding an appropriate level of interaction among learning participants is a key strategy to creating student satisfaction in online courses.

C. Appropriate Level of Learning Community Involvement

1. Key Issue

Appropriate level of learning community involvement is a separate issue from level of interaction with instructor and other students in some cases, since not all effective online courses include learning community involvement as an integral element of their design. However, the key issue here is also one of matching – in this case, the level of learning community involvement with learners' needs. High student satisfaction has also occurred in programs and courses that are not structured for learning community formation, although appropriate levels of student-instructor and student-student interaction are generally essential to success in these programs as well.

2. Current State of Practice

Perhaps not surprisingly, online programs that emphasize learning community formation such as Penn State's World Campus often report that a majority of their students have consistently reported feeling part of a learning community in their programs [17]. SUNY's research has found that high perceived levels of interaction and learning community involvement correlate strongly with high student satisfaction levels [6].

Some studies have started to look more specifically at the factors which facilitate learning community formation and involvement. One promising area of research and practice involves measuring 'social presence,' or the degree to which online learning environments communicate a sense of community building and belonging. Swan [18] has developed a "Social Presence Indicator" research instrument to document "ways [that] participants support community through creating a sense of social presence" in online courses. Using a somewhat different concept to describe similar online behaviors, another study found that the prevalence of "immediacy behaviors" used to reduce the social distance between instructor and students, such as encouragement of discussion and feedback from both instructor and students, addressing students by name in discussions, and the use of humor, were positive predictors of student satisfaction [19].

D. Satisfaction with Online Academic and Administrative Support Services

1. Key Issue

Satisfaction with the amount and quality of online student support services provided is another key element of attaining student satisfaction with online learning (e.g., [20]). Perhaps reflecting a relative lack of attention being paid to student satisfaction with online services as compared to courses, a study conducted by the Western Cooperative for Educational Telecommunications (WCET) in 1997 determined that for a quality distance (or online) learning program, development of services must be equal to the development of courses. Mirroring the chief concerns about student satisfaction with online instruction, the WCET study concluded that effective services must be convenient, feature one-stop, anytime anyplace delivery, be equal to campus services and based on learners' identified needs, and enable learners to feel connected to their campus [21].

Most student satisfaction studies in this area tend to focus either globally on student support services provision or specifically on one or several support services. Of particular interest in the latter category are student satisfaction levels with technical support, especially with regard to computer hardware and software training to assure that students have the requisite skills to navigate online courses. The picture in this area is somewhat unclear. For instance, the SUNY studies found that computer knowledge does not seem to a barrier to satisfaction in online courses, since students with the least prior computer knowledge reported the highest level of learning [22]. However, another study found that computer self-efficacy, or students' perceived ability to use computers effectively, was a significant factor affecting satisfaction for adult learners in web-based courses [23]. Computer self-efficacy appears to be a critical element in learner confidence, and students tend to be dissatisfied and drop out of distance learning courses if they are not confident in the learning process or environment [24, 25]. Some of the quality standards sets that have been developed in recent years, such as the American Distance Education Consortium (ADEC) Guiding Principles for Distance Learning and the National Education Association (NEA) Quality Benchmarks, emphasize the importance of providing students with adequate computer training before and during online courses.

2. Current State of Practice

In general, more attention is starting to be paid to evaluating student satisfaction with online support services; several substantive studies of various services at several institutions have been published. Most student satisfaction studies in this area tend to focus specifically on one or several support services. For instance, extensive surveys of students taking online courses at Pace University indicate high levels of satisfaction with online testing, technical support, basic program information provision, and tutoring services [26]; other studies have found high levels of student satisfaction with the availability of library services, technical help, and ease of registration [10], with online library and testing center services [27], or with a potpourri of services provided by a specific support unit within a program [9].

On the other hand, it is difficult to determine how extensive such evaluation has become at present. Many institutions are performing such evaluations, but the results are kept internally and not shared with a larger audience. Some institutions report providing online student support services but having inadequate or even no mechanisms in place to assess student satisfaction level with these services. In addition, relatively few studies thus far have comprehensively examined online student support services provision at the institutional level, and even fewer have examined the role of integration of student services and its effect on student satisfaction.

E. Dealing with Student Expectations

1. Key Issue

What is optimal student satisfaction? At first glance this may seem like an easy question to answer: the more satisfied the students, the better. In reality, however, to some extent there is a fundamental contradiction between maximizing student satisfaction and providing the best possible learning experience. Some of this is due to practical constraints such as limited resources or the law of diminishing returns; it may not be cost-effective or practical to increase student satisfaction from, say, 95% to 98% in some cases. Even more relevant are the various gaps between the wants and needs of the major stakeholders – students, faculty, institution, employers and parents.

The concept of student satisfaction is often perceived as focused primarily on student wants (Figure 2). On its most basic level, the notion of the "student as customer" has the same focus, as expressed by such statements as "the customer is king" or "the customer is always right." To the extent that satisfying students means giving them what they want, this conception is accurate.

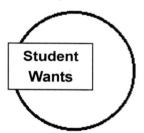

Figure 2. Focus on Student Wants: The Student as Customer

However, students do not always know what they want, and there are gaps between their wants and needs (Figure 3). Thus there is a gap between providing students what they want (which presumably leads to maximum satisfaction) and providing them what they need (which may reduce reported satisfaction, at least in the short term). This gap can be closed to some extent by attempting to create "educated consumers," i.e., students who learn to want what they need, but this does not address the issue entirely because there are other stakeholders in the learning process with their own wants and perceptions of students' needs.

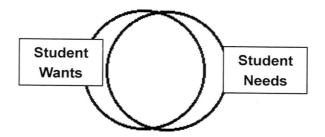

Figure 3. Focus on Student Wants and Needs

Many higher education practitioners, faculty in particular, contend that what students should not always be given what they think they want, at least in some areas. Proponents of this view point to situations which suggest that simply giving students what they say they want often descends into pandering, such as instances where tying faculty performance evaluation to student satisfaction surveys has resulted in grade inflation and lowered academic standards in classroom courses. These observers contend that learners bear some of the responsibility for their own satisfaction because a certain level of performance is expected from them, and that the learning performance process can be inherently difficult, even painful, or otherwise not conducive to maximizing reported student satisfaction. This view also presumes that students do not always know what they want or what is best for them. However, it also implies that other parties – faculty, the institution, employers, parents – *do* know what is best for students. Inevitably, then, there are also gaps between students' wants and needs and those of the other stakeholders in the process. The more one considers these gaps, the less clear the picture becomes (Figure 4).

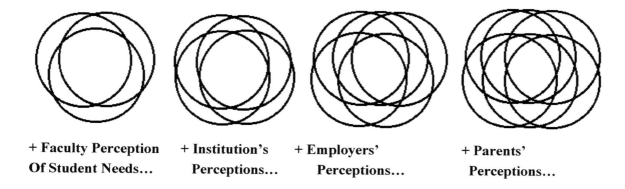

+ **Faculty Perception**   + **Institution's**   + **Employers'**   + **Parents'**
Of Student Needs...   **Perceptions...**   **Perceptions...**   **Perceptions...**

Figure 4. Focus on Student Wants and Needs + Others' Perceptions of Student Needs

The issue of what to focus on becomes important when considering how to deal with student expectations and the resulting impact on student satisfaction. Online learning programs face a host of decisions about the extent to which they need to meet student expectations relative to instruction, technology use, student services, and many other areas. Some cases are primarily a question of expectations management, for instance training students to expect a reasonable instructor response time to online communications. In other cases, for instance provision of online student services, institutions appear to have much less control over student demand than the term "expectations management" implies.

2. Current State of Practice

It is extremely difficult if not impossible to assess the current state of practice regarding how well institutions are dealing with the gap between student wants and needs. At the very least, it seems reasonable to conclude that there is a growing awareness of this gap and increased efforts to treat the student as customer. Recent online discussions of this topic by higher education practitioners on the Sloan-C listserv suggest widespread agreement that the higher education student is a customer, at least in some respects. Program and student services administrators seem more inclined to accept "student as customer" as an "exact" or sufficient descriptor of the student role, while faculty tend to view students as more than just customers and often perceive the customer role as much less relevant to the instructional process. So perhaps it is useful to differentiate between students' roles as learner and as consumer of student services: students are more clearly customers in the latter case with more closely aligned wants and needs, while the role of student as learner is more of a balancing act between student and institutional wants, needs, and responsibilities.

Practice standards such as those created by ADEC, NEA, and others are useful tools for meeting and managing student expectations since they identify many of the areas where gaps are likely to occur as well as recommended practices for dealing with them. Many institutions are either following these recommended practices or developing their own, resulting in numerous new practices for meeting and managing student expectations in a wide variety of areas, for instance specifying instructor response protocols to online communication with students, or monitoring and continuously improving help desk operations, or providing online registration. As noted earlier, actual student satisfaction with these practices is generally unknown, or evaluation results are not shared with a greater audience.

At the same time, many institutions are reporting a struggle with rising student expectations regarding the provision of online instruction and student services. On the instructional side, there is evidence of a possible disconnect between faculty and student technology use. A Pew Internet and American Life project reports that teens are becoming so "Net-savvy" that they report a 'substantial disconnect" between how they use the internet outside of school and how they use it in the classroom. Teens use the Internet to multi-task -- instant message (IM), reserve books at the library, order online, participate in an online quiz or games – and are frustrated that teachers don't use the web more effectively. A July 2002 Pew survey indicates that 78% of teens 12-17 go online, suggesting a possible huge disconnect coming up the pipeline as these students enter college [28]. Of course, many of these students are already in the pipeline; in a 2001 course inventory project of distance courses at RIT, for example, an online chat feature was used in 29% of the 82 courses surveyed, and ease of use increased frequency of use considerably.

On the student services side, some online services, for instance online registration, bookstore ordering, or library research and document retrieval, are proving to be far superior to the previous level of service and convenience provided in person. This, coupled with students' increasing "Net-savviness," perhaps explains the rapid rise in student expectations regarding provision of online student services that some institutions are reporting. These consumer expectations are shaping institutional direction at least to some extent, as some of these same institutions often report that they have no choice but to dedicate resources and launch new technologies to offer a comprehensive array of student services online in response to student demand. In a 2002 EDUCAUSE survey polling members about their most pressing information technology-related challenges, respondents rated administrative system/enterprise resource planning (ERP) as the primary issue for institutions to resolve for strategic success. Online student services was another top concern in this area and was rated in the top five issues in terms of potential to become even more significant in the coming year [29].

III. PROMISING FUTURE DIRECTIONS AND NEEDED DEVELOPMENTS

There are currently a number of likely future directions in the field of online learning. Most of them are exciting and promising, but a few of them will be extremely challenging. As the preceding discussion should indicate, there are also many developments that are needed to facilitate the continued healthy evolution of online learning. Several of the most significant promising directions and needed developments are discussed below.

A. Longitudinal Studies

Now that online learning has been around for a number of years, program-oriented longitudinal studies evaluating the longer-term results of online learning are starting to emerge. The RIT paper on student satisfaction discusses a longitudinal study of graduation and retention rates of online students as well as differences among student populations within that data set. The SUNY paper provides a unique and valuable look at student satisfaction in online courses by combining longitudinal data on student satisfaction along with the findings of a pilot survey implemented this summer to measure the relationship between "teaching presence" and student satisfaction and reported learning. Several other institutions have reported their results of student satisfaction studies or have begun the process.

More longitudinal studies are needed. An accumulation of such studies will have several beneficial effects: as a longer-term verification that online learning is satisfying and is here to stay; as a means for online learning programs to continuously improve their quality; and, indirectly, as a means to elevate the practice of higher education in general as online learning programs offer something that classroom programs often cannot – verification of their effectiveness.

More large-scale studies on student satisfaction would also be extremely helpful. Studies such as the recent Pew Internet & American Life survey "The Internet Goes to College" [30] get considerable attention from the academic media [31] and often mainstream media as well [32]. Upon closer examination, however, these studies are generally much less substantive than the research done by many Sloan-C members and cited in this paper. For instance, the recent Pew study surveyed 1,027 college students about their academic experiences on the Internet; 6% responded that they had taken an online course, of which only around half (52%) said the course was worth their time. Thus the survey's conclusions (as well as those of the media) are based on a sample of roughly 60 students, around 30 of which stated dissatisfaction. By contrast, there are now dozens of institutions that offer online education and routinely generate student satisfaction data on a regular basis from much larger population samples. More studies from these institutions need to be performed, published, and disseminated.

Despite its flaws, the Pew study raises some important questions about both the reality and perceptions of student satisfaction with online learning in higher education. Are the Pew results more representative of online learning as a whole, and the student satisfaction results reported by Sloan-C members anomalous, perhaps because of a greater attention to quality or some other unknown factor? If so, why? Or are the Pew results the anomalous ones? If so, why are researchers and the media so willing to make such sweeping statements based on such scanty data? Such studies also remind us that online learners are far from a monolithic population, and different sub-groups (non-traditional vs. traditional, adult vs. college age, degree-seeking vs. enrichment-seeking, first-timers vs. experienced online learners, etc.) may be more satisfied by different course designs, learning communities, student services, and other factors.

Student-oriented longitudinal studies, i.e., studies that track the progress of students over many years, would also be useful but are probably also wishful thinking at this time, given the effort and expense involved.

B.   Student Satisfaction with Instruction, Interactivity, Learning Community

Previously discussed developments in this area – development of a variety of interaction-appropriate learning models, or exploring the role of social presence in creating learning community and how to enable and measure it – are also promising future directions.   A possible desirable outcome is to educate and inform students about the variety of choices available to them in online learning environments, so that they can make more informed and suitable choices.   What is needed in this area is more granularity in general – what is satisfying to students and why.

A particularly challenging direction is *automated interactivity*.   Work in the development of intelligent agents attempts to produce software that acts as an intelligent assistant [33].   It is believed that intelligent agents will eventually be able to provide certain types of interactivity – answering frequently asked questions or providing basic feedback on assignments, for example – at least as effectively as online instructors currently do, saving them time and allowing them to redirect their efforts into more higher-level online interactions.   Some initial work has been done in this area (e.g., [34]), but considerable effort will likely be required to develop useful tools in this area.

C.   Student Satisfaction with Online Support Services

There are a number of promising developments related to student satisfaction with online support services which appear highly likely to continue in the future.   First of all, an *increased focus on student satisfaction with online support services* is starting to occur, as evidenced by studies underway from the Southern Regional Electronic Campus, Western Cooperative on Educational Telecommunications, and others.   There is also a *growing recognition that online support services provision benefits campus students*, as it blurs the distinction between online and classroom students. Campus-based students can often easily use online support services; more institutions are realizing this and are designing their services provision accordingly.   However, some reports indicate that integration of online services with campus-based support services is happening effectively at the departmental or unit level but not at the institutional or system level.

There is also a *greater recognition of the student as customer role*, which is a welcome response to the many institution-centered, student-unfriendly practices of the past.   There is a need to treat students even more like customers, especially with regard to student services provision.   The likelihood that students will become more educated consumers of online education also has implications for student services provision; for example, as more students learn to 'shop around' for the best online services, institutions that offer superior online student services will raise the bar for all institutions who serve online learners. At the same time, there is a need to delineate more clearly the student role as customer vis-a-vis students' other roles.   More specifically, a focus on students' needs, as expressed for instance by O'Banion's concept of "the learning college," [35], is more likely to optimize student satisfaction. The concept is based on the assumption that educational experiences are designed for the convenience of learners rather than for the convenience of institutions and their staffs.   It encourages engaging learners as full partners in the learning process, but with learners assuming primary responsibility for their own choices, thus supporting a balance with students' wants and needs.

D. Student Satisfaction and Blended Learning

Although this paper has focused primarily on fully online learning, the rise of *blended learning opportunities* is happening at least as rapidly as online learning, and promises to be diffused much more thoroughly in higher education. Blended learning, as with online support services provision, increasingly renders the distinction between online and classroom learning meaningless. Instead, learning designers are starting to focus more on figuring out the qualities of individual "ingredients" (delivery modes and media) and how combine them to create effective new "recipes" (appropriate mixes of delivery modes and media). Finding out what satisfies students about these various recipes and why will contribute greatly to the evolution of online learning.

IV. CONCLUSION

The search to provide and document student satisfaction with online learning has progressed well beyond its original focus of trying to determine whether pioneering online students liked their courses. A substantial body of student satisfaction research has verified that there are many learners who have been satisfied with their online courses, programs, and learning experiences. Further studies are beginning to explore and uncover the sources of student satisfaction on a more granular level throughout the entire range of the online learning experience. As with any expanding universe, the need to broaden and deepen our knowledge of satisfying students is growing in all directions. There is a lot of good work being done; more good work is needed, and the experiences of researchers and practitioners need to be shared with others.

VI. REFERENCES

1. **Sener, J.** Myths and Realities of Online Learning. *The Long Term View.* 5(3): 102-118 (Spring 2002).
2. "Fully online learning" refers to learning environments where the Internet is the principal delivery medium and does not preclude the use of other media (e.g., textbooks or other print media, CD-ROM, videotapes, etc.).
3. "Blended learning" is defined here as learning environments in which online learning is used to complement 'face-to-face' classroom instruction or vice versa.
4. **Saba, F**. Research in Distance Education: A Status Report. *International Review of Research in Open and Distance Learning*, (1) 1: 1-7 (June 2000).
5. **Diaz, D.** Carving A New Path for Distance Education Research. *The Technology Source*, March/April 2000. http://ts.mivu.org/default.asp?show=article&id=648
6. **Shea, P., Fredericksen, E., Pickett, A., Pelz, W., and Swan, K.** Measures of Learning Effectiveness in the SUNY Learning Network. In: Bourne, J. and Moore, J. (Eds.), Online Education: Learning Effectiveness, Faculty Satisfaction, and Cost Effectiveness, Volume 2. Needham, MA: Sloan-C, 31-54, 2001.
7. **Trippe, A.** Student Satisfaction at the University of Phoenix Online Campus. In: Bourne, J. and Moore, J. (Eds.), Elements of Quality Online Education. Needham, MA: Sloan-C, 173-187, 2002.
8. **Sener, J**. Bringing ALN into the Mainstream: NVCC Case Studies. In: Bourne, J. and Moore, J. (Eds.), Online Education: Learning Effectiveness, Faculty Satisfaction, and Cost Effectiveness, Volume 2. Needham, MA: Sloan-C, 7-30, 2001.
9. **Southern Connecticut State University, School of Communication, Information and Library Science**. Results of the Student Satisfaction Survey, March 2002. http://www.southernct.edu/departments/ils/satis_survey_results.html

10. **Connecticut Distance Learning Consortium**. Student Evaluation Survey Results: Spring 2001. http://www.ctdlc.org/Evaluation/index.html

11. **Benedetti, D**. Penn State World Campus Team Wins National Award [press release, 5/12/02]. http://www.worldcampus.psu.edu/pub/home/campnews/

12. **Shea, P., Swan, K., Fredericksen, E., and Pickett, A**. Student Satisfaction and Reported Learning in the SUNY Learning Network: Interaction and Beyond. In: Bourne, J. and Moore, J. (Eds.), Elements of Quality Online Education. Needham, MA: Sloan-C, 145-156, 2002.

13. **Hiltz, S.R., Coppola, N., Rotter, N., Turoff, M., Benbunan-Fich, R**. Measuring the Importance of Collaborative Learning for the Effectiveness of ALN: A Multi-Measure, Multi-Method Approach. In: Bourne, J. (Ed.), Online Education: Learning Effectiveness and Faculty Satisfaction, Volume 1. Needham, MA: Sloan-C, 101-120, 2000.

14. **Yacci, M.** Investigating the Affective Value of Instructional Interactivity. To be published.

15. **Vignare, K. and Sener, J**. Fighting Bioterrorism with Instructor-Led Online Learning. To be presented at the 8th Annual International Conference on Asynchronous Learning Networks, Orlando, FL, November 2002.

16. **Sax, B.** New Roles for Tutors in an Online Classroom: Report of a Program at Mercy College. To be published in the *Journal of College Reading and Learning*, 2002.

17. A detailed description can be found at the Sloan-C Effective Practices web site, http://www.sloan-c.org/effective/SortByStudentSat.asp .

18. **Swan, K.** Content Analysis of Social Transcripts: Social Presence. ALN Web Center on Learning Networks Effectiveness Research. www.alnresearch.org

19. **Arbaugh, J. B.** How instructor immediacy behaviors affect student satisfaction and learning in web-based courses. *Business Communication Quarterly*. 64(4), 42-54, 2001.

20. **Mason, R. and Weller, M.** Factors affecting students' satisfaction on a web course. *Australian Journal of Educational Technology*, 16 (2), 173-200, Winter 2000.

21. **Kendall, J.R., Moore, C., Smith, R., and Oaks, M.** Student Services for Distance Learners: A Critical Component. Washington State University, April 2001. http://www.naspa.org/netresults/PrinterFriendly.cfm?ID=229

22. **Fredericksen, E., Pickett, A., Shea, P., Pelz, W., Swan, K.** Student Satisfaction and Perceived Learning with Online Courses: Principles and Examples from the SUNY Learning Network. In: Bourne, J. (Ed.), Online Education: Learning Effectiveness and Faculty Satisfaction, Volume 1. Needham, MA: Sloan-C, 7-36, 2000.

23. **Lim, C.K.** Computer Self-Efficacy, Academic Self-Concept, and Other Predictors of Satisfaction and Future Participation of Adult Distance Learners. *The American Journal of Distance Education*, 15 (2), 41-51, 2001.

24. **Chacon-Duque, F.J**. A Multivariate Model for Evaluating Distance Higher Education. College Park: Pennsylvania State University Press, 1987.

25. **Keller, J.** Development of the ARCS Model of Instructional Design. *Journal of Instructional Development,* 10(3), 2-10, 1987.

26. **Sachs, D. and Hale, N**. Pace University's Focus on Student Satisfaction With Student Services in Online Education. In: Bourne, J. and Moore, J. (Eds.), Elements of Quality Online Education. Needham, MA: Sloan-C, 127-144, 2002.

27. **Claggett, C.** Distance Education Center Final Evaluation Report. Frederick, MD: Frederick Community College, September 2001.

28. **Levin, D., and Arafeh, S.** The Digital Disconnect: The Widening Gap Between Internet-Savvy Students and Their Schools. Pew Internet & American Life Project, August 14, 2002. http://www.pewinternet.org/reports/toc.asp?Report=67

29. **Kobulincky, P., Rudy, J**. Third Annual EDUCAUSE Survey Identifies Current ITS Issues. Educause Quarterly, 2002. http://www.educause.edu/issues/

30. **Jones, S.** The Internet Goes to College: How Students Are Living in the Future with Today's Technology. Pew Internet & American Life Project. September 15, 2002. http://www.pewinternet.org/reports/toc.asp?Report=71
31. **Kiernan, V.** Students Embrace the Internet, but Not as Replacement to Classrooms, Study Finds. *Chronicle of Higher Education*, September 16, 2002.
32. A radio broadcast news segment on Marketplace, September 16, 2002, also implied that online learning was not yet up to snuff based on the survey results.
33. **Murch, R. & Johnson, T**. *Intelligent Software Agents*. Upper Saddle River, NJ: Prentice Hall, 1999.
34. **Thaiupathump, C., Bourne, J., and Campbell, O.** Intelligent Agents for Online Learning. Journal of Asynchronous Learning Networks, 3(2), November 1999. http://www.sloan-c.org/publications/jaln/v3n2/v3n2_choon.asp
35. **O'Banion, T**. *Launching a Learning-Centered College.* League for Innovation in the Community College, 1999.

VI. ABOUT THE AUTHORS

John Sener is a consultant whose private practice focuses on supporting the evolution of on-line and other learning environments in higher education institutions and consortia, government agencies, and non-profit organizations. He currently serves as Project Evaluator for Maryland Faculty Online's Project Synergy and for a joint pilot project by Rochester Institute of Technology and Monroe County (NY) teaching bioterrorism courses using instructor-led online learning. He is also currently leading a project to survey online student services provision in Maryland higher education institutions for MarylandOnline (www.marylandonline.org). During his seven years at Northern Virginia Community College's Extended Learning Institute, Mr. Sener directed development of associate degrees in engineering, information systems technology, public management, and business management, available through home study and on-line distance education. Mr. Sener's career in education and training over the past twenty-three years includes directing a number of foundation and federally funded projects; he has also been a trainer, teacher, administrator, instructional designer, and tutor in the areas of adult literacy, basic skills, information systems, and English as a Second Language. He holds a M.S. degree in Education from Johns Hopkins University and a B.A. in Psychology from Oberlin College.

Joeann Humbert is the Director of Online Learning at the Rochester Institute of Technology, one of the oldest and most successful asynchronous online learning programs in the country. She is responsible for managing all facets of online learning: faculty development, course design and development, and online student support. Joeann also oversees the Teaching, Learning and Technology Lab, the rollout of the campus courseware system and the training and support for on-campus faculty using the campus courseware. Joeann is a member of the Institute Effective Teaching Committee and the Provost's Learning Innovations Grant Committee. Previous to her position as director, she was manager of Distance Learning Student Services at RIT. Joeann has an MS in Instructional Technology.

LONGITUDINAL SUCCESS MEASURES FOR ONLINE LEARNING STUDENTS AT THE ROCHESTER INSTITUTE OF TECHNOLOGY

Karen K Vignare
Rochester Institute of Technology

- Good longitudinal data and sharing data among higher education are lacking.

- It is critical that higher education get better at sharing and publishing data, so students can make more informed choices.

- A continuing longitudinal study at RIT found that:
  - Course completion rates in distance learning courses average 94.5%, for the past seven years.
  - Online learning students return at a higher rate than campus-based students.
  - There were no differences in cumulative graduation rates between males and females, but females and part-time students earned slightly higher grades.
  - The number of students relying completely on online learning for all their course work has been growing and expected to continue.

I. HISTORICAL BACKGROUND

With over 8000 enrollments in 2002 and 12 years of experience offering anytime/anywhere education, The Rochester Institute of Technology (RIT) is a leader and early pioneer in the asynchronous learning field. Its commitment to real quality and distance learning is validated by the over 2500 distance learning graduates from various programs since 1994. RIT has begun a longitudinal study of online learners. Although the data set is not complete, the data is extensive and revealing. The Online Learning Department will continue to investigate issues of importance in ALN and welcomes suggestions for the investigation from other ALN practitioners.

In 1991, RIT began offering a limited number of asynchronous learning courses through the local UNIX based computer network. Other types of technology were also employed in the early years. Since 1994, most all of the distance courses used a combination of the internet and computer conferencing along with other multimedia technologies—mostly VHS video to deliver the classroom to the personal computer. The same faculty who teach distance-learning courses teach on campus courses, using the same syllabus and learning outcomes objectives. Designed to allow adults with professional and personal obligations to get a full graduate or undergraduate degree without coming to campus, an underlying motivation of RIT's ALN program is to make sure distance offerings are accessible to students, so delivery technology complies with Americans with Disabilities Act (ADA) standards.

In 1996, a strategic distance-learning plan was designed by the University administration. The comprehensive plan integrated the work of distance learning into as many mainstream university services as possible. Additional funding for infrastructure, personnel and marketing was allotted to grow distance-learning programs. All students were eligible to take distance courses, but it was intended that academic departments would offer programs specifically aimed at new distance students. Efforts focused on faculty support, instructional designers offered training and advice, and faculty were given the leeway to design online courses as they saw fit.

A. Rationale for Continued Investigation

Defining and improving student satisfaction for distance learning courses has been of major importance to the Online Learning Department. As reported in various instruments through the last ten years, satisfaction has always shown very high, positive levels. While results were used to help improve various aspects of asynchronous learning, the Online Learning Department decided to initiate a detailed analysis of student records to complement the student satisfaction data. For the past two years the Online Learning Department has led a concerted effort to work with the RIT Institutional Research Office to locate and study online learning student records.

B. Methodology—Defining the Data Set

In 2000, the Office of Distance Learning initiated data analysis beyond the normal quarterly and annual information kept on hand. All student record data is owned by the Registrar and housed in the Information Technology Services department, and Institutional Research must be involved in any data gathering process. Data tracking from RIT Student Information System for RIT distance learners is a technological challenge. RIT's database is a legacy, home grown system which means that research often requires culling multiple reports. In addition, data must be then be manipulated by several other software programs like spreadsheet, database and SPSS (statistical analysis and data mining software). The lack of data integrity and continuity throughout the years, 1994 –2001 limits the job of data analysis. The good news is that student record data integrity improved greatly in 1998 and will provide more reliable findings in the future.

RIT needed to define how we would track the progress of distance learners. The population starts with any student taking a distance course [1]. A subset of students enrolled in distance courses are students matriculated into distance learning program codes. At RIT, 31 of the 33 distance programs also run on campus programs, and all the students matriculated into DL programs can also take on campus courses. After reviewing data from 1996 and 1997 graduates, it was clear that the number of students taking 100% of their course work online was less than 10% of the total distance population. As a result, RIT set a benchmark which defined any student taking more that 50% of his or her courses online as a distant learner. The rationale for choosing to flag all online students taking 50% or more of their course work in asynchronous online learning comes from the Online Learning Department which views the choice of distance learning as a choice of delivery style. Thus, what is most important is not that a student stays with online learning, but that the student obtains a distance learning experience that will be as good as or better than any classroom experience.

The initial data set (see Table 1) included student records from 1993 onward. The size of the population was limited, so after some debate we decided to look at retention, attrition and graduation rates for cohorts starting in 1995. The table below shows the diversity of students taking distance learning. There are matriculated students registered in distance learning only programs, matriculated students registered in other RIT programs and many non-matriculated students taking distance learning.

Table 1. Number of RIT students choosing distance learning courses

Percent of distance courses as a percent of total courses		1993	1994	1995	1996	1997	1998	1999	2000	2001*
Students matriculated into distance programs	0 %	17	29	33	51	54	79	97	130	7
	10 %	14	25	37	59	62	78	112	165	10
	20 %	23	41	32	65	57	83	136	147	24
	30 %	15	21	27	64	48	71	94	113	30
	40 %	5	12	22	25	23	22	44	30	21
	50 %	16	28	35	104	80	67	101	145	43
	60 %	4	11	22	78	43	62	54	68	28
	70 %	3	8	10	26	34	16	27	35	10
	80 %	2	3	7	43	49	14	26	31	10
	90 %		1		2	3	1		2	0
	100 %	18	47	61	252	371	505	604	671	502
	Total	117	226	286	769	824	998	1295	1537	685

		1993	1994	1995	1996	1997	1998	1999	2000	2001*
Enrolled in non-distance programs	0 %	338	277	229	222	299	354	483	710	966
	10 %	216	156	147	151	186	231	264	396	668
	20 %	90	110	93	98	104	129	138	162	265
	30 %	44	62	58	41	48	58	82	71	139
	40 %	19	14	18	8	20	20	31	29	51
	50 %	50	45	63	45	34	48	59	63	134
	60 %	23	29	39	13	14	21	16	22	65
	70 %	13	10	16	2	4	7	4	8	28
	80 %	8	13	33	2	9	7	4	9	15
	90 %			2	1			1	1	1
	100 %	74	120	178	76	59	64	83	96	262
	Total	875	836	876	659	777	939	1165	1567	2594
Non-matriculated students	0 %	2				1		1	1	2
	10 %	8	5	8	8	2	6	3	14	6
	20 %	12	11	11	29	27	18	23	12	7
	30 %	15	11	7	36	43	29	15	21	17
	40 %		4	1	1	3	2	4	2	3
	50 %	37	35	35	65	54	50	34	94	27
	60 %	12	9	9	21	14	9	9	12	7
	70 %	3	2	1	2	4	3	4	5	7
	80 %	1	2	6	2	2	7		2	4
	90 %	1								1
	100 %	100	131	179	287	316	390	470	607	100
	Total	191	210	257	451	466	514	563	770	181
TOTALS		1183	1272	1419	1879	2067	2451	3023	3874	3460

Table 1. Continued

* Data are incomplete for academic year 2001.

The data shows that the number of students relying completely on online learning for all their course work has been growing. We expect that trend to continue as more students feel comfortable that they can learn successfully with the asynchronous learning method. Students at RIT will continue to have a choice of asynchronous or classroom or blended. Most of RIT's online students are within 30 miles of the college. So if students feel that they will be better served for whatever reasons, they will be able to continue to choose distance courses one quarter and campus courses the following quarter.

Chart 1. Online courses taken as a percent of total course work in a year

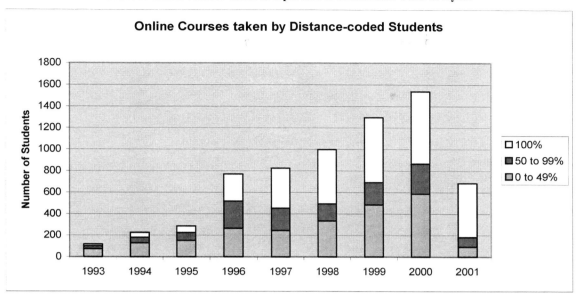

Chart 1. Online courses taken as a percent of total course work in a year

C. Results of Data Analysis

1. Graduation rates imply high levels of success

Measuring student satisfaction from the first year of enrollment through graduation is innovative. Establishing and sharing benchmarks should be a goal of asynchronous learning networks. It is critical that higher education get better at sharing and publishing data, so students can make more informed choices [2]. Thus it is interesting to know that at RIT, persistence through graduation is better than published on campus rates. The graduation rate for the university undergraduates was 55% in the 1995 cohort. For the graduate population at RIT it was nearly 70%. The online learning population at RIT is almost 65% undergraduate. RIT relies on a six-year graduation rate time frame. The same time frame was used for distance learning students.

Table 2. Cumulative graduation rates

Year Started	Number Students	Current Year	After 1 Year	After 2 Years	After 3 Years	After 4 Years	After 5 Years	After 6 Years
1995	136	2.94	26.47	45.59	54.41	63.24	67.65	71.32
1996	505	5.35	26.93	43.56	55.25	62.18	67.72	
1997	580	6.9	25.52	43.1	55.52	64.48		
1998	665	4.81	23.16	38.65	51.13			
1999	812	7.76	22.66	37.93				
2000	952	7.04	25.63					
2001	593	10.12						

Note: Data incomplete for academic year 2001.

Chart 2. Comparison of cohorts, graduation rates

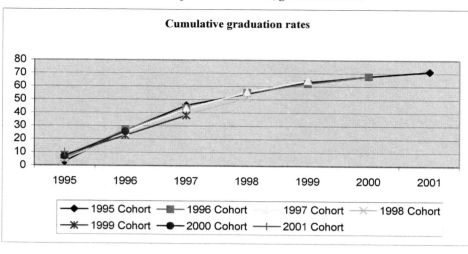

The cumulative graduation rates (see Table 2) have been relatively consistent throughout the seven annual cohorts reviewed. Viewed graphically (see Chart 2) this pattern of success throughout the last seven years becomes even more evident.

It is clear that online learning students are driven to complete their degrees. This is a finding that has been recorded in both marketing and in student satisfaction surveys. When asked why they are attending RIT Online, students respond overwhelmingly that they are here to complete a degree. The rates of completion seem to be staying constant. There are many reasons the trend remains the same. Student satisfaction with distance learning at RIT has remained constant and high over the years. Academic programs in which most online students are enrolled are ones in which students see a financial reward that is compelling enough to make them stay with the program. In addition, tuition investment cost to attend RIT is very high. Between 60 to 80 percent of non-traditional students receive employer support, but even those who don't receive employer reimbursement simply recognize the value of getting a degree. To reap the financial rewards of college, a student must graduate [3]. One more reason for the graduation rates remaining consistent may be that distance learning continues to meet student expectations. Evidence from other studies does show correlations between student satisfaction and fulfilled expectations.

However, there is some concern about these numbers. Online learning at RIT has matured. Continuous improvement over the years has led to improvements in academic content, course design, student services and support. The graduation rate seems to indicate the changes have only served to keep students at the same cumulative levels as before. What are the implications of this lack of change regardless of continued improvements? In some ways it would seem to support the notion that maturity of the product and of consumers means that RIT has kept pace with changing expectations.

2. Gender Differences

RIT is still a bit of an anomaly in today's college world. The number of females attending is closer to one-third than the fifty percent or higher on average reported by the Department of Education [4]. RIT's biggest curriculums are more male dominated than many other colleges. A gender equity team continues to review and recommend policies to change this ratio. In the last decade RIT has made great progress. Overall the gender make up of online students is more female than on campus. In the cohorts reviewed, 1995 through 2001, this trend was supported continuously throughout with the exception of 1995 cohort that was 78% male. However, that proportion was consistent with the university gender ratio that year. On average, two-thirds of the distance population was male and one-third female. A further review by program shows a slightly higher ratio of females in certain academic programs, for example, in the graduate information technology program.

Given the ratios, we further investigated whether there were any differences in cumulative graduation rates between males and females. There were none. Males and females followed graduation patterns similar to the cumulative distance population. There does seem to be a drop in female cohorts beginning in 1998. Yet, this drop reflects a pace similar to male graduation rates. More females graduate than men. This seems to support national data as well.

Table 3a. Male graduation rates as percentage

Year Started	Number Students	Current Year	Year 1	Year 2	Year 3	Year 4	Year 5	Year 6
1995	106	0.94	23.58	42.45	51.89	61.32	66.98	71.70
1996	329	3.95	22.49	38.91	50.76	57.75	64.44	
1997	394	7.11	24.62	40.36	52.28	62.18		
1998	452	4.42	21.02	35.62	49.56			
1999	550	7.64	20.91	37.27				
2000	639	6.10	25.04					
2001	407	11.06						

Chart 3. RIT Online males, cumulative graduation rates

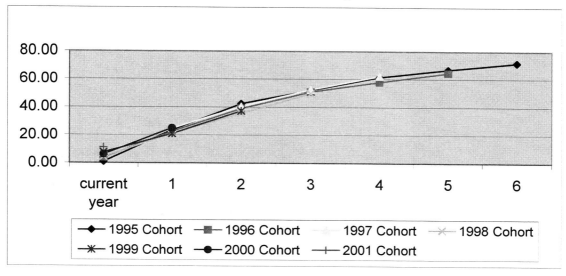

267

Table 3b. Female graduation rates

Year Started	Number Students	Current Year	Year 1	Year 2	Year 3	Year 4	Year 5	Year 6
1995	30	10.00	36.67	56.67	63.33	70.00	70.00	70.00
1996	176	7.95	35.23	52.27	63.64	70.45	73.86	
1997	186	6.45	27.42	48.92	62.37	69.35		
1998	213	5.63	27.70	45.07	54.46			
1999	262	8.02	26.34	39.31				
2000	313	8.95	26.84					
2001	186	8.06						

Note: Data is incomplete for year 2001.

Chart 4. RIT Online females, cumulative graduation rates

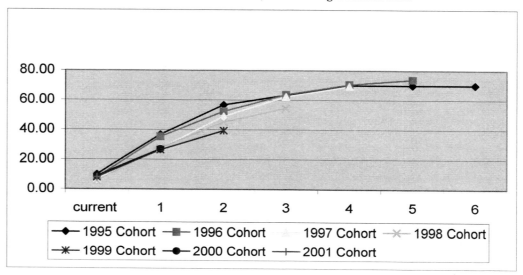

3. Retention and Course Completion Rates

Retention and attrition were also measured. Retention is measured as it would be on campus, on a year-to-year basis. Retention rate for online learning is the number of students returning to take at least 50% or more of their courses in distance learning. At first glance the attrition rate seems to be high. But once graduation rates have been taken into account, the data show almost 90% of the students continue with distance learning after the first year. Campus figures have improved at RIT, but the attrition rate in the 1995 cohort was over 20% for the freshman class. The comparison is also limited by that fact that 35% of online students are graduate students, who also tend to stay with the program more than undergraduates do. Comparable university wide data are non-existent, but from a RIT June 2000 report on retention, it is clear that online learning students return at a higher rate than campus-based students [5].

Moving from retention and attrition rates into course completion rates the Online Learning Department found course completion rates in distance learning courses average 94.5%, for the past seven years (see Table 4). Comparable university data is not available. Given RIT's unique distance population, Online Learning was able to investigate whether students in online course completed at different rates than students who were not enrolled in an online course that quarter. The students to whom they are compared are shown in chart 5. The comparable data on course completions for these students not currently taking distance was nearly the same as those take courses online. Correlation tests on the two sets of data did show the data was almost perfectly correlated.

Table 4. True attrition rates of students

Year	% Return After 1st Year
1995	9.56
1996	13.27
1997	8.45
1998	9.17
1999	11.58
2000	11.03
2001	
Average	10.51

True attrition rates show the number of students retained plus those who have graduated

This data also seems indicate that students who choose distance at RIT complete courses regardless of how the courses are delivered. It is interesting to postulate that personality is likely to dictate the choice of an online classroom. If that is the case, then this data would seem to support that: students who choose distance will do as well in both traditional classrooms and online ones. Essentially, distance education offers the flexibility to learn and complete courses when students want. Another comparison may well be with customer experience data for online businesses. That is, if a customer is already buying your brand giving them access to more ways to buy will increase both the number of transactions and the amount spent on transactions, indices of customer loyalty [6].

Chart 5. Course completion rates

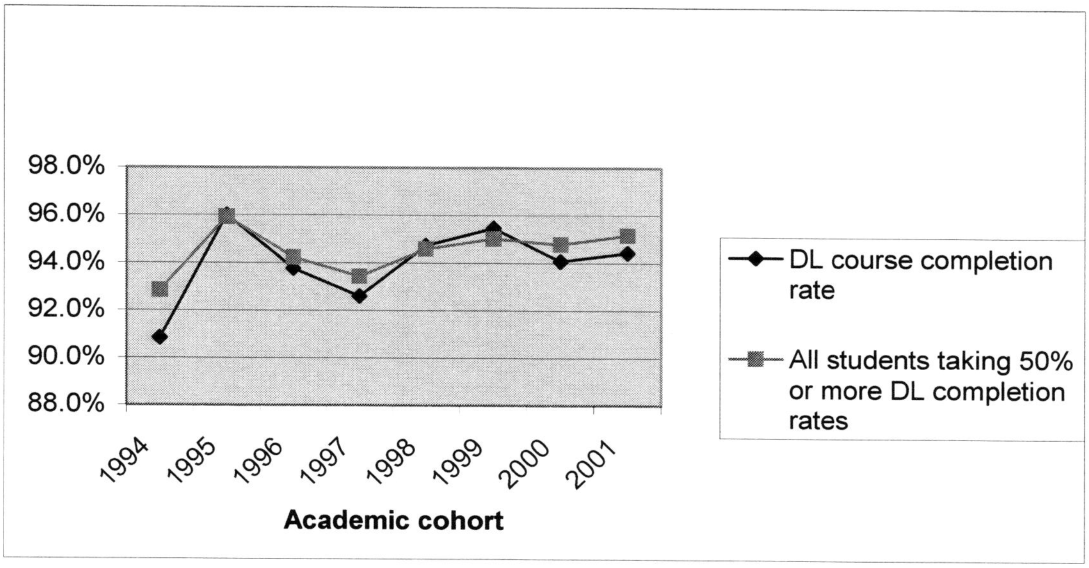

4. GPA, Status, Gender and Grade Comparisons

Analyses of GPA and course grades also support the evidence that distance students are performing very well. The mean GPA for cohorts 1994 through 2001 continues to match the same cohort not taking distance courses at the time. Both populations take at least 50% of the course work in distance learning. The students taking online courses each quarter are a subset of the larger population of students.

Table 5. GPA by group

	1994	1995	1996	1997	1998	1999	2000	2001
All Students taking 50% or more DL courses	3.05	3.09	3.19	3.20	3.12	3.21	3.18	3.02
Students in DL courses only	3.05	3.18	3.26	3.28	3.17	3.22	3.26	3.10

Further investigation using SPSS analyzed means and correlations in each cohort. Each cohort was tested for relationships between GPA and gender, course grade and status. While relationships were found to be significant in some cases, none was strong enough to indicate any relevant information. The simple means test compared the same data and regularly (each year) found that GPA was higher for women and those attending part-time.

Course grades were also scrutinized for information. No strong correlations existed. A distribution of grades across the two populations shows the grades to be distributed nearly the same year after year. The means test revealed that students receiving the highest grade also had higher GPAs. The pattern also followed the GPA pattern for gender and status. The means test showed each year that if a student was female on average she received a slight higher grade. The means test also revealed that part-time students were more likely to get better grades than full-time students. There are obvious reasons for this. Full-time students are likely to be younger and therefore less skilled in time management. Full-time students focus their energies across many courses while part-time students take only one or two courses a quarter. In 2001, RIT also began offering distance courses to students in the RIT Croatia College, American College for Management and Technology. Further an economic incentive also exists for part-time students that may not exist for full-time students. Many part-time students are reimbursed by employers when they receive a B or above.

Table 6. Distribution of Grades by Year

Grades	Students in DL Programs	All Students taking Distance Courses	Students in DL Programs	All Students taking Distance Courses
Year	1994		1995	
A	205	383	302	441
B	124	242	183	300
C	58	111	58	115
D	7	26	3	14
F	22	48	29	55
W	42	63	24	41
Year	1996		1997	
A	482	671	404	568
B	246	407	294	431

C	84	135	57	101
D	18	34	10	26
F	59	31	21	29
W	59	83	67	89
Year	**1998**		**1999**	
A	534	711	690	970
B	331	466	342	506
C	104	168	131	144
D	18	41	30	29
F	44	65	85	74
W	62	41	109	105
Year	**2000**		**2001**	
A	942	1352	682	1155
B	478	756	490	893
C	131	269	218	445
D	30	62	58	125
F	85	118	51	109
W	109	152	99	151

However, traditional students do seem to have as much success in distance courses. Student satisfaction surveys of day students support this finding. Day students respond regularly on surveys that they choose distance for its flexibility. Every year since 1998, RIT survey a subset of students who are considered full time students. They are asked in a short survey instrument why they choose distance. From a list of ten exclusive options, the overwhelming and consistent reason (70%) is for convenience and flexibility. The second most frequently chosen reason is because the course was not offered any other way. For those who choose distance willingly, it would seem that they are just as likely to perform and be satisfied with their experience. The recognition that traditional students may benefit from choosing their own learning delivery preference supports the decision RIT made to allow those students to take online courses.

5. Student Age Factors

An initial comparison of age, success and satisfaction was difficult. What we are able to determine is that the number of undergraduate students taking distance learning at RIT is much higher than reported national averages. A new survey by the Pew Internet & American Life Project reports that approximately 6% of all undergraduates age 18 to 22 have taken online courses [7]. The comparable sample from RIT is almost 15% of undergraduates have taken online courses.

Table 7. Student age factors

	22 & Under	23 - 25	26 -34	35 - 44	45 - 54	55 over	Total Students
1994	35%	11%	28%	22%	4%	0%	872
1995	21%	14%	32%	24%	8%	1%	1003
1996	15%	16%	32%	26%	11%	1%	1434
1997	25%	13%	24%	27%	11%	1%	1207
1998	28%	14%	26%	25%	7%	0%	1675
1999	25%	15%	28%	22%	9%	1%	2100
2000	28%	18%	27%	20%	7%	1%	2910
2001	48%	14%	20%	12%	5%	1%	3083

Unlike many other distance providers, RIT allows its undergraduates to take online courses as the age analysis shows. While the students above age 25 take more classes, there are more unique students in the traditional college age population than any other age group. For many years, RIT's Online Learning Department counseled traditional students not to enroll in distance courses. That advice was based on the lower performance those students exhibited, not the fact that they would be unsatisfied with the course experience. Online Learning has now made a policy of simply asking students if they believe they have the time-management skills for the asynchronous online classroom. This change in procedure seems to be more effective for all students regardless of age. RIT recognizes that different students prefer different learning styles, but that older students are often encumbered by more responsibilities—professional and personal obligations which make them opt more for the online class than do the traditional aged students who have more choices because their outside obligations are often less.

Chart 6. Age of students in online courses

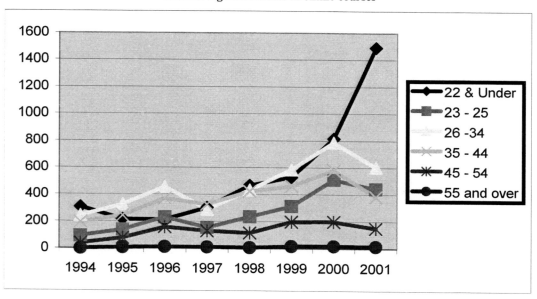

6. Location Analysis of Online Learners

RIT's online student population includes many students who take on campus courses. While the numbers of full-time undergraduate students were growing, many of those students in the last two years were just as likely to be located in Croatia (where RIT has a college) as they are located at RIT. Quite unexpectedly, RIT now has a very large international population. If we ignore traditional students attending online courses, the location has not changed much over the past five years. Most (50%) are within driving range, another 25% are located within New York State and finally the rest are located around the country. Less than one percent is located outside of the US.

At RIT students may enter three addresses in the system: local, home and alternate. Most often the Online Learning Department uses the home address as the mailing address. The data downloaded from the system used local only zip codes. A check of the two files indicated that there were indeed differences in the same social security records. Because of the inconsistency, no further analysis on location was possible at this time.

7. Academic Level Programmatic Data

A sub-sample of three distance learning student majors and non-matriculated students was reviewed to see if withdrawal, course retention or GPA statistics varied from the larger population. The programs chosen were the MS in Information Technology, the BS in Electrical Mechanical Engineering Technology and the non-matriculated population.

A previous study done by the James Scudder, department chair at RIT in 1999, evaluated the results of moving the part-time engineering program to an online format. While the results did show that online students were performing better than students coming to campus, these results were not statistically significant. The results below (see Table 8) simply attempt to see if this program is within the entire distance population. The population is well within those boundaries. GPA and course completion rate shows high levels of student success. This particular program is well known for its high retention level. It is less known for achievement of high academic grades. The students who attend this program are generally older and working in manufacturing facilities and thus have not had to use academic skills for some time. Yet, this program is a true success in distance. It is one of only two accredited BS level engineering technology programs in the country.

The MS in Information Technology attracts many different students. Those seeking to change jobs are typical students according to the department. As a result, many of these students face a bridge program (building undergraduate level skills first) before they can start in the graduate level courses. The course completion rates stand as a measure of student satisfaction for this program as well. While they are lower than the undergraduate program, they are within the range of larger population. The GPA averages are also within the range of the larger online population. The drop in average GPA is likely the result of a departmental attempt to increase the academic rigor of the program.

Table 8. Program population data

Year	BS Electrical Mechanical Engineering Technology		MS Information Technology		Non-Matriculated	
	GPA	Course Completion Rate	GPA	Course Completion Rate	GP A[1]	Course Completion Rate
1996	3.09	97%	3.47	93%	NA	93%
1997	3.2	96%	3.4	95%	NA	96%
1998	3.17	98%	3.32	91%	NA	94%
1999	3.19	99%	3.38	96%	NA	95%
2000	3.17	95%	3.36	94%	NA	92%
2001	3.18	98%	2.87	93%	NA	95%

*GPA stats are not reliable for non-matriculated students since nearly 90% have no previous GPA.

The most interesting results are revealed through the statistics on non-matriculated students. Generally, these students are choosing online for their first academic experience at RIT as recorded through entering term data. These first time students do not have a recorded GPA at RIT. The course completion rate is well within the range of the entire population of students. Most non-matriculated students either intend to enroll or are in the process of enrolling in a degree program. However, many of them choose to start without the commitment of a degree. Even without that commitment, they still complete the course overwhelmingly. The environmental factors supporting this behavior are clear to RIT.

New students are overwhelming satisfied and comfortable with the online process. RIT runs first time student surveys every quarter. These surveys indicate that first time students are indeed comfortable and satisfied with initial experiences. The review of their course completion rates complements this data. These students are given access to both customized online pages that prepare them for the online classroom experience, a CD-ROM to orient them to the online learning, and toll-free access to customer and technical support. In addition, these surveys indicate that physical contact with RIT is not a barrier. Students in the survey report they know whom to contact and using either the phone or email for customer service with a no difficulties. As a result the RIT Online Learning Department, feels that new and non-matriculated students at RIT are comfortable.

D. Measuring Satisfaction through a Course Inventory Project

The desire to describe online learning student satisfaction initiated another project to determine whether knowing more about activities in online classrooms could help explain success with satisfaction. In the winter of 2002, the Online Learning department decided to expand a course inventory project started in 2000. Of the 113 courses offered in the fall of 2001, a review of 82 courses was undertaken. For various technical reasons, all courses could not be reviewed. The purpose of the project was to catalog what was done in the course. Unlike many projects, no attempt was made to judge qualitatively what was going on; the inventory would simply acknowledge whether a teaching strategy or a teaching tool was in use. Applying terminology to describe all the activities was difficult. A teaching strategy refers to an activity undertaken to help students learn. A teaching tool is used to support the content being discussed. Some 43 items were reviewed in each course.

In the inventory project, at least two findings support the data analysis on student satisfaction online. Courses taught at RIT use asynchronous learning environments. For RIT this is an acknowledgement that faculty do listen and understand that using flexible online learning technologies will add to student satisfaction and lead to student success. Faculty typically follow the seven principles of good practice when setting up their online courses. The faculty have also adopted standard practices to assure students get the highest quality educational experience.

The second related finding from the inventory project is that much of the teaching done online uses text primarily. While many types of teaching strategies and activities are used, many are accomplished using text. Thus the online classroom is rich in activity and does not need at this time to add many supplemental tools to enhance student success. There are no classroom-based comparison inventories. Tying the inventory project to reasons online learning is chosen, helps make the inventory more useful. Students reported choosing online for convenience and flexibility, not for the diversity of classroom technologies available.

Chart 7. Inventory of design elements

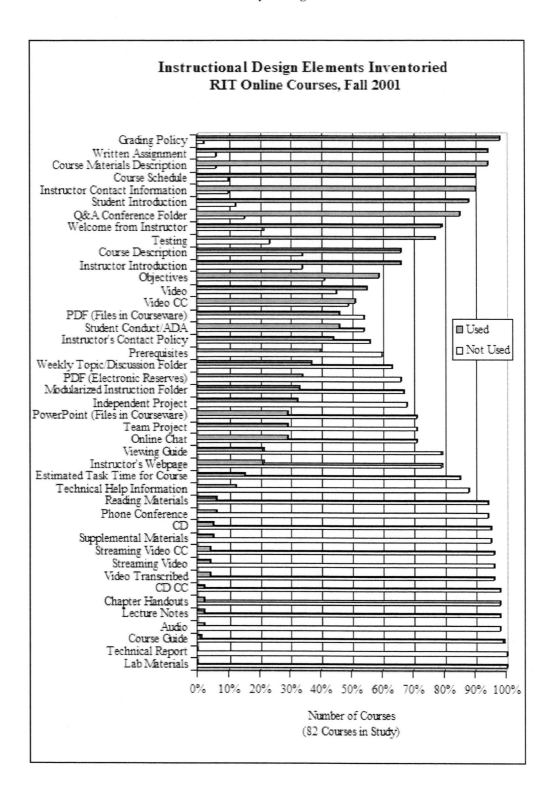

II. CONCLUSION

Measuring student satisfaction through longitudinal data analysis is only part of determining how online learning compares to traditional classroom based learning. Yet, RIT Online Learning feels this is an important facet that has not yet been thoroughly scrutinized by many others in this field. The reasons are clear. Good longitudinal data and sharing data among higher education are lacking; the lack explains why little is known about online learning student success. With the addition of the RIT data set and analyses, other colleges offering asynchronous learning will have some benchmarks. The data no doubt support the efforts of the Sloan Foundation to have Asynchronous Learning recognized for its effectiveness as a method to deliver high quality academic programs. RIT online learners have not only succeeded in the online classroom—they have successfully graduated. While RIT will still need to further investigate its data and create sub-populations to look for variations among the samples, the RIT Online Learning Department feels confident that insight gained through this analysis will be extremely useful to the future plans for asynchronous learning at RIT.

The clear success of RIT's asynchronous learning program has given us the willingness to move beyond the "good as or better" criteria. The Office of Distance Learning now under the direction of the Assistant Provost for Teaching and Learning will attempt to create quality measurements which assess whether asynchronous learning can actually improve upon the classroom experience.

III. AUTHOR BIOGRAPHY

Karen Vignare currently serves as the Senior Research Analyst for Online Learning Services at the Rochester Institute of Technology. In that position, she coordinates efforts to research all facets of online learning to improve online learning for students. She is responsible for communicating the research through meaningful and actionable information. She is an adjunct professor teaching Customer Relationship Management and Marketing on Internet courses at RIT. She has served as the Distance Learning Marketing coordinator and Director of Business Development for Elearning at RIT before moving to her current position. Before coming to RIT, Karen was a full time faculty at SUNY Alfred State in the Marketing, Retail and Computer Technology department. She also served as a Vice-President and Political Economist for a Wall Street financial firm. She has published several pieces of research and instructor manuals on elearning and the internet. She has an MBA in marketing and public policy from the Simon School at the University of Rochester and a BS in Political Science & Economics from Frostburg State University.

IV. REFERENCES

1. **Lewis, L., Snow, K., Farris, E., and Levin, D.** (1999). *Distance Education at Postsecondary Education Institutions: 1997–98* (NCES 2000–013). U.S. Department of Education, National Center for Education Statistics. Washington, DC: U.S. Government Printing Office.
2. **Graham, Amy and Nicholas Thompson.** "Broken Ranks: U.S. News' college rankings measure everything but what matters. And most universities do not seem to mind." *Washington Monthly.* September, 2001.
3. **Day, Jennifer Cheeseman and Eric Newburger.** Current Population Studies, *The Big Pay-Off: Educational Attainment and Synthetic Estimates of Work-life Earnings*, July 2002
4. **Snyder, Thomas and Charlene Hoffman.** Digest of Education Statistics, 2001, 2002 US. Department of Education, National Center for Education Statistics 2001, 2002
5. **Mayberry, Katherine, et al.,** Rochester Institute of Technology, June 2000 Report by Retention Taskforce, 2000.

6. **Hoffman, Donna and Thomas, Novak**. "Profitability on the Web," eLab Position Paper, Vanderbilt University, March 2002.

7. **Jones, Steve.** Pew Internet & American Life Project, "The Internet Goes to College: How Students are Living in the Future with Today's Technology", September 15, 2002.

8. **Bradburn, Ellen.** (2002) *Distance Education Instruction by Postsecondary Faculty and Staff: Fall 1998* U.S. Department of Education, National Center for Education Statistics. Washington, DC: U.S. Government Printing Office

A PRELIMINARY INVESTIGATION OF "TEACHING PRESENCE" IN THE SUNY LEARNING NETWORK

Peter J. Shea, Eric E. Fredericksen, Alexandra M. Pickett, and William E. Pelz
State University of New York

- The best learning environments appear to be learner centered, knowledge centered, assessment centered and community centered.

- Assessment centered environments provide learners with many opportunities to make their thinking visible and to get feedback in order to create new meaning and new understanding.

- Teaching presence has three components: instructional design and organization, facilitating discourse, and direct instruction.

- Faculty can browse a broad selection of previously delivered and now archived courses across disciplines to examine them for ideas designing their own courses.

- Well-articulated time parameters facilitate effective interaction for engaging in co-construction of knowledge.

I. BACKGROUND

The SUNY Learning Network (SLN) is the online instructional program created for the sixty-four colleges and nearly 400,000 students of the State University of New York. The primary goals of the SUNY Learning Network are to bring SUNY's diverse, high-quality instructional programs within the reach of learners everywhere and to be the best provider of asynchronous instruction for learners in New York State and beyond.

Strategic objectives for this initiative are threefold:

1. to provide increased, flexible access to higher education within and beyond New York State;

2. to provide a mechanism for maintaining consistently, high quality online teaching and learning across the SUNY system; and

3. leverage the resources of the State University of New York system to contain the costs associated with the development, design, and delivery of online education.

This paper focuses primarily on the second goal - that of providing a mechanism for maintaining consistently high quality online teaching and learning that supports student satisfaction.

The annual growth in courses, from eight in 1995-1996 to over 1500 in 2000-2001, and annual growth in enrollment, from 119 in 1995-1996 to over 40,000 in 2001-2002, with courses offered at all undergraduate and graduate levels from fifty-five of our institutions, illustrates that the project has met, and in many ways exceeded, original projections. The program has recently been recognized by EDUCAUSE as the 2001 award winner for Systemic Improvement in Teaching and Learning and by the Sloan Consortium for its 2001 Excellence in ALN Faculty Development Award and its 2002 award for Excellence in Institution-Wide ALN Programming.

II. CONCEPTUAL FRAMEWORK

The SUNY Learning Network represents a formal online teaching and learning environment. In order to understand how best to structure such an environment to ensure effective pedagogy it is useful to begin by looking at what works well in traditional learning environments, and in so doing, attend to models of best practices identified for effective education. Of course, such an examination must be done in light of our understanding that differences exist between online and classroom-based teaching and learning. But starting with best practices in structuring traditional learning environments is a good foundation for further investigation.

The National Research Council's Commission on Behavioral and Social Sciences and Education, provides guidance in this area, especially in the publication *How People Learn* [1]. The authors offer a model for effective learning environments in which a system of four interconnected components combine and mutually support each other. These interconnecting components are foci that provide a foundation for learning environments, the best of which appear to be *learner centered, knowledge centered, assessment centered and community centered*. The model may be seen as a set of overlapping circles, as illustrated in Figure 1.

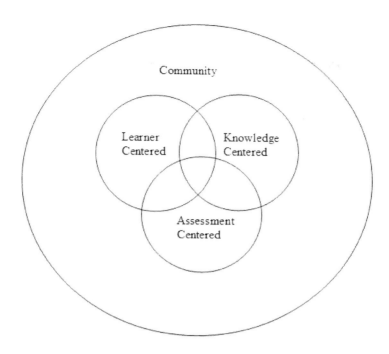

Figure 1. Perspectives on learning environments. (Source: Bransford et al. [1]).

The authors detail each of these foci - briefly summarized here. Good learning environments *are knowledge centered* in that they are designed in consideration of desired outcomes. Guiding questions for creating a knowledge-centered learning environment include - what do we want students to know and be able to do when they have completed our materials or course? How do we provide learners with the "foundational knowledge, skills, and attitudes needed for successful transfer" [1]?

Good learning environments are also *learner centered*, that is they function in a manner that connects to the strengths, interests, and preconceptions of learners [1] and help students to gain insight into themselves as learners. In such environments teachers work to bridge new content with students current understandings and facilitate growth, while attending to the learners' interests, passions, and motivations.

Another characteristic of good learning environments is that they are *community centered*, that is they promote and benefit from shared norms that value learning and high standards. Ideally good learning environments connect to relevant external communities and provide a milieu within the classroom where students feel safe to ask questions, to work collaboratively, and in which they are taught to develop lifelong learning skills.

Finally, the Bransford, et al. [1] emphasize that good learning environments are *assessment centered* meaning that they provide learners with many opportunities to make their thinking visible and to get feedback in order to create new meaning and new understanding.

The guidelines in *How People Learn* [1] provide an excellent framework from which to consider the design of online learning environments, in that they summarize much of what is known about good learning environments generally. However, in addition, we must also consider the specific needs of higher education learners, and focus on lessons learned from research in college level teaching and learning, as these are most relevant to SLN. Are there guidelines that help to determine how to implement a learning-, assessment-, knowledge-, and community-centered environment - one that is designed to engage higher education students specifically?

Certain institutional practices are known to lead to high levels of student engagement. Perhaps the best-known set of engagement indicators is the "Seven Principles of Good Practice in Undergraduate Education. [7]

The seven principles of good practice in undergraduate education identified by Chickering & Gamson [2] reflect much of what is identified by Bransford et al. [1] in the design of good learning environments. These principles distill decades of research on the undergraduate experience, providing some guidance on how best to structure learning in higher education. Chickering & Gamson [2] encourage the following general conditions and behaviors for successful learning: 1) frequent contact between students and faculty; 2) reciprocity and cooperation among students; 3) active learning techniques; 4) prompt feedback; 5) time on task; 6) the communication of high expectations, and 7) respect for diverse talent and ways of learning.

We feel that the principles of good practice outlined by Chickering & Gamson [2] are at the heart of the model presented by Bransford, et al. [1] and provide a focus specific to higher education learning environments. Figure 2 details this relationship.

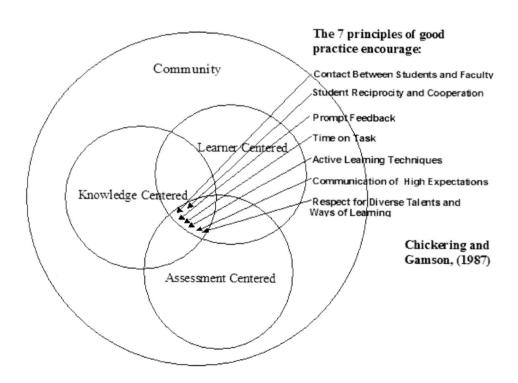

Figure 2. Principles of good practice and perspectives on learning environments. (Source: Chickering & Gamson [2]).

While these principles provide guidance in developing higher education learning environments, they are written at a relatively high level of abstraction without a specific focus on the needs of higher education students *learning at a distance* as in the case of the SLN. Further, SLN was specifically designed as an asynchronous environment, and for many courses in the program, depends largely on text-based forums to carry out teaching and learning interactions. A specific set of indicators that *does* focus on higher education at a distance in primarily text-based, asynchronous environments may be found in the model proposed by Garrison, Anderson, & Archer [8]. This framework also reflects, the principles of good practice and, we propose, the model presented by Bransford et al. [1]. It is to the Garrison et al. [8] framework we will now turn with the goal of providing a more comprehensive conceptual background and to provide a more developed and detailed set of categories through which to examine issues of pedagogy, faculty development, student satisfaction, and reported learning in SLN.

In the model of critical thinking and practical inquiry proposed by Garrison et al. [8] three overlapping lenses - cognitive presence, social presence, and teaching presence provide mutual support to create a framework in which interaction in an asynchronous online educational experience may be assessed. The model seeks to explain how to best analyze and ultimately promote higher order learning in computer mediated, largely text-based, environments such as SLN. This paper will focus primarily on one aspect of the model, "Teaching Presence" and briefly summarize the other components.

The authors define cognitive presence as "the extent to which students are able to construct and confirm meaning through sustained discourse in a community of inquiry" and it is achieved in concert with effective teaching presence and satisfactory social presence.

In this model social presence is viewed as the "ability of students to project themselves socially and affectively into a community of inquiry" and is deemed critical in the absence of physical presence and attendant teacher immediacy necessary to sustain learning in the classroom.

Teaching presence is referred to as "the design facilitation and direction of cognitive and social processes for the realization of personally meaningful and educationally worthwhile learning outcomes." Teaching presence has three components Instructional Design and Organization, Facilitating Discourse, and Direct Instruction. We discuss these in greater depth below.

The authors provide a visual representation of the model, reproduced in Figure 3.

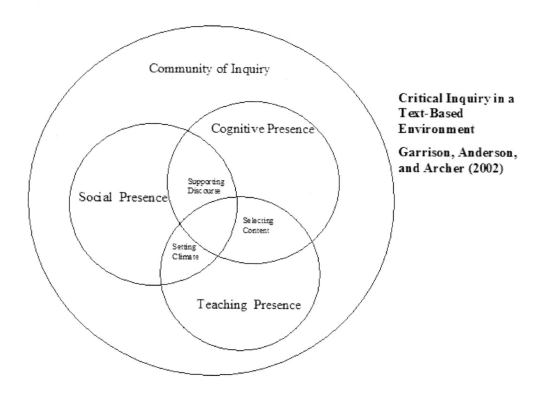

Figure 3. Elements of an educational experience. (Source: Garrison, Anderson, & Archer [8]).

How does this model relate to the principles of good practice in undergraduate education espoused by Chickering & Gamson [2]? Again, one might revise the model to locate the seven principles of good practice as shown in Figure 4.

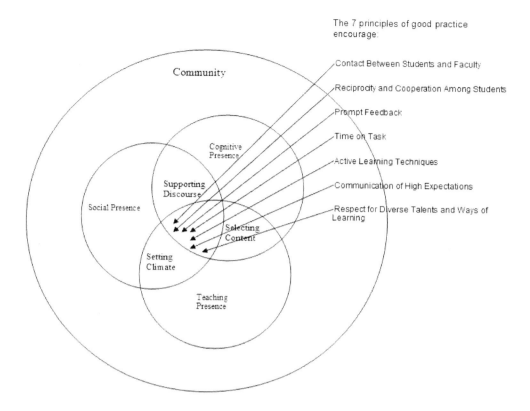

Figure 4. Principles of good practice and elements of an educational experience.

We feel that the principles of good practice are also essential elements of the teaching and learning transaction and crucial in creating and sustaining student engagement and learning. We feel that the Garrison et al. [8] model helps to identify and enact these principles in a specifically online learning environment.

Because it was designed for online learning environments, the framework and indicators articulated by Anderson et al. [3] is useful in analyzing the SLN faculty development efforts. While it is not the original intention of the authors that this model be used for assessing faculty development programs, it does provide a "checklist" against which efforts to create an effective online learning environment can be analyzed.

Below we will describe the faculty development process and identify elements of support for the creation of "teaching presence" that are embedded in SLN training. We will also explain how faculty become aware of and enact these in the online courses they teach to create and sustain cognitive presence. By attending to both the general principles of good practice in higher education articulated by Chickering & Gamson [2] and to how they are identified and enacted in online, asynchronous environments in the Anderson et al. [3] framework we will attempt to discover whether the faculty development efforts were likely to result in good pedagogy, student satisfaction, and learning.

III. HELPING FACULTY CREATE AND SUSTAIN QUALITY ONLINE TEACHING AND LEARNING

How can a faculty development process help faculty to engage in behaviors that are likely to result in productive learning environments, high levels of learning and student satisfaction? Clearly, to achieve this goal there is a need to focus on the elements put forth by Bransford et al. [1], i.e., the trainings need to emphasize the importance of learning-centered, knowledge-centered, assessment-centered, and community-centered environments. Additionally, because SLN is a higher education learning environment, we need to emphasize the importance of the specific principles of good practice in undergraduate education outlined by Chickering & Gamson [2]. Finally, because the goals of the trainings are to help faculty understand the nature of online, asynchronous learning we need to emphasize many of the indicators of social presence outlined by Rourke, et al. [9] and teaching presence outlined by Anderson, et al. [3] that lead to better online learning. Below we will discuss faculty development in greater detail, especially as it relates to teaching presence, and examine how faculty learn about these ideas and practices through SLN trainings.

A. Helping Faculty Create and Sustain Teaching Presence

Anderson et al. [3] define teaching presence as "the design, facilitation, and direction of cognitive and social processes for the realization of personally meaningful and educationally worthwhile learning outcomes." While the authors were principally concerned with analyzing course discussion transcripts for evidence of these categories, it is our belief that teaching presence is also evident in other areas of online courses. Anderson et al. [3] acknowledge this, and encouraged others to investigate teaching presence beyond course discussions. We will use the categories devised by Anderson et al. [3] and provide additional examples of teaching presence (beyond what may be found in discussion transcripts), and describe how faculty are supported to understand and create teaching presence in SLN online courses.

Teaching presence in this model has three components - I. Instructional Design and Organization, II. Facilitating Discourse, and III. Direct Instruction. We will discuss each of these in some detail below. Under the category, "Instructional Design and Organization" the authors include: a) setting curriculum, b) establishing time parameters, c) utilizing the medium effectively, and d) establishing netiquette and e) designing methods. This aspect of the model equates with Chickering & Gamson's [2] concern for active learning techniques, time on task, communication of high expectations, and prompt feedback, again, providing more consideration of the affordances and constraints of *online* environments.

1. Instructional Design and Organization

Support for instructional design and organization is provided in many ways for SLN faculty. For example all faculty are provided a shell structure from which to build their learning materials within the SLN course management system (CMS). The SLN CMS embeds a common instructional design format and organization into each course. It is however, flexible, and faculty can alter the format to suit their needs and the specific learning outcomes for their courses. This CMS provides several advantages for achieving the goals of building an asynchronous learning network on the scale of SLN. Each course has a common look and feel, so students do not need to learn a new interface every time they enroll in a new course. Placeholder documents also serve to remind faculty to include information that students will need to feel well oriented in any course. The CMS helps faculty to establish teaching presence in accordance with several of the categories identified by Anderson et al. [3]. These are - *a) setting the curriculum, b) establishing time parameters, c) utilizing the medium effectively,* and *d) establishing netiquette.* Below we will also discuss faculty development support for *e) designing methods.*

a. Setting the curriculum

Common course information shell documents provide a reminder to faculty of the importance of this element of teaching presence, and that they need to inform the students about the course, how it will proceed and how students can succeed. Common issues confronted include the sequence, quantity, and pacing of learning activities in each section of the course.

Each course contains documents into which course-specific information may be inserted. Trainers, using the hard copy and online-faculty development guide provided to all faculty, give examples of appropriate content that can be tailored for a standard set of course information documents. Documents that touch upon setting the curriculum include: a welcome document, a course overview, course learning objectives, "how you will be evaluated" and "my expectations" documents, as well as readings and course materials. Such signposting begins to fulfill the role of creating a "narrative path through the mediated instruction and activity set such that students are aware of the explicit and implicit learning goals and activities in which they participate." [3] In addition to creating the narrative path, we feel it is also important to provide a "table of contents" to the narrative. So faculty can also create course-level and section-level overview documents with the goal of reminding students where they are and what they will be working on throughout each section of the course.

b. Establishing time parameters

This element of teaching presence is critical - keeping students moving along at a similar pace is foundational to supporting meaningful interaction in asynchronous learning environments such as SLN. For students to engage in co-construction of knowledge, they need to work together, and well-articulated time parameters facilitate effective interaction.

Faculty in SLN learn about the importance of establishing time parameters in several ways. Again, the SLN CMS provides standard documents and instructional cues that help establish time parameters. For example, it contains a preformatted course schedule, into which learning activities, topics, assignments and due dates may be recorded. Each course segment (module) contains a standard "What's Due?" document for that section of the course. At the document level, "discussion starter" documents contain start and end date reminders so that faculty remember to provide these time parameters to students. Assignment starter documents contain similar due date reminders to help faculty to keep students on track. Additionally, the SLN CMS permits faculty to activate and deactivate learning modules in order to control course pace.

c. Utilizing the medium effectively

Under this category Anderson et al. [3] include helping students understand how to use the technology appropriately, for example the proper use of the reply and quote functions in online discussion. Again, the SLN CMS contains standard course documents that help faculty to help students understand these functions and they are placed immediately before the task to which they refer or in which they will be used. Such shared documentation on effective use of the medium reduces the burden on individual faculty to "reinvent the wheel" in each course.

Frequently students will need extra help with the technology - so in addition to documentation within each course, a central student helpdesk exists to assist students to make effective use of the medium. But rather than take a merely reactive role, the Helpdesk facilitates an interactive, online orientation to SLN. This online course, modeled on all other SLN courses is offered each semester and helps students understand the medium and its effective uses, as well as practice the skills necessary for success before they enter a specific, credit-bearing course.

To help faculty understand and address instances when students are not using the medium well, one of the roles of the SLN instructional design partner is to monitor each course, especially in its very early stages, and to make sure that the faculty member is aware of communication breakdowns, such as misplaced postings, unanswered questions etc., so that they may be repaired.

Utilizing the helpdesk and instructional design partners to support elements of teaching presence may represent a more productive approach to online learning environment design.

d. Establishing netiquette

Rourke et al. [9] refer to "netiquette", i.e., behaviors that are deemed appropriate in online communication. Newcomers to online communication are often unaware that certain acts may violate established norms. One example is typing in upper case, which is viewed as "shouting" in online communication and thus inappropriate for most messages. Dominating conversations with long postings is another potentially problematic violation of netiquette. Trainers review these concepts and the hard copy and online versions of the SLN handbook provide examples of simple policies for acceptable interaction in online college courses.

e. Designing methods

Under this category the authors include the provision of instructional strategies that help structure learning activities. One of the greatest challenges in online learning is the clear articulation of how learning activities will be structured and paced, and new online faculty frequently struggle with providing clear instructions on how to accomplish a particular activity. Cooperative learning methods in particular require clear directions and close monitoring. The ability to draw on hundreds of courses that have been developed, designed, and delivered through SLN provides some assistance in overcoming these challenges. Faculty are able to review examples of learning activities that were either successful or unsuccessful to understand how their design and method may impact their effectiveness. Examples include student-designed surveys, journals, observations, individual and collaborative projects, jointly constructed annotated bibliographies, etc. Through the SLN Faculty Developers Center, and the all-faculty conference, instructors can view entire archived courses, "sit in" on live courses, and access excerpted examples of well-designed, or previously successful learning activities. These resources, which assist faculty to understand the design of effective methods, are detailed below.

2. SLN Faculty Developers Center

Through this online resource, faculty can access their SLN email, explore a common set of library resources, search a repository of discipline specific learning objects (MERLOT), access the online version of the SLN Handbook, participate in an online faculty orientation, and access instructional design tips and online teaching tools, beyond those included in the SLN CMS. The Faculty Center is one resource for promoting understanding of designing methods.

a. Archived courses

Faculty are encouraged to browse from a broad selection of previously delivered and now archived courses across disciplines and to examine them for ideas regarding how they will design their own course. These courses provide a "static" view of previous designs that have proven effective in the eyes of the instructional designer, faculty members and students.

b. Live courses

New faculty may enter a selection of live, ongoing SLN courses to get an understanding of how experienced instructors conduct and facilitate a course. This guided discovery process occurs during the all faculty online conference and allows faculty to see and discuss the dynamic process by which a course unfolds and through which teaching, social, and cognitive presence may evolve.

c. Excerpted activities

Instructional designers have developed a database of innovative online teaching and learning activities from previous courses that new instructors can access. This resource is smaller than a complete course but represents a greater concentration of examples from across many courses.

d. Facilitating Discourse

Another element of teaching presence in the Anderson et al. [3] framework is facilitating discourse. The task of facilitating discourse is necessary to sustain learner engagement and refers to "focused and sustained deliberation that marks learning in a community of inquiry" (Anderson et al.). The authors provide indicators of the act of facilitating discourse, which include a) *identifying areas of agreement and disagreement; b) seeking to reach consensus and understanding; c) encouraging, acknowledging, or reinforcing student contributions; d) setting climate for learning; e) drawing in participants and prompting discussion;* and *f) assessing the efficacy of the process.* This aspect of the model equates in some ways with Chickering & Gamson's [2] encouragement of contact between students and faculty and reciprocity and cooperation among students – further delineating these for *online* learners. Facilitating discourse is also essential for sustaining the knowledge-centered and community-centered learning environment emphasized by Bransford et al. [1]. We will look at the components of facilitating discourse and identify how faculty in SLN learn about this skill.

Trainers and instructional design partners encourage faculty to consider the early stages of their courses as an opportunity to begin to create a non-threatening environment in which students can begin to engage in discourse. A standard practice designed to help meet this goal is the use of an "ice-breaking" module. In this initial course section, students engage in ungraded activities where they can practice the skills needed to participate in the course. These might include open class and small group discussions, submitting a profile or taking a learning style quiz. These activities are designed to encourage class discourse in a safe, supportive and un-assessed (at least in terms of course grade) environment.

Two indicators of discourse facilitation, *identifying areas of agreement and disagreement* and *seeking to reach consensus and understanding*, depend on the ability to frame a thought provoking topic of discussion. Students need to be encouraged to engage in dialogue in order to express thoughts that others may then acknowledge or refute. Before consensus can exist, ideas must be expressed and examined. Faculty learn how to start and extend such discussion in several ways. Though face-to-face and online forums, faculty explore resources that document effective, engaging online discussion practices. For example, in face-to face trainings faculty examine and discuss a list of fourteen ways to enhance online discussion that correspond to the categories identified by Anderson et al. [3]. Faculty "experience" these tips by participating in facilitated discourse in the online all faulty conference. Examples of discourse facilitation tips to faculty are included below:

Include a grade for participation.

Be clear about how students can succeed in discussion with reference to quality and quantity guidelines as well as requirements for timeliness. Entering an asynchronous discussion after it is nearly over can be unproductive (though there are ways around this problem - such as asking a late student to summarize the discussion that has already occurred)...

Provide an overview of what is due for each week.

This weekly agenda will help keep students working as a cohort and ensure a "critical mass" for getting discussions off the ground...

Make the discussion interesting or provocative.

Asking students to respond to "known answer" questions is unlikely to generate sustained involvement. Discussion questions should be open-ended, focused on learning objectives and likely to spur some controversy or interaction…

Participate "wisely".

The instructor should not dominate the discussion. Nor should he or she be absent. It is the instructor's job to keep the discussion on track by guiding without "pontificating". Frequently an instructor will provide a comment that students perceive as the "official answer" and discussion can come to a halt…

Require a product that is based on or the result of discussion.

A "hand-in" assignment that is based on class discussion can help students to synthesize, integrate and apply what has been discussed…

With the ongoing assistance of an instructional design partner for implementation, tips such as these help faculty to understand how to facilitate productive discourse in the service of creating teaching presence and ultimately cognitive presence.

3. Direct instruction

Anderson et al. [3] also include indicators of direct instruction in their framework for the analysis of teaching presence. These indicators include a) *presenting content and questions, b) focusing the discussion on specific issues, c) summarizing discussion, d) confirming understanding, e) diagnosing misperceptions, f) injecting knowledge from diverse sources* and *g) responding to technical concern*. This aspect of the model equates with Chickering & Gamson's [2] concerns for prompt, assistive feedback, again with emphasis on the needs of *online* learners. Attention to direct instruction is also essential for sustaining the knowledge-centered learning environment emphasized by Bransford et al. [1].

Regarding the final indicator of direct instruction, responding to technical concerns, it should be noted that faculty in SLN are specifically instructed not to respond to student technical difficulties, as this diverts instructor resources away from their primary role, facilitating learning. It is the role of the SLN Help Desk to address all technical issues and faculty are advised to refer all such questions to the Help Desk to avoid students becoming dependent of instructors for technical support.

New online faculty struggle with how to engage in direct instruction. Novice instructors frequently raise questions about how they will "teach" in the absence of visual and aural clues reflective of students misunderstanding. So, how do new SLN faculty learn about effective practices for direct instruction in the "lean" ALN medium? Again, there are a variety of forums in which this topic is explored. For example, new faculty interact and learn from experienced faculty in the "Managing and Teaching your Course Workshop", the last in a series of three face-to-face workshops for new instructors. In this meeting, experienced instructors present lessons they have learned from designing and facilitating their own courses, including how they present content, focus and summarize discussions and issues, and identify and remedy misunderstanding.

New faculty learn that direct instruction takes place most commonly through dialogue with the instructor (as well as more able peers). Some examples of suggestions for effective dialogue discussed in training forums include:

Resist the temptation to respond to every student's response. Otherwise, the discussion may become a series of dialogs between you and each student, rather than among you and the students.

Assign individual students the task of summarizing the discussion, and check for accuracy and comprehensiveness.

Employ student-led discussion where assigned students devise critical thinking questions and are evaluated on the quality of their questions and how they facilitate the discussion.

Create a discussion response that calls on specific students that have not yet participated in the discussion.

Create a discussion response that asks a specific student to clarify a point, or that asks a student to reassess a response in light of another student's response.

Create a discussion response that asks a follow-up question of the group or of an individual student.

(SLN Faculty Developers Guide)

The SLN CMS also provides some scaffolding for effective direct instruction practices; for example, there is a built in "Question Area" through which misunderstanding may be resolved. Standard course documents provide an arena for the presentation and effective organization of content. Faculty can also use a pre-formatted "shared reference" form also embedded in the template to inject knowledge from diverse sources.

Through suggestions, tips, and elements of the SLN CMS such as those mentioned above, as well as participation in online forums, new faculty gradually learn from trainers and experienced faculty how to engage in effective dialogue and to implement direct instruction online.

IV. STUDENT SATISFACTION, REPORTED LEARNING AND "TEACHING PRESENCE"

As part of the revision cycle of the course design and faculty development processes we have engaged in systematic efforts to evaluate and analyze online teaching and learning in SLN. Each semester we conduct surveys of participating faculty and students through an integrated, web-based data collection infrastructure. In the Summer 2002 semester, we piloted a questionnaire on students' perception of teaching presence. To define create the survey, we framed questions around teaching-presence indicators identified by Anderson et al. [3].

In the most recent survey (Summer 2002) we received responses from 1150 students, about 15% of student enrollments for that period. Due to the low response rate, we must consider these result to be a pilot of the instrument, and not generalizable to all students enrollments in SLN. This response rate, while low, is unfortunately typical of email and web-based survey returns, which have been declining in recent years [10].

Students are asked, via email and through messages posted online, to complete the web-based survey by both SLN administration and their instructor. Follow up reminders are sent to non-respondents two weeks and four weeks after the initial request. While the survey is completely voluntary, the format of the instrument requires that all questions be answered before the survey may be submitted successfully, so for these surveys, students respond to all items. Students are instructed that the results of the survey will not be revealed to their instructor and that it is a voluntary activity that will have no bearing on their grade.

V. RESULTS

What follows are the frequencies of student responses to the questions we asked on the Teaching Presence Survey as well as those responses that correlated highly with student satisfaction and reported learning. Questions are organized by the components of teaching presence identified by Anderson et al. [3]. Survey items were followed by a five point likert type scale that asked students to express their level of agreement or disagreement to statements eliciting responses related to teaching presence. Frequencies of response are presented for each question followed by the correlation between the responses for that item and student satisfaction and reported learning.

A. Instructional Design and Organization

Overall, rating for questions about instructional design and organization were quite high. Approximately 85% of respondents expressed agreement about statements reflecting good practices in instructional design and organization as defined in the survey. In attempting to determine how relevant this group of indicators are to student satisfaction and reported learning we correlated these variables. On average, students who reported high levels of instructional design and organization also reported high levels of satisfaction and learning ($r=.635$ for satisfaction and $r = .588$ for reported learning).

B. Facilitating Discourse

Summary: Compared to results for Instructional Design and Organization the ratings that indicate effective discourse facilitation were somewhat lower. For this category students were asked to rate both their instructor as well as their fellow classmates. This dual scoring system reflects the belief that, in a learner-centered classroom we would expect to see students facilitating some of the discourse supportive of their learning. Approximately 73% of respondents agreed with statements indicating that their instructor helped facilitate productive discourse and approximately 72% agreed with statements indicating that their classmates helped facilitate productive discourse.

Facilitating Discourse		
Ratings of Instructor	Agree	73%
	Nuetral	15%
	Disagree	12%
Ratings of Fellow Students	Agree	72%
	Nuetral	21%
	Disagree	7%

Table 1. Average student ratings for statements reflecting effective discourse facilitation. (see appendix for statements and individual responses)

On average, students who reported effective discourse facilitation on the part of their instructor also reported high levels of satisfaction and learning ($r=.64$ for satisfaction and $r = .58$ for reported learning).

	Satisfaction	Reported Learning
Correlation	.64	.58
Significance	.000	.000

Table 2. Instructor average: facilitating discourse (see appendix for statements and individual responses)

While students rated their classmates almost as high as their instructor on effective discourse facilitation, the correlation between their rating of their classmates discourse facilitation and their satisfaction and reported learning were not as high. (r=.36 for satisfaction and r = .37 for reported learning).

	Satisfaction	Reported Learning
Correlation	.36	.37
Significance	.000	.000

Table 3. Student average: facilitating discourse

C. Direct Instruction

Summary: Regarding direct instruction approximately 76% of respondents agreed with statements indicating that their instructor provided helpful direct instruction and approximately 66% agreed with statements indicating that their classmates did so.

Direct Instruction		
Ratings of Instructor	Agree	76%
	Neutral	11%
	Disagree	13%
Ratings of Fellow Students	Agree	66%
	Neutral	24%
	Disagree	10%

Table 4. Average student ratings for statements reflecting effective direct instruction. (see appendix for statements and individual responses)

Students who reported high levels on these measures of teaching presence also reported high levels of satisfaction and reported learning. On average, students who reported effective direct instruction on the part of their instructor also reported high levels of satisfaction and learning (r=.64 for satisfaction and r = .61 for reported learning).

	Satisfaction	Reported Learning
Correlation	.64	.61
Significance	.000	.000

Table 5. Direct Instruction: Instructor

Again, while students rated their classmates relatively high on effective discourse facilitation, the correlation between their ratings of their classmates and their satisfaction and reported learning were not as high. (r=.39 for satisfaction and r = .39 for reported learning).

	Satisfaction	Reported Learning
Correlation	.39	.39
Significance	.000	.000

Table 6. Direct Instruction: Student

VI. CONCLUSIONS

In general, students rated their experience of teaching presence as relatively high in these courses. Approximately 85% of respondents reported agreement with statements describing the first category of teaching presence, instructional design and organization. On average, students who reported high levels of instructional design and organization also reported high levels of satisfaction and learning (r=.635 for satisfaction and r = .588 for reported learning). The relatively higher ratings on this category can probably be attributed to the greater high proportion of resources applied to instructional design and organization through faculty development and the SLN CMS design. Inasmuch as design is accomplished before a course begins, opportunity to impact this area of teaching presence is relatively greater.

Survey respondents also reported relatively high levels of the other categories of teaching presence, facilitating discourse and direct instruction. Approximately 73% of respondents agreed with statements indicating that their instructor helped facilitate productive discourse and approximately 72% agreed with statements indicating that their classmates helped facilitate productive discourse.

For the categories of facilitating discourse and direct instruction, the survey measured interaction behaviors of both instructors and students. The assumption here is that in a learner centered environment we'd expect "shared roles" or collaboration such that students engaged in behaviors that lead to co-construction of knowledge. Survey respondents indicate that their classmates do frequently engage in these behaviors. However, for the students who responded to this survey, instructor behaviors correlate more highly with satisfaction and learning than do student's teaching-presence behaviors. So, while students actually scored their classmates higher on several indicators in these categories of variables, their perception of instructor behaviors for facilitating discourse and direct instruction correlated more highly with satisfaction and learning then their perception of fellow students.

There may be several interpretations of these results. Certainly, students have traditionally expected the instructor to play the central role in teaching. Upon reflection they may be pleasantly surprised to discover that their classmates also fulfilled this role, but their expectations are more stringent for the instructor than for their fellow students. As to why students might rate their classmates higher on certain categories, the same explanation may apply – student may have higher expectations of the instructor than their classmates, and therefore be more "strict" in their rating of the instructor and lenient in rating their classmates. Alternatively (or perhaps additionally), students far outnumber the instructor, so their interactive behaviors should be higher in number and therefore more evident. In either case, the result indicating that students perceive that their classmates engage in teaching presence behaviors at high levels, either by facilitating discourse or by providing direct instruction, should not be interpreted as inappropriate. Best practices in teaching and learning advocate this shared role, and these results indicate success in this area.

For one category, direct instruction, it is probably more appropriate for the instructor to play the "stronger" role. As the resident expert, we would expect the instructor to provide more direct instruction than other students, at least from a traditional view of teaching and learning. That being said, the evidence presented here suggests that students are playing an active role in their online courses, which, again, is congruent with good practices in teaching and learning.

The results we have reported here are useful in informing decisions regarding enhancements to the faculty development process. This study has provided evidence pointing to areas of potential strength (instructional design and organizations) and areas that may need improvement (facilitation of discourse and direct instructions). We have begun the process of revising training based on these results. In cooperation with our instructional design team we have created a new training, the goals of which are to communicate to faculty these general findings and to provide a forum for reflection and revision. Using collaborative learning techniques faculty will partner with peers to examine categories of discourse facilitation, direct instruction, and to a lesser degree, instructional design and organization. Through guided learning activities these online instructors will reflect on how they currently accomplish tasks in these areas, identify where their courses need improvement and, with the assistance of their instructional design partners, implement the necessary revisions.

In summary we feel that an emphasis on multiple perspectives may be a step forward in the development of online learning environments. Attention to the principles espoused by Bransford et al. [1], Chickering & Gamson [2], as well as Garrison et al. [8] and Anderson et al. [3] may be the best approach to ensuring high quality in the development of future online learning forums. We will endeavor to facilitate understanding of this emerging model (Figure 5) to the SLN community as we seek to improve the experience of students and faculty in the SUNY Learning Network.

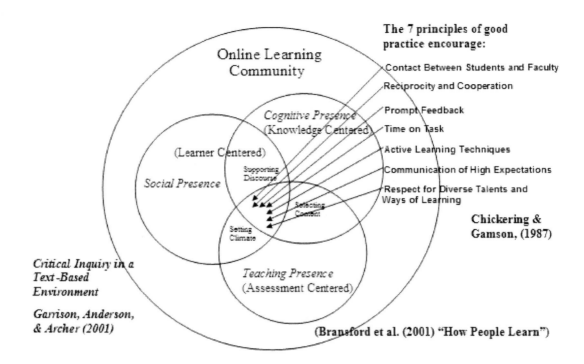

Figure 5. A conceptual framework for high quality, higher education, online learning environments.

VII. REFERENCES

1. **Bransford, J., Brown, A., Cocking, R., Donovan, M., and Pellegrino, J. W.** *How People Learn,* National Academy Press, 2000

2. **Chickering, A. W., and Gamson, A. F.** *Seven Principles for Good Practice in Undergraduate Education.* Racine, WI: The Johnson Foundation, Inc/Wingspread, 1987

3. **Anderson, T., Rourke, L., Garrison, D. R., and Archer W.** Assessing Teaching Presence in a Computer Conferencing Context. *Journal of Asynchronous Learning Networks*, 5(2) (September 2001).

4. **Shea, P., Fredericksen, E., Pickett, A., and Pelz, W.** Measures of Learning Effectiveness in the SUNY Learning Network, *Online Education: Learning Effectiveness, Faculty Satisfaction, and Cost Effectiveness,* Needham, MA: Sloan-C, 2001.

5. **Shea, P., Pelz, W., Fredericksen, E., and Pickett, A.** Online teaching as a catalyst for Classroom-based Instructional Transformation, *Elements of Quality Online Education,* Needham, MA: Sloan-C, 2002.

6. **Shea, P., Swan, K., Fredericksen, E., and Pickett, A.** Student Satisfaction and Reported Learning in the SUNY Learning Network, *Elements of Quality Online Education,* Needham, MA: Sloan-C, 2002.

7. **Kuh, G.** The National Survey of Student Engagement: Conceptual Framework and Overview of Psychometric Properties 2001. http://www.indiana.edu/~nsse/acrobat/framework-2001.pdf

8. **Garrison, D. R., Anderson, T, and Archer, W.** Critical Inquiry in a Text Based Environment: Computer Conferencing in Higher Education. *The Internet and Higher Education*, 2(2-3): 1-19, 2000

9. **Rourke, L., Anderson, T., Garrison, D. R., and Archer, W.** Assessing Social Presence in Asynchronous Text-based Computer Conferencing. *Journal of Distance Education*, 2001. http://cade.athabascau.ca/vol14.2/rourke_et_al.html

10. **Sheehan, K.** Email Survey Response Rates: A Review. *Journal of Computer Mediated Communication,* 6(2), 2001.

11. **Barnes, M.** Questioning: The Untapped Resource. (ERIC Document Reproduction Service No. 1888555). Paper presented at the Annual Meeting of the American Educational Research Association. Boston, MA. (April 1980)

12. **Bradburn, N. M.** A Response to the Non-response Problem. *Public Opinion Quarterly,* 56: 391-397. (1992).

13. **Brehm, J.** Op cit. In T. W. Smith, Household Survey Non-response. Paper presented at the 5th International Workshop, 1994.

14. **Buckley, D.** In Pursuit of the Learning Paradigm: Coupling Faculty Transformation and Institutional Change. *Educause Review*, 37(1): 28-38, 2002.

15. **Chickering, A. W., and Ehrmann, S. C.** Implementing the Seven Principles: Technology as Lever. *American Association for Higher Education [Online].* http://www.aahe.org/Bulletin/Implementing%20the%20Seven%20Principles.htm

16. **Flashlight Group Current Student Inventory.** The Teaching, Learning and Technology Group, The American Association for Higher Education, and the Corporation for Public Broadcasting. 1997

17. **Fulford, C., and Zhang, S.** Perceptions of Interaction: The Critical Predictor in Distance Education. *American Journal of Distance Education*, 7(3): 8-21, 1993.

18. **Hox, J. J., and De Leeuw, E. D.** A Comparison of Non-response in Mail, Telephone and Face-to-face Surveys – Applying Multilevel Modeling to Meta-analysis. *Quality and Quantity*, 28: 329-344, 1994.

19. **Karp, D., and Yoels, W.** The College Classroom: Some Observations on the Meanings of Student Participation. *Sociology and Social Research*, 60: 421-439, 1987.

20. **Lave, J.** Cognition in Practice: Mind, Mathematics, and Culture in Everyday Life. Cambridge, UK: Cambridge University Press, 1988.
21. **O'Rourke, D., and Johnson, T.** An Inquiry into Declining RDD Response Rates: Part III a Multivariate Review. *Survey Research*, 30(2): 1-3, 1998.
22. **Stones, E.** Students' Attitudes to the Size of Teaching Groups. *Educational Review*, 21(2): 98-108, 1970.
23. **Wenger, E.** Communities of Practice – Learning as a Social System. *The Systems Thinker,* June 1998. http://www.co-i-l.com/coil/knowledge-garden/cop/lss.html

VIII. APPENDIX

Survey questions, responses and correlations with student satisfaction and reported learning.

A. Instructional Design and Organization

1. Setting the curriculum

Overall, **the instructor** for this course clearly communicated important course outcomes (for example, provided documentation on course goals).

	Frequency	Percent	
strongly disagree	37	3.2	6.9%
disagree	42	3.7	
neutral	77	6.7	6.7%
agree	405	35.2	
strongly agree	589	51.2	86.4%
Total	1150	100.0	

	Satisfaction	Reported Learning
Correlation	.668	.617
Significance	.000	.000

Overall, **the instructor** for this course clearly communicated important course topics. (For example provided a clear and accurate course overview)

	Frequency	Percent	
strongly disagree	36	3.1	6.6%
disagree	40	3.5	
neutral	84	7.3	7.3%
agree	403	35.0	
strongly agree	587	51.0	86%
Total	1150	100.0	

	Satisfaction	Reported Learning
Correlation	.664	.617
Significance	.000	.000

2. Designing Methods

Overall, **the instructor** for this course provided clear instructions on how to participate in course learning activities (e.g., provided clear instructions on how to complete course assignments successfully).

	Frequency	Percent	
strongly disagree	37	3.2	8.0%
disagree	55	4.8	
neutral	93	8.1	8.1%
agree	407	35.4	
strongly agree	558	48.5	83.9%
Total	1150	100.0	

	Satisfaction	Reported Learning
Correlation	.652	.596
Significance	.000	.000

3. Establishing Time Parameters

Overall, **the instructor** for this course clearly communicated important due dates/time frames for learning activities that helped me keep pace with the course (for example, provided a clear and accurate course schedule, due dates etc).

	Frequency	Percent	
strongly disagree	32	2.8	5.5%
disagree	31	2.7	
neutral	59	5.1	5.1%
agree	376	32.7	
strongly agree	652	56.7	89.4%
Total	1150	100.0	

	Satisfaction	Reported Learning
Correlation	.608	.544
Significance	.000	.000

4. Utilizing the medium effectively

Overall, **the instructor** for this course helped me take advantage of the online environment to assist my learning (for example, provided clear instructions on how to participate in online discussion forums).

	Frequency	Percent	
strongly disagree	38	3.3	7.5%
disagree	48	4.2	
neutral	96	8.3	8.3%
agree	441	38.3	
strongly agree	527	45.8	84.1%
Total	1150	100.0	

	Satisfaction	Reported Learning
Correlation	.652	.606
Significance	.000	.000

5. Establishing Netiquette

Overall, **the instructor** for this course helped student to understand and practice the kinds of behaviors acceptable in online learning environments (for example provided documentation on "netiquette" i.e. polite forms of online interaction).

	Frequency	Percent	
strongly disagree	31	2.7	7.3%
disagree	53	4.6	
neutral	162	14.1	14.1%
agree	455	39.6	
strongly agree	449	39.0	78.6%
Total	1150	100.0	

	Satisfaction	Reported Learning
Correlation	.569	.547
Significance	.000	.000

B. Facilitating Discourse

1. Identifying areas of agreement/disagreement

Overall, **the instructor** for this course was helpful in identifying areas of agreement and disagreement on course topics that assisted me to learn.

	Frequency	Percent	
strongly disagree	45	3.9	12.8%
disagree	102	8.9	
neutral	186	16.2	16.2%
agree	434	37.7	
strongly agree	383	33.3	71%
Total	1150	100.0	

	Satisfaction	Reported Learning
Correlation	.656	.611
Significance	.000	.000

Overall, **other participants** in this course were helpful in identifying areas of agreement and disagreement on course topics that assisted me to learn.

	Frequency	Percent	
strongly disagree	22	1.9	7.6%
disagree	66	5.7	
neutral	209	18.2	18.2%
agree	551	47.9	
strongly agree	302	26.3	74.2%
Total	1150	100.0	

	Satisfaction	Reported Learning
Correlation	.344	.362
Significance	.000	.000

2. Seeking to reach consensus

Overall, **the instructor** for this course was helpful in guiding the class towards agreement/understanding about course topics that assisted me to learn.

	Frequency	Percent	
strongly disagree	53	4.6	12.3%
disagree	89	7.7	
neutral	195	17.0	17.0%
agree	438	38.1	
strongly agree	375	32.6	70.7%
Total	1150	100.0	

	Satisfaction	Reported Learning
Correlation	.662	.599
Significance	.000	.000

Overall, **other participants** in this course were helpful in guiding the class towards agreement/understanding about course topics that assisted me to learn.

	Frequency	Percent	
strongly disagree	25	2.2	7.0%
disagree	55	4.8	
neutral	255	22.2	22.2%
agree	547	47.6	
strongly agree	268	23.3	70.9%
Total	1150	100.0	

	Satisfaction	Reported Learning
Correlation	.378	.370
Significance	.000	.000

3. Reinforce student contributions

Overall, **the instructor** in this course acknowledged student participation in the course (for example replied in a positive, encouraging manner to student submissions).

	Frequency	Percent	
strongly disagree	64	5.6	11.6%
disagree	69	6.0	
neutral	121	10.5	10.5%
agree	383	33.3	
strongly agree	513	44.6	77.9%
Total	1150	100.0	

	Satisfaction	Reported Learning
Correlation	.639	.555
Significance	.000	.000

Overall, **other participants** in this course acknowledged student participation in the course (for example replied in a positive, encouraging manner to student submissions).

	Frequency	Percent	
strongly disagree	21	1.8	4.8%
disagree	34	3.0	
neutral	151	13.1	13.1%
agree	553	48.1	
strongly agree	391	34.0	82.1%
Total	1150	100.0	

	Satisfaction	Reported Learning
Correlation	.393	.382
Significance	.000	.000

4. Setting climate for learning

Overall, **the instructor** for this course encouraged students to explore concepts in the course (for example, encouraged "thinking out loud" or the exploration of new ideas).

	Frequency	Percent	
strongly disagree	40	3.5	8.8%
disagree	61	5.3	
neutral	164	14.3	14.3%
agree	424	36.9	
strongly agree	461	40.1	77.0%
Total	1150	100.0	

	Satisfaction	Reported Learning
Correlation	.620	.573
Significance	.000	.000

Overall, **other participants** in this course encouraged students to explore concepts in the course (for example, encouraged "thinking out loud" or the exploration of new ideas).

	Frequency	Percent	
strongly disagree	27	2.3	6.3%
disagree	46	4.0	
neutral	262	22.8	22.8%
agree	514	44.7	
strongly agree	301	26.2	70.9%
Total	1150	100.0	

	Satisfaction	Reported Learning
Correlation	.383	.390
Significance	.000	.000

5. Drawing in participants, prompting discussion

Overall, **the instructor** for this course helped to keep students engaged and participating in productive dialog.

		Frequency	Percent	
Valid	strongly disagree	64	5.6	16.4%
	disagree	113	9.8	
	neutral	178	15.5	15.5%
	agree	426	37.0	
	strongly agree	369	32.1	69.1%
	Total	1150	100.0	

	Satisfaction	Reported Learning
Correlation	.568	.529
Significance	.000	.000

Overall, **other participants** in this course helped to keep students engaged and participating in productive dialog.

	Frequency	Percent	
strongly disagree	32	2.8	7.8%
disagree	57	5.0	
neutral	219	19.0	19.0%
agree	547	47.6	
strongly agree	295	25.7	73.3%
Total	1150	100.0	

	Satisfaction	Reported Learning
Correlation	.325	.344
Significance	.000	.000

6. Assessing the efficacy of the process

Overall, **the instructor** for this course helped keep the participants on task in a way that assisted me to learn.

	Frequency	Percent	
strongly disagree	49	4.3	12.0%
disagree	88	7.7	
neutral	154	13.4	13.4%
agree	483	42.0	
strongly agree	376	32.7	74.7%
Total	1150	100.0	

	Satisfaction	Reported Learning
Correlation	.655	.618
Significance	.000	.000

Overall, **other participants** in this course helped keep us on task in a way that assisted me to learn.

	Frequency	Percent	
strongly disagree	26	2.3	8.7%
disagree	74	6.4	
neutral	331	28.8	28.8%
agree	494	43.0	
strongly agree	225	19.6	62.6%
Total	1150	100.0	

	Satisfaction	Reported Learning
Correlation	.403	.395
Significance	.000	.000

C. Direct Instruction

1. Present content/Questions

Overall, **the instructor** for this course presented content or questions that helped me to learn.

	Frequency	Percent	
strongly disagree	47	4.1	9.0%
disagree	56	4.9	
neutral	99	8.6	8.6%
agree	427	37.1	
strongly agree	521	45.3	82.4%
Total	1150	100.0	

	Satisfaction	Reported Learning
Correlation	.689	.672
Significance	.000	.000

Overall, **other participants** in this course presented content or questions that helped me to learn.

	Frequency	Percent	
strongly disagree	22	1.9	9.0%
disagree	82	7.1	
neutral	237	20.6	20.6%
agree	541	47.0	
strongly agree	268	23.3	70.3%
Total	1150	100.0	

	Satisfaction	Reported Learning
Correlation	.423	.436
Significance	.000	.000

2. Focus the discussion on specific issues

Overall, **the instructor** for this course helped to focus discussion on relevant issues in a way that assisted me to learn.

	Frequency	Percent	
strongly disagree	47	4.1	9.7%
disagree	64	5.6	
neutral	128	11.1	11.1%
agree	468	40.7	
strongly agree	443	38.5	79.2%
Total	1150	100.0	

	Satisfaction	Reported Learning
Correlation	.661	.623
Significance	.000	.000

Overall, **other participants** in this course helped to focus discussion on relevant issues in a way that assisted me to learn.

	Frequency	Percent	
strongly disagree	28	2.4	7.3%
disagree	56	4.9	
neutral	251	21.8	21.8%
agree	553	48.1	
strongly agree	262	22.8	70.9%
Total	1150	100.0	

	Satisfaction	Reported Learning
Correlation	.427	.411
Significance	.000	.000

3. Confirm understanding

Overall, **the instructor** for this course provided explanatory feedback that assisted me to learn (for example responded helpfully to discussion comments or course assignments).

	Frequency	Percent	
strongly disagree	90	7.8	16.8%
disagree	104	9.0	
neutral	107	9.3	9.3%
agree	385	33.5	
strongly agree	464	40.3	73.8%
Total	1150	100.0	

	Satisfaction	Reported Learning
Correlation	.666	..603
Significance	.000	.000

Overall, **other participants** in this course provided explanatory feedback that assisted me to learn (for example responded helpfully to discussion comments or course assignments).

	Frequency	Percent	
strongly disagree	29	2.5	8.2%
disagree	66	5.7	
neutral	270	23.5	23.5%
agree	526	45.7	
strongly agree	259	22.5	68.2%
Total	1150	100.0	

	Satisfaction	Reported Learning
Correlation	.385	.390
Significance	.000	.000